C

CR

CREW MEMBER

Answers to All the Questions Every Passenger Wants to Ask

Fourth Edition

by Joshua Kinser

All names and some genders of people in this book have been changed to protect confidentiality.

ISBN: 9781728758787

This book is dedicated to all cruise ship crew members. Without you, these ships would never leave port. The cruise ship companies should be paying you much more than they do.

And this is for the guardian angel who watched over me during these sea voyages. Thank you for talking some sense into me when I wanted to throw that cruise ship manager overboard. I owe you one.

INTRODUCTION

I never expected to find myself out at sea unless that rafting trip I always wanted to take down the Mississippi River went horribly wrong. Nonetheless, I ended up working on cruise ships for more than five years. It was the wildest time I've ever had. For someone who loves to travel, there's possibly no better job than working on a cruise ship. As a travel writer and a musician, I've traveled all over the world, and I can honestly say that the crew area aboard a cruise ship is one of the most fascinating places you can visit.

In this book, I'd like to show you what it's *really* like to work on a cruise ship, what really takes place down below the waterline in the crew-only area, and what happens when a person decides to batten down the hatches and trade in their normal life on land for a life of port-hopping maritime adventure and worldwide travel. It's a story that takes us around the globe, from the mountains of North Carolina to the coast of Florida, and sails around the Bahamas, the Caribbean Islands, Mexico, and then across a stormy Atlantic to England, Germany, Spain, Turkey, Greece, Italy, and France.

At its heart, this book is a true story about love: my love of sailing, of the sea, of traveling, and of life aboard cruise ships. This is also a tale about the dark perils of falling in love with this peculiar brand of life aboard cruise ships, and at some points, it's a story for anyone who has ever wondered what it's truly like to be lost at sea. It's a maritime voyage that follows a crew of young, hopeful, adventurous friends through the ups and downs of life as cruise ship crew members. It begins the moment they walk up the gangway for the first time, and it ends the day they disembark the ship, possibly for the last time in their lives.

This is absolutely a true account. Yet please keep in mind that I view ship life through a periscope with a comedic lens that seems to distort the life of a cruise ship crew member into a nautical comedy, and so you can't take everything I write literally. For example, the rusty washing machines in the crew laundry were not salvaged from the *Titanic,* even though they did look as if they were.

I hope to give a balanced account of my time on cruise ships, and I won't focus too much on the negative. But please allow me to give you fair warning before our adventure at sea begins: working on a cruise ship is not all piña coladas, monkey-shaped towel animals, leggy and lovely showgirls, sun-drenched beaches, and cheap vodka-cranberry cocktails in the crew bar. There is a wonderful and sunny side of ship life (which mainly takes place off of the cruise ship and on some beautiful, palm-covered beach in the tropics), but there is a dark side too (which almost always takes place somewhere between port and starboard). We will explore all sides of the cruise ship hull, barnacles and all.

I'm sure what I say in this book will offend some people. Good. If this book doesn't offend at least a few people in the cruise industry, then I'm not doing a very good job of telling the truth, the *hull* truth, and nothing but the truth. So to all the people in the cruise industry who may read a little of this book and immediately want to light it on fire, throw it over the cruise ship rails, and laugh as they watch it sink to the sea floor, I just want to say, "Hey, don't get your whale-and-anchor-patterned panties in a wad. Please keep reading. This book is especially for passengers and crew members, but it's for you too."

My goal here, apart from telling an entertaining story that will make you laugh, is to hopefully make some positive change in the cruise industry and therefore make some positive change for those thousands of crew members who are out at sea right now, having to deal with the same problems that I had to deal with. I just hope that what I say here will make a positive difference in one crew member's life. That's enough for me.

In the cruise industry's defense, it has an exceptionally difficult task, running all of those ships around the clock, all around the world. And for the most part, it does an exceptional job. I'm forever grateful to the industry for the opportunity to work and travel aboard its ships. However, sometimes cruise ship managers out on the ocean, away from the oversight of cruise ship supervisors on land, don't do right by their crew. So not all of the blame can be laid at the bow of the cruise ship companies.

I can only draw from my own experiences, and I can only tell this story from my perspective, so I'm sure some crew members may disagree with what I've written. Each cruise line is different, and every seafarer certainly has a different perspective on ship life. However, I would wager a sailboat anchored off the coast of St. Barts that most crew members, no matter what position they hold, would completely agree with nearly everything that you will find in the following pages.

No matter how you feel about what I've said in this book, I hope you find the book entertaining and enjoy reading it. It will show you that ship life is a lot like sailing in rough seas; there are a lot of ups and downs. And after you read this book, I guarantee you'll never be able to hear the deep and thundering bellow of a cruise ship's horn the same way again.

Now let's climb aboard our cruise ship. Come on. Don't worry. I'm a cruise ship crew member, and I know how to operate the lifeboats if we need to escape. And I know where they store all of the cheap Duck Nipple–brand champagne that they serve on the cruise ship, so it should all be quite fun.

Just walk up the creaky gangway, and please present the Indian security guard standing by the X-ray machine with your vaccination card. This ship will be sailing into international waters and roping up at many distant ports, so please, present proof that you've been vaccinated for mumps, measles, and rubella. And you may want to close your eyes before our ocean escapade begins so that your vision will have time to adjust—it can get rather *dark* aboard this ship at times.

But before we begin our cruise, there's something we must do. Please put down your margarita, get in a straight line, place your life vest over your head, and fasten the straps like so. In the event of an emergency in which we are forced to abandon ship, you should place your right hand over your nose and cover your mouth. With your left hand, firmly hold down the front of your life jacket and slowly walk off the side of the ship and into the water. Remember to take a deep breath before you hit the ocean below.

Okay, the passenger book drill is now complete. You may return to the buffet and start your cruise, and now we can start having some fun. So let's untie this vessel from the safety of the dock and see what adventures lie ahead.

I see reading and writing as a leap of faith, but I like a thrill, so let's jump overboard. Bon voyage.

PART ONE

CHAPTER ONE

WHAT TIME IS THE MIDNIGHT BUFFET?

About two weeks is the breaking point. At least that's when I hit my breaking point on my first contract. Let me explain. There are two hundred or more cruise liners floating out at sea right now. On average, there are two thousand passengers on each ship. So at any given moment, there are more than four hundred thousand passengers wandering around lido decks, standing in the hot sun, waiting for lifeboat drills to start, or searching for the next buffet.

Crew members quickly learn that every passenger has great potential—potential to ask a crew member a stupid question—and most passengers absolutely live up to this potential. Sometimes it's not the stupidity of the questions but the maddening repetition of these questions that drives crew members over the edge. It's enough to send us running for a gallant leap over the ship rails and into the dark-blue waters below while we whistle the melody to the classic cruise-ship song "If I Were Not Upon the Sea." In that cold and choppy ocean, crew members will at least find eternal bliss in the certainty that there will be no passengers asking stupid questions.

When crew members are asked their first stupid question, they often stop in mid-stride, like a cruise ship that has run aground off the coast of Italy. One moment the crew members are smoothly sailing down the promenade with their company name tag on, and the next they're wrecked on a rocky shoal, wondering if they've made the right decision to go sailing for a living. There is a wide variety of questions that can cause this sudden explosion in the engine room of a cruise ship crew member's life.

Questions like "Why can't I drink alcohol at the emergency boat drill?"

"Why is the ship rocking so much?"

"Do the crew members sleep on board?"

"Do I have to go to the mandatory boat drill?"

"I don't remember my room number, but could you tell me where my stateroom is?"

And "What time is the midnight buffet?"

I hit my breaking point about two weeks into my first contract. I'm pushing a cart, one similar to the luggage carts you find in a hotel lobby, and it's loaded down with a poorly balanced pile of drums that could topple at any minute. I'm a drummer in the orchestra, or showband as it's called in the biz (*wink, wink*). I'm the drummer in the band you'll see in the production shows in the main theater if they haven't replaced us with animatronic robots yet, which I'm pretty certain is their ultimate plan. If you're on a cruise right now, I'm one of the musicians (or robots, like I said) that are dressed in all black like we're going to a funeral. If you don't see us, you can probably find us in a broom closet, practicing our instruments at all hours of the day and night, out scrubbing bird turds off the breezeway, or down in the crew bar, drinking and trying to drown the memory of the last passenger talent show we performed at.

The showband also performs with the singers, magicians, jugglers, contortionists, accordion virtuosos, and banjo people that perform on the cruise. And yes, banjo people are a real thing, and you haven't fully lived until you've heard the theme song to *Jesus Christ Super Star* played on the banjo while sailing aboard a cruise ship.

So, I was trying to move my drum set to the atrium for one of our biweekly jazz sets, which usually sounded to me like the sort of noise you'd create if you threw a group of musicians down a flight of stairs. For these performances, I had to move my entire drum set from the bow of the ship to the aft, twice a week.

Have you ever tried to walk from one end of a cruise ship to the other as fast as you can? If you're on a cruise right now, go do it and come back to me. Okay, that wasn't much fun, was it? Yes, cruise ships are big. Remember all of those people walking around aimlessly that were in your way? You know how I know all those people were there? Because they are always there.

The *cones* are always there.

On cruise ships, *cones* are what crew members call passengers. I'm not sure where the name comes from. Maybe it's because passengers are always eating ice cream cones or maybe because passengers are always in the way, blocking where crew members are trying to go like traffic cones.

Back on the promenade, I'm pushing my cart of drums.

I'm carrying a case of cymbals in one hand while trying to direct the cart through a crowd of passengers with the other hand, and the *cones* are not getting out of the way. I make it about halfway across the ship after nearly clipping a few piña coladas from a couple wearing matching tropical shirts. They look like they came from the set of a *Magnum PI* episode—one of the early ones before there was a decent budget.

I carefully steer my cart through the crowd, and then I see her from across the promenade. She has that look, that annoying inquisitive twinkle in her passenger eyes. I cringe. I know I've been spotted and identified as an employee of Festivus Cruise Lines—that's what we'll call the cruise ship company I worked for. Before I can jump ship and disappear behind one of the doors that lead to the crew-only area, she's already across the room.

She taps me on the shoulder. "Do you work here?" she says.

I look at my name badge. "Yes, and what can I help you with?"

"Do you know where my room is?" she says.

"Well, what is your room number?" I ask.

"I don't know."

Here we go again. Another day in paradise. "I really wish I could help you. I have a performance in about ten minutes, but I recommend that you go to the purser's desk. It's forward of the atrium, on the starboard side."

"Where is that?"

"Forward. Starboard. Mid-ship."

"Which way is the front of the ship? Is that what you mean by forward? Star what? Where's the middle of the ship? And where's the nearest ice cream machine? And what should

I do when I get to port? And how do I tie my shoes when the ship is rocking so much?"

This went on for five more minutes and then continued for five more years. It happened nearly every time I'd peek out of the crew area and find myself face-to-face with passengers.

So, what time is the midnight buffet? Well, that's a pretty silly question, because the cruise ship is one massive, never-ending buffet. The midnight buffet is no different from all the other multitude of buffets that happen the rest of the day. Sure, there are the lulls when the buffet is closed in an attempt to encourage passengers to get out and do something other than eat. But if you want to eat when the buffet is closed, you have the dining rooms that serve you three meals a day, just in case you feel like eating six times a day while you're on vacation. And if you want to eat more, you can visit the grill on the lido deck and stuff yourself full of hamburgers, hot dogs, and french fries. You have the sandwich shops and the twenty-four-hour pizzeria, and on most ships there are sushi stands, steak houses, Italian restaurants, and a window café that serves a rotating list of Asian menus. It's absolutely remarkable how much food there is on a cruise ship. On average, 105,000 meals that require more than twenty thousand pounds of beef, twelve thousand pounds of chicken, and twenty-eight thousand eggs are prepared every single week aboard a cruise liner.

So before you go out on your next cruise ship and find the showband drummer to ask him, "What time is the midnight buffet?" I'm going to save the drummer from having to answer one more question. The midnight buffet is whenever you want it to be. And it never ends. So enjoy your cruise, whether it's three days to the Bahamas, seven days in the eastern Caribbean, or a month cruising around the incredible ports of the Mediterranean.

When I first climbed aboard a cruise ship, I thought I'd work on the high seas for a few months and then move on with my life. Little did I know I'd wake up five years later to the sound of that cruise ship horn blowing, and I'd still be sitting in a tiny bunk bed down below the waterline in the crew area, wearing my Festivus Cruise Lines name tag, and getting up to push another cart of equipment across the ship. Ship life is a funny business, indeed. You never know what ports of call it may take you to, or how far down below the waterline you may go.

CHAPTER TWO

HOW DO YOU GET A JOB ON A CRUISE SHIP?

I think most of us dream of a life at sea during some point in our lives. Perhaps we'll always harbor a curious fascination with the sea and those who venture upon its waters. More than a hundred years later, we're still fascinated by the *Titanic*. When we do imagine our lives as sailors or pirates, we often envision the life in a highly romanticized way. But the truth is that pirates of yore didn't have it so good. A pirate's life wasn't all rum, swashbuckling, dark eye shadow, and wrestling-giant-squid fun. Pirates had to suffer through squalls on the high seas, hardtack Thanksgiving dinners, and months without women. It's not so different today, really, unless the call to go to sea is a call to a luxury cruise liner. Well, the hardtack Thanksgiving dinner is about right on some ships.

For me, the call to the sea came out of the blue. It came in on my cell phone, and it caught me completely off guard. I never tried to get a job on a cruise ship. I had never even been on a cruise before I spent five years on one. I had spent most of my life at that time living on the Gulf Coast of Florida, and back then I could have counted on *two* fingers the amount of times I had stepped aboard a sailboat. Even after working as a musician for fifteen years, I had never met anyone else who had worked on a cruise ship.

Most people who become cruise ship crew members get a

job on a ship by walking into a recruiting office. There are cruise ship agencies all over the world, from Mumbai to Mexico City. Agents pass out glossy pamphlets that paint ship life as the proverbial land of milk and honey—a life filled with windfall paydays, all-you-can-eat cheesecake buffets, and endless days spent on sunny islands, slathered in cocoa butter, where the only work you have to do is on your beautiful tan. There are agents for every position on the ship, and they generally take 10 to 20 percent of your wages.

People from many countries like Russia or India are often required to go through an agency to get a cruise job, but if you want to work on a ship and you live in a Western country, you can often go online and contact the cruise lines directly, which will require you to negotiate with the cruise line. As a result, you may end up with a lower wage and find yourself on board one of the less-desirable ships in the fleet than if you had gone through an agent. If you're a musician, dancer, or a singer, and you're interested in working on a cruise ship, feel free to email me (my email is in the back of this book), and I'll try to get you connected with an agent or someone at the cruise lines that can help you get a job.

And before I get into some of the negative aspects of working on a ship, I'd like to say this: If you're dreaming of working out at sea, then follow your dreams and go do it. Overall, for me, it was a blast. Once in a while, you might have to suffer through food that looks like chicken-beak stew, and you may have to physically restrain yourself from throwing your cruise ship manager overboard here and there. You may have to perfect your duct-tape skills in order to repair the washing machines in the crew laundry that look as if they were pulled from the wreckage of the *Costa Concordia*.

Yet you *will* have those days on perfect islands where the only work you have to do is enjoy the sun, sand, and sea. If you try, you'll have a wonderful ship life sailing aboard those floating cities that charge through the ocean and rope up at port after port, beach after beach, and paradise after paradise. At the end of the day, even though I went through some difficult challenges and could have done without a few of the ships that I worked on, there were times that I wish I could go back and live all over again, especially those early days as a cruise ship crew member.

For me, I never knew that working as a musician on a cruise ship was an option. I assumed if you wanted to work as a musician on a cruise ship, you had to know how to read music really, really well, and I didn't. You had to know how to play all the musical styles (rock and roll, jazz, Latin, funk, reggae, calypso, Broadway, gospel, and most importantly, a two-beat polka feel), and I didn't. You had to own a nice suit and a snazzy bow tie and have a respectable collection of tropical shirts. For the most part, the ship provided the tropical shirts, which I didn't own except for the single one I had picked up on a Hawaiian vacation a few years back.

Before I first stepped foot aboard a cruise ship, I was working as a staff writer at a newspaper in northwest Florida by day and as a drummer by night. I was working in one of the newspaper's satellite offices north of town, where they sent the rookies until they lost their greenhorn status. I loved the job. I had my own desk for the first time. Someone was actually paying me to sit and write. Right around the corner, Mama Bass's Kwik Burger was serving up the best Southern cooking in the South. There was free coffee at the office and fresh pecan pie down at Mama Bass's, so I was in heaven.

Then my cell phone rang. It was a guitar player named Gary. I hadn't heard from Gary since I'd toured with him and his band in Europe. We had performed for American troops that were stationed in the Mediterranean. We spent most of our time traveling across Italy, but we also made stops in Portugal, Egypt, Spain, Greece, Turkey, and France. It had been great to leave behind the low-paying gigs in local bars, where I had sometimes found myself performing for the worst audience members since John Wilkes Booth.

"Listen," Gary said. "Me and the band, we're out here working on a cruise ship in the Bahamas, and we're having a little problem with our drummer. We want to know if you want to come out and join us."

I asked him what the job was like.

"We play for about four hours a night, and we usually have two nights off a week. We're doing the same stuff we did on the tour, with maybe a few extra tunes. We rehearse about twice a week to add some new stuff. It's an easy gig, but you have to play by the rules, and there are a lot of rules out here. You get fed, and the food is all right, but you'll get sick of it eventually. You get a free room. You'll probably be bunked with the showband drummer. That's where our last drummer was."

As usual, everyone always talks about the good stuff first. This was a mixed bag. He really sounded kind of down about the whole thing. He sounded really tired of it—tired of the food, tired of the gig, or tired of something. *How could anyone get tired of playing music on a cruise ship in the Bahamas? How could anyone get tired of free food?* I took a sip of my free coffee. I wasn't tired of that. Also, as usual, he hadn't mentioned money. It always comes last, although it's often the first thing on every musician's mind. The gig probably didn't pay beans. *I'll be lucky to get $1,200 bucks a month for this sort of gig,* I thought. Playing drums on a cruise ship in the Bahamas sounded like something most people would pay to do.

"So what's the pay? And when do you want me out there?"

"We need you out here as soon as possible. We're playing with a drum machine right now." I heard the pain in his voice. "You'll need to get a physical done, but I've talked to our agent. He said we can fast track you if you want the job. We could get you out here in two weeks, hopefully sooner. The gig pays $2,600 a month, and the only thing you have to pay for are the drinks you want on board the ship and what you want to do and buy when we're in port. Room and food are free. You can save a lot of money working out here."

It sounded incredible, but I needed time to think about it. A few minutes ago, I was sitting at my desk, writing a story about a garage fire and planning the rest of my life on the coast of Florida. Now I was being asked if I want to throw caution to the wind and set sail on the high seas and join the cruise ship navy traveling around the world for a living. It was a lot to take in. It was a huge decision that would alter the course of my life forever.

"How long can I have to think about it?" I said.

"I can give you 'til later tonight," Gary said. "I need someone fast, and I have other people I can call."

While Gary was talking, I imagined myself in a tropical shirt, sipping a piña colada on the deck of a cruise ship. I was standing on the bow of the ship with the wind rushing all around me. I put my arms out like Leonardo and yelled, *I'm the king of the world.* I was surrounded by beautiful women in bikinis. Passengers were high-fiving me and saying, *"Hey, that's the drummer!"* And then I thought about the endless free cups of coffee, the endless free slices of pecan pie, and the free whatever-the-heck-I-wanted to eat. I thought about what it would be like to only have to worry about playing drums and having fun for the next few months.

"Gary, I don't need to think about it," I said, interrupting him mid-sentence. Then I made a decision that would change my life forever. It was a decision that would send me out to a life at sea for the next five years.

I held the phone close. "Gary, I want the job."

CHAPTER THREE

WHAT IS IT LIKE TO WORK ON A CRUISE SHIP?

I was put in touch with the agent so I could complete a "little bit of paperwork" before I climbed aboard the ship and started my maritime adventure. That "little bit of paperwork" turned out to be a medical evaluation form about the length of the Encyclopedia Britannica. It turned out that this web of red tape was actually an appropriate introduction to the sometimes-maddening bureaucracy that a crew member encounters on a daily basis while working aboard a cruise ship, as you will soon see.

The band wanted out of their drum-machine nightmare, which had them sounding like a bad version of the Talking Heads, so I was told to get everything done as quickly as possible. The medical evaluation seemed to require every type of test: chest X-ray, blood-work for every known disease, a collection of vaccinations as long as the *Titanic*'s passenger list, the rub your belly and pat your head test, walk and chew bubblegum at the same time test, white-rice and noodle-cup allergies test, response to stupid questions asked by passengers test, and the ability to live too close to a bilge tank for months on end test.

The evaluation cost me $1,100, which was a huge sum of money for me at the time, but I reluctantly forked over the cash. This $1,100 membership fee wasn't going to stop me from joining and having my good time aboard club cruise ship. But why couldn't I get this medical evaluation done aboard the cruise ship? Every cruise ship in the world has its own medical facility and medical staff on board. Allowing me to get my medical evaluation completed for free by the doctors aboard the cruise ship would have been a nice gesture before I went and worked for them on a six-month contract. Yet it's one more thing I'll probably never understand about the world of cruise ships.

The inner workings of the cruise industry are a maritime mystery wrapped inside a riddle wrapped inside a drunken pirate wrapped inside a noodle cup and then wrapped inside another maritime mystery.

I assumed this was the only medical evaluation I would ever need for the cruise company, but I soon discovered that medical evaluations were required every two years. And if I took a break from working on a ship that lasted longer than three months, yes, I would need to pay $1,100 again and complete yet another medical evaluation that was as long as the complete list of passengers who've been shocked when they received their bill at the end of their cruise.

However, a lengthy medical evaluation does make perfect sense. Getting seriously ill or dying is a costly and complicated process when it happens while you're out on a ship in the middle of the sea. Take something like appendicitis, for example. I was on board when a musician in the orchestra developed appendicitis while we were sailing in the Atlantic Ocean. Earlier in the day, we had been hiking around the Bay of Fundy in Canada. A few hours later, he was in the ship's infirmary. He was put on a stretcher and loaded onto a helicopter and flown to Boston for surgery. I'm sure this wasn't cheap. When crew members die, are injured, or become ill on board, it's expensive for the cruise ship companies. There's the expense of caring for the victim and replacing them if needed and also the expense if the lawyers are called. So cruise companies want healthy employees.

I was assigned to a ship sailing out of Fort Lauderdale, about thirty miles north of Miami, Florida. The ship was sailing around the Bahamas. Our itinerary would alternate between three- and four-day cruises. Starting in Fort Lauderdale, we'd disembark around five p.m. and then cruise all night, roping up at Nassau in the morning. We'd spend seven hours in port, and then we'd head back out to sea. The next morning, we'd anchor off the coast of Half Moon Cay, a private island that's apparently owned by several cruise companies. On a four day-cruise, we'd sail to Grand Turk in the Turks and Caicos. The schedule sounded like a slice of tropical heaven.

I had to bring my own drum set, and there's a lot of gear involved with playing drums. You have the drums themselves, which are often large, awkward to carry, heavy, expensive, and easily scratched pieces of musical equipment. Then there are the stands, the cymbals, the sticks and brushes and mallets and other various bundles of plastic and wood that you use to make different sounds on the drums, the shakers, the tambourines and maracas, the pedals, the extra parts in case something breaks while you're performing and you need to do a quick repair, the oil for keeping the moving metal parts of a drum kit well lubed and squeak free, and the microphones, microphone stands, microphone cables, drum heads, and all the drum cases and bags that all the equipment goes in. The best part of being a drummer is when the guitar players show up with all of their equipment in one hand, plug in their guitar, sit down and kick their feet up, and then watch you load in and set up an entire semi-truck worth of gear while they sip on a piña colada and watch funny cat videos on YouTube. Every time I load up a drum kit, I wish I had become a harmonica player.

I packed my drums into the car, as happy as a clam being served on a cruise ship buffet, but then I stopped. I had never been on a cruise. What do you pack for a cruise? More importantly, what do you pack for a cruise that will last six months? I grabbed a suitcase and threw in a few pairs of swim shorts, the tux that I bought from a second-hand shop, a snazzy clip-on bow tie, a variety of other clothes, and a few bottles of sunscreen. I figured I'd be working a lot, but what if I had a good bit of free time on the ship? I decided to bring a few books along—a medium-sized duffel bag's worth. I love to read, and I figured this was my chance. This was going to be the adventure of a lifetime, and I wanted to be prepared to waste it with my nose planted squarely between the pages of used paperbacks.

I began driving toward my new ship life at two in the morning. I was a young kid, speeding down the highway, racing toward the unknown, cruising through the darkness toward all the uncertainties of a life at sea. Gary had told me two things: (1) there were a lot of rules and (2) we'd have a lot of fun. How could I not have fun getting paid to play music on a cruise ship that was sailing to some of the most beautiful islands in the world?

I was a little nervous when I pulled through the gate at the Fort Lauderdale seaport. I bit my lip and tapped on the steering wheel. It was the nervous excitement and wonder that accompany anyone who uproots their life and takes that leap of faith toward something profoundly new and challenging. I thought about how fast my life had changed. I was committing, for the next six months, to live on...and then there it was—a hump like a snow hill with a giant, funny-shaped smokestack towering above the lido deck—my new home for the next six months. This was one of the smaller ships in the worldwide cruise ship fleet, but even from a distance, the ship looked enormous to me. The ship's name was painted on the hull in big bold letters, the *MS Bilge Tank,* or at least that's what we'll call it. I parked my car and walked up to the cruise ship for the first time. As I stood beside the ship, the towering hull rose to the sky like a white metal canyon wall.

The bass player for the band was waiting for me on the dock. Everyone called him Star Man. We loaded my drums onto a cart, and Star Man grabbed the duffel bag of books.

"What's in here?" he asked.

"Books," I said. "In case I get bored."

Star Man laughed. "Trust me. You're not getting bored on *my* ship. I own this ship. If you get bored on *my* ship, you might as well give up. Because if you can't have fun on a cruise ship, then you can't have fun *anywhere.*"

He turned out to be right. I never opened a book while I was aboard the *MS Bilge Tank.* I was too busy having fun. We took my drums and luggage to the top of the steep and rattling metal gangway and entered the ship through a large opening in its side.

This was a threshold that led from real life to ship life, a passage from which I would never return. This was the beginning of my transformation from landlubber to sea lover, from a citizen of the United States to a citizen of the United

Ships. And even though I didn't know it, my life of flexible schedules and complete freedom would be traded for a life of regimented itineraries and hierarchical governance.

I walked up to an X-ray machine, where an Indian (from India) security officer stood watch, and I placed my luggage on the conveyor belt. This first encounter with cruise ship security was about as pleasant as each of the ten million experiences that I would have with ship security guards over the next five years.

My luggage moved through the X-ray device. There was no hello, no welcome, really, no pat on the back for suffering through my medical evaluation and finally making it aboard the cruise ship. The Indian security guard with dark bags under his eyes walked over and began to pat me down. It felt a bit like prison. Perhaps I was going to the delousing unit next. The security guard watched my luggage on a small screen. He pushed a button, and the conveyer belt stopped, and then he pushed another button, and the conveyer belt reversed direction.

"Upin-ja-ba-blee," the security guard said and pointed toward my luggage. "Upin-ja-ba-blee," he said again.

"What?" I said.

"Upin. Ja. Bag. Blease."

"Ah, open my bag, please," I said as I opened the duffel bag.

"What is this?" he said.

"Books," I replied.

"Why you bring so many books with you?" he said.

"In case I get bored."

The security officer scratched his chin and squinted. He looked at me and shuffled through the pile of books, opening a few to make sure I didn't have any contraband hidden inside. He zipped up my bag and pointed toward the inside of the ship. "Okay, dank you berry much. You go now."

I walked past the security station and stepped into the crew area for the first time. I have to admit, I was expecting the *Titanic*. Not a devastating iceberg-collision scenario, but beautiful formal ballrooms filled with crystal chandeliers and dramatic maritime scenes starring Poseidon and busty mermaids painted on the ceilings. I expected every lady and gentleman aboard the ship to be expertly outfitted in finely fitted tuxedos and evening gowns. Perhaps waiters would call me sir in posh Central London accents as they offered palm-tree-shaped slices of *pâté* from silver platters. I wanted red-carpeted, spiraling staircases with an endless march of slender, sexy bachelorettes clad in gorgeous sparkly and feathered cocktail dresses and sliding down the rails while they giggled.

I stepped into the crew area. It was almost as nice as the lobby of a quarter-star motel I stayed at once outside of Newark, New Jersey.

However, while the industrial carpet and fluorescent lighting were similar to the motel in Newark, the crew area's wasn't quite as nice. But what the crew area lacked in charm and style, it made up for in obnoxious noise and constant racket. Crew members from all over the world filled a long, cavernous hallway that stretched the ship's length. Forklifts moved piles of luggage crammed into massive metal crates, stacks of tenderloin, loads of flour sacks, and heaps of fruits and vegetables that seemed like enough food to feed the world for a day. A forklift hauling an amazing mountain of bananas zoomed past. I could now finally strike "see Banana

Mountain" off my bucket list, which felt very rewarding. The crowd of crew members parted as the forklifts zoomed back and forth. The forklifts barely fit through the narrow and crowded hallway known as the I-95, the main thoroughfare for crew foot-traffic among the hundreds of branching hallways within the labyrinth of the ship's crew area beneath the waterline.

I heard many languages being spoken, mostly Filipino, Italian, Russian, the various languages of India, and English. I also noticed a lot, and I mean a tremendous amount of cursing. I came to quickly learn that the phrase "curse like a sailor" exists for a reason. Nearly everything being said was punctuated with a heavy helping of profanity.

Listening to a cruise ship crew member talk is often like getting hit in the face with a loose boom after you forget to duck.

At first it caught me off guard, but soon I wouldn't even notice the effing cursing. Sailing vessels are filled with potty mouths, and it's nearly impossible to avoid being transformed into one when you are constantly surrounded by a sea of swearing. I don't care how strong willed you are—if you spend enough time on a cruise ship, you're going to find yourself producing a profound amount of profanity. If Mother Teresa had become a spa girl, she wouldn't have left the ship with just an unfashionable number of highlights—she also would've sworn as much as someone in a scene from Goodfellas.

It happened to me, and I never even realized that I had been infected with a ship mouth until after I finished my first contract. I walked into a Cheesecake Factory for my first real meal in five months and said, "Wow, that effing piece of effing cheesecake looks effing great." Now that I'm a reformed crew member, I hardly ever curse—at least, I try not to.

Cursing has been a phenomenon among sailors throughout history. But why the dirty talk? Perhaps it's because ship life is effing frustrating. Maybe instead of blowing their tops and losing their jobs, crew members blow profanity out of their mouths. This epidemic seems to be found across the blue-collar workforce. Perhaps cursing is the universal release valve for everyone who works in the service industry. And for most people who work out at sea, there's a lot of effing tension that needs to be released on a daily basis.

Nearly everyone was wearing a uniform and a name tag. No one had a trace of facial hair. There was a lot of short, spiky hair, as if everyone got their hair cut by the same crew barber, and it seemed to be a place where the only hair product was gel. Just a few moments ago, I had been in America, standing in Fort Lauderdale, Florida. Now I was stepping into a whole new society that had an entirely unique culture, and it smelled very bad.

The crew area's aroma is a very special thing. These days, if I want to bring back all of the memories of my time aboard cruise ships, all I have to do is breathe in through my nose a little while standing too close to a pile of garbage. But that doesn't capture the unique and complex scent completely. In the foreground is the unmistakable stench of body odor. I firmly believe there is a cruise ship agent somewhere that recruits only the worst-smelling people on the planet and then sends them all to whatever ship I'm working on at the time. You see, it seems some cultures on the planet don't find body odor particularly unpleasant, and I can respect that. I understand we are all different, and I respect all cultures.

However, this wasn't the culture I came from, so at times, it was a bit much for me. And it just so happens that some of these cultures, many of which I grew to absolutely love, make up a large segment of the employees on cruise ships.

Beneath this body odor is the wonderful fragrance of wet industrial-grade paint. Keeping the ship well painted is a religious activity for the cult known as cruise ship crew members. Cruise ships are huge. The salty sea air and harsh maritime environment take a rough toll on a ship's exterior. By the time a painting crew has coated the ship from back to front, the back of the ship is ready for more paint again, so the painting crew just starts over. As a result, the ship almost always harbors that wonderful aroma of fresh, wet, pure-white paint.

Blending with the scents of fresh paint and body odor is the fantastic smell of cigarette smoke. When I first worked on cruise ships, the crew could still smoke in their cabins, as well as at designated smoking areas in open-air breezeways. Thankfully, this has changed on most cruise ships. But back then, even those smoking rules were loosely enforced, so it was common to see crew members smoking in the crew area hallways or huddled around cabin doorways, chain-smoking before their short work breaks were over.

Rounding out the crew area cologne was a strong note of rotting food. Mostly, this smell emanated from the garbage room, where unfortunate crew members spent more than ten hours a day sorting through every bit of discarded food and garbage that the cruise ship generates.

I looked at the crew members as I walked down the I-95. There were a lot of smiles, but there was a lot of exhaustion underneath those smiles, too. I wondered why many of the crew members seemed rather unhappy. I told myself then and there that I wouldn't allow myself to become unhappy. I would know when it was time to move on from ship life. And when it was time, I promised myself I would leave ship life in my wake. It was obvious that there was so much I could learn from this new job and this fascinating new environment. I felt there was something here for me, so much to experience, so much that could help me grow. I also promised myself that once I learned what I could, and once I grew as much as I felt I could from the ship life experience, I would move on from it and not allow myself to become unhappy and stagnant. This was a promise I wanted to keep.

Star Man and I shuffled through the crowd and crossed the I-95, nearly getting flattened by a forklift hauling enough corn to run a tortilla factory for a week or two. We walked into a stairwell and began our descent into the bowels of the cruise ship, down beneath the surface of the sea, where the crew creatures lived and where I'd be living alongside them for the next six months.

We passed deck after deck, each level looking nearly identical, a seemingly endless maze of tan walls, tan doors, and white stairwells that broke up the tan monotony every one hundred feet or so. Each stairwell looked as if it had been painted about fifteen minutes before we climbed aboard.

The hallways were tiny—barely enough room for two people to pass each other without rubbing shoulders. There were ratcheting, grinding, rumbling sounds that made the walls vibrate and the ceiling hum. I heard footsteps from crew members walking on the deck above us. I hoped with all my heart that we'd turn a corner and find the captain greeting us and welcoming us into a cleaner, newer, more spacious, less smelly section of the crew area.

As we walked down the hallway, I began fantasizing about what my new life was about to be like aboard the cruise ship. I imagined myself sailing at sea, standing inside my absolutely luxurious and stunningly spacious crew cabin. Foamy waves crashed against an impressive floor-to-ceiling porthole window. I imagined a regal four-poster bed topped by a comforter with images of lighthouses, ship bells, anchors, and whales stitched on the front. Antique-brass nautical lanterns cast a comforting golden glow across the wall-to-wall teak floors. Wooden ship's wheels and maritime-masterpiece artworks by Winslow Homer and J. M. W. Turner adorned the white shiplap walls. I imagined that my crew cabin would look more like the interior of a Red Lobster restaurant than any other room I had ever seen. There was a four-person cedar-framed hot tub, where I imagined myself sitting amongst the bubbles, reading passages from *Moby-Dick*. From the hot tub, I could fetch my collapsible brass spotting-scope and observe whales and dolphins and giant squid cresting from the sparkling sea outside while shafts of light, dramatic enough to induce a spiritual awakening, pierced through clouds like a silly, nautical Kinkaid painting. In all honestly, this was what I thought my crew cabin would be like.

I was more wrong than a person who thinks Cap'n Crunch has good enough credentials to pilot a cruise ship through the deadly Drake Passage.

I imagined I would find a large wooden door with a shiny brass name plaque on the front. Instead, when we arrived at my room, it was just a tan door like every other tan door in the hallway. This was what we call a learning experience. There are important moments in our lives when we are humbled by the fact that most of the world doesn't really give a crap about us, when we realize that the rest of the world feels we are about as special as the seaweed pulled from a cruise ship's propeller. This was one of those special, humbling moments.

The door was decorated with a lovely variety of filthy fingerprints. My name was printed on a small paper card that was tucked into a plastic sleeve beside the door. There was no brass plaque. The captain was nowhere in sight. Star Man handed me the key to my room, which looked like a plastic credit card. I placed the key in a slot on the door handle, heard the door unlock, and opened the door.

What had they done with my beautiful teak floor? In its place was wall-to-wall tan-colored vinyl flooring that was ripped and chipped here and there. Standing in the doorway, I could reach out and nearly touch my bed on the other side of the cabin. Next to the room's entrance, I found the smallest bathroom on planet Anywhere. The bathroom made the facilities in a Barbie Playhouse feel like a spacious modern-living design. It still amazes me that you can fit a toilet, sink, and shower into a space that most people would be unable to comfortably brush their teeth in without causing debilitating damage to their elbows. However, I like to look on the bright side of life, and nothing makes me want to jump for joy like discovering how to do something more efficiently. So I immediately recognized the silver lining of being able to poop, shower, and shave without having to move more than approximately 2.2 centimeters.

A shoddy-looking bunk bed was bolted to the far wall. The beds looked as if they were inspected for safety about as regularly and thoroughly as the nuclear plant at Chernobyl had been examined. The bottom bunk was mine, and I guess the good side to this was that when the beds collapsed and crushed me in my sleep, at least I'd have the person in the top bunk to say my last wishes to before I died. The bed was about as wide as a countertop, and the mattress looked about as hard. I hadn't slept in a bunk bed since I was eight years old, and I didn't feel particularly excited about regressing to my childhood right at the moment at which I felt I was coming of age.

There was certainly no hot tub. In fact, there was no *tub* tub. A hot tub would have taken up the space you'd find in two or three crew cabins. And where was my porthole window? There was no round window. There was no square window. There was no rectangular window. There was no window at all. Just a tan wall with a tiny desk, a scratched-up wardrobe, a single chair in the middle of the room, and my roommate's clothes and dirty socks spread around the room so that they covered as many square inches of the available space as humanly possible.

At least it's free, I thought. *That's the spirit! This isn't a windowless sardine can with a countertop bunk bed. It's a* free *windowless sardine can with a countertop bunk bed. And it's all yours. Everything will be fine. Who needs a window, anyway? I can go out on the breezeway and look across the sea and breathe that fresh sea air as much as I like. I'd probably get tired of staring out at that boring old sea after a few months, anyway, and besides, I'm getting paid for this.*

With that, I accepted my fate. I'd live in this pint-sized sailor's shack, and I'd be happy. I threw down my bags and followed Star Man on a grand tour of the ship, my new home. We headed up the stairwell and marched down the I-95 toward the middle of the ship.

We stopped by the purser's office and picked up my "welcome aboard" packet, which included my name tag. I was told I had to wear the name tag at all times.

We continued down the hallway. Star Man dodged forklifts and Filipinos. "You ever been on a cruise ship?" he asked.

"No."

"Let's go to Lido."

As we walked, I flipped through the welcome packet. There was a map of the ship's crew and passenger areas and a section that detailed the dress code for crew members in passenger areas. It was specific and detailed: No open-toe shoes like sandals or flip-flops. No jeans; khakis or slacks only. No T-shirts; polo shirts or button-up dress shirts only. On formal nights, men had to be in a suit and tie at all times, jacket on and tie snug. I looked at Star Man. He had on flip-flops, swim trunks, and a sleeveless T-shirt. *So much for the rules. This place must be relaxed.* I was wrong. Star Man just didn't give a crap.

Star Man opened a door that read Passenger Area. It was hard to believe these two vastly different worlds, the crew area and the passenger area, were connected by only a thin door. We stood on an expansive oval-shaped deck, like a giant balcony that wrapped around the entire perimeter of the lido deck. For those of you who have never been on a cruise, the lido deck is the main outdoor deck on a cruise ship. It's where you'll find the swimming pools, lounge chairs, hot tubs, and water slides. And for all you trivia people, *lido* is actually an Italian word for beach.

The Atlantic Ocean sparkled to one side of the ship, and

passengers were still boarding on the other side. Passengers were milling around, exploring the ship for the first time, most of them holding tropical drinks with little umbrellas sticking out the tops. Now, a word of advice to those of you on a cruise right now; any drink on a cruise that your bartender takes the time to decorate with any sort of umbrella or cutesy chocolate ship's wheel or plastic flamingo or something is unbelievably expensive. Receiving your bill at the end of a cruise where you spent every day on the lido deck, sucking down piña coladas before you asked how much they cost, is the quickest way to have all of the relaxation that you experienced on your cruise sucked right out of you. Most passengers sneak alcohol aboard the cruise ship in water bottles or those bladders they sell on Amazon. That brings the shipboard fun to a whole new level.

On the lido deck, there were a pair of pools, several hot tubs, and a stage in the center, where a reggae band was setting up for its sail-away-party performance. Behind us, there was a set of water slides, where kids sailed down into pools, sending huge splashes onto the wooden decks. Crew members at the Lido grill cooked up heaping piles of hot dogs, hamburgers, and French fries. An ice cream cone was squarely planted in nearly every palm of the hundreds of passengers exploring the party deck. Swimsuits, sunglasses, and flip-flops were the dress code. There was a lot of pale skin that looked as if this was the first moment it had escaped from the stuffy confines of a winter jacket all year long. I had never seen so many people simultaneously getting sunburned at one time in my life. Passengers from the upper reaches of Canada and coldest stretches of North Dakota were changing from the subtle shade of snow white to cheap-rosé pink faster than a cruise ship captain can say, "No, you leggy and young, sexy, cruise ship showgirl, I'm not married. This is my high-school graduation ring."

I turned to Star Man. "Can we swim in the pool?" I was ready to jump right in.

"No."

"Can we use the hot tubs?"

"No. But we have a crew hot tub on the crew deck, forward, in front of the crew bar."

"Well, that's not so bad," I said.

"This is it. Your new home. Enjoy it while you can. We're going to have a blast. Come on."

We walked through a door that led back inside the ship, and it was as cold as an icebox. You learn quickly as a crew member that the ship only has two temperatures. When the air conditioner is broken or off, it is blazing hot. When the air conditioner is on, the interior of the ship is freezing cold. There's no in between. Ship life prohibits moderation, and in more ways than one. I'd need to buy a jacket, because ironically, crew members spend most of their time in the Caribbean wearing hoodies and sweatshirts.

We walked through beautiful dining rooms with elegant sculptures made from the finest Italian molded plastic. There were Impressionistic murals of colorful coral reefs, tropical fish, and romanticized depictions of some of the coastal Mexican villages the ship sailed to, and in every painting the artist had thoughtfully removed every single cigar-smoking driver that asks you if you want a taxi. Every metal rail had been polished to a mirror finish. Oversized porthole windows, like the one I imagined I'd discover in my room, lined the wide hallways and framed the ocean outside like a masterpiece oil painting. The air was fresh, crisp, cold, and smelled like suntan lotion with a hint of sea air, ice cream cone, and freshly opened Dramamine packets.

Built in the 1980s, the *MS Bilge Tank* was no *Queen Mary II*. The *MS Bilge Tank* had as much elegance and grace as a contestant in a cruise ship hairy-chest contest. There was as much neon along the promenade as you'd find in a Las Vegas brothel. Much of the ship looked as if it had been decorated by Debbie Gibson and whoever designed the sets for Olivia Newton-John's *Xanadu* (which I actually love). There were hints of class here and there: gorgeous marble countertops on the promenade bars, plush leather swiveling stools, massive wine racks backlit with purple lights. In the atrium, I found that spiral staircase I had imagined, as well as a colorful glass chandelier hanging above a grand piano. A towering glass elevator was at the center of it all. This was quite the classy affair, and I loved it—that is, until we arrived at the Cat's Purr.

We walked into the club where we'd be performing, the Cat's Purr. The round booths and tables were designed to resemble open cans of cat food, complete with labels on the outside. This meant that when you walked into the club and sat down at a table, it looked like you were sitting inside a can of cat food. Large paintings of giant bags of Meow Mix–brand cat food covered the walls. In the center of the bar was an elevated, circular dance floor that was designed to resemble a tire laid flat on its side. The Goodyear brand name was painted onto the tire/dance floor's surface. Here and there were neon geometric shapes, evidence of Debbie Gibson's contribution to the club decor.

The Cat's Purr didn't resemble a place where a cute kitty

cat would come strolling into the club in a tight miniskirt but rather a re-creation of the scene where your favorite cat had been fatally run over. Maybe it's just me, but tires and cats don't exactly mesh and conjure up positive associations like, say, rum and sun. But it was our club, and so we'd make it work. The magic of music would find the muse, even within this club catastrophe.

You have to do your best to stay positive in ship life, no matter where your anchor happens to land.

Mostly, I was just grateful for the opportunity to be out here sailing on the sea and playing music with excellent musicians. Thank you, Gary, wherever you are.

I wanted to get settled into my new, wonderful, king-sized crew cabin, so we walked back down to the crew area. After about two seconds below the waterline, I wanted to go back up to where all the pretty passenger people got to live in their Poseidon's playground.

Star Man stopped in the hallway and pointed a finger in the air. "Wow, I almost forgot my milk."

"Do I need to get milk?" I said. "What's with you and this ship milk?"

Star Man looked at me as if he was about to tell me where the secret lifeboat time machine was kept aboard the cruise ship. "Cruise ships have the best milk, but this ship always runs out before the end of the cruise. They always put a new bag in the machine at the beginning of the cruise. So I need to fill up my milk jug before they run out. And don't come around my cabin, asking me for some ship milk, because I'm not giving you any."

At the time, I didn't understand the seriousness of something as seemingly small as getting your share of the ship milk, but I decided to take his advice and get some ship milk like a smart sailor. On ships, I'd later learn, it was the little things that helped you get through the tough times at sea, those dark sides of ship life. And you could get the little things in ship life by keeping track of the big schedule that the ship operated on. You had to be in sync with the cruise clock, with ship time. This meant knowing things like when the gym or crew Laundromat would be empty or when it was possible to sneak up to the passenger area and eat at the Asian restaurant without a manager catching you or when to get ship milk before it ran out.

It was the little things that made the ship world go 'round. Well, and knowing who to bribe. That helped even more.

I was trying to get my crew effects stuffed into the four drawers I had to my name, which was a geometric mystery requiring a PhD in mathematics, when an announcement came over a loudspeaker that was mounted into the ceiling of my crew cabin.

"All crew-ah member. All crew member." The voice was distinctly Italian, and the English was about as easy to understand as the first time you tried to read Shakespeare. Every few words were interrupted with an "ah," the national Italian punctuation. "All crew-ah member, report to your-ah muster station-ah and prepare for the lifeboat drill-ah. At this time-ah, all crew member-ah, must report to their muster station for the boat-ah drill-ah."

Hey, he said crew member. That's me! Yep, that's me, Mr. Perky Greenhorn McPerkyson, and that was the beginning of my life being entirely dictated by the cruise ship's schedule, by ship time. And the schedule would express itself at any waking moment by using the proxy of an Italian man yelling at me through the obnoxious loudspeaker bolted to the ceiling of my stateroom. I'd joyfully attend these boat drills once or twice a week depending on the length of the cruise for the next five years. I attended at least three hundred cruise ship safety drills. During my last 4.999999 years of the five that I was out at sea, watching the barnacles grow on the cruise ship's hull would have been more rewarding and exciting than attending another cruise ship safety drill.

The boat drill ended, and not a second too soon. As I walked to the Cat's Purr, I heard the ship's horn blow for the first time. The ship broke loose from its dockside mooring of the Fort Lauderdale port. My maiden voyage had begun, and moments later, I felt my first sway of the ocean as the boat gently rocked back and forth on its bearing toward Nassau.

The band performed later that night, and it felt wonderful to be on stage with them again, performing all the Earth, Wind, and Fire classics and Aretha Franklin hits we had played before. The young female vocalist, Shelia, was an excellent singer, and she could really work the crowd. The guitar player, Gary, was outstanding and precise in his rhythmic playing as well as a fantastic soloist. That band was anchored by his perfect chord placements. Star Man never met a spotlight he didn't like, on or off stage, but he didn't need one. His bass playing was so skilled that it naturally drew attention to him. The crowd didn't once fall asleep during his bass solos, and that's really saying something. Sorry, bass players, but it's true.

We played for four hours that night, my first night aboard a cruise ship. After our first performance ended, I walked back to my crew cabin. The ship swayed, and I had to brace myself in the hallway several times to keep from running into the walls. I wasn't a sailor yet. I hadn't found my sea legs. I settled into bed and pulled the thin solid-blue blanket over me. Waves crashed above me against the hull of the ship. The room gently rocked as the cruise ship sailed through the ocean waves. The cruise ship was rocking me to sleep, like a baby in a crew-cabin crib. Before I fell into a deep sleep, I thought about how ready and excited I was for this new and unexpected chapter of change and growth to begin. I was ready to wake up and do it all over again the next day.

And that was exactly what I did. I woke up and did it all again, over and over and over again, for the next five years. Ship life, if any one word can define it best, is a life of repetition, and every crew member is the star of their own maritime *Groundhog Day*. However, this is just the scheduled part of ship life. This is just ship time.

For now, for me, this ship was the ship of dreams. It was a dream come true, and it was time to live that dream. Everything has its time, and for now, it was time to kick back, put the dial on cruise control, and enjoy the ride.

CHAPTER FOUR

WHAT IS THE CREW AREA LIKE?

Below the waterline, under the sea, and in the deep depths of the metal-clad behemoth of a ship is where the crew sleeps, lives, plays, and most of all, works. They toil and sweat down there below the polished railings, smooth teak decks, glitz, glamour, and clean air of the passenger areas. The number of man-hours worked every day on a cruise ship is staggering. An average-sized cruise ship has around one thousand crew members, and most of them spend nearly all of their ship life down in the cramped crew area. The majority of them work no less than ten hours a day, many working twelve to sixteen. This means that if you tallied up all the hours that all of the crew members work on a ship every day, you'd have around ten thousand hours. It requires a remarkable amount of effort to keep the cruise ship puttering along toward Nassau, China, Bora Bora, or wherever it's headed and to make sure that the two thousand passengers on board can sit comfortably in the sun, sip that rum punch, eat that sizzling steak, and most importantly, do it all on a safe and (of course) well-painted ship.

If you divide all of this work, you would see that each crew member works for at least five hours every day for each single passenger aboard every cruise ship. And probably around 80 percent of this work occurs out of sight of passengers, concealed in the crew area beneath their feet. Like a well-oiled machine or a bee colony hive, there are workers folding towels, cooking steaks, ordering more steaks, maintaining the engine, printing photos, perfecting dance moves, baking pastries, washing dishes, shucking corn, counting money, practicing drums, painting the same stairwell they painted last week, and most importantly stacking more bananas onto the amazing Banana Mountain. And the crew works at every hour, day and night.

It's an amazing feat, really, to smoothly pull off the day-to-day operations and logistics that cruise ships require. A cruise ship is a massive hotel that must cross oceans, and it relies on a complex assortment of extremely sophisticated navigational, mechanical, and culinary equipment. And all of this must operate on a tight schedule so that the ship arrives at port on time and the crew gets paid on schedule to avoid the ever-present threat of mutiny at sea. It's a challenging supply-chain environment in which passengers are consuming a historical amount of food, yet the ship is only able to resupply once a week or so. Most importantly, it's a death-defying sea quest from which every passenger expects to return to port alive. As a result of these high-pressure circumstances, the crew area is often an understandably chaotic place to work, and those who work within it are largely underpaid, in my opinion.

It's also in this chaotic environment of the crew area that crew can take a break from the people of passenger land and relax with fellow shipmates from cruise country, fellow citizens of the underground. In the safety of the underwater world, away from the sunburned ears of the passengers, we can complain to the choir of crew who understand the frustrations of working in cruise-liner land. It's our own slice of heaven and hell on the high seas in some ways, where the crew gathers to eat, celebrate, love, and play. It's where we can get away and watch the sun rise over the sea without being asked directions to the purser's office for the millionth time and where we can tuck into a hard bed and sleep for a few hours in absolute darkness with the sound of the merciless sea continuing its epic and eternal battle with the side of the ship. It's where the crew plays their often odd mix of foreign dance music from all around the world and a place where the ocean is always there to rock you to sleep.

The crew area is also terrifically dependable; you can always depend on finding a good curry in the crew mess, no matter how many times you've told the Indian crew chef you couldn't eat another bite of curry even if the alternative was to walk the plank. And in the crew area, we cabin-party like there's no tomorrow, which is appropriate, since you never know when the cruise ship may run aground on a coral reef and the last thing you remember thinking as a crew member is how odd it is that a dolphin and the cold sea busted through the hull of the cruise ship and came to the party in your crew cabin like the Kool-Aid Man busting through a brick wall.

However, as you will see, crew members have a love–hate relationship with the crew area of a cruise ship. On one hand, it's where most of the wonderful memories with their shipmates are made, and therefore it's a place that they will cherish forever. On the other hand, every time a crew member steps into an old, rundown, one-star motel late at night, the stunning resemblance to the crew area on some ships is enough to make them cringe and then smile as they are filled with the distant and fond memories of their adventurous life at sea.

So, let's take a quick tour of the crew area, shall we? If you're on a cruise right now, go and grab a map of the ship, preferably one with a cross-section diagram of the ship. If you're not on a ship, let's exercise our imaginations. Find the point at which the ship meets the surface of the sea. On most ships, one deck above the waterline is where the crew area begins. The crew deck below this is often right at the waterline, and these crew cabins dip in and out of the foamy ocean when the ship is sailing in calm seas. In high seas, powerful waves splash and crash against the small porthole windows. Interesting is the sailor's life when your pleasant view of the ocean is a constant and frightening reminder that only a plate of glass separates you, the ocean, and certain death and where the waves ceaselessly pound at this plate of glass like liquid fists wrapped around saltwater hammers. The remaining crew decks below are submarine style, completely submerged in water world (apart from the officers' and management quarters, which are often near the bridge).

One of the most important places for crew on a cruise ship is the crew bar, and thankfully, the crew bar is nearly always above the waterline and has a crew deck attached to its front. Perhaps this wonderful combination of crew bar and crew deck is testament to the mercifulness of maritime architects and ship designers, or perhaps it's located here since the floor-to-ceiling glass windows of the bridge are nearly always directly above the crew bar open-air deck, where the captain and officers can keep a watchful eye on the intoxicated crew below and perhaps get the pleasantries associated with having a bird's-eye view down female crew members' tops. Even though we are cruise ship crew members, salty sailors and dirty pirates still lurk among us, after all. At the crew bar, seafarers can purchase their endless rations of perhaps the greatest morale booster known to anyone who ever took ship to sea: $1 rums and beers. And after purchasing a fabulously ice-cold $1 beer, a crew member can walk right out a back door and into the fresh air and sunshine of the crew deck. This moment, as a crew member tilts the beer back, is often the first time in many hours that the sun has touched the crew member's cheeks.

The crew deck, more importantly, is where crew members can go to admire the exceptionally fit and leggy and very hard-working cruise ship showgirls as they lounge and sun in their bikinis or soak in the crew-deck hot tub as the ship cuts through the ocean and beautiful islands glide past. That particular morale booster has quelled the worst of impending mutinies, in my experience.

However, the cheap booze in the crew bar occasionally boosts crew members straight to the gangplank with a one-way ticket home. I remember a particular night on the crew deck when a crew member, who wasn't one to allow the intoxicating perks of ship life pass them by, took a running start and leapt into the crew pool. This would have been unremarkable if it hadn't been for the fact that the crew pool was empty. In their defense, the pool did have a loose net covering its top. Apparently, he expected the rope netting to catch him, allowing him to bounce like a tightrope trapeze artist at a classic circus show. This would be the appropriate place to mention that nearly everything on a ship is made from metal, from the ship's bell to the cruise ship hull to the—yes, you guessed it—the crew-deck pool. Anyone with two eyes that were not blurry from drunkenness could see that the net would probably not support the weight of a fly on the lido deck buffet. It's a curious fact that the gong-like sound a body makes when it bounces from the bottom of a crew-deck pool is something that will never leave your memory once it is heard. The crew member was lucky to escape the incident with only a cast on one arm. This left his other hand with the ability to wave from the airplane window as it returned him to his home.

The crew bar is where the cruise ship party begins. Once the bar is closed, crew members pour out onto the crew deck and continue, often until security is called. Then crew members move to hallways, stairwells, inside lifeboats, broom closets, dressing rooms, someone's cabin, anywhere they can find until security is called once again. Eventually, the party winds down about the time that crew members must show up for work, and then they do it all over again. I partook in this for a while. We were all young once. Then I realized that operating on two hours of sleep and working a full-time job at sea weren't particularly compatible, a realization most of us come to somewhere around our thirtieth birthday after our brains have finally fully developed. Besides, this is the sailor's life. Have you ever heard a song about sailors and pirates that didn't feature pulling in the lines, casting out the sails, battening down the hatches, firing the cannons, and then swigging down the casks of rum aboard the ship? Sailors and drinking go together like cruise ships and overpriced champagne. Most crew members may not have parrots on their shoulders, wooden legs, and eye patches, yet the tradition of drinking like sailors and partying like pirates lives on among the cruise ship crew. The spirit of the sailor is alive and well down below the waterline. And while most crew members wouldn't know a jib from a mast, by the end of their contract they definitely could be blindfolded and tell you if they were drinking light or dark rum.

The main attraction of the crew bar is often a wood-topped bar capable of seating ten or twenty seafarers. And of course it makes perfect sense to have a twenty-top bar when a thousand plus crew members would like to get a drink every night. The crew bar often has all the glamour of a passenger cruise ship bar with all the glamour removed and thrown into the sea where no crew member can retrieve it. It's often a dimly lit affair with a snooker table and dartboard off to the side. The furniture often has that mismatched quality that resembles what happens when you take random pieces of damaged furniture, no longer seaworthy for the passenger area, and put them down in the crew bar.

If you love karaoke, then you've come to the right place. At almost any given moment, you can find crew members from every part of the world passing the microphone around, channeling a foreign version of Michael Bolton or Whitney Houston. A dance floor is often found in the center of the crew bar, complete with all the spinning lights and disco balls of a real but somewhat seedy and low-budget nightclub. Providing the most entertainment are the cheap drinks: $1.50 shots and mixed drinks, and $1 beers. And there's not much else to spend your money on aboard a cruise ship, which results in some exceptionally fun and memorable nights at sea.

The crew deck is often connected to the crew bar, and at night, the captain will sometimes turn off the lights around the bridge and crew deck so that the navigational crew can more clearly see the faint glows of buoys and the lights of smaller watercraft that are also sailing upon the sea. It's much easier to stargaze when the ship lights are out, and so at these times, the crew would drift from the crew bar out onto the open deck to see the stars sparkle in the night sky, which has a darkness only sailors have seen from the middle of the sea. On these nights, crew members who had traveled to the ship from around our big world would converge atop this small, teak-deck space and gaze together, wonder together at the universally admired and unifying beauty of the universe beyond.

Some of the best times I had upon cruise ships were spent lying on my back, admiring the undeniable beauty that worked and moved in delightful and mysterious ways above me, and some of those moments were spent lying on my back on the crew deck, looking up at the stars.

We listened to the ocean waves crashing against the side of the ship, the stretching of the metal cables as the cruise ship sailed through the ocean and cruised through the darkness of the Caribbean night. The ship would crest wave after wave, lifting us up toward the stars and then pulling us back down to the sea—the only living things between the ocean below and the twinkling universe above.

On the crew deck, crew members watched city after city come into view until the cities' buildings towered above us as we roped up at harbors from St. Thomas to Shanghai. It was the best seat on the ship, whether it was a sunset sail through the Philippine Islands or a sunrise cruise beneath Australia's Sydney Bridge past the Opera House. It's where crew went for their rejuvenating long, deep breaths of fresh, crisp, clean air—a highly prized and rare commodity for crew. It's where we'd go to watch dolphins ride the waves that were pushed from the side of the ship and the perfect place to stand on the ship's bow, throw our arms out as wide as they could go, and yell, "I'm the king of the world!"

And we'd stand on the bow of the ship, look out over the ocean, and search that horizon for what was coming next. We were always sailing somewhere, always cruising toward the next adventure, and the crew deck was the first place you'd discover what was out beyond the sea.

If you're on a cruise ship right now and you'd like to see the crew deck, go and find the lowest open-air passenger deck on the front of the ship. Walk out to the railing and look down. Usually, the crew deck will be right below you. There is often a hot tub that doesn't work and has no water in it, and sometimes a small pool that also has no water in it.

When the hot tubs and pools are working, it's heaven after a hard day of work to go and relax in them, watching the ship sail through the ocean as the sun dips below the horizon. Unfortunately, this is rare. Like many crew amenities, the crew pools and hot tubs on most ships are often either closed to crew or in a seemingly eternal state of disrepair. While passenger saunas, steam rooms, pools, and hot tubs are always shipshape, crew amenities are usually in, and please excuse the language, shit shape. I once worked aboard a ship that cruised Alaska. There is no better place in the world to sit in a crew hot tub than when you're sailing through Alaska's beautiful Inside Passage, surrounded by crisp and cold sea air, snowcapped mountains, icy-blue waters, and Alpine maritime forests. On my first day on the job, I finished my work and then donned my swimsuit, grabbed my *Master and Commander* novel by Patrick O' Brian, poured hot cocoa into my favorite mug that had "I Love Sitting in Hot Tubs on Cruise Ships" printed on the side, and ran toward the crew deck as fast as a passenger can run to the dining room on steak and lobster night. I arrived, with my monogramed towel thrown over my shoulder, to a hot tub that was as dry as a crew-deck hot tub is 99.9999999 percent of the time.

Dear whatever cruise ship manager is responsible for crew hot tubs,

An Alaskan cruise is no time to abandon your duties.

Sincerely,
Every cruise ship crew member that ever worked on cruise ships.

P.S. We dislike you very much. But if you repair the crew hot tubs, we will love you again.

That crew hot tub wasn't open one time on my entire three-month Alaskan-cruise contract. I know it's just a little thing, and I didn't let it ruin my good time, but it's the little things on a cruise ship that help you get through the tough times.

Now let's continue with the tour. Next to the crew bar is where you often find the crew internet room—the crew's lifeline to the outside world. Now, most cruise ships have wireless internet for the crew to use. Unfortunately, internet access on a ship is very expensive for passengers and crew; at least it was when I worked aboard ships. Crew members are already low paid, and then cruise companies were charging them more than ten cents a minute to use the internet and send emails and pay bills back home. The coal-mine company stores always came to mind every time I bought an internet card aboard the ship. I understand that cruise companies are in the business of making profits, and they do this very well, but perhaps there is a fine line between savvy business practices and tacky employee bilking. While I was working on ships, it was my understanding that many crew members were paid little more than $300 a week for more than sixty hours of work. So one internet card for two hundred minutes of time costs many crew members 10 percent of their weekly wage. Most crew members only have a half day off a week, and they have families back home that they desperately want to keep in touch with, so they spend their money at the company store.

If I stacked up all the little plastic internet cards that I bought over the five-year period I worked on cruise ships, the stack would probably stand higher than a two-story house. If you stacked up all the internet cards that have been purchased by every crew member since the cruise companies started selling them, the stack would probably stretch to the moon and back. And each one cost a crew member twenty hard-earned dollars. Here I'd like to advocate for the crew and ask the cruise companies to give them free internet access. This is the least cruise companies can do for the people who are working so hard for them. Besides, consider how much the cruise line is charging passengers for internet access. Don't you think the cruise line is already making enough money off of passengers to make excellent profit from their internet service? Do you think they really need to make money off their own crew as well?

Nowadays, crew members on most ships can access the internet anywhere on the ship, including in their crew cabins, and so crew members are probably buying more internet than ever before. Two hundred minutes of internet time for twenty dollars may not sound like such a bad deal. It may sound like a lot of time, but you have to understand that the internet on most ships was dreadfully, pull-your-hair-out slow. This isn't the high-speed internet on land that you know and love. This is 1990s-dial-up-AOL slow. And perhaps the cruise companies don't have much motivation to try to improve the speed of their internet, since everyone is paying such a high price per minute. My advice is, if you're a passenger, fill out one of those nifty little comment cards. Maybe we can make some positive change if we all pull together as a team.

Now, let's move on. As you would probably imagine, a large percentage of the crew area is taken up by crew cabins, food storage rooms, officers' cabins, crew offices, and the engine control room. Occasionally, the ship offers tours of the engine room, and it's well worth the time if you're interested in machinery and how things work. Nearly all parts of a modern cruise ship are remarkably large, which always fascinated me. The sheer size of the anchor cable-and-winch system alone is jaw-dropping. If you'd like to take a tour of the ship, ask at the purser's desk on board, and they'll point you in the right direction.

The engine room is a wonderful place to visit, but I wouldn't want to live there. I would know. I have lived there. Many crew cabins are located directly on the other side of a thin wall from the engine room, anchor winch, or crew maintenance facility. These cabins are the undesirable properties, the low-rent duds on the cruise ship Monopoly board. Once, I had a room adjacent to the maintenance facility. Every morning, sometimes as bright and early as six or seven a.m., I'd awaken to the cheerful sound of crew members chiseling and hammering paint chips from metal ship railings.

It was a lesson in chronic sleep deprivation from which I may still be recovering. However, it was a most effective alarm clock. Unfortunately, the beautiful sound of metal on metal was not reserved for the mornings. The painting on a ship never stops, and so the chipping of paint never ends, either. I also lived at different times in crew cabins next to the anchor-and-winch room. The cabin wall would vibrate violently every time we'd arrive or disembark from a port, which you come to learn is quite often when you're living next to an anchor winch the size of most people's houses. To complete the trifecta of bad location deals in ship land, I've been assigned cabins beside the engine room, where the loud humming and clanking and grinding of the engine never stopped.

To top it all off, most crew cabins are below hallways, and if you're unlucky enough to live below the I-95, that main hallway for crew, you'll enjoy an entire symphony of annoying sounds, including one that occurs at regular intervals day and night that sounds like a prisoner in heavy chains is being dragged by his feet by a crazed horse along the deck above you. To this day I still don't know what that was. Earplugs are a crew member's first ship-life love affair.

The crew must eat, and there are four different dining halls for seafarers aboard the ship. On many ships, the hierarchy determines the sumptuousness of the dining facilities. The crew is at the bottom, and then there is staff, the officers, and the captain at the top. Aboard many ships, each rank has its own dining hall. As you go down the hierarchy, each dining hall offers a progressively less-refined experience, as you can imagine, fitting the rank of the seafarer. The captain's dining room boasts a beautiful long wooden table and a team of servers to take his order and pour his wine.

I once had the opportunity to dine with the captain in the captain's dining room. It was truly an honor. I had been selected as employee of the month. As a result, I received an extra $100 in pay, a special name tag, my photo on the I-95, and the chance to finally eat some excellent food with the captain. After eating in the crew mess for many months, dining at the captain's table was comparable to finally eating at the French Laundry after eating nothing but Taco Bell for six months. No—Taco Bell may indeed be better than much of the food that is served in a cruise ship crew mess.

The irony of the food the crew eats is that the crew is literally surrounded, every day, by the best food money can buy. Yet the crew is often fed the bottom of the barrel of the cruise ship's food supply. Crew members are the bottom-feeders of cruise ship marine life. Perhaps the frustration with crew food arises from the fact that the crews eat so much of the same food for months on end. Crew members are often faced with the prospect of a menu that reliably repeats itself for the length of their eight-month contracts. Then again, some of the frustration is there because much of the food just isn't very good. While the tradition of hardtack is a thing of the past aboard these cruise ships, something closely resembling it lives on in the form of lentil curry and pork-knuckle stews.

On a cruise ship, getting to eat a well-prepared meal that hadn't been sitting under a heat lamp for six or seven hours was a cause for celebration. So you can imagine the joy when a crew member gets to eat steaks and drink wine at the captain's table. I had hoped to hear wild sea stories from the captain—perhaps stories starring giant squid or battles with pirates off the coast of Somalia—but no such luck. However, after many glasses of the best red wine you can find on a cruise ship without actually going into a passenger area, we were laughing and singing like a group of cheerful sailors who had just won the naval battle that turned the tide of war. Mostly we sang random Indonesian folk songs that several of the other employees of the month taught us.

There often isn't much to sing about in the crew mess, the large dining hall for crew members. Either whoever designed crew areas really loves the color tan, or it's the cheapest color paint available. Nearly everything in most crew areas is tan—the floors, the walls, the tables, the chairs—and the crew mess is no exception.

A large buffet is at one side of the room, with a collection of culinary favorites such as the rejected cuts of beef from the passenger area, hot dogs, yoghurts, several strange gelatinous desserts, pizza with random Indian-food toppings like curried squid and octopus, a fish-head stew or two, a collection of cereals, and the three major food groups for most crew members: the plate of white rice, the pile of white rice, and the mountain of white rice. You'll find a wonderful variety on the crew mess buffet, but it's often the same variety every day, and after three or four months, many crew members are can't-bring-their-fork-to-their-mouth-without-gagging sick of it.

On some cruise ships, the hierarchy is further divided into crew and staff, and often in these situations, staff will have a separate dining hall. Sometimes the staff will have waiters and white tablecloths, can order off a menu that includes several of the meal choices served in the passenger dining rooms, and can order free white or red wine with meals. In these cases, musicians are often considered staff. When lucky enough to find ourselves aboard one of these golden ships, the musicians would spend as many hours as possible in the staff mess, sipping our fifth cappuccinos and polishing off our third apple crumble desserts after eating several plates of filet mignon and drinking several glasses of wine.

It's easy to assume that one would not grow tired of filet mignon. But after eating the same filet mignon, prepared the same way, for six or eight months, crew members will find themselves choosing to buy filet mignon in port to avoid eating the ship filet mignon that they could have for free. I realize this filet mignon conundrum does not exactly draw sympathy from the peanut gallery, but the point is that the cruise ship will teach a crew member a great deal, including the fact you can get tired of anything no matter how good it is—even free filet mignon.

Next to the staff mess is the officers' dining hall, but I was not allowed in there as a crew member, so I don't really know much about it. All I know is what I've seen from the threshold that separates the chosen ones from the peasantry. I've seen the white tablecloths, the steaming plates of better-prepared meals, a larger menu, and excellent waitstaff with posh British accents serving baked Alaska and lobster tails on silver platters with one hand while they give officers a backrub with the other. To a crew member, the officers' mess is cruise ship dining-hall heaven. It's where all the hard working, talented, or bribery-inclined crew members go after they die and become cruise directors, officers, staff captains, and payroll managers.

Interestingly, I have known quite a few officers who wouldn't eat in the officers' mess. They chose to eat in the crew mess with the rest of the crew as a gesture of camaraderie. When I was considered a staff member and could eat in a staff mess or the crew mess, I always chose the better of the two whenever possible, but I did feel for the crew who never got to order off a menu, order decent coffee, drink free wine, or get tired of filet mignon (because you haven't lived until you have become tired of filet mignon). Instead, the crew seemed to live mostly off of piles of white rice. However, every ship and company is different. On some ships, there isn't much difference, if any at all, in the quality of food between the crew and staff mess, as you'll see.

Now let's journey into the real heart of the ship—the crew office, where the crew members get paid. Usually located mid-ship just off the I-95, the crew office is where the money flows. Unfortunately, all crew members are often paid at the same exact time, on the same day, by the same single person sitting behind a single window dispensing checks and cash as if they were selling tacos from a taco truck in northern California. In all the years I worked on cruise ships, not once was I paid late, but I would always have to wait in a line that often stretched around the crew-area block, where I'd wait behind hundreds of other crew members to get my pay. Everything on a cruise ship operates on ship time, and a crew member's time largely takes a back seat to the seamless operation that's required to keep the ship on schedule.

From the crew office, we'll walk down the I-95, where you'll find an enormous variety of food storage and preparation facilities. In one room, crew members are wearing aprons and carving tenderloins, slicing steaks, and trimming roasts at all hours of the day. In another, there are crew members whose single objective is to slice vegetables for ten hours a day or so. These crew members robotically feed endless supplies of green peppers, tomatoes, onions, and potatoes into the spinning silver blades of mechanical slicers. The vegetables are sorted into individual colorful piles like the daubs on a painter's palette, and these piles often fill the room. You've never met someone who smelled more like onions until you stand alongside a cruise ship onion slicer during a long ride in a tiny crew-area elevator.

At the end of the I-95, you reach the front of the ship, where a stairwell often leads down to the ship's main laundry facility. Think of every person on an entire cruise ship—all two thousand-plus passengers and one thousand-plus crew members. Imagine how many towels, sheets, blankets, and pillowcases they all use every day, and that's not counting the monkey towel-animals too. When I worked on ships, I used about two towels a day, and I wasn't going to the pool two or three times a day like most passengers do. So if, on average, passengers and crew use three towels a day, and four sheets and four pillowcases are stripped and washed every day from each room, this means that at least nine thousand towels, twelve thousand sheets, and twelve thousand pillowcases must be carted down to the ship's main laundry room at the bottom of the ship, washed, dried, and then returned to staterooms all over the ship, every single day.

The entire bottom of most ships is filled with washing machines, dryers, industrial-sized soaking tanks, and massive spinning machines that can hold these hundreds of sheets and towels at a time. All of the clean laundry is then funneled into a single room, where tireless crew members work to stack, fold, and deliver this unfathomable amount of laundry to every corner of the sailing city, ensuring that passengers and crew members are always provided with their linens, perfectly white and clean. As a result, every time a passenger reaches out for a towel, whether at the gym or the pool or in their staterooms, they will always find a perfectly clean stack of towels just at the end of their chocolate-melting, cake-stained hands. A passenger can stop anywhere on the ship and ask a crew member for a towel, and they will have one in their hand within a few minutes, often not folded in a boring square but magically transformed into the shape of a monkey or a dolphin or a detailed towel replica of Buckingham Palace, complete with a hand towel folded to resemble the Queen of England having her afternoon tea inside. It's astounding what these crew members do, and it's so easy for all of us, passengers and crew alike, to overlook how much work goes into a single cruise.

While the passengers' laundry facility consistently and reliably putters along and the laundry machines there are often sparkling clean, the washers and dryers in the crew laundry facility often contain more duct tape, dents, and broken parts than you'd find on the last-place car in a demolition derby. Usually located just above the main laundry near the front of the ship, it is possibly the smallest and most poorly maintained community laundry facility that has ever been shared by one thousand people in all of human history. Naval battles occur daily to determine who gets to use the single working dryer. Though they often harbor around twenty machines, the title of "laundry facility" is hardly apt. It should instead be referred to as the "place crew go to get rust in their clothes and find them half dried because none of the machines *effing* work properly" facility.

It's rather ironic that this is the laundry room provided to the same crew that works so hard to ensure passengers always have clean laundry. It would seem that this would induce some sort of shame in every cruise line executive that has crew laundry facilities in this poor condition, but at the time I wrote this book, apparently that shame was not enough to change the situation for the crew. I hope this will help create some positive change for the crew. It only takes one heart to be touched to change the course of this ship. Let's all hope and pray that the cruise ship companies discover the moral compass that will guide them to a future of lower stress and clean clothes for cruise ship crew members.

Officers often have their own laundry room. As you can imagine, the machines work, there's no duct tape on the machines, and officers share this facility with around a hundred other people. It's the ship-life hierarchy at its finest. And I understand creating an environment that motivates crew to advance up the ship-life ladder. However, we are all human on a cruise ship. Just like officers, crew members deserve the ability to clean the sweat and blood and dried hair gel out of their clothes so they can work again the next day in clean shirts and trousers.

Filling all the remaining nooks and crannies of the crew area is a maze of tiny crew cabins, where crew members sleep two to four or more in each room. Each room has one bathroom, bunk beds, a desk, and a wardrobe. Two chairs are often enough to fill the remaining available space.

Real estate is a premium commodity on a ship, so the Spartan nature of the crew quarters is understandable, and crew members make it work. And after the work is done, crew members, sometimes more than ten in a room, will cram into a crew cabin and celebrate ship life, celebrate the fact that they are working out at sea, floating for a while in the ocean with real life on hold, riding the waves, working hard at their jobs, getting tired of filet mignon, drinking the cheap rum in the crew bar, looking out of their porthole windows (if they are officers) or from the doorway of their little crew cabins (if they are not officers), and worrying about nothing else but where the sea will take them next.

All in all, the crew area may be shabby and cramped, but the crew area is merely where we live. Ship life is what we experience, and to have a good experience, each crew member should perhaps choose to enjoy and explore ship life to the fullest and perhaps try to stay positive even when the ship environment can be difficult to handle and can sometimes be disheartening to live in. It's only the ship, and there's an entire world of sea and ports to explore.

Perhaps the ship you're assigned to mustn't always determine your navigational course. Much of your experience in ship life is determined by what crew you bring aboard, which ports you choose to sail to, and whether you can muster the strength and wisdom to catch the natural currents of the sea, fill your sails with the strongest winds, and battle the ocean's many storms, no matter what type of sea creatures you may encounter along your ocean voyage.

And now, ladies and gentlemen, we have come to the end of our crew-area tour. I think this would be the appropriate place to say thank you to all of the hardworking crew members who make these wonderful cruises possible. And if you're on a cruise right now where there has been a waiter or a room steward or an officer or (and I know this is a stretch) a drummer in the showband that has made your cruise exceptionally enjoyable, I encourage you to pull them aside and say thank you. As a crew member, I know how rare it is for a passenger to say this, and I know how much of a difference it can make in ship life, especially during the tough times. We often live in a compassionless world, but on a cruise ship, we have the ability to transform our world into the world we wish existed. Cruising is the ultimate escape from the real world. So let's also take a short break from how heartlessly we often treat one another and make the fantasy of cruising just a bit more fantastic.

And if you are on a cruise right now, have taken one in the past, or are planning one as we speak, I want to say thanks to you. You and every other passenger make ship life possible for every crew member, and I sincerely thank you for the opportunity to experience what it's like to live and work aboard cruise ships.

Finally, if there's a crew member that has made your cruise memorable, I encourage you to tip them, and tip them well. Many of these crew members have very low wages and come from countries with poor economies. An extra twenty dollars can make a huge difference in their lives. Tip them, and tip them well. They certainly deserve it.

CHAPTER FIVE

WHAT IS IT LIKE TO WORK AS A MUSICIAN ON A CRUISE SHIP?

On land, I never knew where the next job would come from. I beat the pavement and hustled to eke out my living as a writer and a musician, always hoping that big break into the major leagues of the music business or the publishing world was just around the corner. Musicians, like writers, live on the edge of massive possibilities, and it's certainly exciting. But being a musician is also like living at the base camp of Mount Everest. You have a boatload of heavy gear to carry around, and you often live off of ramen noodles and trail mix until you have the chance to see what the world looks like from a higher vantage point.

The hustle was fortunately left standing on the dock when I walked up the gangplank and joined the cruise ship band. On my second day on board, we pulled into Nassau in the Bahamas, my first stop on a long adventure of ports that would lead around the world. I had never been closer to the Caribbean than the outer edges of the Everglades on a canoe trip. And the Florida Everglades—a swamp filled with alligators, pythons, Florida's state bird called the mosquito, and other prehistoric creatures that can eat you whole—is not exactly a tropical-island holiday hot spot.

I bounced with excitement at the thought of seeing my first Bahamian island. I grabbed my beach bag and filled it with sunscreen, snorkel gear, and a container of crab soup that I had snuck out of the crew mess that looked as if it had been made with horseshoe crabs. I skipped down to the gangway, slid on my sunglasses, and walked up to the security station. They slid my ship ID card into a slot in a wooden kiosk, and then I heard the sound you hear every time a game-show contestant gives the wrong answer: that universally understood auditory-rejection noise that's a combination of a car horn and a loud fart. That wasn't what I had wanted to hear at all at a time like this.

"What was that?" I asked the security guard.

"You can no get off ship," the security guard said.

"Why?"

"I have no idea. Next."

The security guard waved me away. I stood next to the gangway and looked out the side of the ship, where sunlight was beaming in. There was beautiful blue water out there, babes in bikinis, everyone smiling and laughing, beautiful Bahamians passing out free samples of coconut-and-rum daiquiris, stands with men wearing tropical shirts and selling roasted iguana on a stick. I heard angels singing. I was steps away from paradise but locked out of heaven.

I walked to the crew office.

"I tried to get off the ship, and the security guard said I couldn't go out."

The purser looked up my name. "You have training. You won't be getting off the ship for a while."

I had a special reservation with new-employee training, and the training would last the next four days.

I wouldn't be seeing Nassau or Half Moon Cay or Grand Turk. I wouldn't see *any* of the ports on my first cruise. While the ship docked alongside those palm-tree-lined beaches with rum bars, bikinis, and tiki torches that faded into the misty salt-air horizon, I could be found in yet another tan-colored crew room, memorizing how to use a fire extinguisher and where all the muster stations are located on the ship, just in case my drum set spontaneously burst into flames. I sat in the tiny room and listened to the corporate drone recite the same environmental regulations and safety procedures he had been reciting to the endless flow of new employees for the past thirty-five years with as much focus and interest as a passenger at an emergency boat drill, the trainer's voice resembling Charlie Brown's teacher (wah-wah, wah-wah-wah-wah). I stared out the window as fellow crew members filed down the gangway wearing sleeveless shirts, sunglasses, and flip-flops, headed to some tropical paradise where women played beach volleyball topless, I presumed.

After a few years on cruise ships, I began to appreciate the safety training and take it seriously. This is the natural course of ship life after witnessing near-disasters at sea and hearing stories from other crew members who had lived through maritime mayhem. Back then, however, I felt as if I had gone through that entire medical evaluation fiasco just to spend another four days trapped in corporate liability-risk-reduction misery; and it was a completely tan-colored misery that smelled like paint fumes, to boot. I poured myself a big glass of the best free milk on the planet, which made it all better. After the long day of training, it was time for me to go to work.

Over the next week, it was a repeating schedule, and every night we packed the Cat's Purr with passengers. The night often ended at the crew bar, where I was making friends with the other musicians, dancers, entertainers, and crew members on board. The cruise ship showgirls were, as you may imagine, the most alluring for me. We all know that cruise ship dancers are the most beautiful creatures to have ever set foot on this Earth. They also seemed to be the only thing in this world that's more flexible and more fun to play with than a Slinky. Combine this with charm, intelligence, sexy foreign accents, the talents of dancing and singing, and all-hours access to a variety of feathery and leathery provocative showgirl costumes, and you have an irresistible recipe for falling in love at sea. I wouldn't stand a chance against the powers of a cruise ship showgirl.

One afternoon, during a break from safety training, I walked to the main theater to watch a bit of the production show, in which the singers, dancers, and orchestra musicians perform. The musicians were top notch. They were reading charts and playing all styles of music that included traditional jazz, Latin music, Motown, and rock. Huge folders on stands were stuffed with music. At the time, I was mostly playing music by ear. I could read music but not on the level that the orchestra musicians could. I'll never forget standing in that auditorium doorway and watching that cruise ship orchestra. The lights were flashing and the dancers twirling, and the band broke into an up-tempo mambo number. I knew instantly that was what I wanted to do. I would need to learn how to read music as well as the musicians in the orchestra.

A cruise ship is often an inspiring place for a musician to work. When I worked on ships—and I know it's different now—Jamaican musicians performed on the lido deck for five hours a day, playing reggae and calypso, the music of the Caribbean performed by people who have lived it all of their lives. Jazz players filled the large orchestra with a full horn section, many of them having studied at the top music schools like Berkeley and Texas A&M. There were jazz trios in the cigar bars, pop and country bands in the lounges, solo guitarists on the promenade, and string quartets in the atrium. Once I got to know the different musicians on board, I'd often be able to hop around and play a few songs with each group every night. I remember joining the Jamaican band on the lido and playing "Red, Red Wine" and then hopping over to the cigar bar and playing "Caravan" with the jazz trio. A cruise ship can provide a great education for a young musician if they apply themselves to their instrument more than applying themselves to the $1 beers in the crew bar, which is a temptation that is often difficult to resist.

I quickly learned that there are a lot of rules on a cruise ship, many of them seemingly petty, which can take a lot of the fun out of the job and, given time, negatively affect a crew member's attitude and morale. When I first climbed aboard the cruise ship, out of ignorance, I was living on a cruise ship without rules. An example occurred during this first week on board. A passenger walked into the Cat's Purr. She was wearing brown leather boots and a white backless shirt, and she danced all night. We talked after my last set, and she said she wanted to see the crew area. *Why not?* I thought. I would later find out that I was about to break one of the top three rules for a cruise ship crew member:

(1) Do not fraternize with guests.
(2) Do not bring passengers into a crew area.
(3) Do not bring drugs aboard the cruise ship.

These are the big three, and if you break these rules, you will be fired and sent home immediately. No ticket home. You must pay your own way back. Nonetheless, these rules are often broken, in my observations.

We walked down to the crew deck, to the bow of the ship. I didn't realize at the time that the crew deck was directly below the bridge, where all of the officers and the captain work. We looked out over the sea, and then she climbed atop the ship's rail. We were sailing through the ocean. The wind whipped her hair in all directions. She laughed at seeing that I was more concerned about her safety than she was. The ship hit a small wave. She wrapped her legs around the rail to keep herself from falling overboard. She smiled. I tried to convince her to come down, but she was enjoying herself. I eyed the life ring at the bow of the ship, and then a bright spotlight was shone onto her face. I looked up to see that the light was coming from the bridge. A voice came over the loudspeaker.

"Get down-ah from the rail of the ship-ah!"

She curled her lip and gave me a pouty baby-face, and then she slowly hopped down from the rail and back to the safety of the deck.

Only later did I realize I would have been fired if the captain or officers had known she was a passenger. I realized I needed to learn the ropes of ship-life rules. The bandleader, Gary, had warned me there were a lot of rules when I first took the job. The first cruise ship rule I learned was that I couldn't have passengers hanging over the rails of the crew deck at two o'clock in the morning. Got it.

After the first week on the cruise ship, the band continued to pack the Cat's Purr. I was enjoying the financial freedom and the amount of time I had to work on my drumming, since I no longer had to cook, clean, or do many of the other everyday tasks one must do on land such as grocery shopping. Many musicians spend a great deal of time practicing their instrument, and a cruise ship job is an excellent place to become proficient in your performance. Professional musical equipment, especially drums, is rather expensive. Just one professional ride cymbal often costs between $300 and $500. A complete professional drum kit with drums, cymbals, stands, pedals, and sticks often costs around $3,000 or more. Most cruise ship companies provide at least some of the professional gear musicians will need to perform aboard the ship, which can be a great opportunity for musicians who may have the talent but don't have the means to perform on top-notch equipment.

By the second week on board, I was able to have some time ashore away from the ship for the first time. I had hoped to step off the end of the gangway and plop my toes in the sand on a beautiful beach. Instead, I was introduced to the practice of tendering. I waited in line, swiped my crew member ID card, walked down the gangway, and then, to my surprise, climbed aboard yet another boat. It felt rather counterproductive. Maybe after the boat they'd put me on a raft, then a life ring, then put me in those arm floats children wear, and then finally throw me a line and pull me to shore.

I walked down the gangway and climbed aboard the tender. If you're not familiar, tenders are the boats that take passengers to shore when the waters surrounding a destination are too shallow for the cruise ship to sail. Sometimes passengers will tender if there is no dock at the port or the port is already at full capacity. In these cases, the cruise ship will anchor offshore, and passengers and crew will ride the little boats called tenders to shore. Tenders often carry about fifty passengers at a time, and you're often taking a risk when you climb aboard a tender.

Most people cruise in the Caribbean, where the weather is extremely volatile. For example, we once anchored off the coast of Saint Thomas. Tenders were bringing passengers back to the ship. The seas were building a little, but the skies were blue. The weather report called for a day of sunshine, but then a squall suddenly swept over the coast, happening faster than a crew member can consume a mountain of white rice. The sea became a choppy mess. A fleet of six or seven tenders was still attempting to return to the ship. The tenders couldn't rope up to the side of the ship; the seas were too high. They were in no man's land, forsaken castaways trapped between ship and shore. All they could do was just bob around out in the storm. Many passengers and crew members gathered on the lido deck to watch, hoping for their safe return.

The tender would disappear behind a wave, and everyone feared it would capsize and the Coast Guard would be called. I imagined them dredging the bottom of the Caribbean Sea, only to recover the badly sunburned bodies of passengers with braided and beaded hair, each clutching their soggy boxes of Tortuga Rum Cakes, perfectly sealed bags of illicit Cuban cigars, unopened bottles of rum, and their winnings from hermit crab races.

This went on for what felt like several nail-biting hours. All we could do back on the ship was sit on the lido deck and eat chicken fingers and pizza and sip frozen margaritas while we watched those poor souls turn as green as avocados. Eventually, the seas died down and the tender passengers, wobbling and dehydrated and ready to punch the lights out of the captain, stumbled back aboard the ship. When you step onto a tender, you are putting yourself at the mercy of the sea. Do it at your own risk, and bring a paper bag, Dramamine, seasickness patches, and plenty of water, and be sure to check the weather report.

The day I took my first tender, the seas were calm. The Caribbean water was as blue and beautiful as a tub of Blue Kool-Aid on a hot summer day. I got off the tender and walked down the beach. The cruise ship was anchored off the coast. A warm sea breeze rolled in off the coast. A Jamaican reggae band played under a tiki hut, and several crew members grilled hamburgers and hot dogs for anyone on the beach who wanted them. The island, Half Moon Cay, was an idyllic location for a beach party hideaway. I didn't think it could get any better. And then there she was—a beautiful cruise ship showgirl from New Zealand in a bikini. She had canyons for dimples and a particular topography of mountains that would make any young man forget about the widely celebrated Banana Mountain back aboard the cruise ship. She was the leggy, gorgeous, and tropical port of call that every male who has ever had two properly functioning eyeballs dreams about. And by some divine intervention on this beautiful, sandy, sunny island in the middle of paradise, she was walking toward me.

Now, I'm not exactly the catch of the day, so when she asked if I wanted to take a walk on the beach, I assumed it was a friendly gesture from a fellow crew member who wanted to extend a welcome to her new shipmate on board. We walked to the end of the beach and found a little private cove to swim in, a little ways from the part of the beach crowded with passengers. And let me put this into perspective here. Just a few days before this, the highlight of my corporate-drone life on land as a newspaperman was getting a five-minute break from a long, hard day spent hunched over a keyboard to drink a cup of free coffee. And free coffee is great and all, I know, but there I was, doggie-paddling in the Caribbean Sea with a showgirl in a bikini who was looking at me in the same way I looked at free cups of coffee, and the sea was sparkling around us, and I could hear the reggae band down the beach, and I could smell her suntan lotion, and I wanted to taste her lips that were splashed with drops of saltwater until the day I died.

This was the exact moment that I absolutely, completely, and entirely fell head over hulls in love with this wonderful thing called ship life. The rudder on my ship had been snapped right off. I was now at the mercy of the ocean's mysterious currents. There was no turning back, no recharting this navigational course. I knew I wanted to be a cruise ship crew member for as long as the ships sailed the sea.

And everything continued to sail smoothly for the next couple of weeks. The band continued playing well and filling the Cat's Purr with passengers. One evening, the cruise ship dancer from New Zealand asked if I wanted to watch a movie with her in her crew cabin. We sat on her little bunk bed and talked most of the night. Even though I knew it was too soon, I wanted to kiss her the entire time, but I was young and an idiot at the time, so I never told her how I felt. However, I felt there was a spark, and so I was excited to see where this ship was headed. I thought, given time, perhaps we could move from shipmates to soulmates.

However, in ship life, I would soon discover that finding

love, while difficult, is not the hardest part; it's keeping that love anchored in a life where the merciless and violent sea is always washing love away, even when that love is bound by the sturdiest of ropes and the strongest of moorings.

On the last night of my second week on board the ship, the band was about to perform our last song of the night. Star Man put his bass down on its stand and asked everyone in the band to come out to the front of the stage. He turned off all the guitar amps and killed the switch on the sound board. All the hums and buzzes coming from the music equipment were silenced. He dimmed the lights, and all of us sat on the edge of the stage. We put our arms on each other's shoulders, and then Star Man grabbed his bass and plucked the first few notes to "Lean on Me" by Bill Withers. Shelia, the incredibly talented and beautiful female singer of the group, took the lead. Her voice was pure, clean, and perfectly pitched. She had the power of Aretha Franklin combined with the crisp, flawless, and steady quality of Alison Krauss. The rest of the band joined in for an *a cappella* version of the chorus.

We had finally come together as a band. This was the moment that I felt would mark the beginning of a great musical relationship that would take us across all the great oceans and to endless perfect ports. We walked off stage, and the cruise director, who was sitting at a table to the side of the stage, called Gary over, I assumed to compliment the band. Then Gary waved everyone in the band over and told us we had been fired.

"Is this our last night?" I asked.

"Yes," Gary said. "We have to pack our equipment up and be off the ship at six a.m., as soon as we arrive in port. No ticket home. No gas money. They're kicking us to the curb."

I never really got the full story of why the band had been fired. It seemed to have something to do with something that had happened before I had arrived. There are so many rules on a cruise ship that if the cruise director doesn't like you because you happen to look like the kid in elementary school who bullied him, he can easily find a way to get you kicked off the ship. Shelia and I seemed to be taking it the hardest. We were both young. She was very talented, and I can't speak for her, but I definitely felt this was an excellent opportunity we were losing, and perhaps she did too.

Word spread among the passengers that we had been fired. Several passengers who had listened to the band on their cruise tried to talk to the cruise director, but nothing was going to change our situation. Eventually, the only people left in the Cat's Purr were the band. We packed up our gear in that empty room with cat food bags on the wall and a fake tire for a dance floor. Star Man quickly packed his bass up and left, possibly to fill his milk jugs with ship milk one last time, which I wouldn't blame him for doing. I wanted to fill up a few jugs of ship milk too, and maybe get one last look at Banana Mountain before I went on my way.

At six in the morning, we carried our gear off the ship. I didn't know what I was going to do next. I couldn't believe that I was standing on the dock with a banana from the very top of Banana Mountain in one hand and a twenty-ounce soda bottle filled with ship milk in the other. This felt like no time to be leaving ship life behind. My ship life was just getting started. There was so much rice still to be eaten and so many elbow injuries to have while trying to brush my teeth in my tiny crew-cabin bathroom. There were so many tropical ports left to explore. And how could I leave when a beautiful showgirl from New Zealand with canyons for dimples was just starting to look at me like a seafarer looks at land after weeks at sea, and when I had just learned that she had all-hours access to the production-show costumes that the dancers wear in the Welcome Aboard Show where they dress like the most scandalous female sailors since the pinup dolls of World War II? I bit off the tip of my banana from Banana Mountain and drank my last sip of ship milk. I took a deep breath. *Why does my ship always run aground right as the beautiful, deep harbor and the welcoming, warm ports come right into view?*

Gary apologized about how things had turned out. He was a good guy. I loved that band. They were all excellent musicians and, more importantly, great people. We all wanted to stay on board, but on a ship, often the only person that can change most things like this is the captain, and apparently the band had been fired through captain's orders.

I had one last chance to go aboard the ship and grab a few of my personal belongings. I walked into my crew cabin and saw the showband drummer, my roommate at the time, sleeping in the tiny bottom bunk.

That sparked an idea.

I grabbed a notepad and wrote a letter to the orchestra's music director, who was the leader of the band that performed in the production shows. The letter asked if I could audition for the orchestra. I wrote down my email address and phone number. It was a shot in the dark, but I refused to just walk away from the job without trying for a second chance. This cruise ship job was too good and too fun to just let slip through my fingers. I climbed a flight of stairs to the music director's room. He answered the door. It was six a.m., and he looked thoroughly unimpressed that I had woken him up, but he took my letter.

"I'll see what I can do," he said before shutting the door.

Back at the seaport parking lot, I loaded the rest of my equipment into my car. Soon I'd have to leave ship life behind and go back to real life. The hustle would be back, sooner than I had expected. Perhaps I could beg for my newspaperman job back, like an embarrassed lover who tries to beg back his longtime girlfriend after cheating on her with someone he met on the third day of a three-day cruise.

A few of the friends I had made came down to say goodbye. The New Zealand dancer came down the gangplank too, one long, perfect leg at a time, as graceful as a Russian ballerina. I threw my banana peel down in the seaport puddle and reluctantly gave her a hug, trying to smile and hoping somehow I'd see her again. It was one more love and life that could have been that was ripped from the realm of possibility by the life of ship and sea. It's a story that happens every day in cruise liner land. You fall in love. You fall deeper in love. And then you watch them sail away into the sea, never to return home to you again. Often someone's heart is left struggling, battling in that ocean storm, and over time, that heart sinks deeper below the surface, until one evening you're standing on the bow of the ship and you realize that it's hard to feel love at all, and after years of ship-life love being lost, all you know is that one day you feel like you're drowning in a darkness and in a sea and on a ship where you doubt love can exist at all. And then a fellow shipmate ropes up alongside you and rescues you from the wreckage. And then you watch them sail away again, and then you're struggling, then you're sinking, then you're drowning. Then you're a crew member, and ship-life love doesn't exist.

I stood at the edge of the port. The ship blew its horn, and the sound shook me awake. It was the final note to the band's final set, a jarring end to my two-week career as a cruise ship musician. I got in my car, and I drove away, looking back at the ship in my rearview mirror. The ship was headed to more Caribbean Islands of paradise, where the reggae band played and sandy beach stretched on forever. It would sail away without us. I looked at the ship one last time. It drifted out of sight. From this perspective, my short ship life felt like nothing but a fantasy. I thought back to that feeling I'd had the first day that I walked onto the cruise ship. There was a lot to learn in this ship life. I felt I could grow so much from this experience of traveling the world and working with crew members from every corner of the globe. I also remembered the promise I had made myself, to know when it was time to leave ship life behind. I hoped this wasn't the last that ship life had seen of me.

CHAPTER SIX

ONE-TWO-READY-PLAY

I had spent my savings on the medical evaluation to get aboard the ship, and the little money I had left over from that I had spent on a grilled iguana, a coconut with my name carved in it, and getting my hair braided in the Caribbean. So when I heard back from the music director and had an audition set up for the orchestra, also known as the showband, I was pretty much saved from a life of braiding hair and carving people's names on coconuts on the streets of Northwest Florida.

The showband mostly performed with written music, so I hit the books, focusing on playing jazz, which was the majority of the music the band played at the time. Now, as I understand it, the showbands on most ships play mostly pop music. But back then—and thank God I had the chance to experience the tail end of what many consider the showband glory days—the cruise ship was one of the last bastions of big band music performance.

So I started listening to jazz records and practiced along with them the best I could, and I did my best to brush up on the wide variety of musical styles I would need to play well in the showband. On the day of the audition, I received an email with music charts attached. I had thirty minutes to print out the charts and look them over. Then I received a call from the recruiter and performed different sections of music for him. The audition was fairly high speed for me at the time. Thankfully, I got an email a few days later with an offer to join a cruise ship in the Caribbean again. This time the ship was sailing to St. Thomas, St. Martin, Puerto Rico, Jamaica, Cozumel, and Grand Cayman, all places I'd never been. The itinerary sounded like a perfect tour of beautiful islands. I was most excited about Grand Cayman, where I imagined stopping and opening that offshore bank account I'd always wanted. I wouldn't have any money to put in it, of course, but I could put that coconut with my name carved in it there for safekeeping, and perhaps if I hit it big in the publishing world or the music biz, it would come in handy someday.

Festivus Cruise Lines flew me to Miami. I only had to bring cymbals this time. Everything else would be provided. This, of course, made me very happy, as happy as a drummer who had been lugging around his stupid drum kit for the past fourteen years. I arrived in Miami around seven p.m., and I took a shuttle to downtown Miami, which at the time, during the recession, had all the charm of a homeless shelter and a crime rate as high as a cruise ship embarkation day when passengers are sneaking alcohol aboard the ship. Miami is much nicer now. The recession turned it into a newt. It got better.

I checked into the hotel room, tired from traveling, so I decided to get some sleep. However, I didn't stay asleep long. I was awoken by my room door flying open. I jumped out of bed. A dark, shadowy figure walked into the room. This was it. This was the end of my life. My life flashed before my eyes. The last thing I saw was me grabbing that banana from Banana Mountain and drinking the last of my ship milk. This was no time to die. Not when I was about to climb back aboard the cruise ship and have the chance to see Banana Mountain once again and the chance to drink as much ship milk as I wanted. I was going to die before having my chance to buy a *guayaba y queso* pastry in downtown Miami, which is one of the greatest parts of the entire city alongside South Beach on a Saturday night. It's a cruel world out there. A cruel world indeed.

"Who are you?" I said toward the shadow in the doorway and then grabbed my pillow and pointed it at him, hoping this would scare a hardened Miami criminal from my hotel room. He had luggage in his hand. I assumed he'd grab my cymbals and bow ties and run out of the room.

"Is dis room 157?" he asked. His voice was unmistakably Indian.

"Yes. This is my room. How did you get in here?"

"I am afraid dis is my room as well," he said very kindly. I looked at him. My eyes adjusted to the low light of the room, and then I understood.

"Are you a crew member?" I asked.

"Yes, are you?"

"Yes," I said. I rubbed my eyes and looked around the room. There was only one bed. I looked back at my new roommate.

"I'm sorry," I said, "but there's only one bed." He turned around and let the door close behind him. It didn't surprise me that the cruise ship company would try to save money by booking me in a single-bed hotel room with another crew member. *Welcome back to ship life.*

Early the next morning, I took a shuttle bus to the ship. I walked up the rickety gangway and through the large opening on the side of the cruise ship once again. A different but equally tired-looking Indian security guard was there to meet me. He pushed my bags through the X-ray machine, and

I walked back onto the I-95, finding the same rushing city of internationals that I had left on my last ship but populated by new faces. The forklifts were there, moving the crates of passenger luggage. And then there it was, Banana Mountain. I took a deep breath. That familiar odor of bananas, fresh paint, cigarette smoke, trash compactor, and body odor welcomed me at the door. *Ahhhh, it's great to be back.*

The music director, Ricky, was waiting to welcome me on board and show me around the ship. First, we stopped by my room, where my new roommate, the bass player in one of the lounge bands, proceeded to give me the lowdown on the rules of what he considered "his" room. He pointed around the room.

"This is my stuff, and this is where you can put your stuff. Don't touch my stuff, and don't eat my food. I sleep after the gig, so there's not going to be any late-night partying and no girlfriends over to spend the night or anything. Keep your stuff off the floor, and clean the sink after you shave. Don't be all loud and stuff when you come in at night, and don't smoke or drink alcohol in the room. Don't play the TV loud while I'm asleep or turn on the lights while I'm asleep. If you come in at night, use a flashlight. I've got an extra one if you need it. I snore at night, so if you got a problem with it, use earplugs. You got two drawers here and half of this thing over here to store your clothes, so there's no reason why they should be on the floor. We got one chair, and don't bring another one in. There's no room for it. This is where I keep my bass and my guitar, so don't put any of your stuff there. I'm going to the crew mess. I'll be back in an hour or so. Welcome aboard." Then he walked out of the room.

"Charming," I said. Now, after living aboard a cruise

ship for many years, I understand where he was coming from. It's hard living in a rat hole with another person for months on end. He actually ended up being a really nice guy. He had just had a string of disrespectful, irresponsible, selfish roommates, and it had gotten him down. Anyone who works on ships long enough has had a roommate like this, and many on land have too. It took a while, but eventually he came around, and we had a great time on the ship together.

"Well, he had his own room for a few weeks. Now that you're here, he has to give it up and share. Having your own room is kind of a big deal," Ricky said.

Ricky was right. And let me put this into perspective. Finding a banana in the crew mess that's not rotten is a really big deal. Having a cook who puts chicken fingers on the crew mess menu two nights in a row is considered an act of divine intervention. And you know you're living a life deprived of decent food when chicken fingers and the gooey, orange-colored, honey-mustard syrup send you and your fellow crew members into a frenzy to match the best water-chumming scenes during Discovery Channel's *Shark Week*. However, getting your own room on a cruise ship is better than being the couple that the crowd crowns the winners of that Newlywed Game that occurs on nearly every cruise ship in the world. There's nothing better when you live and work in one of the most cramped and chaotic environments on the planet than having your own space to get away from it all, relax, stretch out, sleep when you want, and have your significant other spend the night whenever you want to. Unfortunately, the percentage of crew members who get their own room while working on a cruise ship is precisely .000000000000000000000000000000000000000000000000000

0000000000000000000000000000000000000000000000000000000
000000000000000000000000000000000000000000001%.

This is for the crew. However, there are a few jobs on a cruise ship that will often guarantee that you'll have your own room. If you are thinking about working on a cruise ship, then pull out that highlighter and start taking notes, because these are the jobs you want: They include working as an officer, the captain, music director, dance captain, doctors, nurses, for some bizarre reason art auctioneers, and a few other positions high up in the ship hierarchy such as staff captain, marketing manager, and the like. On the other side of this cruise coin, when you get a great roommate, it can be way more fun than living alone, and I've had a lot of wonderful roommates who I am certainly grateful to have met and to have had the opportunity to get to know so well, an opportunity that most likely would not have occurred if we had not been roommates.

Ricky and I left the room and walked a few hundred feet to the stage. I could already tell this ship was much nicer than the last one. My last ship with the Cat's Purr had been built in 1982 or so, and it certainly looked its age. My new ship, built in 2000, was much larger and had a more classic cruise ship interior, leaning more toward the formal, classy cruise ship look of old.

This new ship could hold just over two thousand passengers, nearly twice as many as my last ship, which it seemed to dwarf in size. And cruise ships since then have only continued to grow larger. The sea race to have the largest and most luxurious cruise ship in the world has pushed companies to build behemoths of the seas. When I wrote and released this latest of edition of this book, the largest cruise ship in the world was the *Symphony of the Seas*, built by Royal Caribbean. The 230,000-gross-ton ship can transport more than 6,700 passengers and 2,300 crew members. On any given cruise, there are often more than ten thousand people on this one ship. It has eighteen decks, and according to the Royal Caribbean website, it took five hundred thousand parts to complete the building of this impressive sea monster. Astoundingly, the *Symphony* is only slightly smaller than a Nimitz-class aircraft carrier. On one seven-day cruise, its food and beverage department will often use three hundred fifty tons of ice cubes, 2,100 pounds of lobster tail, 2,500 pounds of salmon, and more than fifty-five thousand eggs. The future looks bright and big for the cruise industry, and I hope the cruise companies continue to innovate and build ever-more-beautiful ships for us all to enjoy.

Ricky and I were standing backstage of the main theater. My eyes adjusted to the low light, made even darker by the light-absorbing black-painted walls, the black stage floor, and the floor-to-ceiling black curtains with tiny, dim, fiber-optic lights running their length, which twinkled like stars against a pitch-black, middle-of-the-sea sky. The parted curtain gave me a view of the empty theater.

The stage seemed to be waiting for its performers, creating a tension for what was to come later that night. The curtains twinkled. Empty seats, upholstered in dark-red velvet, curved upward. A balcony wrapped around the back of the room, its front finely carved with scenes of ships and sea and ballroom dancers in dreamy gowns and suits. The empty stage waited for the best hopes and dreams of these young dancers and musicians and singers and jugglers and magicians to be made or to be tossed over the cruise ship rails, where they would sink down to the seafloor and join the wreckage of the *MS Artist's Aspirations*.

We walked to the edge of the stage, and Ricky pointed down into a dark hole, where a platform at stage-front had been lowered below the floor of the auditorium. I saw a drum kit to one side, a keyboard and chair in front of it, and about twelve other chairs lined up in rows beside the drum set.

Ricky pointed down into the dark hole in the ground. "That's where you'll be performing."

You see, orchestra musicians often do not perform on stage but instead in something affectionately known as "the pit," a small platform that can often be mechanically lowered and raised. The walls of the cruise ship pit were painted black. At the time, the cruise ship uniform for musicians was all-black attire. This meant that if a passenger were to look down into the orchestra pit during a show, they'd likely see little lights illuminating sheet music on stands and an odd collection of floating heads and hands in the darkness.

We walked over to the pit, and Ricky handed me a folder that was two-inches thick and literally bursting at the seams with sheet music. I know "bursting at the seams" is an oft-used cliché, but this dark-blue sea-colored folder had actual cracks in the seams from years of sheet music stuffing, the paper edges of the sheet music worn, ripped, and stained with the sweat of the hundreds of showband drummers who had come before me.

"This is the show we're playing tonight," Ricky said, "so give it a look. We'll be performing this at seven o'clock." The folder was packed with music charts for the production show.

A production show on a cruise ship is a nonstop, hour-long music performance. Everything you play is written out on the sheet music. All the breaks, sometimes-complex transitions, often difficult drum fills, segues, drum patterns, time signature changes, volume dynamics, and important setups for the horn section are all written out on the charts. And in just two hours, Ricky expected me to play everything on those charts at an expert level.

"This is what we're playing two hours from now?" I asked, trying to conceal my concern as best I could.

"Yep," Ricky said.

Sight-reading charts with the orchestra would become routine after several years playing in the showband, but this was my first contract, and I didn't have the best ability to read music charts at the time. When I played with bands back home, we would sometimes spend months getting shows together. We would practice five or six hours a day for three or four days a week to put together a two-hour show. In college, the jazz band I performed with would spend two months or more rehearsing for a one-hour collection of songs.

On a cruise ship in the orchestra, we would often have a twenty-minute rehearsal to prepare an hour-long performance of music I had never seen or often heard before in my life. I found it amazing and refreshing how fast the showband worked. My performance when sight-reading a piece of music was never expected to be flawless, but the music directors expected it to be close. A musician who didn't play his parts well would often drive everyone else in the showband banana-cakes and leave the especially talented musicians wanting to hurl their saxophones, trombones, and drumsticks at the weakest musical link. I remember a certain trumpet player who was an exceptional musician, and at the time, I wasn't up to his level, which I felt seemed to frustrate him. I wish I had been as accomplished as him when I first joined the showband so that he could have had a more fulfilling musical experience. Sorry, Chris. I hope you're still out there playing your trumpet somewhere and loving every minute of it.

"Let me show you the Aviom system," Ricky said, "and then you can look over the music for the show."

I had no idea what he was talking about.

"The Aviom system," Ricky said and pointed, "is that little blue box attached to your music stand." The little box had knobs and buttons all over it, and an Aviom box was attached to all twelve or so stands in the pit.

"The Aviom box is where you can adjust the volume of each player in the band as well as the singers on stage," Ricky explained. "You can adjust the volume of the metronome and the backing tracks. There are two backing tracks that guide the band through the shows. There is a backing track for the horn section and a backing track for the rhythm section. We all wear headphones when we play, and you can hear the metronome, the band, the backing tracks, and the singers in your headphones. It's totally up to you as to who you want to hear and the volume level of each member of the band. Many drummers don't listen to the singers; they often throw them off rhythm. You definitely want the metronome, and you most likely will want to hear the backing track for the rhythm section in case you get lost in the show. But don't get lost, or it will mess everybody up." Ricky chuckled. I can still hear his laugh today and see his smile. He was an extremely nice guy, so I'm certain he meant this in a very nice way. He was one of the best music directors, or MDs, I ever had, and I'm extremely grateful that he was the first MD I had during my cruise ship career. Thanks, Ricky. You're golden, and I hope you're still playing music and smiling and being so nice to everyone. You made a huge impact on my life, and I really appreciate that.

Got it. Don't screw up, I thought.

"Oh yeah, and you can't always trust the metronome. Sometimes it's wrong," Ricky said and chuckled again.

For the non-musicians who are reading this book, a metronome is a device that keeps perfect time. The sound is produced digitally, and it can be whatever sound you want: a cowbell, a beep, a sound like the snapping of fingers, for example. The metronome keeps time for the band during the production shows. Everything in the show is synced to the metronome—what the band plays, the lighting for the show, the moves the dancers make, and the set changes. This is often how Broadway and Vegas production shows operate as well.

"So what do I do when the metronome is wrong?" I asked.

"You just have to play through it and do the best you can do. You'll learn where the metronome is wrong and feel your way through it," Ricky said.

What Ricky was telling me was that in some sections of the production shows, the metronome wasn't going to match or sync up with the music we were playing. Often during these times in the production shows, the metronome was embarrassingly off time. So imagine trying to play a song on an instrument flawlessly and in perfect time. For difficult pieces of music, that is quite hard to do, of course. Now imagine playing that song "in time," or in perfect sync with the metronome, while wearing headphones that are playing a ridiculously loud beeping sound that has no relation whatsoever to the tempo or feel of the song that you are trying to perform flawlessly. What this meant for me was that my job, a job that I was going to need a *Matrix*-style infusion of information and skill to successfully execute that night, had just become much more difficult.

"OK," was all I could say. I had to either do it—make it work and play the show—or lose the job. It was pretty simple.

I had a zillion questions, but a cruise ship is a fast-paced environment. Ship time struck again. After finding a broom closet in which to practice on a practice pad for several hours, I was back in the orchestra pit with the sheet music for the show in front of me, seated behind the drum set. Show time.

The bass player was seated next to me, the keyboard player in front. The pit was crammed tight. I looked over at the bass player. He was a friendly guy with a square jaw and a crew cut like a marine. He was practicing an up-tempo jazz section in the show.

"Hey, how does the show start?" I asked.

The bass player lifted a brow. "Hey Ricky," the bass player said, "the FNG wants to know how the show starts."

What exactly does FNG mean? I wondered. I soon learned—and I'm not one for cursing, so I'll modify the term—that it meant "effing new guy."

The rest of the band didn't look too pleased with the prospect of playing with an FNG drummer for the next several months, but nonetheless, everyone in that band was very welcoming and friendly toward me while I worked on that ship. I had a lot to learn, and many of them showed me the ropes of cruise liner land along the way.

I think I heard one of the showband guys mutter, "Effing new guy."

Ricky explained to me what was about to happen. He probably explained it in a very nice and slow way, but at the time, it was so much new information that it felt as if he were talking at ninety miles an hour.

"I'll point to you, and you do a drum roll on the floor tom. While you're rolling, someone will introduce the cruise director, and then I'll count off the band for the first chart in your book. The cruise director will call some passengers up on stage, and I'll count again, and the band will play "St. Thomas" while they walk up on stage. The passengers are going to participate in a comedy bit, and then we'll play the *Flintstones* theme song to play them off stage. When I count it off, I'll count in double time, and we're going to swing it really fast, so be ready. Then we'll play "St. Thomas" again, and then the *Rocky* theme song at the end of the cruise director's spiel. At this point, put on your headphones. After a few minutes, I'll point at you to do the drum roll on the floor tom again, and then you'll hear a voice in your headphones that will count off the show. That's the signal to start the first page of the production show. Got it?"

"Yes," I said. I had no idea what was going on. I scribbled notes of what he'd said on the margins of the sheet music, said The Lord's Prayer ten times, and hoped for the best.

This was the way of the showband drum chair. Virtuoso banjo players would come aboard with a folder of music for their show. I'd attend the twenty-minute rehearsal in which they'd explain the millions of cues in their show, declaiming long, detailed instructions twenty minutes before we performed the act in front of a thousand passengers. The banjo player would, with a completely straight face, tell me to remember that when he plucked the fifth string on his banjo for the third time, during the second song of the fourth routine, the drummer should hit the bass drum six times and then shout, "Hey, who stole my banjo?" I was the FNG. There was a lot to learn, and I had to learn it fast.

The theater lights dimmed. I grabbed my sticks. Ricky pointed at me. I rolled on the floor tom and stopped when the cruise director came out on stage. Divine intervention is the only possible explanation for how I made it through my first pre-production show routine, with all of the finger pointing, cues, fast-tempo *Flintstones* theme and all. Then the light dimmed lower. I put on my headphones. The music director pointed at me. I rolled again on the floor tom, and I felt the ship list a little to one side. We had left port a few hours before the show, and the ship had now moved into open ocean, where the waves had picked up.

As you can imagine, rough seas often make the job of performing on an instrument or dancing on stage much more difficult. I continued rolling on the floor tom. I looked up toward the opening of the pit and saw a bright glow as the stage lights were turned on. It was show time. I listened to my headphones for the cue. I fiddled with the Aviom system, readjusting a few volume knobs for the backing tracks and checking to make sure the vocalist channel was off, as Ricky had suggested. Then I heard a voice come through my headphones. "One-two-three-four-one-two-ready-play." The hydraulic platform began to move upward as the band played the opening sequence of the show. The pit was lifted to stage level, giving me a view of the audience that filled the theater. The curtain opened behind us. A group of dancers wearing feather boas and sparkling sequined bodysuits with thigh-high fishnet stockings pranced on stage.

A production show on a cruise ship is often a nonstop medley of seamless music. For example, in just five minutes during a Motown-style production show, the band may play small bits of "I Heard It Through the Grapevine," "Signed, Sealed, Delivered," "Let's Get It On," "Ain't Too Proud to Beg," "Ain't No Mountain High Enough," and "Dancing in the Street." The shows often last for an hour without much of a break for many of the orchestra musicians.

I ripped the sheet music from my stand as we went through the show, with no time to keep the music organized as it fell to the pit floor. I did my best to quickly read the notes as they flew by. An hour later, the band hit the final note, and the curtain closed. The dancers clapped to celebrate another performance. I was drenched in sweat and surrounded by sheet music, having avoided serious disaster many times during the show but far from drumming up a particularly great performance. I realized the showband gig, at least for the foreseeable future, was going to be a one-way street that led straight to the practice room for hours on end.

I slipped back into cruise control, back into the repeating pattern of ship life, which at the time mostly consisted of practicing drums, performing the shows, exploring the ports, and occasionally going down to the crew bar for a crew party or a little R & R. The production shows were becoming a little easier to manage every day. Everything was smooth sailing, until one day I was sitting in my crew cabin between performances on the thirty-minute break I would have. We had a small television in our crew cabin that had an old VCR attached to it. I would record *Jeopardy* and *Wheel of Fortune,* which came on during the hour of our production show. After the first show ended, I would go to the crew bar and buy a bag of popcorn and a glass of cranberry juice and bring it back to my crew cabin to watch game show power hour, as it's called here in the States.

I was answering a question to *Jeopardy* when I smelled cigarette smoke in the room. I looked around. *No, I didn't suddenly take up smoking without knowing it.* I breathed in a little through my nose. *Yes, that's definitely cigarette smoke.* I walked around the room to try and find where it was coming from, and I found the source at the small air-conditioning vent on the ceiling of my crew cabin. I stood on a chair and could see the light cloud of smoke slowly flowing into my room. I'm not sure what caused this to happen on this particular day. Perhaps there was a smoker a few rooms down from me who had just moved in. All I know is that I had reasonably fresh air for a few weeks, and then suddenly I was living in a box that seemed to have a nearly constant stream of secondhand smoke flowing into it.

CHAPTER SEVEN

TAKE A DEEP BREATH. EVERYTHING WILL BE FINE.

In crew areas on some ships, the amount of air that is healthy to breathe is equal to what you'd find below the surface of the sea when you're not wearing a snorkel mask or diving equipment. Passenger areas have excellent air filters, usually one for each cabin. They also have properly functioning ventilation systems, which help out a bit too. If you're ever in a passenger room on a cruise ship, just look up. Those fancy little boxes that are plugged into the ceiling are cleaning the air at least enough so that it doesn't smell unbearably bad. Hopefully, they are also cleaning the air enough so that it's healthy to breathe.

Unfortunately, on many cruise ships, most crew members don't have air filters in their crew cabins. We don't have nifty little boxes in our ceilings. Instead, we have holes. There is a tan (of course) cover over this hole and a little dial on it that does exactly absolutely nothing. This dial is presumably designed to give the illusion that the crew member has some amount of control over the amount of or temperature of air that is flowing into their room, which they do not. And the air that comes out of this hole often smells so bad that it's a common practice for crew members to stuff fabric-softener sheets into these holes to mask the smell. I've had cabin stewards stuff the holes with fabric-softener sheets without me ever asking them to.

Air is circulated throughout the cruise ship. Air is taken

from the outside and pulled inside the ship. Now, I'm not a shipbuilder or a maritime engineer, and I won't pretend to know with certainty how these ventilation systems work exactly, but from what I've observed, there was a chain of crew cabins that the air on a cruise ship passed through before it arrived at mine. So everyone in my hallway seemed to be breathing much of the same air, and sometimes that air that was pumped into the ship from outside wasn't very clean to begin with. If the wind was blowing hard or blowing the wrong direction, it sometimes seemed to blow some of that dark smoke that constantly billowed from the ship's smokestack right into the intake vents that sucked the air into my cabin. And if someone was smoking a cigarette a few cabins down from my quarters, then I would be smoking that cigarette too. On one ship, the outdoor crew smoking section was located directly in front of the intake vent that pulled the air (yes, I think you guessed it) right into my crew cabin.

Now, before every person who smokes stops reading this book right here, let me say I don't have a problem with people smoking. I think there should be an area of the ship where smokers can go where it's not going to affect the health of other crew and passengers. That seems fair to me, and I assume that would seem fair to those who smoke.

When I first started working on cruise ships, crew quarters looked like a scene from a Quentin Tarantino film. Everyone smoked, all the time, everywhere. The official smoking policy at that time, at least as I remember it, was limited to the single rule that you shouldn't smoke while lying in bed because you might fall asleep and start a fire.

From what I understand, since the time that I originally published this book, the cruise ship companies have changed the rules regarding smoking for the better, and I hope that's true. During this first contract with the showband, I started to see the rules begin to change. At this time, the cruise ship company first announced that crew members could no longer smoke in their rooms, but none of the managers on board were enforcing this no-smoking policy.

After weeks of having smoke, and all sorts of other unpleasant odors that humans produce with regularity, waft into my crew cabin through the hole in my ceiling, I decided to bring up the issue at one of the weekly meetings that were held for the entertainment department. At these meetings, we were encouraged to vent our frustrations and bring up any issues that concerned us.

I raised my hand and let the cruise director know about the issue I was having with smoke coming into my cabin.

The cruise director gave me a blank stare. After a lengthy pause, she said, "I think this cruise ship is my home. I think you should be able to do whatever you want in your own home. So if people want to smoke in their own home, then they should be allowed to do it." This line of logic seemed about as rational as the amount cruise lines charge for a margarita on the lido deck, but the cruise director was in charge. The cruise director squinted and said, "I don't think this is something you really want to fight on this ship, anyway."

I decided to make an effort to try to talk with someone who would perhaps be a bit more sympathetic and reasonable about this issue. At the time, I was mostly hoping to get a positive resolution to this issue for myself, but I also felt that there were probably many other crew members that felt the same way I did but perhaps didn't want to make any waves, as they say, and make trouble in cruise liner land for themselves. I asked around about who would be the best person to talk with about this issue, and several veteran crew members let me know that I might have the best chance speaking with the staff captain, so I made an appointment.

The staff captain is as high up the chain of command a crew member can go before being given permission to speak with the captain of the ship. The staff captain has the power to make significant changes in a crew member's life. There are many excellent staff captains out at sea, as well as cruise directors. Most of the managers I worked with during my time at sea were truly incredible, compassionate people whom I admired and respected deeply for their professionalism, skill, dedication, and excellence at their jobs. And perhaps some of the issues I had with others were simply a result of them having a bad day or year, and therefore perhaps we cannot fully judge their character on one interaction they had with me. However, on this ship, the case was somewhat complex.

I arrived at the staff captain's office in high spirits, and I knocked on the door.

"Come in," the staff captain or someone on the other side of the door said. I opened the door. The staff captain was seated behind a large wooden desk. He had an officer on each side of him. All three of them were smoking cigarettes in the tiny office. They appeared to take me for a fool.

"What is this about?" I asked the staff captain.

"I'm not-ah sure-ah what you mean-ah by that-ah?" the staff captain said. He pulled hard on his cigarette and blew the smoke up into the cloudy air.

"I've been having an issue with cigarette smoke coming

into my cabin," I said. "As I understand it, crew members shouldn't be smoking in their cabins. And now I come here, and you knew why, and all three of you are smoking. Is this some sort of joke?"

"I don't-ah know what you mean-ah." The staff captain stood up and walked over to me with the cigarette in his hand. "I don't-ah see anyone-ah smoking here-ah." He took a deep drag of his cigarette and blew the smoke in my face.

As if on cue, the cruise director walked out of a nearby crew cabin. The cruise director smiled and then took a drag from a cigarette. The cruise director stopped in front of me and repeated, "I don't think this is something you really want to fight on this ship." *Unbelievable.* I walked out of the room and tried to slam the door behind me, but a little mechanism kept it from slamming and instead the door shut slowly and quietly, which wasn't the effect I was going for at all. I could hear laughing as I walked away.

Many cruise ship companies since then have apparently announced that they will no longer permit smoking inside any crew areas at all. Bravo. Now all they have to do is enforce it.

Of course, it made sense that the officers, staff captains, and cruise directors didn't care much about the air-quality issues for the crew at that time. They didn't have holes in their ceilings that they had to stuff with air-fresheners. Those with a rank of officer and above had air filters and an ultra-convenient thermostat in their rooms to control the temperature at the touch of a button. The crew members got the holes. The crew members got the smoke, the exhaust, the body odor, and all the farts that circulated from room to room.

CHAPTER EIGHT

HEY, SHIPMATE, OLD PAL

It was about this time that I got a new roommate. My old roomie had shipped off to a short vacation at home before joining a different ship. I was always nervous about getting a new roommate on the cruise ship, which is like playing roulette; the odds are extremely high that you're going to lose big time. Many times you're going to be stuck working and living with this person for months on end and share a ten-by-ten-foot room with a four-by-four-foot bathroom. And when getting a new roommate, you sometimes know right away if you've won or lost. I had never known more, with all my heart, that I had lost miserably at the roulette table of cruise ship roommates than at the time I met this particular roomie.

I walked down the I-95 and went through the list in my head of things I did not want my roommate to be:

(1) A drunk. There is an exceptionally high number of drunks out at sea. We are sailors. Having a bottle of rum in hand is almost part of the official uniform. Besides, there is cheap booze, a huge amount of time to kill, nowhere to go when the cruise ship is out at sea, and almost always a party going on in the crew bar. So most people decide they might as well drink. However, having a roommate that stumbles into your cabin every night at four in the morning and then decides it's going to be acceptable and hilarious to throw crew-mess salami at your face while you're sleeping starts to

wear thin after two or three months. Unfortunately, often you'll have to bunk with this roommate for six to eight months.

(2) A smoker. Sometimes having a smoker as a roommate isn't that bad. There are plenty of considerate smokers. But this is a gamble as well. Many times, you end up living with a smoker that asks you if they can smoke in the room. When you tell them no, they do this thing where they stand halfway out the door and blow the smoke into the hallway, as if this makes the situation any better.

(3) The depressed guy that never leaves the room. Cruise ships can be fun, but they can be lonely and depressing places for some people as well. Some crew members have a hard time coping when they only get a few hours of sunlight every day, are isolated from their family and friends, must eat food like chicken-beak soup in the crew mess, and must live under strict and often petty rules. Ship life can send some crew members into a downward spiral of depression, and sometimes they turn into people who never leave the room. They just sleep and sleep and sleep in the darkness whenever they have time off. When I'd have a roommate like this, I'd try to cheer them up, and that was most important. However, not being able to use the room very much could make ship life more difficult than it already was at times.

(4) The control freak. We have all had to deal with living with control freaks at some point in our lives. Nowhere is it more difficult to live with a control freak than on a cruise ship where you live in a ten-by-ten room and it is very easy to control every square inch. You know you're dealing with a control freak when your roommate is thrown into a frantic fit of rage because you moved his Darth Vader coffee mug from

the *Star Wars* shelf to the *Battlestar Galactica* shelf.

(5) The "interesting person." These are very common, as there are plenty of "interesting people" on cruise ships. Once, I shared a room with a very "interesting person" who had rather strange sleeping habits. He snored so loudly he would wake *himself* up. His snoring sounded like the noise a cruise ship engine would make if you threw a bucket full of wrenches into the oil compartment. He also had a Spanish girlfriend and was fluent in Spanish. He apparently would dream in Spanish and yell in his sleep in Spanish, which would also startle him awake. Every time he woke himself up—and this is the cherry on top here—he would yelp like a sea lion that had gotten his flipper slammed in the car door, and then he'd yell in Spanish a little more for good measure, go back to sleep, and then do the whole damn thing over again approximately 3.52 seconds later. I didn't sleep a wink for nearly three days until I got transferred to another room, which might have been his evil-genius play from the beginning. Note to self: develop loud sleeping issues on the cruise ship so that I can deviously acquire my own crew cabin (*mu-ah-ha-ha,* tapping fingers together creepily).

(6) The lifer. You find them in every line of work. They are employees that have no life outside of work, are completely obsessed with the office, and only talk about their job... all the time. They are the employees that are going to work at that job for the rest of their lives. Lifers. And you find plenty of them on cruise ships. You can always quickly identify these crew members because all they ever talk about is their last contract and their last ship.

"On my last ship, the dance cast was incredible."

"On my last ship, the food was way better."

"On my last ship, we had chicken fingers three days in a row once."

"On my last ship, the drummer in the showband was much better looking."

"On my last ship..."

"On my last ship..."

"On my last ship..."

Ahhhh! Someone tell them no one cares about their last ship!

These were the types of roommates I didn't want. I walked up to my crew cabin, positive and optimistic. I crossed my fingers and opened the door. It was one p.m. on a Sunday. My new roommate was sprawled out on the bathroom floor, a small bit of drool running down one side of his mouth. A cigarette hung loosely between his lips, smoke billowing into the room. He was clutching a nearly empty bottle of rum. His eyes were bloodshot, half open. He stuck out his hand. "Hey, shipmate, old pal, I'm your new roommate."

He sounded chipper, the way sailors do when their brain is floating in their skull cavity on a thick, liquid cushion of rum. Then he got sick in the toilet. The room was spotless, all of his clothes folded on the bed and organized into piles by clothing type, his underwear ironed and folded too, the official neat-freak red flag. A box of snoring strips sat on the desk. An announcement came over the loud speaker in the ceiling of the room.

"Crew-ah member. Crew-ah member. Please-ah report-ah to your designated muster station-ah."

The boat drill was about to begin. My new roomie, smelling like a passenger after taking a Caribbean catamaran ride on which they serve free rum punch, stumbled around the room and eventually donned his lifejacket in a tangled mess. He sloppily threw on his neon-colored cap, the bill of the cap cocked to one side, making him look more like a member of the Beastie Boys than someone you would want to rely on while the ship is sinking, unless you wanted to have a last-minute freestyle rap battle.

My roommate headed straight out the door toward his muster station. I was right behind him. I watched as he stumbled down the hallway and bumped into guests that were unenthusiastically attempting to form a line for the boat drill. He was fired that afternoon and walked down the gangplank the next. No ticket home. He had to figure it out for himself. He didn't care, though. He had been on the ship for eight months straight and was ready to go home. Eight months on a ship can do that to a sailor.

CHAPTER NINE

BOAT DRILL, SWEET BOAT DRILL

I walked to the boat drill. It's no secret that passengers have a special hate/hate relationship with the emergency boat drills that take place at the beginning of each cruise. For most passengers, it only takes one boat drill to become instantly aware that they are something you absolutely dislike, similar to what happened the first time you saw your picture in full display on the promenade from when the cruise ship photographer took your photo while you were drunk and chewing your food in the dining room, the one where you're as sunburned as a lobster, smiling so wide everyone can see each of your purple-stained teeth, your breasts are halfway out of your bikini top, and you have mayonnaise running down the side of your mouth.

I fully understand the desire to throw the boat drill over the rails. Nothing says *care-free holiday* like starting it off donning your life jacket and standing in the hot sun for half an hour so you can listen to an officer tell you what to do if an iceberg slices the hull of the ship wide open like a can opener or how to jump overboard if the cruise liner runs aground and becomes the world's largest artificial reef off the coast of Italy.

Imagine for a moment what it would be like to be a crew member who has the maritime pleasure of running these wonderful boat drills, having to deal with grumpy, tired, stressed-out passengers at nearly every one of them. Many passengers go on a cruise because they are in desperate need of a vacation, so they're often stressed out before they even walk out the front door of their house to begin their journey to the cruise ship. Their base-line stress levels are already equal to that of a crew member at the end of an eight-month contract who worked in the garbage room sorting drink-stirrer straws from piles of chocolate-melting cake and lobster tail shells for twelve hours a day with only a half day off a week. Then many of these people endure the stresses of an airport or a Greyhound bus (God forbid) or a car full of whining children or a spouse who's in one of their "moods" (Lord have mercy). Then these same people get to join the fun that is the fiasco of parking at the gargantuan port and then waiting in that massive line of passengers and going through security before climbing aboard the cruise ship.

Passengers navigate the stressful labyrinth of the cruise ship and then arrive at their stateroom after walking around the ship for a few hours like they did as children the first time they were lost in the grocery store. Then they finally drop off their luggage and head for the lido deck. They tuck into their first burger from the lido-deck grill, buy their second $40 piña colada (with plastic souvenir cup, so of course that's a fair price), at which time they discover there are no laws governing price gouging in international waters, and then, by some miracle on the high seas, they find the perfect cushioned lounger overlooking the ocean. They've finally escaped it all. They tilt the lounger back, slide on their sunglasses, lace their fingers, put their hands behind their head, and take a deep breath. *Let the vacation begin.*

Then, like a scratched record ruining the best part in your favorite song, the passenger hears the announcement for the emergency boat drill. "All-ah passenger, all-ah passenger. Please reenter the stressful maze-ah of the cruise ship-ah and find your-ah stateroom-ah and secure your-ah life jacket-ah and report-ah to your muster station-ah. This is mandatory and-ah all-ah your fun-ah will be ruined-ah. Thank you-ah. Your captain-ah."

And then after all of this fun, all of these same people show up to my boat drill, many of them rather grumpy, full of attitude, and looking for someone to complain to about the stupid boat drill that could save their life. Enter me stage right. They find me standing in my life jacket with a big goofy smile on my face (only because it's required by cruise ship company law whenever crew is in passenger areas) and a bright neon-colored hat on my head that reads CREW in big black letters. The hat might as well read COMPLAIN HERE.

At a boat drill, there is always that one passenger who shows up holding a dewy, punch-bowl-sized glass of frozen margarita, or the pudgy kid inhaling a massive plate of chicken fingers with honey mustard sauce, or the guy in the Florida Gators hat sipping Bud Light through his mustache. Most of them would get an attitude when I told them they couldn't drink a big, dewy glass of margarita or sip Bud Light through their mustache or eat plates of chicken fingers at the emergency boat drill. None of them were happy when I had to take their drinks and food away.

In theory, a crew member's job at a boat drill is simple. They form passengers into straight lines as they arrive at their muster stations and then continue to form neat little rows of passengers as more drag in at the last minute. However, passengers at boat drills are notorious for being insubordinate nonconformists who refuse to get in or stay in said line. It never failed that William Wallace of the high seas would come waltzing into my boat drill line and then proceed to rouse up his Scottish clansmen into a mutinous mob. I quickly grew to understand that most people who are on vacation have the same motto of: *I'm on a cruise. Don't tell me what to do.* This often made ship life hard for the lowly crew member who was just trying to do their stupid job at the boat drill and then move on with their life, getting back to sorting plastic stir straws in the garbage room or taking embarrassing photos of passengers in the dining room while they're chewing their food.

I would kindly ask someone to stand in line so that I could create a row of people in front of them, and the minute I turned my back, *whoop* (in a Chris Berman voice), they would slip right back out of line and mess up the whole process. The repetitive monotony of having to battle the rebellious William Wallace of the high seas every three or four days for five years was enough to make me feel as if I had contracted the norovirus every time I heard that boat drill announcement come over the loudspeaker of my crew cabin. But as crew members, you, over time, develop a high threshold for stress. I became rather desensitized to the triggers of buttheads, rebels, and drunken rabble-rousers. So if you're about to go on a cruise right now, please get in line and stay in line at the passenger boat drill. In all seriousness, these emergency boat drills could save your life. And cruises are such a wonderful thing that everyone would like to live to see another cruise.

CHAPTER TEN

HURRY UP AND WAIT!

It was around this time that I was sitting in the crew bar after my nightly showband performance, looking out the small porthole window as the moonlight cast silvery rays over the Caribbean Sea. I had just taken a sip of my $1 Stella Artois when I heard the loud *clank* of glass on wood. I looked down to see a bottle of vodka sitting on the table in front of me, and through the clear glass bottle I saw Svetlana, the dreamy Russian casino dealer on the ship that I had been trying to flirt with whenever I happened to be walking past her card station at the promenade casino.

"This is for me," she said and pointed at the bottle then winked and smiled, "...and you." I melted at the sound of her biting Russian accent, a sound that I had associated with mischievous Russian vixens ever since I started watching Natalia in the *Rocky and Bullwinkle Show* as a kid. I assumed this was about to be the best night of my life. I heard Phil Collins's "In the Air Tonight" play in my head, starting at that point with that big incredible drum fill, *bop-bop...bop-bop...bop-bop...bop-bop...bop...bop.*

That night I finally understood why Russians, after a few drinks, dance in a squatting position while kicking and singing with their arms crossed. After a few drinks of vodka shared with a beautiful Russian woman, you become so giddy that a Russian nesting doll can seem like the most entertaining device since Al Gore invented the internet.

She was beautiful, exceptionally intelligent, and direct and confident in a way that I had experienced very little with American women. She had an excellent education in world literature, and so we were able to talk at length about writing and books, and I felt that if we were to stay together, she could save me the boatload of money that I was spending on hiring editors for my books, just icing on the cake. We seemed to be a match made in Cold War heaven.

I'm not one to drink much these days, but back on this night in my early days as a cruise ship sailor, I had consumed so much vodka that I could've been convinced that spending the night in a Siberian prison wasn't such a bad idea.

Our relationship took a slow and natural course, which was a good thing. Most of us know that taking things slow is nearly always better than jumping into the sack with someone right away, especially when you know as much about their values and true character as what you've gleaned about Vladimir Putin from interviews with American journalists.

Our ship-life romance came easy, and I remember exploring the Caribbean ports and beaches together. I pretty much stayed in a state of ship-life bliss during this time. In celebration of our relationship surviving two months at sea, I bought us a bottle of Dom Perignon and bribed an Indian cook in the crew mess to make us a dozen chocolate-covered strawberries. She brought a blanket and two glasses, and we found a quiet spot on the upper crew deck and spent a great evening sipping champagne and clinking glasses as we sailed through ship life and the sea together, two young and hopeful foreigners in love, hoping to form a lasting unity between two cultures that are often at odds, and from two countries which often react like a rocky shoal and the hull of a ship when they happen to collide.

It wasn't much later that I was called to the crew office, and while there I was told that I'd be transferred to a different ship. This was two strikes for me now in the baseball game of ship-life love. The next morning, I packed my bags and said goodbye to Svetlana. As of now, it seems as if I may never see her again.

I cleaned out the pile of old internet cards from the bottom of my crew cabin drawers and wiped down the walls in my room, a nice gesture for the next crew member to take my place. It was five in the morning, and I had been told to be at the immigration procedures at 5:10 a.m. on the dot, captain's orders. I was running late, so I grabbed my heavy luggage and tore down the I-95. I was breathing heavily by the time I walked into the room for immigration, where another hundred or so crew members who were also disembarking the cruise ship that day in Miami were gathered. I wiped the sweat from my forehead and looked at the clock. It was 5:09, thank God. I sat down and then waited… and waited… and waited.

If I had to sum up what it's like to be a cruise ship crew member in four words or less, I would say, "hurry up and wait." You hear this phrase constantly being used on the ship, and quite appropriately. Crew members get rushed into a training room, a meeting, a line, or a boat drill, and then they sit and they wait… and wait… and wait, sometimes for hours, until whatever was so important to rush toward actually begins. Immigration is the best (and therefore the worst) example of this hurry up and wait phenomenon in ship life. Every time I boarded a new ship or left my old ship, I had to go through immigration procedures. Crew members are packed into one room, always exceedingly early in the morning, and then they sit and wait for hours and hours until the immigration officers actually arrive. These immigration officers then often process crew members' paperwork at a pace similar to the speed at which glaciers eroded the North American mountain ranges. It doesn't matter if you're Indian, Italian, English, or American. It doesn't matter what country you're "immigrating" back to. It doesn't matter if you're an American who is getting off the ship in America. You have to immigrate, and so you have to hurry—to arrive at immigration "on time"—and then wait.

I sat in a passenger dining room, thinking about Svetlana and how much I was going to miss her and the Cold War–era games from her childhood she used to teach me, like the one where we would pull strands of loose fabric from the ripped parts in her jean knee-holes to see who could pull out the longest strand of cotton. Two or three hours had passed by when I heard a commotion coming from a few rows down. An American like me seemed to have had enough.

He was standing up, waving his arms around, his face flushed, spittle coming out of his mouth as he talked rather loudly. "What the heck is this? Why am I even sitting here waiting? I'm an American! Why am I at immigration? Why do I have to immigrate to my effing own country?"

The other crew members and I kept quiet, most of us half asleep, and ignored him. Seeing a crew member go bonkers really wasn't that uncommon for me at this point, even this early on as a crew member; it was only evidence of the way ship-life frustrations can mount. I remember riding on a crew elevator when a Food and Beverage manager stepped in and smiled at me. As soon as the elevator door closed, he turned around and started punching and kicking the metal walls, leaving big dents and yelling profanities the entire time. I remember one crew member who constantly complained about his life on the cruise ship. He had gone *dark,* as we say in ship life. He was in bad need of a long vacation on land. One night after drinking heavily at the crew bar, I woke up hearing someone yelling from a few rooms down the hallway. He was smashing lamps and kicking the walls, and the next day he was gone. He had been on the ships for something like nine months straight at that point. Fortunately, episodes of this severity do not happen that often, from what I've observed.

I would venture to say that 70 percent of cruise ship crew members love and enjoy their jobs on the ship. However, after six months on a ship, all of the monotony, cramped quarters, poor air quality, crew mess food, bad roommates, the waiting, the petty rules, the rickety laundry facilities, and the red-alert days can start to do funny things to a crew member. That's when we have to remember what the great philosopher Star Man said: "If you can't have fun on a cruise ship, then you might as well give up."

I wasn't giving up, not on finding love aboard the ship or on ship life, either. I was headed to a new ship, a new adventure, and even though I wished Svetlana could have been by my side, I was ready to climb aboard and see where the next cruise ship would take me.

CHAPTER ELEVEN

EVERYTHING IS MUCH BETTER IN THE BAHAMAS

Nowadays, I always bring a pack of pens along with me on the plane whenever I travel to the Bahamas. All different colored pens: sea-foam green, coconut brown, sunshine yellow, Customs-and-Immigration-holding-cell blue—all the colors of the Bahamian rainbow. You see, once upon a time, in a Latin country called Miami, I boarded a plane on a hot summer day, and I took wing over the Caribbean Sea. It was a little puddle-jumper of a plane, the kind you see pictured in newspaper articles with headlines like, *Midday Plane Crash, No Survivors.*

As the plane drifted toward the patchy cotton-ball clouds, I watched all the little islands off the coast of Florida—each of them with beach cottages painted the same neon colors that you find on poisonous snakes and spiders in the Amazon—shrink into small dots among a vast expanse of deep blue sea.

I was being transferred, catching my next cruise ship in Nassau, and I was on a tight schedule. I had just three hours to get through customs and get aboard the cruise liner. I was on ship-time, and I knew the captain waited for no man.

After a few minutes on the plane, I drifted asleep. I didn't wake up until I heard the sound of plane tires screeching to a halt. Outside my window, the coconut palms that bordered the tarmac were blowing in the breeze. *Caribbean life, baby.* I'm always willing to travel for decent work, especially when the job is on board a cruise ship with the bow pointed toward the tropics.

Off my flight tray, I grabbed the little square sheet of paper with a heading at the top that read: *IMMIGRATION FORM.* One of the friendly Bahamian airline stewards must have left it there for me, not wanting to wake me up as they passed them out. *How nice.*

I stepped off the plane and grabbed my bags from among the luggage laid out on the runway. I pulled down my shades and walked into the airport terminal.

Big banner sign: *WELCOME TO THE BAHAMAS.* I felt a blast of air conditioning. A steel drum ensemble with a female singer played Lionel Ritchie's "All Night Long" as I walked in.

Yes. Wonderful. What a welcome! All I needed was a guy with dreadlocks selling fresh steamed lobsters and little cups of butter, and I would have been in heaven. I could smell the beach from there.

I was the last one off the plane, and so when I walked into the terminal, I was at the end of the line of people waiting to get through Customs. I watched as every one ahead of me breezed through without a problem. Customs: just a slight inconvenience, and a small price to pay for an all-access pass to paradise.

There was a long line of customs workstations, like an electric fence to keep the gringo goats from freely grazing on the green Bahamian grass on the other side, but there was only one woman working behind a single station.

The moment I stepped up to the counter, the steel drum band stopped playing, as if they had been contracted to play only until the last person walked up to the counter. That was just like a band, never playing a second more than they're paid for. That last tinny note of the steel drum echoed through the terminal. The band walked out the back door, and the room became quiet. It felt larger than it had before, now that it was just me and the customs agent, all alone on the edge of Nassau.

I put my Customs and Immigration form on the counter and noticed that the agent had a pen clipped onto the front pocket of her shirt. I looked at her and smiled. "Do you have a pen I could use to fill out the immigration form?"

She did not smile back. Red flag number one.

She pointed to my form on the counter. "What is dis (this)?"

What an odd question. Has she not seen a customs form before? "Um, this is my immigration form."

"Why it not be filled out?"

"Um, well see, I didn't have a pen, and I must have fallen asleep. I—"

She pointed to the form, to a section near the top. I looked down and read it. It said something like: *All persons entering the Bahamas must fill out and sign Immigration and Customs form and have form in hand at all times prior to entering the country.*

"I'm really sorry," I said. "I seem to have fallen asleep. If I could just use your pen I—"

"I don't have no pen."

"Actually, there is a pen right there on your shirt. If I could just use it, I'll—"

She looked down at her shirt pocket. "Dis is my pen. Why don't you have no pen to fill out de form?"

Was I still dreaming? Should I try and slap myself awake? What kind of bizarre-o world had I awoken to here? I felt as if I was in a *Seinfeld* episode. *No pen for you.*

I looked around at the other security stations. No pens. No pencils. No crayons, even. "Are there any other pens in here that I could use?"

"I *don't* know. Keeping track of pens for you isn't my job."

Geesh. Wouldn't you know it? I'm on a tight schedule to catch a ship that's pulling out of harbor in T-minus two hours, and I'm trapped inside the Bahamian air terminal with the pen Nazi.

I grabbed my form, admittedly displaying a bit of frustration and disbelief, which certainly didn't help my cause. I walked toward the back of the terminal, toward a waist-high bench running the length of the back wall, the type of bench you see in banks that people use to fill out deposit slips. As I got closer, I saw one of those silver chains, the kind with the little beads, that you always see connected to (Could it be? Had I been saved?) pens.

I grabbed the chain. Nothing. I looked down the long counter. There was a line of chains, all of them just dangling off the end of the bench with no pens attached.

This place had been the victim of a crack pen burglar. I walked down the line, grabbing each chain as I went, hoping to find a pen on the end of one of the chains. Nothing. Just lousy silver beads that I could spin in my hand. I rummaged through my bags. Nothing.

I turned around to face her. She was waiting, like a shark circling my life raft, knowing that eventually I would fall overboard and eventually the shark would have its bloody meal. As long as she was patient, she knew she would win, because this shark had the only stupid pen in the sea.

I approached cautiously; this was going to require the diplomatic skills of a Naval-war-college graduate. She was writing something in a notepad—with her pen.

"I can't seem to find a pen anywhere," I said. "What would you suggest I do?"

"You cannot go through customs until de form is completed."

"So you want me to wait here until I can find a pen?"

"I don't care what you do, but you be not coming tru (through) here until dis form be filled out."

"When is the next plane landing?" I asked.

Someone on board would have a pen. I'd beat her at her game, after all.

"Hmm, I'm not sure. Maybe three or four hours."

The ship would be gone by then. I would have to call my boss back at showband headquarters in Miami and explain why I missed the boat. But it wouldn't matter. The ship I was boarding was taking seven-day cruises. I'd be stuck in Nassau at the height of tourist season. I would have to pay for food and a hotel room for seven days until the ship was back in port. This wasn't going to be cheap.

All over a stupid pen. A pen that she had right there in her hand. A pen that was less than a foot away from me. A pen that, to me, was worth—oh I don't know, maybe a thousand dollars or so.

I took a few deep breaths. "I'd like to speak to your boss."

"Go sit over there." She pointed toward a line of chairs in the back of the terminal. Then she tucked her pen into her little shirt pocket and waddled away.

I walked toward the line of chairs, but didn't sit down. Surely her boss would have some common sense. He would be reasonable, go fetch me a pen, and this whole wacky episode would be over.

She returned with a man in tow: linen pants, linen shirt, leather sandals, big white smile. He walked through the customs gate. "So, another one without a pen." Then he laughed and motioned toward me. "Come with me. We have a place where you can wait."

I picked up my bags and followed him to a tiny room on the side of the building. Plaque on the door said something like: *CUSTOMS HOLDING ROOM.* There was a small desk in the front of the room: deep-blue-sea-colored carpet, bright white walls, two metal chairs in front of the desk—the kind of chairs designed by chiropractors to keep them in steady supply of clients with chronic back pain.

"Have a seat," the man said and motioned toward one of the chairs. I sat down and put my bags beside me, keeping them close. He sat on the edge of the desk, one leg hanging off the ground a little. He leaned forward. "Seems like we have a little problem here."

Yes. I had a problem. I was trying to enter a country where the locals were fiercely territorial over pens. I looked at the desk. There was a coffee mug with an illustrated palm tree and a slogan across the front in bright yellow letters: *WELCOME TO THE BAHAMAS! EVERYTHING'S MUCH BETTER IN THE BAHAMAS.* "I just need a pen."

The man leaned back, then stood up, and started pacing around the room with his hands behind his back, as if in deep thought, as if I had just asked him some complex riddle that he was trying to solve. "Why have you come to the Bahamas?"

I felt as if I was in one of those cop movies. It had all the right components. The crime, the holding cell, now I was in the scene where they interrogated the bad guy, maybe rough him up a little. It even had the two cops. Good cop, bad cop. Except, there was no good cop. This was bad cop, bad cop situation.

"I'm boarding a ship."

"What kind of ship?" He said it in the way that the lead investigator on *CSI* says, *Where were you on the night of June 25, 1994?*

"A cruise ship."

"Uh-huh. And what do you do on the ship?"

"Come on. I just need a pen. There's a whole mug full of pens right there. Right in that—"

"What do you do on the ship?"

"I'm a drummer."

"What kind of drummer."

"A drummer that does the laundry. What? A drummer that plays drums. In the band."

"We're going to have to search your bags."

"Really? Geez, go ahead."

As he rummaged through my bags, taking every single thing out one at a time, he kept asking me questions. *What's my name? Where was I born? Am I sure?* I was starting to get worried. Could this all really be over a pen? Did I trigger some type of alarm in the back office? Did I look like some big-time cocaine smuggler they'd been trying to snag for years?

This could be serious stuff here. I might end up in the

slammer over a case of mistaken identity. And not just any prison, but a Bahamian hoosegow where I'd serve a life sentence living off my one meal a day of watered-down conch chowder and grapefruit soda, and where they have a special cell in the psychiatric ward for all the other gringos who didn't have a pen. After about five minutes, the man walked back in, grabbed one of the pens from the mug, and tossed it over to me.

My belongings were scattered all over the desk. No cocaine anywhere. I was starting to think I might make it out of this place alive. I pulled the chair to the edge of the desk and filled out the form as fast as I could.

"Follow me," the man said.

We walked to the customs security station. "Passport please?"

I didn't say a word. I just slid my dark blue booklet across the counter. He grabbed the stamp and punched both documents. He slid them back to me and put out one hand, motioning toward the other side of the gate, toward freedom, toward a land filled with pens and pencils and crayons, toward the cruise ship that was leaving port in less than an hour.

A half hour later, I was walking up the gangway, and I had my bags, my passport, my liberty, and a little souvenir that I had tucked into my pocket before I left the Customs Holding Room—a little, stupid, plastic pen that read *WELCOME TO THE BAHAMAS! EVERYTHING IS MUCH BETTER IN THE BAHAMAS.*

CHAPTER TWELVE

AS HOT AS A CRUISE SHIP FEVER

I climbed aboard my new ship and started the process over again: immigration, getting my old folder of music, attending safety drills for the first week, learning a new batch of often difficult production shows that required ceaseless practice for me for the first several weeks, making new friends, finding my niche in my new life at sea, and looking for a ship-life love who hopefully would want to continue life on land together one day.

This new ship had a similar Caribbean itinerary. We alternated seven-day cruises between the Western and Eastern Caribbean ports, which included wonderful stops at St. Martin, St. Thomas, Cozumel, San Juan in Puerto Rico, Nassau in the Bahamas, Grand Turk in the Turks and Caicos, Grand Cayman in the Cayman Islands, and different ports in Jamaica. These were some of my best times aboard cruise ships. It was early enough in my career that I hadn't grown tired of the ports, and ship life had only just started to wear thin.

The travel was certainly one of the best parts about working on a cruise ship. The world was a place that I felt should be explored, and the cruise ship gave me a first-class ride to the most beautiful ports on the planet. I felt a part of the great seafaring tradition. And while sailing through the seas, bays, and inlets of the world, I began to get a true sense for how massive and marvelous the planet really is. I was having the chance to explore the sea more deeply than I probably ever would have been able to otherwise. Crew members got to feel the spray of the ocean when high seas thunder against the hull. They watched dolphins and whales follow the wake of the mysterious metal ship that has entered their waters. We would stand at the bow of the ship at sunset and sail away from the coast as dolphins playfully jumped and led the way forward, as if they were towing the cruise liner to our next tropical destination.

As crew members, we had the opportunity to travel around the world. We were able to experience destinations and forge lasting relationships with people from every corner of the globe, eating the exotic and strange foods, exploring foreign landscapes, and feeling the sand of a thousand beaches between our toes.

The ship was always moving forward, a feeling I rather enjoyed. There was nothing behind a cruise ship but exhaust and the wake. The past was not a destination that the cruise ship sailed to. The calm waters were always in front of the ship, and the horizon was at once the ending of the landscape and the beginning of new possibility. There was always the next port, that next island, that next great adventure to look forward to, and that is something that I will always miss on the days that I'm not sailing aboard a cruise ship.

It was early on in this contract, while drumming for a full-cast rehearsal with the production-show band, that I met the person who would be the most important friend I would make while working on cruise ships. Many times, the first time you meet the most important people to come into your life, you sense it immediately. And I was never one who had believed in love at first sight—until I saw her. She was wearing a backless yellow top and black tights that instantly made me say a short prayer thanking God for creating yoga pants.

She was beautiful, but every cruise ship showgirl is one of the most beautiful girls in the world, from my observation. Before I ever talked to her, it was the way she moved that captivated me most. Many dancers acquire refined, formal, and graceful movements, the result of countless years of ballet training. Many of these dancers on the cruise ship were top-class, natural talents; they took their very first steps as toddlers in groups of eight. The girl in the yellow top was certainly graceful, but she also had a rather unique cheerful and joyful approach to stepping and hopping her way through her dance routines. Even her bright-yellow shirt turned out to be an apt representation of her sunny personality and joyful outlook on life.

She had long blonde hair that was cut short at the bangs and a small waist, and she had been hired as the seamstress for the cast, which literally made her a tiny dancer, the seamstress for the band. She finished her dance routine and came hopping down the stairs, smiling. When she reached the bottom of the staircase, she curtsied, laughed, and twirled around, her hair flinging to the side. She instantly reminded me of Olivia Newton-John in the music video for "Xanadu" (pronounced Zanadoo), the feature track to the futuristic, roller-skating, rock-opera musical of the same name. It had an excellent soundtrack written and performed by Jeff Lynn and his band, the Electric Light Orchestra, who still to this day do not get the credit they deserve for this masterpiece. As a young kid—and I know this may sound strange to many people—this was my absolute favorite movie for quite some time. And here was my first crush, Olivia Newton-John, twirling in front of me on the cruise ship as if I'd died and gone to Xanadu heaven.

I felt she was certainly out of my league, but after seeing chicken fingers in the crew mess three days in a row, you quickly learn that anything is possible in life, and everything is possible in ship life, where you're a member of a crew that's working on a ship that's the size of a small city, and it's all sailing through the sea, which is a miracle in itself.

However, this particular ship wasn't all days of wine and roses. Our itinerary had many more sea days than my last ship, those days when the ship doesn't dock at port and stays out at sea all day. Eventually, I found ways to deal with sea days, but at the time, they were beginning to give me a case of the ship version of cabin fever. Crew members who sail aboard ships headed to Hawaii and back or partake in an ocean crossing from New York to England can have many consecutive sea days in a row, and these crew members can easily develop ship fever.

Ship fever occurs when you begin to have a difficult time being isolated out in the middle of the ocean, and the only cure is to get off the ship. I was able to reduce the temperature of my ship fever by getting off the ship and exploring a port, but this was only temporary. The minute I would get back on board the ship, my ship fever temperature would slowly begin to rise until I ran off the ship again. I began to feel a bit trapped while aboard the ship, and I wasn't ever going to have a long break from it until my contract was over and I could go home for a short vacation, which was still three months away.

My ship fever would grow until the ship reached a port, and then I'd run down the gangway, practically foaming at the mouth, ready to leave the confines of that smelly ship in my wake for as long as possible. I can't imagine the level of ship fever those crew who are only able to get off the ship once a week for a half day must develop, and that's if their day off happens to fall on a port day. That's a ship fever I never want to experience, and my hat goes off to all the crew members who are able to work in those conditions and still keep a smile on their faces day after day.

The main reason ship fever occurs is because most crew members are required to work out at sea for such long periods of time, often in eight-month stretches, without a vacation home. In my opinion, requiring these long contracts is a poor business decision. From what I have observed, about three months is the perfect length of time for a contract. After three months, most crew members have grown tired of being on the ship and could use a short vacation before they're ready to go back out to sea. However, perhaps in an effort to save money on travel expenses and the cost of turnover on a ship, it seems most cruise companies often require crew members to be out at sea for no fewer than six months. I worked one eight-month-long contract, and at the end of it, I didn't want to see a picture of a cruise ship for at least a full year. There are a lot of exhausted and often rather miserable crew members out at sea right now as you read this. Crew members become burned out. For the cruise lines' bottom dollar, this means crew aren't able to offer that high level of customer service and high level of productivity that all cruise companies really want out of their employees. Many if not most crew members want shorter contracts, and I believe the cruise companies should offer this to those who want them. Give a crew member a three-month contract and then a month off, and I believe that, most importantly, the mental health of crew members will improve, and crew members will also gladly return to a ship refreshed, rejuvenated, and ready for their next adventure at sea. This could increase the quality of customer service, increase passenger satisfaction on cruise ships, and therefore increase repeat cruisers. This could also reduce employee turnover and the cost of training, which must be exceptionally high for cruise companies. In my opinion, by requiring six- to eight-month-long contracts, the cruise industry is effectively shooting itself in the hull. My hope is that if I and others advocate for this, the result could be a positive change in the lives of crew members and a positive increase in cruise industry profits. I see it as a real win-win, and I hope one day shorter contracts are offered, especially for the improved mental health of crew members.

I didn't see much of Lisa, the dancer with the yellow top, over the next few weeks, but somehow she kept popping back into my mind. I'd imagine her twirling at the bottom of the steps, looking like Olivia Newton-John, as hot as a cruise ship fever, while "Xanadu" played in the background.

And then, once upon a time in a little crew bar floating somewhere in the Caribbean Sea, Olivia Newton-John walked right up to me and asked me if I'd like a glass of wine. She had a posh London accent and that cute rabbit mouth with slightly large front teeth that so many British women have that makes them irresistible to Americans such as myself. Listening to her talk made me feel as if I were listening to a BBC newscast with the most beautiful newscaster they had on staff. Now, let me be clear: I'm no Brad Pitt, so please don't mistake these types of descriptions here and later in the book as arrogance on my part. However, to *me,* she was the most beautiful girl I had ever seen. More importantly, we seemed to get on very well. I was looking for physical chemistry, sure, but I was also, and more importantly, hoping to meet someone of great character, someone who shared my values, and since I loved to talk, someone I could have great conversation with. In land life and in ship life, I found that having the ability to find someone who can be a wonderful companion is much more important than finding someone to sleep with for the short time aboard that ship. Over the next several weeks, we discovered we shared much of the same politics and enjoyed lengthy conversations about this, as well as our love of the arts, performance, music, and everything involved in the production shows.

One Halloween night, I went to a crew party where everyone was dressed in costumes. She arrived in a skin-tight black costume with cat ears and a cute little nose and whiskers painted on her pretty face. We sat at the bar for a bit, and then some of the other dancers in the cast grabbed us to join a group that was headed outside to the crew deck to look at the stars and the full moon that was rising over the Caribbean Sea. We walked together onto the teak deck. She took my hand and led me up to a small platform near the bow of the ship. We looked out over the sea as the ship sailed past small islands, the wind whipping her long blonde hair, and the moon rising on the distant horizon. I looked in her eyes, and she smiled. I was pulled toward her like a passenger is pulled to the free champagne at a cruise ship art auction. I couldn't stop from leaning in toward her lips. She moved toward me, too. And then I kissed her, and it was one of the most electric first kisses I've ever had. I had finally done it. I had finally kissed Olivia Newton-John! But the important fact here is that she turned out to be better, in all ways, than I could have ever imagined Olivia Newton-John to be. In that moment, with that one kiss, I felt as if all my searching was now over. I felt that I had truly found the perfect harbor for my lonely, wandering ship, and I hoped with all my heart that she would want to climb aboard.

CHAPTER THIRTEEN

CRUISE SHIP APPRECIATION DAY

Several months later, Lisa and I were roommates. The cruise ships encourage coupling, and they allow crew to room together and often accommodate this request as quickly as possible. I had never known exactly how many shoes and dresses women have and how important they are to them until I shared a ten-by-ten-foot cabin with a cruise ship dancer named Lisa. I will say that Lisa was an exceptionally fair-spirited person, and she allowed me to have the same number of drawers as she did. And even though as the contract progressed most of those drawers slowly became filled with her shoes, makeup, and sparkly cocktail dresses, she was nice enough to let me know that they were still technically my drawers.

It was around this time that we had decided to attend a crew party. I parted my hair with gel to make my best effort at looking like George Clooney for her. She was sitting in a small chair in front of the desk in the middle of the room, using the mirror on the wardrobe door to apply her makeup in the skillful way that only showgirls know how to do, which requires the dexterity of a surgeon to use those small mascara applicators and lipstick tips as deftly as they do in rough seas. The ship rolled with the sea, and the waves pounded against the hull of the ship. I took a deep breath and had the chance for everything to slow down for a moment so that I could fully appreciate what was happening.

Ship life had found that special path into a place deep inside my soul. I felt the love of the unknown horizon, a passion for the adventurous future, an obsession with racing forward. I was embracing this constant movement, this enduring dedication to battle toward paradise. My life aboard the ship had become so much a part of me that whenever the ship roped up to the dock—and the engine would shut down, and the creaking and the moaning of a ship at sea quieted, and the hum of the metal hull as it pushed through the sea went silent, and ship life suddenly became still and hushed—I was left with an empty feeling, a feeling as if I were no longer whole.

I watched Lisa brush her long blonde hair and continued to get ready for our crew party adventure together, and I was grateful for every moment this ship life was giving me. I picked out a white button-down and slipped it on. I thought about all the things I truly loved about ship life. First, I never had to drive a car. Imagine a life without traffic. Imagine a life without ever having to slip into the driver's seat for months on end. I would walk to work every day; and Lisa and I could go to the bar and drink as much as we wanted and not have to worry about crashing into someone on the way home, getting pulled over and issued a DUI, or having someone else crash into us.

We had the world's best commute to work. We would wake up and walk fifty feet or so to get backstage to where we performed. There was no sitting and waiting in bumper-to-bumper wasteland. We never had to drive to get to a restaurant or go to a movie theater—we could walk to them on the ship. We never had to ride in a plane to get to a tropical paradise—the ship went to one nearly every day. In the United States, motor vehicle crashes are the leading cause of death for individuals between the ages of five and thirty-four, so there was no better and safer place to spend our days as crazy youths than sailing around the world on a cruise ship and never having to step foot inside of a car the entire time.

Lisa slipped into a little black dress. I fastened my belt, adjusted my slacks, and slipped my wallet into my back pocket. I thought about how I never had to worry about money while working on a cruise ship. I never worried about whether I could pay rent or buy food, because rooms were free, and even though sometimes the food tasted like ketchup-covered raccoon snouts, it was free too. The price of gas was about as important to me as what passengers had on their dining room menus; it didn't matter. I wasn't getting any. I thought about how my total expenses were about $50 a month. At the time, I had a car back home that was paid off. My only expense was a small car insurance policy. I had canceled my phone plan because we were sailing in an area where I couldn't get reception. I had no mortgage, no gym membership, no medical bills (because the clinic was free for crew members), and no health insurance. All I had was $50 going out the crew-cabin door every month. All my wages, well, I spent them on whatever I wanted in port, taking excursions and exploring the islands, buying $1 Stella Artois in the crew bar, but most of it I saved. Living and working on the cruise ship proved to be an excellent way to save money and pay off debt. Much of what I made went toward paying off the student loans I had at the time.

Lisa walked over and sat on the edge of the bed. Her dress was open in the back, exposing her toned shoulders.

"Will you zip me up?" she asked in her British accent.

I kissed her on the neck and zipped up her dress. I slid on my black dress socks and black dress shoes that were polished to a shine. I thought about how we never had to cook. There was a chef who was paid to cook as much food as we wanted, as long as we wanted lentil curry, white rice, chicken-beak stew, pizza, boxed cereal, and whatever else was on the crew mess menu that day. We never had to do the dishes, take out the trash, clean our room, clean our own bathroom, or make our bed. We had been assigned a room steward who would do all of this for us for about $1 a day, although most crew members tipped them very well.

Lisa walked over to our wardrobe and sat in the chair in the middle of the crew cabin, trying on different pairs of heels. I picked out a bow tie and tied it beneath my shirt collar. We were headed to another crew party, like so many nights before. I thought about how we never had to walk far to find a celebration on the ship. Once a month on most ships, the cruise ship company paid for an official crew party, usually with a theme like "'70s Disco Party" or "Dress Up Like a Superhero." These parties were often helpful when ship life began to get us down. I especially enjoyed the "Band Nights," where the showband would set up in the crew bar and play for the crew for several hours. It was always enjoyable to have the opportunity to bring music to the crew and entertain those who worked so hard on the ship. We could also attend the occasional deck parties, where an open-air area of the ship would be roped off for the crew to gather out under the stars as the ship sailed through the night, dancing to that odd mix of international dance music that is only played by cruise ship DJs. Still to this day, every time I envision a crew party, I see a group of Russians, Indians, Filipinos, Americans, Australians, Scots, Brits, Irish, South Americans, New Zealanders, and Canadians, all dancing together under the stars to "Gasolina" by Daddy Yankee while dressed like scantily clad pirates for the pirates-and-wenches–themed night.

The true camaraderie and morale that buoyed the ship were formed at the crew parties, where that crew was kept happy and unified. They were the best parties on the seven seas. And if we hadn't had enough at the crew party, we could wander around the ship until we found a group of fellow seafarers celebrating ship life in their crew cabins. Hopefully, we'd be invited to a cabin party hosted by the cruise director or someone else with officer status that was high up on the food chain so that we could enjoy the spacious crew quarters, the porthole window, the air filter, and the living room with a couch for a little while before heading back to our rat holes down below the waterline where the peasantry lived. But they were our rat holes, and the crew area was our safe zone, where we could get away from passengers for a while and all the questions they asked. Our crew cabins were one of the few places on the ship where we could take off our name tags for a bit, remove our clip-on bow ties, clean the gel out of our hair, and get out of our uniforms. Our little cabins on the sea were the perfect places to unwind and celebrate until it was time to get back to scrubbing the decks and hoisting the mizzen and main again the next morning in the passenger areas.

Lisa was choosing between two pairs of black heels. I straightened my bow tie and thought about our friends aboard the ship. When we had climbed on board, we had joined that fraternity and sorority of cruise ship crew members. It was easier to make friends on the ship than it was on land, it seemed. We were all in the same boat, so to speak, all experiencing the same ship life together, which often created an instant bond between us. We were all aboard for this cruise through an eternal summer, always sailing to where it was warm and sailing to the islands and ports when it was the most beautiful time to visit. We didn't sail to destinations during the rainy seasons, mosquito seasons, blizzard seasons, or hottest times of the year. We always sailed with an endless bearing that was nestled into that perfect little warm, dry, and cozy sweet spot where the ports were at their best and crew members could always find a secret, quiet spot ashore to work on their tans. If there was a hurricane brewing or heading for our port of call, we simply sailed around it and changed our course toward a different tropical island where the palms trees weren't being ripped from the ground.

Lisa dabbed perfume on her neck, and I splashed on a bit of cologne. I thought about how I never would have had the opportunity to travel the world if I hadn't worked on cruise ships. We certainly didn't have the kind of money to buy that type of experience as a young couple, and I assume that a large percentage of crew members feel the same way. We might never have walked through ancient Mayan temples on the Mexican coast or body surfed in the glassy, curling waves at Bondi Beach in Sydney or sipped Mai Tais in Hawaii. These were cost-free experiences, the perks of the job. If I calculate exactly how much free cruising I have received over the five years that I worked on cruise ships, it totals to about three hundred free cruises. An average cruise cost about $500, meaning I took about $104,000 worth of cruises and was paid about $80,000 to take them. And I had some of the best times of my life out at sea, playing music. I'd say that's a pretty fine deal, eh?

Lisa stood up and straightened her dress and made those wonderful small adjustments with her hair that women make to bring out the best of their beauty. I slid on my cufflinks and fastened their tips. I thought about how wonderful it was to have the opportunity to work with people from all over the world. We were able to walk into the crew mess and sit at any random table and talk with crew members from India, Russia, Indonesia, England, Romania, America, wherever, and talk with them about their countries' fascinating history and their experiences growing up and living there. We would sit on sea days over cups of coffee, and if we asked the right questions and practiced the lost art of listening to someone's story, we'd hear gripping firsthand accounts of conflicts and world-shaping moments in modern history that had occurred across the globe. We learned quickly that no news story can capture the grit of conflict like talking with someone who lived or fought through the war. We had the soul-shaping opportunity to deeply understand how different everyday life is for people all over the globe, giving us a stronger appreciation of who we are, the countries we came from, and how much of our fate and experience was determined by the sacrifices and battles of those who came before us, and the culture, values, and state of the economy of where we happened to be born and at what particular time we were born there. We discovered that when we left our hometowns and traveled the world, we not only learned about the world and experienced its beauty; we also discovered our place in this world, our place in time and history, and gained a clear understanding of how special our hometowns, the places we started our journey, had been all along.

We were able to step outside our own lives, the influences of our cultures, our family, and our friends, and see ourselves from afar, looking back at our lives with a new perspective from the sea. We were able to improve ourselves with each new ship we climbed aboard, taking with us everything we had learned from our last ship-life experience and applying those lessons learned to our new cruise-liner home. We became shape-shifters in the most positive way possible. We were shaped by the cruise ship and the sea into people much more aware and much more developed than what we were the first time we walked up that gangway and first stepped foot onto a ship.

Lisa pinned her name tag to the front of her dress, and then she helped me slip on my suit jacket. I looked down at a pair of drumsticks and the pile of sheet music on our cabin desk. The cruise ship allowed me to focus on music more than I would otherwise have been able to during this time in my life. I was still in the minor leagues of music, but I was able to make a good living by doing nothing else but performing. I thought about how I was going to miss this ship life one day, miss the feeling of excitement as the ship thrust forward toward a horizon that led to beach after topless beach. I had already experienced what it was like to miss the cruise ship, which would happen toward the end of my short vacations. I would miss the ship and then climb aboard again and find a quiet spot on the crew deck as the ship sailed out of port for the first time. I would take a deep breath of fairly clean air that was slightly mixed with the exhaust of the cruise ship. I'd nibble on a chicken finger, wash it down with a $1 Stella Artois from the crew bar, and then I'd rediscover that familiar ship-life feeling that I'd finally come back home to the sea where I belonged.

They're called cruise ships, but for crew members, a cruise liner is much more than a ship; it's our country. It's our sailing city. It's our home on the high seas. And aboard every new ship we joined, we'd find our new seafaring family. I'll always be grateful for the opportunity to work aboard cruise ships. Thank you to everyone who ever gave me the opportunity to do so.

I knew I'd miss these carefree cruise ship days. We were young. We were hopeful. We were ready to take on our ship life no matter what squalls the seas brought our way. We were free, in the way that only cruise ship crew members can be.

"Are you ready?" Lisa said. She straightened my bow tie and kissed me on the neck, just below the ear.

"I'm ready," I said. "I'm ready now."

CHAPTER FOURTEEN

OSCAR, OSCAR, OSCAR

Lisa and I hopped from ship to ship for the next several years. Over these many ports and many days at sea, we hardly had a single argument, which is rather remarkable given the fact that two members of the opposite sex were living, working, playing, and spending nearly every waking hour together while sharing a single ten-by-ten-foot space without windows that was surrounded by often extremely stressful living conditions. I was too young to fully appreciate the rarity of this well-matched pairing, and so like many young people, I didn't fully know what I had until it was gone.

One day Lisa received a call for an audition in London's West End. It was also around this time that I had been hired to write my first travel guide for a respectable publishing company. We both took a vacation at home, her in England and I in the United States, and tried to make things work on land with more than two thousand miles of ocean separating us. Our dreams for our careers were both coming true, and this pulled us in different directions in life, neither of us wanting to let go of what had seemed like our life's work to become successful in the arts and neither of us wanting to live in a distant country away from our family and friends. It's a story as old as cruise ships and foreigners coming to work aboard them. The distance between us proved to be too much over time, and we realized that what had brought us together, the far-reaching sea, was the very thing that would eventually tear us apart.

I was assigned to a new ship, ironically one where I would finally get my own room when all I wanted was to be sharing it with Lisa. As I became a more experienced showband musician and paid my dues on the less-desirable ships in the Caribbean, those older ships with three-day cruises to one or two ports for six months, I eventually worked my way up in cruise-liner land and was assigned to a ship with an itinerary that cruise ship dreams are made of. Our home port was Sydney, Australia. We would alternate between fourteen-day cruises circumnavigating Australia and New Zealand, crossing the Tasman Sea between the countries. We sailed this route for two months before embarking on a forty-two-day cruise that sailed to ports at islands off the coast of Australia and then stopped at Borneo and Papua New Guinea, Indonesia, South Korea, China, and Japan before returning for one more trip around Australia and New Zealand.

It was in Darwin, Australia during this contract that I went on one of the most memorable shore excursions of my entire time aboard cruise ships. A friend and I were leafing through a glossy booklet of shore excursions that the ship offered. It was all the usual stuff: snorkeling the Great Barrier Reef, riding dune buggies through a dusty desert in the outback, zip-lining in the Blue Mountains, visiting the aborigines who really know how to play a mean didgeridoo in Sydney Harbor. Nothing was really jumping out at us.

But then we found the excursion of a lifetime. It was titled something like, *Adventure to Death Swamp,* and then below that, *See the Horrifying Jumping Monster Crocodiles.*

The pamphlet was littered with crisp color photos of crocodiles seemingly in midflight, their tails almost completely out of the water as they soared upward and latched onto a bloody hunk of cow tongue that some smiling Aussie, with a crazed look in his eye, was dangling over the side of a pontoon boat. Onlookers cheered and gawked at the carnage and at the incredible feat of reptilian acrobatics. It all looked exceptionally dangerous, extraordinarily violent, and remarkably pointless.

We signed up immediately.

The field trip was supposed to take us deep into the outback of Aussie-land, to some murky river that runs through a dangerous swamp, the kind of place that kangaroos go when they've decided to give up on life. Once there, we would board a rickety pontoon boat and allow two complete strangers to guide us into the darkly depths of crocodile country in search of some of the most violent creatures on planet Earth.

It all sounded too good to be true. When the day finally came, I packed a bag of peanuts in case I got hungry.

Waiting for us outside of the ship was a remarkably new and safe-looking bus to take us into Australian no-man's-land. Our driver was a friendly and animated fellow with leathery skin that was the same shade and texture as his leather hat, which even had a hatband of crocodile teeth. He reminded me of Crocodile Dundee—not the original one, but the version of Dundee that might have been cast in a low-budget sequel that went straight to on-demand video. He kept us rather entertained with stories about his wild adventures in the Australian outback which always seemed to end with him having a campfire and spending the rest of the night drinking

Foster's beers the size of oil cans.

When we reached the swamp, the driver veered from the paved road and took us onto a dusty gravel lane that cut straight through the heart of the wetland, a vast expanse of shrubby tropical plants and inky, still water that stretched to the horizon on both sides of the country road. I found myself daydreaming as I looked out the bus window and over the boggy Australian landscape. I imagined what type of frightening creatures must lurk below the surface of the creepy marsh: swamp snakes, bloodsucking spiders, cold-blooded crocodiles with a discerning taste for American flesh made sweet by a steady diet of chocolate-covered donuts and dollar-menu cheeseburgers, wild-eyed kangaroos that could box like Muhammad Ali (float like a bush fly; sting like a wallaby)—kangaroos that had been driven to insanity long ago by the recurring concussions caused by boomerang enthusiasts.

That's when the bus ran right off the road, drove straight through the barbed wire fence, and toward the edge of said swamp. I heard screams. The driver yelled, "Crikey!" and lost control.

The bus careened into the same bog that had been so benignly described in the pamphlet as "Death Swamp".

The bus nearly flipped over onto its side. I heard the sound of safety glass shattering into tiny dull-edged squares, more screams, and then the most cursing in different languages than I've heard since I went on the Log Flume ride at Disney World. Someone in the back of the bus immediately kicked out the back window. The driver told us to get out of the bus and to go stand on the dirt lane. My friend and I climbed through the back window and trudged through the swamp toward the road, fully expecting to be devoured at any moment by a massive Venus flytrap or confronted by a crocodile who at that very moment had decided to end his month-long fast and give the Atkins diet craze a whirl.

We made it to the road, and I checked to see if all my limbs were still attached to my body.

A few minutes later, a truck arrived to shuttle us to the rickety pontoon boat so we could watch the crocodile version of Hungry Hippos. The crocodiles did "fly" out of the water, using their powerful tails to thrust them from the river. My friend and I shared my bag of peanuts as we watched the crocodiles' teeth chomp onto the cow tongues that were dangled over the side of the boat by the same crazy-looking Aussies we had seen in the glossy pamphlet.

All in all, it was the best excursion I ever went on. However, next time, we decided we'd just play it safe and go visit the Sydney Opera House or something.

It was also on this ship that I had another close call. I was sitting in my crew cabin after watching the ship leave the port of Nagasaki from the crew deck when I heard a loud *bang* against the hull of the ship, which sounded as if we'd had a head-on collision with a whale. My cabin at the time was very near the bow of the ship and still below the waterline, and it sounded as if that whale had hit very close to where I was sitting. It was the loudest sound I had ever heard from the hull of the ship. The entire front of the ship shook. I half expected to see the wall/hull of my crew cabin burst open and watch as the Sea of Japan and a few Japanese white tuna came pouring into my crew cabin to say hello. Months later, after I had left the ship, this ship went to dry dock, where they lifted the cruise liner out of the water to do work on the hull, propeller, and other parts of the ship. A fellow crew member noticed a large dent very near where my crew cabin had been located. That crew member asked what the dent was from, and an officer informed her that the ship had run into a piling for the Nagasaki Bridge as we were leaving port. I'll never know how close I was to needing a diving mask and an oxygen tank to escape the ship, but it reminded me just how dangerous life as a crew member or passenger can be.

Fires, wrecks, and other disasters still occur on modern cruise ships. At the time I was writing this book, the most recent large-scale cruise ship disaster involved the *Costa Concordia*. On January 13, 2012, the navigational officer in charge of the *Costa Concordia* at the time apparently guided the cruise ship too close to a rocky Italian shore. There are conflicting reports about the event, but it has been reported that the officer was navigating this close to the coast so that a crew member could wave goodbye to his family on shore. Whatever the reason, the captain ended up sailing the cruise ship directly into a rock and ripping a 160-foot gash into the port side of the hull. The incident occurred in the Tyrrhenian Sea, which is about sixty-two miles northwest of Rome. The ship was carrying around three thousand passengers and one thousand crew members on board. Shortly after the ship struck the rock, the engine room was flooded and all the power on the ship was lost. Inside the ship, passengers and crew members fought their way through flooded and nearly pitch-black corridors. The ship drifted toward the coast, eventually listing onto one side just three hundred meters from Giglio Island.

Many news outlets also reported that the captain waited more than an hour before ordering an abandon ship. The evacuation of the *Costa Concordia* took more than six hours to complete. Maritime law states that an evacuation should take less than thirty minutes after an abandon-ship order is given by the captain of a vessel. At the time this was originally published, thirty-one people were confirmed dead as a result of the accident, and sixty-four were injured.

Just one month after the *Costa Concordia* incident, a fire broke out in the engine room aboard the *Costa Allegra*. The ship completely lost power and was left to drift helplessly in pirate-infested waters off the coast of Tanzania. Then just days later, the *Silver Shadow*, operated by Silver Sea Cruise Lines, was sailing in heavy fog and accidentally rammed into a cargo ship off the coast of Vietnam. I've heard stories and know passengers and crew who have suffered through a variety of unfortunate situations while cruising, from fires to muggings while in ports to robberies and piracy, not to mention icebergs, of course.

A ship I once worked aboard was docking in New York City. As we approached the dock, I heard a loud thud. Suddenly, the ship came to an alarming stop. I was nearly thrown onto the floor of my crew cabin. I ran up to the crew deck to see what had happened. I saw helicopters and airplanes circling above the cruise ship. News reporters had their cameramen hanging over the edge of the dock to get a shot of where the cruise ship had rammed into the Port of New York City. The thick cement wall of the port was cracked, and the front of the ship's hull was badly dented.

Cruise ships have fallen victim to pirate attacks in which passengers have had to keep them from climbing up the side of their ship by throwing deck chairs and loungers at them. There have been fires that have killed hundreds of passengers and crew. A cruise is all fun and games, all piña coladas, tropical islands, and chocolate-melting-cakes until someone gets *dead*. It all reminded me that I was lucky to have spent as much time as I did sailing through as many oceans as I did and made it back home alive. I'm very grateful to the captains and officers and crew for the fine jobs they did navigating the ships that I sailed upon. As many miles as we sailed, hitting one bridge and running into one port really isn't that bad. On average, the best hitters in baseball strike out 70 percent of the time. Then again, when they strike out, they don't have the potential to kill three thousand passengers and crew. Regardless, my hat sincerely goes off to them. Thank you for getting me back home alive.

It was on this contract that ship life began to wear thin. I was still loving the ports; these were all new places I had never traveled to before. However, the repetition of ship life in general and of playing the same production shows over and over again was becoming tiresome. I had reached the point with the food in the crew mess that all I could eat was the boxed cereal and noodle cups that I could buy from the crew store. I didn't want to eat the gelatinous pumpkin pie they passed off as a palatable dessert in the crew mess. The pumpkin pie would jiggle when you shook it. There were Pilgrims rolling over in their graves. I wanted to eat whatever I wanted to, whenever I wanted, and be able to bake a real pumpkin pie whenever I wanted one. I wanted to live life on my own schedule. It was around this time that I began to grow tired of the petty rules on the cruise ship too.

No one likes to be a subordinate; it can really take the wind out of your sails.

The rules on cruise ships can drive crew members

absolutely bonkers. For example, it was during a slow cruise. We were floating around the Caribbean somewhere. After four or five months, most of us guys in the showband had grown tired of most of the ports. When we were in Cozumel in Mexico and Ocho Rios in Jamaica, we caught up on sleep or spent some time working on our tans on the cruise ship sundeck instead of going ashore. It was simply more relaxing and interesting to watch paint dry on the crew deck than it was to get off the boat and fight the crowds of passengers.

I woke up in the middle of the day, feeling as if I had drunk an entire fish tank of cranberry vodkas the night before—which I possibly had, and I'm talking about one of those impressive floor-to-ceiling fish tanks that you find in fancy seafood restaurants with names like The Captain's Table and The Barnacle Pit.

The phone in my crew cabin rang. It was Marvin, the trombone player in the band. "Hey, you want to catch a movie in the theater?"

The cruise ship always has something going on: shuffleboard playoffs, bingo marathons, hairy chest competitions, Chocolate melting cake–eating contests, unclog-your-stateroom-toilet tournaments. This kind of stuff keeps going even when the ship is in port. Believe it or not, some of the passengers hardly ever get off the ship when they take a cruise. However, the show must go on, and so movies are shown in the main theater.

"What movie are they showing today?" I asked.

"*Shutter Island.*"

An escape. That was exactly what I needed. "I'm in."

Nothing sounded better than to sit in a dark room and watch a movie, to feel as if I was back on land, doing something that might bring a bit of normalcy back to my life.

I met up with Marvin and a few other showband guys. We walked into the dark theater. The place was pretty much empty, but we wanted to be respectful, so we took a seat in the back of the room. There was a Filipino crew member walking around, passing out paper cups of popcorn. I grabbed a cup of popcorn, pulled a soda from my pocket that I had smuggled into the theater, and then popped the top.

When the movie started, I was transported back home for a moment. I forgot all about the shipboard politics that were driving us all crazy. I just crunched on the popcorn, sipped my soda, and let *Shutter Island* steal me away for a moment. It was heaven on ship. An island of refuge from my ship life.

A few minutes later, I felt a tap on my shoulder. I looked up to see an Indian security guard. He had a dim flashlight in his hand. He shined it into my eyes. In his Indian accent, he said, "You. All of you. You are not allowed in the theater during movie time."

"What?" Marvin asked. "We're in the showband. We aren't crew. We're staff."

"I know," the security guard said. "You have to leave, now. Movie time is for passengers and officers only."

We got up and trudged out of the theater. We couldn't believe it. We were in the band. This was the theater where we entertained more than a thousand passengers every single night. And now we were being kicked out. It was the rules.

That night, we were called into the staff captain's office. Each of us was given a written warning for trying to catch a flick on our time off. After a bit of halfhearted protest and attempts to explain our reasoning, we all signed our written warnings and then walked back to work, in the theater that we had just been banned from, to perform another show for thousands of passengers.

Ship life. No movie for you.

I was also exhausted with having to rebuild a group of friends on every new ship. Without Lisa, I was forced back into trying to find love, and I was quickly becoming one of the many cynical crew members who believed the chances of finding real love in ship life were about as good as the odds that the crew mess would serve surf and turf one day.

The crew parties had lost their spark. The ship had lost its shine. The boat didn't float like it used to, and most of all, I had grown tired of watching friends and the few girlfriends I had while at sea sail away, never to be seen again. I would forge deep friendships, but when the contract ended, I'd have to leave them all behind. I'd get on a ship and meet new crew members, and after a few years, I began to see them mostly as people that I would eventually have to say goodbye to.

Falling in love on a cruise ship became a mini tragedy waiting to happen.

The cruise terminal became a place where love was found and lost every day, and whether I was finding it or losing it depended on whether I was arriving or she was leaving. And then it was time to do it all again. At the end of this contract in Australia and New Zealand, I was scheduled to be transferred to a new ship, a ship in Alaska, sailing the inside passage.

The ship I had been on was scheduled to go into dry dock, so most of the crew was leaving at the same time. We had all counted down to the day we were leaving. We counted the months, then the days, the hours, the minutes, and the seconds. Once aboard a cruise ship, there's not much more a crew member loves to do than leave.

Many of the crew was going home, home to a home cooked meal and a room that didn't make us feel as if we were living inside of a submarine. Most of them had been daydreaming for weeks about the day that they'd finally walk down that gangway, and then run for the tarmac, dashing for that plane that would lift them off that hot runway and fly them through the clouds until they were back home. Leaving the ship becomes an obsession for most crew members that have ever worked below the waterline.

When the day finally came, we were all huddled in a passenger dining room, bright and early in the morning, most of us still rather inebriated and without a wink of sleep as a result of the celebrations that always ensue when a crew member knows they'll be saying good-bye to ship life for a while once the sun comes up.

We were a rough-looking lot: dancers still wearing their show makeup from the night before, which had smeared badly from all the crying they were doing while saying good-bye to the other girls in the cast, casino dealers still in tuxedos and bow ties who smelled like the wet bar in a rock star's dressing room, and then a few of us showband musicians who were pretty happy because we finally got to eat breakfast in the crew mess. After all, the only way for a showband musician, who often works until around midnight, to eat breakfast in the crew mess is to stay up all night until five in the morning. All the musicians had the type of smile you can only get from eating bacon after you haven't had any in many months.

We were gathered together in the passenger dining room, waiting for the immigration officers to show up. Big surprise, right? Hurry up and wait.

Of course, we didn't mind waiting. We were used to it. And at this point, those who were going home didn't care about anything. Their bags were packed. They'd said their good-byes. All they had to do now was walk down that gangway and...freedom! Glorious, liberating, sunbeam shining down on us from heaven, *freedom!*

I was talking to a group of dancers—all from England or Australia, all finishing up a very long nine-month contract—when the staff captain walked up to us. He was holding a radio, and he did not look happy. "Excuse me, but there seems to be a bit of a problem."

Had someone died back home? Was the ship sinking? No. It couldn't be. Some of these people were supposed to be eating a roast dinner and sleeping in their very own beds in a few hours.

"What happened?" a dancer asked.

"Well, a volcano erupted and—"

"What?" was pretty much the general response from everyone in the room.

The staff captain put out his hand to calm every one down. "Now hold on. No one has been hurt," he said. "This is in Iceland. A volcano in Iceland has erupted and—"

Everyone looked relieved. "So what does this have to do with us?" one of the dancers asked.

"Well, the ash plume is enormous," he said. "All flights from here to England have been cancelled."

One of the dancers looked as if she was going to faint. But she gathered herself and asked, "For how long?"

"They don't know."

"What do you mean? Can't they just fly around it?"

"No. The volcanic eruption is that large. And they have

no idea how long it's going to last."

"Any idea. Days? Weeks? Months?"

"Unfortunately not. However, there is some good news."

"Okay," the dancer said.

"Since the ship is in dry dock, everyone who has a cancelled flight will be able to stay aboard the ship until they are able to fly home." This was about as good of news as being told that your entire family fell overboard somewhere off the coast of Antarctica. Dry dock: going on a cruise inside of a jackhammer on a ship that sails to nowhere and all the passengers are replaced with construction workers who have perfected the whistle they use to try and get the attention of every woman that walks by. The only time a destination of dry dock is good news is when you are just released from a super-max prison, and then it's pretty much same old, same old.

The dancer's jaw dropped "This is a joke. This has to be a joke. Are you pulling my leg? Ha! You almost had me there."

The staff captain looked down at the deck. "No. This is not a joke. We will let you know as soon as we hear anything else. But for now, I would suggest that anyone scheduled to fly to England today return to their crew quarters. You will not be flying home today."

Those dancers had been counting down for nine months. Now they had no idea when they were going home.

The dancers ended up having to spend an entire week aboard the dry-docked ship, which must have been enough to nearly drive them bonkers. After a week in dry dock, they would have rather been thrown *into* the erupting volcano than spend another day aboard that ship.

The Icelandic volcano finally sputtered out and stopped disrupting international flight patterns for a bit. There was probably an entire plane full of English cruise ship crew members headed back to England that day. As they were flying over Iceland and spotted the still smoldering volcano, they probably all said some very choice words that cannot be repeated here—words to express their extreme gratitude to the volcano gods, of course.

CHAPTER FIFTEEN

WHY WOULD ANYONE EVER STOP WORKING ON A CRUISE SHIP?

The answer to that question is easy. It was a Monday, the fourth sea day in a row, and the ship was under "red alert," the two words that every crew member despises with all of their rum-soaked heart. Those two words are enough to send a crew member running toward the nearest lifeboat, where they climb inside and cut the lines so that the lifeboat will plop down into the sea, where the ocean currents can carry them away from the cruise ship as fast as possible. It doesn't matter where the currents may take their little survival craft. Being shipwrecked on a deserted island like Tom Hanks in *Castaway,* with only a soccer ball to keep you company, is a better fate than staying on a cruise ship during a red alert.

Red alert is a state of emergency that a cruise ship activates when 2 percent or more of the passengers and crew on board contract a contagious illness, and this happens much more often than you might think. Cruise ships, being cramped and crowded places, are the perfect playground paradises for viruses, germs, colds, and all sorts of little bugs that can make you sick. There are, on average, around two thousand or more passengers and one thousand crew members packed onto one ship during a cruise. So it's nearly certain that one of these passengers or crew members will climb aboard the ship on embarkation day and be sick as a dog. And when they come aboard, they often ruin the party for everyone else.

Cruise ships are germs' and viruses' happy places. Everyone is touching the same metal rails, sneezing and coughing into the same circulated air, sitting in the same chairs, working out in the same gym, and swimming in the same pools and hot tubs. No legion of crew members armed with bottles of disinfectant spray and washrags can defeat all of these ubiquitous, stubborn, and resilient viruses searching for a host to take a holiday vacation within.

The most prevalent virus found aboard cruise ships is the norovirus, which spreads so fast and so effectively from person to person that the United States Centers for Disease Control (the CDC) considers it to be the leading cause of foodborne disease outbreaks in the country, and norovirus is often the leading cause of viral outbreaks on cruise ships worldwide.

If you're unlucky enough to contract the norovirus, you will know it fairly quickly. The virus causes what the CDC calls acute gastroenteritis. You develop an extreme case of stomach pain and general nausea, accompanied with all of the other unpleasant experiences often associated with a very bad case of the flu. Most passengers and crew on a cruise ship don't particularly need extra help with nausea when the ship is rolling up and over ocean waves for days on end.

Norovirus isn't the extent of illnesses that are commonly spread on cruise ships, of course. I remember once when we stopped in Vietnam and resupplied the onboard food stores. We brought some particularly special spinach aboard that was infested with *cyclospora,* an overly friendly intestinal parasite that you're better off never meeting.

To help combat these unwanted cruise critters, there is a

color-coded alert system in place aboard cruise ships. The lowest alert level is called green alert. During a green alert, the ship is a happy place in which the crew members conduct a normal level of sanitation, and all eating areas are open for passengers and crew. The ship will activate the more serious yellow alert if two or three passengers or crew members aboard a cruise ship show up at the ship's clinic with symptoms of norovirus or other contagious illnesses. Yellow alert is fairly common. Under yellow alert, ship passengers and crew members are required to use hand sanitizer before entering food serving areas, the cleaning crews are kicked up a notch, and the chlorine content in the cleaning solutions is boosted.

However, sometimes this isn't enough. If the norovirus, or whatever else happens to be spreading on the ship, wins the battle against the cleaning crew and infects more than 2 percent of the passengers and crew members on board, then the ship is put into red alert. It may seem like a small number of people, but remember that most ships have three thousand or more people on board. So when 2 percent of the passengers and crew aboard the ship are sick, there are more than sixty people walking around infecting everyone else. The virus spreads fast when you have sixty people spraying entire colonies of norovirus in every direction. This is considered an outbreak.

This is when you want to act fast and get the heck off that ship. Here are my suggestions. We shall call this Plan A:

(1) In complete secrecy, gather a group of your most trusted and reliable friends. Choose wisely. It is preferred to select those with military skills, navigation abilities, and those crazy friends that we all have. Experience handling small

watercraft is a plus. Choose one expendable person that you don't necessarily like to come along with you. We will codename this person "The Pawn." He or she will come in handy at a later time.

(2) Dress in all black. If you don't have black clothes, find a group of showband musicians and steal their all-black uniforms.

(3) Head to the midnight buffet with several empty gallon jugs and an empty backpack. Fill the backpacks with bottled water, chicken fingers (do not forget the honey mustard sauce), and as many bananas from Banana Mountain as they can hold. Fill the jugs with ship milk.

(4) Find a social host and force them to tell you the location of the storage room for the cheap Duck Nipple–brand champagne on board. Waterboarding may be required. This is acceptable. Take as many bottles as possible, and then kidnap the social host. They know lots of good cruise ship jokes and can call bingo during the long voyage ahead.

(5) Under the cover of darkness, seize control of a lifeboat. Make sure to leave The Pawn aboard the virus-infected ship. The Pawn must lower you safely onto the surface of the calm Caribbean Sea. Now paddle, paddle, paddle as fast as you can until you reach a beautiful beach where you can feast on your chicken fingers, drink your cheap champagne, listen to funny cruise ship jokes, and play bingo with the social host as everyone else aboard the cruise ship faces the good times of the nautical nightmare known as the norovirus. You can thank me later.

While the above may be written in jest, the red alert is no laughing matter. If crew members or passengers contract the norovirus, they are quarantined. There are no exceptions. The cruise that you paid for could be happening during your honeymoon or your grandmother's hundredth birthday party, and you will still be quarantined, unable to leave your stateroom for any reason. Your cabin steward will deliver your daily rations, which include Alka-Seltzer, Jell-O, crackers, and possibly a bowl of chicken broth. All those steak and lobster dinners in the dining room can be kissed goodbye.

If you ever find yourself with the norovirus or *cyclospora* or something like this, an option other than Plan A mentioned above is to cover the room with wall-to-wall plastic. Tape the seams. Lie down in the middle of the room and start a slow drip with enough horse tranquilizers to keep you comatose and completely oblivious to what is happening around and inside of you for about the next five days. Spend the time you would have spent pleading for your life to end in this safe little plastic-wrapped room, dreaming about the Dallas Cowboy cheerleaders running in slow motion or being trapped with Matthew McConaughey on an island with no T-shirts or whatever it is that you dream about. When you wake up, roll up your filthy plastic wrap, take a shower, stash the horse tranquilizer for your next cruise, and move on with your life.

For passengers and crew, one of the worst parts about being on a ship under red alert is that the buffets are often closed. Crew are no longer allowed in passenger areas unless they are required staff. During these times, the food in the crew mess also goes downhill as fast as a kid on a cruise ship waterslide. Eating the food in the crew mess that's served during a red alert for weeks or months on end is as close as cruise companies come to medieval torture without bringing out a row of pillories and two horses to draw and quarter.

It's during times like these that I've seen crew members go to remarkably great lengths just to get a decent meal aboard the cruise ship. For example, I remember when I first climbed aboard a ship that was scheduled to sail north from New York City into Canada. I immediately set off to explore the crew area. I was searching for the perfect place to read, a quiet breezeway or open deck where passengers couldn't find me and ask me stupid questions. A cruise ship is one big maze, and if you look hard enough you can discover quiet spots on the ship that are difficult for most passengers to find, little nooks that are off the beaten path. I finally discovered this one tiny deck on the back of the ship that was really difficult to get to. You had to take several different staircases up, then cut through a passenger area, and then take a few different staircases down in a very small and isolated crew area at the back of the ship just to reach it. It looked like the perfect spot to read. You could look out over the wake of the ship and see the sky above. It seemed really off the radar for most of the crew, and there was no way a passenger would ever find their way back there.

One night, I walked to that little deck and found a group of four or five Filipinos sitting out there smoking. Something didn't look right. They looked guilty, like a lineup at a police station. They had pulled a few deck chairs from the lido deck and were sitting close to the ship's rail. I noticed that a rope was tied to the rail, and so I walked over and looked down. The rope stopped about halfway to the water, and attached to the rope was some heavy-duty fishing line.

I asked the Filipinos if they were fishing. They said they were catching all kinds of good stuff and then having the crew chef cook it up for them. It didn't surprise me. You have to work hard to get a decent meal when you're on the crew.

During one particularly terrible red alert, crew members were served nothing but noodles with olive oil and an assortment of bread rolls for an entire week straight. The stress and vitamin deficiencies that result from eating not much more than noodles with olive oil and bread rolls for anything longer than a couple of days is probably enough to lower your immune system functioning to a point where you wouldn't want to come within a few thousand cruise ship lengths of Hugh Hefner in fear of contracting an STD, which seems counterintuitive when the goal of red alert is to reduce transmission of contagious illness. Crew members, during red alert, are also only permitted to leave the crew area for work. This means that apart from the crew deck, crew members must stay in the all-tan, crowded, stuffy confines of the crew area, where you often receive approximately zero sunlight for 95 percent of the day. On top of this, every time crew members go to the crew mess, there is a manager there making sure they wash their hands every time they even so much as look at the buffet line. For crew, red alert is a stressful situation that has driven even the most strong-willed crew members slightly banana-cakes. I'm still not entirely convinced that the cruise company's guidelines as to how crew members are treated during red alert are well thought out.

So if you find yourself on a cruise ship and you so much as hear a rumor about red alert—run. You don't want to go where that ship is sailing, especially if you're a crew member.

And the fun doesn't stop with the norovirus and *cyclospora*. In the honorable mention category for the worst sicknesses you can contract on a cruise ship are the common flu, Legionnaires' disease, *E. coli, salmonella infantis,* and *salmonella typhi,* which is commonly known as typhoid. In 1996, 330 passengers aboard an Italian ship cruising in the Mediterranean contracted severe cases of *shigella dysenteriae,* probably as a result of eating contaminated cod or swordfish. In 1989, seventy-two passengers and twelve crew members developed *shigella flexneri.* The company determined it was most likely a result of eating German potato salad. And then there are cases of *staphylococcus aureus* contracted from raspberries, *vibrio cholerae* from Asian rice, SRSV from contaminated bathrooms, and all sorts of nasty bacteria and viruses from eating seafood and meats.

There have even been several deaths as a result of these food poisonings as well. One minute you're sitting on the lido deck with a big silly grin on your face, watching islands float by at sunset while stuffing down heaping spoonfuls of German potato salad, and then the next day you're searching for horse tranquilizers because some mindless dolt forgot to put the mayonnaise back in the refrigerator or wash the spinach or rinse the raspberries. On cruise ships, perhaps passengers should do what the kings of old did and buy an extra ticket to bring a food tester along with you. If your food tester gets sick and dies after eating a chocolate-and-vanilla-swirl ice cream cone, you will probably want to find a different ice cream machine to use.

So it was on this particular contract that way more than 2 percent of the ship had contracted the norovirus. I was searching for a horse tranquilizer, and I had already decided which friends would be the best crew members to take with me when I escaped on a lifeboat at midnight. I had spent the last week watching the perfect cruise turn into a nautical norovirus nightmare.

On the first day of the cruise, a few thousand people climbed aboard the cruise ship. They were all smiling, looking forward to cruising Alaska's inside passage, confident they'd see whales or lasso a bald eagle and ride it over the snow-capped mountains or whatever it is that passengers dream about doing on their Alaskan cruise. Then the norovirus showed up to the party. These same giddy passengers devolved into stumbling through the hallways as they scuttled toward the medical center.

In our crew mess, there was nothing to eat but steamy noodles with olive oil and a clear plastic bin full of bread rolls. Just to top it all off, lurking somewhere on the dessert buffet were especially bland and gelatinous slices of pumpkin pie that looked as if they'd been made with culinary care from the innards of a jellyfish that had washed ashore. The crew was officially banned from passenger areas. Captain's orders. Crew were trapped in the stuffy and cramped crew areas, where we could all rest easy and breathe the same virus-infused air together. Everyone was praying for the day that the ship would reach our home port in Seattle.

The hot tub on the crew deck, of course, had been closed the entire time I had been aboard the cruise ship. As I said before, if there's ever a time that you want to grab a cappuccino from the crew mess and sit in a bubbling hot tub set to 105 degrees with a cast full of dancers who are as hot as a cruise ship fever, it's when you're cruising through Alaska's inside passage, watching snow-capped mountains drift by while the cruise ship dodges breaching killer whales and arctic dolphins.

These are the times when I felt ready to pack it up, head

home, and never see a cruise ship again as long as I lived. Every crew member gets tired of the monotony, the noise, the petty rules, the smell, the smoke, and the food. However, this time, my ship fever had developed into full-blown ship meningitis. I absolutely had to get off the cruise ship, at least for a very long break, but perhaps forever.

I was hungry, so I walked to the crew mess for some more noodles, bread rolls, and jellyfish pie. The crew mess was sterilized from floor to ceiling. I was surprised to see that the cruise company didn't have some of the smaller, lightweight crew members using suction-cup shoes so they could scrub down the ceiling with bleach. The crew mess smelled like a swimming pool, which is exactly the type of environment we all would like to eat in for every meal of the day for weeks on end. At nearly every entrance to the crew mess, there was a manager making sure that every crew member washed their hands. I had to wash my hands when I walked in the door. Then I was told to wash my hands before I went up to the buffet and then wash my hands before I poured a drink. I had to wash my hands for just looking at the guy telling everyone to wash their hands.

At times like this, the crew often gets a bit edgy. When the ship is under red alert, most crew members are required to work longer hours than normal to ensure that the passenger areas are thoroughly cleaned. Combine long working hours with the fact that crew members can't leave the crew area, and you end up with a ship full of rather exhausted, stressed, and exceptionally edgy sailors.

After repeatedly washing my hands, I finally made it to the bread roll bin. That's when I noticed something interesting. Crew members were coming into the crew mess from a small side door. This small entrance effectively bypassed all of the hand-washing police, and so the crew members who came into the crew mess from this side entrance were not washing their hands at all. I watched several of these crew members walk right through the side door, wipe their noses with the front of their hands or touch their mouths, and then grab the bread roll tongs and serve themselves a couple of bread rolls.

I didn't want to contract norovirus. I hadn't located any horse tranquilizers yet, and a lifeboat escape might have been too dangerous to attempt while sailing in the cold Alaskan waters. I certainly didn't want to get sick. So there was no way I was going to touch those grimy tongs in the bread roll bin.

I left the tongs alone and simply grabbed a few bread rolls out of the bin with my hands, making sure I didn't touch any of the other bread rolls that were inside. I placed the rolls on my plate. That's when an Indian security guard with a thick mustache, like an extra from the set of *Three's Company,* materialized out of thin air as if he had been instantly generated from the spool of a low-budget Bollywood movie.

"Did jou jus take a bread roll with your hands?" he said. His head bounced from side to side as if he were a bobble-head as he accused me of bread-roll touching in the first degree.

"Well," I said, "there's this door here, and crew members are—"

"Did jou or did jou not just touch these bread rolls? Do you not know we are under red alert? Do you understand that you are supposed to use the tongs?"

"Well, look, that's what I'm trying to explain. I don't want to get sick, and..."

"So you don't think you have to follow de rules dat everyone else has to follow?" he said. "Everyone has to use these tongs. There are strict rules that we must follow, and you're breaking these rules and could cause everyone else to get sick." He turned around and walked off. I never had the chance to explain how I had become involved in Bread Roll Gate, the cruise ship scandal of the century.

Later that night, I finished my performing with the showband. I was called into the cruise director's office. I had completely forgotten about what had happened in the crew mess. When I arrived at the cruise director's office, he said he might have to fire me for touching the bread roll. After a great deal of debating, the cruise director decided to simply give me a written warning. I was thirty years old, and I was getting written up for touching a bread roll. It felt like high school again. It was ridiculous, but this is how ridiculous ship life can often be. I was ready for a very long break, and luckily my contract on the cruise ship would be ending in just a few days, and I decided that it would be a long time before I would voluntarily set foot on a cruise ship as a crew member again.

Ironically, I needed a vacation from my cruise vacation. I wanted one more night under the stars on the crew deck and one more long night in the crew bar, and then I'd be ready to batten down the hatches, hang up my ship-life pirate's hat, and never look back. I wanted my freedom of land life. I didn't want to eat one more bowl of donkey-balls soup in the crew mess. I didn't want to touch my door handle and worry about contracting the norovirus again. I didn't want to be on ship time anymore. I was ready to take control of the helm and steer my own ship. I wanted to look my life right in the eyes and say, "Look at me. Look at me. I'm the captain now."

Two days later, I had reached the end of that long Alaskan contract, and I took that last walk down the rickety metal gangplank. I turned around to look at the ship one last time. The cruise ship had been my home for the last six months. I smiled when I realized that I wouldn't have to be back aboard the ship in six or seven hours, and I wouldn't have to eat another bowl of lentil curry for a long, long time. For a crew member, it's a great feeling to know that you're leaving red alert, emergency boat drills, and your sardine-can-sized cabin behind for a while.

So once again, like so many times before, I said all the long and hard goodbyes to all of the great friends I had made on my contract, and then I ran down that gangway as fast as I could. I walked out into the port and caught a taxi to the airport, where I boarded a plane that would take me home and back to a life that I controlled—a plane that flew a one-way route to freedom.

When I arrived home, I ran to my room, climbed into bed, and turned off all the lights. I pulled the covers over me and then celebrated for a moment the gargantuan size of my bed, which had suddenly become an exceptionally novel thing. After making snow angels under the covers and thoroughly stretching out in every direction possible to take full advantage of the bed's remarkable width, I closed my eyes.

What I realized was that the world outside of a cruise ship, the world above the waterline, is a chillingly quiet place, unnervingly quiet. The world is still—and without the hum of the hull as the ocean roars past the sides of the ship, and without the creaking of the walls, floor, and ceiling as the cruise ship battles over waves and fights against the ceaseless watery fists of the sea—there is only silence. Land life is motionless. The sea had rocked me to sleep for months, and now that I was out of its arms, I felt lost somehow. I felt strange without those familiar sounds and movements of the ship. There was no ocean splashing and spraying outside the bedroom wall, and there was light everywhere. The streetlights, the headlights of cars, and the dim lights from nearby rooms seeped through the crack at the bottom of the door. All of them seemed like jailbreak spotlights shining into my room. On the ship, there is no light in the room at night. When you walk into your crew cabin and turn off the lights, you are left with the most absolute and complete darkness. You are nestled below the ocean and tucked into a room with no windows.

I lay in bed and realized that I would have to make that bed when I woke up. I would have to cook my own breakfast and clean my own dishes. Days later, I was thinking about money—something I hadn't done in months. I had to go to the grocery store, and I hadn't driven a car in months. I hadn't been in bad traffic in years. When I arrived at the grocery store, I couldn't believe how much they were asking for chicken fingers, real pumpkin pie, or a single banana. On the cruise ship, I could grab a banana from Banana Mountain whenever I wanted to, and it was absolutely free.

For a crew member, the transition from ship life to land life can take months before they're entirely rehabilitated. Often, the difficulty of the transition is enough to send them running back up the gangway and drive them back to the ship life they know so well. They want to return to the familiar and back to a life where they will be able to sleep in the arms of the sea and won't have to make their beds when they wake up.

No matter how much time passes, the sea and my life as a cruise ship crew member will always be a part of me. I will never be able to leave it completely behind. There will always be a little more salt in my blood—and probably a lot more rum from those youthful days aboard the ship. Once you work on a cruise ship, you will *always* be a crew member, always belong to that group of people forever scattered around the world that know what you're talking about when you say "red alert" and double over in exaggerated pain and anguish, or when you smile about a cabin party. They have fought the Filipino Mafia in the crew laundry room. They have lived in a windowless crew cabin. They have battled through the sea, night after rocky night, and looked up at the same brightly shining stars into a pitch-black Caribbean sky from the edge of the crew deck.

They know what it's like to live a life of adventure on the sea and the difficulty of leaving it behind. They know what it's like to travel the world, see thousands of miles of the planet's coastline, and live a life in an endless summer aboard a sailing city that's always moving from one paradise to the next. They know what it means to live their life on cruise control.

And after it was all over, my memories of ship life still carried on within me. No matter how much time passed and no matter where I was in the world, I was never able to hear the deep and thundering sound of a cruise ship's horn the same way again. When that ship's horn would blow and echo across the sea, I would always be filled with the often fond and sometimes nauseating memories of my life as a cruise ship crew member. The sound of that ship's horn leaves crew members with a feeling like the first time they saw a clown at a friend's birthday party as a child. They feel completely uncertain whether they should run toward it or run away as fast as their little legs can run.

PART TWO

CHAPTER ONE

HELLO? YES, THIS IS THE SEA CALLING. I'D LIKE YOUR LIFE, PLEASE.

Before Gertie and I got the call to go back to the deep blue sea, I had everything a man could ever want—which is to say, everything that you can't have when you're working as a cruise ship crew member. I had a bed that was larger than a breadbox and a mattress that was less than ten-years old, both things that only exist in a crew member's dreams—but only daydreams, of course, since crew members hardly ever get any sleep. To a reformed crew member, the best part of that mattress was that it didn't contain a single broken spring that tried to commit murder-by-knifing every time I tried to get some shut-eye.

In our little home, I had several windows from which I could receive a healthy amount of natural light, which helps greatly in warding off deep depression. This is something you don't realize is so important until you work aboard a nuclear submarine that's forbidden to surface, or until you work as a cruise ship crew member. Best of all, my bedroom didn't rock violently each time a small squall blew through our neighborhood. It's amazing how well things stay on shelves when you live on land. I still find myself running to catch the bottle of wine from my kitchen counter each time I hear a gust of wind.

It was nice that we didn't need to turn on the television

and tune in to the live video-feed from the camera overlooking the bow of the ship to see what the weather was like outside. We could just go outside, at will, which was quite a luxury after working on a cruise ship for five years. We had a grocery store right down the road, where we could get all the fresh food we wanted. We could eat whatever we wanted, whenever we wanted to, which we took great delight in. Sometimes we'd sleep in until a shameful nine in the morning, and then we'd be sent into a state of joyful mania after discovering that our mess hall (our own kitchen) was still open. This meant we could still have eggs and bacon, a proper glass of orange juice, and a cup of coffee that wasn't made from that delicious combination of Ethiopian coffee-syrup concentrate and bilge water.

I was also very happy to stop sleeping on the bottom bunk of a bunk bed. Those who have never worked on a cruise ship may not understand this. Sleeping on the bottom bunk in a cruise ship crew cabin is a frightening experience, only equal to waking up and finding that the clown from Steven King's *It* had been having a staring contest with you while you slept.

Think about it. How many safety-related cruise-ship accidents have you seen on the news in the last few years? If the safety oversights that resulted in the *Carnival Triumph* and the *Costa Concordia* fiascos (I-ah accidentally-ah fell-ah into the lifeboat-ah) are any indication, imagine how likely it is that a bunk bed in a crew member's crew cabin might collapse at any given moment. The rusty bolts that hold some of these beds in place look as if they were salvaged from the wreckage of the *Lusitania,* and they probably haven't been inspected since *Space Invaders* was considered a high-tech video game.

The best thing about life on land was that we were living in reality—at least, in a form of reality where we were not subjected to an arbitrary hierarchy where we were regarded as peasants.

However, occasionally (and as hard as this may be to believe) I would start to have the creepy feeling that I might want to go back and work on a cruise ship again. I would really start to miss ship life. I knew deep in my heart that this feeling was simply a dangerous episode of optimism-induced amnesia, but it was hard to fight. I'm sure some of the people reading this book are former cruise ship crew members, and so I have some advice for you. Whenever you have one of those mini-strokes and start to miss ship life again, I want you to do three things.

1) Simulate what it is like to live in a crew cabin by bringing a handful of lit cigarettes and a bowl of lentil curry into one of your closets.
2) Have one of your best friends stand outside of the closet and play a recording of a jet taking off to simulate the sound of the ship's engine.
3) Then have this dear friend repeatedly slam the bedroom door while simultaneously stomping their feet loudly on your hardwood floors. This should closely reproduce the sound of crew members walking past a crew cabin and then slamming the doors nearby, which is something that happens at all hours of the day and night on a cruise ship.

See, don't you feel better about living on land again? You're welcome.

This easy test was usually enough to bring me back to my senses, and to keep me from thinking that going back on the cruise ship was such a good idea. However, if you're still walking around like a zombie and mumbling about how much you miss those sunny Caribbean islands, I want you to take the test to level two.

1) Have your friend stand guard at the front door to your house.
2) Every time you try to walk outside for a trip to the coffee shop or a walk in the park, your friend must ask you for your ID card.
3) Then have your friend glance at the ID and, in an Indian accent, say, "You can't leave the house today because you're on port manning."

And for readers who don't know, port manning is the regulation that requires a certain percentage of crew members to be on board the cruise ship at all times. Even when the ship is in port, some crew members are required to stay on board, to man the port. You can imagine how much crew members *love* port manning.

This fun reenactment will usually do the trick, but sometimes you just can't get those dreams of shuffleboard, midnight buffets, and late-night crew parties out of your head.

That's exactly what happened to Gertie and me.

We had a small house that was about nine hundred square feet, which is around 899 square feet larger than a crew cabin, so to us it felt as though we were living in Windsor Castle. Our little cottage was tucked away in a small community in the southern Appalachian Mountains near Asheville, North Carolina. Once in a while, we would want to revisit what it was like to live on a cruise ship and reexamine what it's like to live in the trappings of a nineteenth-century social order, complete with a working class that lived in squalor on the lower level. Whenever this happened, we would just go and visit the Biltmore Estate (the largest privately-owned home in America, built by the railroad mogul George Washington Vanderbilt II), which was only a few miles from our house. If that didn't refresh our memories of ship life, we would simply turn on the telly and watch an episode of *Downton Abbey*.

I was comfortable, absolutely content, had finally found the elusive inner peace...and then the phone rang.

That's how it seems to go, isn't it? The universe seems to have an affinity for chaos. And so the phone just had to ring right at the moment when I had become comfortable and happy in my life on land.

I know it sounds cliché, but if I had known then what I know now, I would have handled things quite differently. I would have asked Gertie to let her phone ring until the voicemail took a message. Then I would have stuffed the phone inside a filet mignon and set it out on our front porch. Hopefully, a bear would have come bumbling out of the forest and promptly devoured the filet, the phone, and the unexpected fork-in-the-road in one lovely and somewhat-electrifying chomp. At the time, Gertie would have believed I was completely mad, but I would have been an unsung hero for preserving our happy land-life.

But that's not what happened at all. Out of the blue, the phone rang.

It was the sea calling.

Gertie answered her phone, mouthing the words, "It's the art company," and then walked into a different room. While she was gone, I thought about the audition video we had made and sent off to Seven Seas Art Adventures. It was Gertie's big dream to work as an art auctioneer. At the time, I liked her quite a bit, and so her big dream had somehow become my dream too.

When Gertie walked back into the room, she had a big, goofy grin on her face, the kind of smile you'd see on a Labrador puppy that was just let loose in a bacon factory.

"You won't believe it," she said. "They watched our video and they just offered us the art auctioneer job."

When we made the audition video, I wasn't overly excited about the idea of working out at sea again. However, the winter had been long. Maybe my brain froze a little, because at some point I started to think that going back on the cruise ship wasn't such a bad idea.

It had been five years since Gary had called and asked me to work on the cruise ship as a drummer. I wasn't the same kid who romanticized about what it was like to live on a sailing party ship in the Bahamas. I knew exactly what it was like. I knew it was a lot like sailing in rough seas, that there were a lot of ups and downs. This time around, I just wanted the facts.

"What would our status be?" I asked.

"They said we'll be officers."

This sounded great. I could finally get some stripes. Maybe I'd get to wear an officer's uniform. Imagine that: me as a penguin, after all. "And what about the cabin?" I asked.

"They said we'd get an officer's cabin."

"Officer's privileges?"

"Yep."

"Where's the ship going?"

"We start out in the Caribbean, and then we'll cross to England. Then after a dry dock, we'll sail around Scandinavia."

"Where's dry dock?"

"Hamburg, Germany."

"How long is the contract?"

"Only two or three months. At first we'll be training. We'll be art associates. Then, if we do well, they'll make us art directors."

"When do they want us on board?"

"In three weeks."

"What do you think?" I asked her.

"I want to do it. This will be incredible!"

And the funny thing is, I agreed. It all sounded amazing. It was winter in the Appalachian Mountains. A blustery blizzard had been blowing through our little town for the past three days, snowing us in. Our options for fun activities had been reduced to wonderful things like watching icicles melt, shoveling snow, and scraping ice from our windshields.

Gertie had also developed a bad case of cabin fever, which now had developed into full-blown cabin pneumonia.

At that moment, I couldn't think of anything I'd love more than to climb aboard a cruise ship. I wanted to sit in the warm sun again and sip a *piña colada* from the crew bar as the ship's horn whistled and the waves gently lapped against the hull. I wanted to lounge on the crew deck and watch the bow turn toward the tropics as we began our sail to the next palm-lined island on our long list of holiday harbors.

It was that, or stay in the mountains with my lifetime supply of snow cones, black ice, and seasonal depression.

The decision wasn't completely easy. We knew this wasn't just a small fork in the road. We knew that taking this job would send our lives on a new sea-bound trajectory. We also knew that working as an art auctioneer was one of the best jobs on a cruise ship. Taking a job on a ship as a musician would have been a very difficult decision and an offer I probably would have refused, but art auctioneers lead very different ship-lives than the seafarers in the band. First off, art auctioneers can often literally make a *boatload* of money. I had heard stories of art auctioneers making upwards of ten thousand dollars a month. I know. Those are jaw-dropping paychecks, and that's why every room steward and musician wants to transfer positions as soon as they get on board.

Art auctioneers also have more shipboard privileges than musicians—at least, *some* of them do (as we came to find out). On many cruise lines, art auctioneers are officers. This means that art auctioneers are appointed to an officer's cabin, complete with the luxury of a bed that's wider than a coffin, an air purifier in the ceiling (oh, boy, could it be true!), and most lavish of all, a porthole window that lets in the sunlight, something that's nearly extinct in the crew area. And on many cruise lines, art auctioneers don't have as many responsibilities as crew members. For us, this translated into one glorious thing: we wouldn't have to participate in the passenger emergency boat drill, an experience for crew members that's equal to falling overboard and being slowly eaten by an inefficient school of great white sharks that are exceptionally picky eaters.

Along with these wonderful privileges, there were other exciting upgrades to look forward to. We could eat at the passenger buffet, which when compared to the crew mess is like comparing the French Laundry to a frozen burrito that you bought at a gas station. We would be able to enjoy the passenger areas during our time off, rather than be held hostage down below the waterline.

Working as an art auctioneer is also, hands down, one of the easiest jobs on a cruise ship, and thankfully you don't have to actually know anything about art to get the job. Some of the art auctioneers that I've met would have been shocked to learn that Leonardo and Michelangelo are something other than turtles with outstanding ninja skills. I've met some brilliant art auctioneers while out at sea, but believe me, there are some real scallywags out there too.

Yet, even with all of these privileges, I was still uncomfortable with the idea of walking up that gangway again. We were happy in our little house in the mountains. I was truly happy with my life as a landlubber, perhaps for the first time in quite a while. We were eating healthy. We lived outside of Asheville, and this meant there were more hippies in town than the high school reunion for Berkeley High's class of 1967. The availability of cheap organic food was comparable to what you would find in the parking lot of a Grateful Dead concert. I was willing to bet a pair of tickets to the Super Bowl that we wouldn't find any organic food on the cruise ship, unless we started deep-sea fishing off the lido deck or got really good at using shuffleboard sticks to bludgeon seagulls. We had mountain-fresh air, and we had a spacious house, but our house wasn't headed to any warm Caribbean islands. No, our house was headed straight into the icy depths of a long, cold winter.

And that was how our adventure began, an adventure that led me back to ship life, a place to which I never thought I would return.

I looked at Gertie, and then I looked out the window of our house. Snow was gently falling outside. The limbs of the oak tree in our front yard were covered with ice. A strong wind was blowing dead leaves down our street. This was no kind of life for a couple of adventurous sailors. This was no kind of place for a couple of pirates.

We deserved to be where bottles of rum were as cheap as water, and to travel to places where people were willing to do something as outrageous and indecent as having a parrot as a pet. We deserved to live a life in the sunshine, in a place where palm trees swayed in the warm tropical breeze. We owed it to ourselves to leave this landlubbing, nine-to-five, grind-of-a-life behind and follow our dreams into the sunset, to a place where no curry is too unsuitable to be served on the crew buffet—a place where long-standing labor laws are often overlooked, a place that knows no such words as "overtime pay", but a place that follows summer wherever it goes and will take us to lands of endless beaches and sparkling seas. We deserved to live a life of aquatic escapades where the spirit of the ocean pushed our imagination and passions to the limit. We would return to a place where the beer in the crew bar is always cheap and the officers are mostly Italian.

And this time things would be different, because we would *believe* that they were going to be different, *believe* that they were going to be better. We would leave the freezing mountains behind, stop living in a town with all the charm of an old snow globe that has been forgotten in a dark freezer, and once again become cruise ship crew members.

We began packing immediately. This time I wouldn't bring so many books. This time I would bring earplugs and horse tranquilizers (just in case I came down with the norovirus during a red-alert). Gertie began tossing bikinis, sparkly high-heels, and Lily Pulitzer dresses (the type with a repeating pattern of tiny sailboats sailing on a sea of hearts) into her suitcase. It was going to be an adventure of a lifetime. We were going to walk up that gangway once again, climb aboard that cruise ship, and trade our land life for ship life. We would become a man and a woman of the mast once again.

CHAPTER TWO

THIS IS MY LAST CONTRACT! WELL, SORT OF.

I'm going to break ranks and tell you a secret motto of cruise ship crew members. There are quite a few sayings that could be considered crew maxims, one being, "I hate boat drills," and another, "Yes, I would like another rum punch, please."

But there is one phrase that takes the chocolate-melting cake. It's an expression that every crew member has said at least three hundred times during their cruise ship career: "This is my last contract!"

I've heard it a million times, and I've heard it from crew members from every department. I've heard it from a room steward as he's trying to dislodge an alpaca-shaped towel animal from a clogged toilet that has flooded an entire deck of staterooms. I've heard it from musicians in the orchestra as they labor through yet another awful rendition of "The Greatest Love of All" at the passenger talent show. I've heard it from entire squads of married Italian officers who have become involved in yet another passionate and scandalous love affair with yet another beautiful and much-too-young cruise ship showgirl. And I've said it myself, at least once, on every contract that I've worked as a cruise ship crew member.

I was just a few days into my first contract, the first time I heard a crew member say—or in all honesty, yell—"This is my last contract!" I was working as a musician in the lounge band and it happened in the crew mess. A musician, who appeared as disheveled as a hobo on a train during the Great Depression, stumbled into the crew dining hall and walked up to the buffet line. He gave the tripe soup a stir, and then moved down to the barbecued blowfish cheeks and gave them a once over. I heard him mutter something under his breath that sounded very close to "Shoot me now" before he marched over to the salad bar and loaded up his plate with nothing but a towering pile of cucumber slices.

He walked over to the table where I was sitting, put down his plate, and then set down a bottle of hot sauce. He squinted and said, "This is my last contract!"

I was left thinking, *Who brings their own hot sauce on a cruise ship?*

Well, most crew members, it turns out. Hot sauce is about as valuable to a crew member as a high tolerance for seasickness and the stupid questions that passengers ask. (*If the ship sinks, will there be an ice cream machine on the lifeboat?*) In fact, hot sauce has many vital uses that should never be underappreciated or overlooked.

First and foremost, it is useful in completely masking the utterly bland and entirely unpalatable taste of nearly all food found in the crew mess. Don't feel like eating another Grade Z hot dog that has been sitting under a heat lamp for the past eight hours again? Just douse it with a liberal soaking of your favorite Africa-hot ghost pepper sauce, and you won't taste anything but fire and brimstone—which, as it turns out, is much better tasting than anything served in the crew mess.

Getting mugged in downtown St. Thomas or on the Caribbean coast of Costa Rica again? Hot sauce is just as effective as pepper spray when doused into the eyes of a renegade Caribbean wallet-hustler.

Is the ship too cold as always? Hot sauce will raise your body temperature to a level that at least will keep your fingertips from blackening with frostbite.

And so hot sauce is a part of a cruise ship crew member's uniform. Seafarers walk around with it in holsters, so that they're ready and quick on the draw when its services are needed.

But I still had a lot to learn on that day when my new friend sat at the table next to me and set down his bottle of Texas Phil's Hotter-Than-Hell Habanero Sauce. He thoroughly doused his cucumbers, took a bite, and then said those five favorite words, "This is my last contract!"

Three months later, I was walking onto a new ship for a new contract, and whom did I see but Mr. Texas Phil himself.

"I thought that was your last contract?" I asked.

"Well, I'm back," he said. "I needed the money. But this is my last contract!"

They say absence makes the heart grow fonder. However, for a cruise ship crew member who worked on those sailing hotels as long as I did, a lobotomy may have been required. Yet, something exceptionally curious did happen to me after I left ship life and looked back on my days as a cruise-liner pirate. A form of selective amnesia began to find its way into my memory, making me forget about all of the junk I had to endure when I lived on the iron giant that sailed the blue highway.

Slowly, the bad times faded away. I was left with just half a brain, one that only remembered the beautiful Caribbean Islands, the gorgeous women in dental-floss sized bikinis, and the occasional meals served in the crew mess that were actually edible. My mind replaced all of the octopus-leg curries and barbecued-chicken-foot pizzas with the filet mignon and lobster tails that the cruise line served to crew members that one time on Christmas Day. Which, of course, was enough to make cruise ship crew members believe in Santa Claus again.

So when Gertie and I boarded the plane in Orlando that was headed for the Port of Miami, I was certainly in ship-life-amnesia mode. Whenever my synapses tried to make a connection in which I would remember a bad memory of my former life as a crew member, my thoughts would be rerouted and I would see myself swaying in a hammock on a sandy beach in Mexico, sipping a sangria that's so strong it's considered toxic. Gertie would be there in her bikini, running into the turquoise-colored sea like Bo Derek.

I packed light for the voyage, but not by choice. I didn't know what to expect when I got to the ship, but I knew that Gertie and I would be sharing a room. That room was going to have a tiny closet, and when you're traveling with a woman who will fall into a deep depression if she has to repeat a dress and heel combination on a single formal night during a two-month long cruise, you learn quickly that the closet belongs to her, which was fine with me.

Gertie brought two large suitcases out to the car with bikini straps and sequin dress parts sticking out the sides. "I couldn't fit everything," she said. "My mom is going to bring me the rest after our first cruise." I figured it was in my best interest to just smile and nod. Smile and nod, boys. Just smile and nod.

Everything I would bring aboard the cruise ship would need to fit under our bed, so I started questioning whether I should bring that vacuum sealer contraption I had bought one night in 1999 while watching an infomercial. This meant there would be a great deal of ironing clothes in my future, which meant there was a high probability that I wouldn't survive the contract, since the most lethal objects known to man are the frayed wires attached to the irons found in the crew laundry room.

But at least I'd die an officer. I began fantasizing about having that special officer's ID card that I could swipe to gain access to the Officers' Laundry Room, the fabled land of properly working washers and dryers. It was rumored that the irons there, unlike those in the *crew* laundry room, actually have fewer confirmed kills than a Navy SEAL Sniper.

Before we boarded our plane, Gertie had to pay overweight-luggage fees, since her bags contained around two hundred pounds of clothes each. As we flew above the coast of Florida and inched our way closer to the gangway, I felt the anxiety began to settle in. We had no way of knowing what we were getting ourselves into.

You see, every ship is different. Every ship has a different captain who has a different approach to running the ship. You would think that even within the same cruise line, ship life would be fairly similar, somewhat predictable, but a cruise ship crew member has no idea what their life is going to be like from one ship to the next. Joining a ship is a shot in the dark. It's a crapshoot, and most of the time you only win crap.

Even with the promises the company had made, we really didn't know what our room would be like, where it would be located, or what our privileges would be once we walked aboard the ship. We did know that we'd be officers, but this distinction still only roughly defined what type of privileges we'd have on the cruise liner. On a ship, unless you are the captain, there is always someone above you who has the power to control your privileges, and so they have the power to take them away on a whim. In ship life, life is like a dock of cruise ships. You never know what you're gonna get.

CHAPTER THREE

THE SHIP-LIFE SIREN SINGS AGAIN.

If you ever have the desire to experience what cattle must feel like as they're being led to the slaughterhouse floor, then sign up as a crew member who must board a ship at the Port of Miami. There is a long series of gates to get through before you get inside the factory, and along the way you are poked, prodded, and herded onto the ship with a large group of easily-spooked animals who aren't completely certain about where they're headed, and they all have the same uneasy feeling that they might not like it once they get there.

We walked toward the pier, dragging our three suitcases, and leaving a trail of Gertie's sparkly sequins behind us. I figured this may be useful if we ever wanted to find our way home. We navigated the maze of the cruise ship port, becoming as disoriented as a cave diver after his flashlight burns out unexpectedly. But We had our lifeline of sequins, so we were okay. We made it through the first of several checkpoints, and then I came face to face with a cruise ship for the first time in many years.

I was astonished at how I felt. It was all very romantic, really. A gentle warm breeze was blowing across the Atlantic. Waves were lapping gently against the hull of the ship, its bow pointed toward adventure. The thick ropes that held the beast at bay creaked and moaned. The smell of the salty sea and the sight and sounds of the ship resurrected old feelings of my love of ship-life and the high seas.

That wasn't what I had expected at all. I felt as if I was coming home at Christmas time, and before I stepped inside my childhood home, I could see my family through the frosty window, all gathered around the Christmas tree, singing carols in front of a crackling fire. It was a warm feeling of returning to a place that I once deeply loved, where people who I loved deeply once lived.

As Gertie walked toward the ship and I struggled to pull her four-hundred pounds of luggage up the gangway, it felt as if I was walking into the arms of my mother. For those of you who have never worked at sea and therefore have never fallen madly in love with life among the waves and the wind, this may seem like a stretch. However, landlubbers beware: the decision to journey into a life inside the hull should not be taken lightly. There really is no turning back. Once you weigh anchor and head out to sea, you will always have the spirit of a seadog deep in your salty, rum-drenched, scallywag soul.

And after you work at sea for many, many years, the ship really does become a second mother. She rocks you to sleep. She feeds you. She calls you when it's time to come home. She always has a berth that is made and ready just for you. She protects you from the big, bad, scary world out there, a world with violent storms and squalls that rage and battle endlessly with the bow. She steers you through the rough oceans and comforts you in the calm seas, and she does everything she can do to deliver you to the next safe harbor. The ship becomes your mother, the beacon of hope and light in the darkest of nights, a tireless navigator through the mystical fogs of life.

Then again, a cruise ship is also like a mother-in-law. She

can be very hard to get along with, it's probably best not to live too close to her, and a visit should never be too long since there is a high probability that you will be driven to the absolute brink of madness and would rather walk the plank and take your chances in Davy Jones's locker than spend another minute on her crew.

For crew members, there is a deep connection to the cruise ship and, often, an intense dependency on ship life that can be very difficult to overcome. This is precisely why leaving ship life behind can be so difficult. We all have to grow up sometime and go out into the real world and make a life for ourselves. We can't just live with our mothers forever, but this transition from a ship life to a life on land is often far from easy.

I had already done this. I had been through the difficulties of finding my way in the world without the ship to cut through the seas and navigate the storms. For example, after the last time I left ship life, I had to learn to make my own bed again, because there wasn't a crew room-steward to do it for me every morning. I had to relearn how to cook and clean, and how to drive a car. My digestive system had to relearn how to digest foods with a high nutritional content, something a cruise ship crew member's stomach forgets how to do after five years of eating food in the crew mess.

As I stood there and peered into the cold, dark interior of the cruise ship, I wasn't sure that I wanted to go back and pass through that threshold again. I wasn't confident that I wanted to go back to ship life, because I knew that one day I would have to break free again, and then I would have to relearn how to cope with living on land once more.

Then I caught a whiff of chocolate-melting cake and

lobster tails, and I heard the luring song of the cruise ship siren, a beautiful topless mermaid who sings from a secluded beach on St. John Island. Her song went something like this:

You got your new black shoes
You got your new black socks
You got your new black suit
You're ready for the cruise ship life

You got a big buffet
You got curry delights
A nice room steward who makes the bed just right
You're ready for the cruise ship life

You got the wind and the waves
You got the sea and the sights
You got more ports than a British wino at night
You're ready for the cruise ship life

You got the crew bar, woo!
Where the drinks are priced right
You got the spa girls, a sight
And showgirl dancers, all right

You got the lava cake
And the crew deck at night
You got the stars in the sky
The moonlight to navigate by

It's all just a dream
So climb right aboard

Let's explore this world
From port to starboard

Ship life's not too bad
Through the rough seas you'll roll
But there's nothing like ship life
And being back on cruise control

You got your new black shoes
You got your new black socks
You got your new black suit
You're ready for the cruise ship life

And so we drifted back aboard, back into the bosom of life on deck Z. As we passed through the threshold and walked onto the cruise ship again, I knew that our life was going to be much better than our ship lives were before. We were no longer in rank and file with the have-nots. We could finally wear too much Drakkar Noir and walk into the crew bar with a brass spotting scope and order a Stella and refuse to socialize with any other crew members of lesser rank.

We were finally going to have some power in this ship life, finally going to be officers. And this pair of proud penguins couldn't wait to see the privileged luxuries that awaited them inside their officer's stateroom.

CHAPTER FOUR

YOU MUST LIE IN THE BED YOUR ROOM STEWARD MAKES FOR YOU.

We wheeled our bags into the crew office to pick up our room keys, and unintentionally discovered the world's grumpiest people all gathered together in one place. We were halfway out the door when a man with as much energy as an F5 tornado burst into the room and started talking at five hundred miles an hour.

He was wearing dark sunglasses fit for a rock star and a preppy sweater-vest over a heavy-starched button-down, the 1973 Jimmy Page look. His hair was gelled and tussled into a mess.

"Welcome aboard!" he said. The two words sounded wonderful, and it was very nice to receive such a warm welcome.

His name was Alex Ashebury, and he used a hurricane of hand movements when he talked. He turned to us and started with the karate chopping. "We're going to have such a blast! But look, I need to run. I got tons of paperwork. It's turnaround day, and we got new art coming on board, and I don't know how I'm going to survive this stuff. I just want to play table tennis in the crew bar tonight. Look. Just get to your room and get your work clothes on. Oh yeah—it's formal night, so don't show up wearing a T-shirt and flip-flops. We'll get you two up and running. We're going to make so much money. It's going to be raining *Benjamins* up on this ship. I'll call your cabin in a few hours when I'm headed to the gallery. I got tons of stuff for you two to read. Okay? Welcome aboard."

And just like that, the hurricane left and moved on to the next town. We walked out of the crew office and headed toward our crew cabin, our new home for the next two months. The ornery crew-office people had told us our room was located approximately two miles down the I-95 toward the aft of the ship. We wheeled our luggage to the closest crew elevator. Instinctively, I pushed the "down" button, but then I stopped and looked at the number on the keycard for our stateroom: 3452. I squinted, expecting to see the numbers shift to something like Z-001, but no, they stayed the same. For the first time in my ship life, I was going to take the elevator *up* from the I-95 to get to my cabin. We were moving up in cruise-liner land, finally living somewhere *above* the waterline.

This was big news. For once, if a leak sprung in the hull it wouldn't be an absolute certainty that water was going to come pouring out of our crew-cabin wall. If the ship ran aground, we no longer had to worry that our last thoughts would be, *"Hey, what the hell is that reef doing in our bathroom?"*

This also meant that there was a chance, but only a chance, that we might have a porthole window in our crew cabin. We might be able to sit up at night, pop a bottle of champagne, and sit on our very own bed as we watch the sea sparkle in the moonlight and listen to the ship cut through the waves as an inky outline of tropical islands slowly rolls past our porthole window. We could wake up in the morning and watch the sun rise over the sea as frothy waves curled from the hull of the ship as we raced toward another palm tree–

lined port. I could sit in the sunlight, and marvel at the beauty of the sea and the stars twinkling in the sky, and each time be amazed that I can see it all from the edge of the bed in our officer's cabin.

Ding! The elevator arrived, but it was packed with crew members who had the healthy glows of Steve Buscemi after three days filming without sleep.

"Well, I guess we'll catch the next one," Gertie said in a chipper tone. "Have a great day!"

One of the room stewards mumbled something that sounded very close to "Effing new guys" and then pushed the button to close the elevator. Let's just say that enthusiasm is not a crew member's strong suit after they've been on board a ship for more than three months.

The elevator returned empty, and so we shoved Gertie's dump truck–sized wardrobe collection into the elevator and had just enough room to wedge my plastic grocery bag of clothes and toothbrush into the corner.

I pushed the up button, and then heard the theme song from *The Jeffersons* playing in my head. The elevator opened to a view of the crew mess. This was perfect. Our room might be close enough for me to run and grab some food anytime that I had a craving for grilled cow tongue or aardvark-bung curry—which would be absolutely never. However, it was nice to know that I could easily smuggle ice from the crew mess (and *smuggle* is the appropriate word here) for all of those rummy nightcaps and daycaps too.

It was late morning, so the crew mess was mostly empty. I could see a few crew members sitting in front of plates piled high with mountains of rice. Some of them were dousing the rice with hot sauce, mostly from bottles with roosters on the front. Nothing had changed.

Nothing except the fact that we would never have to eat in the crew mess again, a room with all the charm of the waiting room at your local DMV. This made me feel good all over, of course.

I was excited to see what the officers' mess looked like. I imagined white linens and Filipino waiters dressed like *Downton Abbey* footmen. *Yes, I would love a cappuccino and another chocolate melting cake please, and while you're standing over me, could you rub my shoulders just a bit? Yes, the ones with the yellow stripes on the shoulder boards. I do say, that is marvelous. Just marvelous.* We had heard rumors that on some ships, officers could drink free wine with dinner in the officer's mess. We had heard that the walls were not just covered with posters from human resources that said things in big block letters like, "ALWAYS REMEMBER TO SMILE AT PASSENGERS, EVEN IF YOU DO FEEL LIKE JUMPING OVERBOARD" and "STAND UP STRAIGHT, OR WE'LL FEED YOU TO THE SHARKS, YOU DIRTY BILGE-SUCKING SCALLYWAGS." Instead, we heard gossip that the officer's mess had framed, albeit severely faded, prints by the likes of J. M. W. Turner and Winslow Homer as well as inspirational portraits of world-famous sailors such as Jacques Cousteau, Horatio Nelson, Captain Ron, Captain Crunch, and Popeye.

We walked out of the elevator, picking up our pace as we got closer to our stateroom that was just around the corner. I looked at the sequence of numbers on the other cabin doors, and calculated that we would actually be on the sea-view side of the hallway.

"Oh my God," Gertie said, sounding as happy as Noah when he was finally able to say "I told you so." She turned to me, her eyes as big as shuffleboard pucks. "We're going to have a porthole!"

We ran down the hall with excitement, counting down the cabin numbers as we went. Then we stopped and came face to face with cabin 3452.

We looked at each other and smiled. I slowly slid the keycard in. The light on the handle blinked green, and we heard the lock click. I waited for a second, just to tease her, and Gertie laced her hands together and put them over her mouth.

I pushed the door open, and there it was, in all of its glass-paned glory, casting a bright ray of light from its round beautiful opening that was surrounded by slightly tarnished brass dogs holding the swing plate in place.

It was our window to the shining sea, a porthole to the oceanic marvels beyond. "Beyond the Sea" began playing in my head. We had finally received our medal for advancing to life above the waterline. I grabbed Gertie, and we stood there, side by side, admiring the pure beauty of the thing, the way passengers look when they first set eyes on the ice cream machine on the first day of their cruise.

But then I looked down below the porthole, and in my head, I heard the sound of a screeching record. I saw a bed, but only one, and it was about as wide as a countertop.

I looked at Gertie. "This must be a mistake."

Then we heard the singsong voice of an Indian man from behind us. "You must be the new art auctioneers."

We turned around. The door was open to the cabin across the hall from us. However, it wasn't a crew cabin at all, but an office. And inside this office was a rather large desk with a friendly looking Indian man sitting behind it. He was wearing an officer's uniform, and he had a refreshingly sincere smile on his face. It was bracing to finally discover the elusive genuine-smile on a cruise ship, like spotting a snow leopard in the mountains of Central Asia.

I glanced at his nametag—ARJUN PATEL, HUMAN RESOURCES MANAGER, INDIA.

It was nice to know that we would only have to go across the hall to find out when the next crew party was happening or to ask what watery grave our paychecks had ended up in.

We introduced ourselves, and then Gertie said, "I think we've been given the wrong room."

Arjun leaned back in his chair and put his hands behind his head. His lips curved upwards, transforming into the snow leopard again.

"No," he said. "I think this is the room that you are assigned to."

"But," I said, moving out of the way so that he could see the culprit at the heart of the matter, "there's only one bed."

Arjun raised his eyebrows and peered over his desk as if he were giving the bed a thorough, albeit very quick, examination. "Well, I hope you two like to snuggle."

We both learned a long time ago that cruise ships are a lot like naval wars, you have to choose wisely which battles you wage. You must always navigate through your maritime conflicts with as much skill as John Paul Jones. (Not Led Zeppelin's bass player; the other bloke.) Likewise, there's also a high risk of developing scurvy from improper nutrition, and you have to keep one eye on the attacking armadas and the other eye on the loyal-less crew where the line that divides order and mutiny is as sharp and thin as the edge of Blackbeard's bloody blade. So, the last thing we were going to do was make a first impression that we were complainers or that we were anything other than grateful for the officer's cabin that we had been appointed, which we were, immensely.

"So I guess this *is* the right room," I said. "Everything else is very nice." I enthusiastically fiddled with the novel thermostat on the wall, which apparently had been set to "meat locker" along with the rest of the ship. I was extremely grateful to see the thermostat. When you don't have a thermostat, (like the other eighty percent of the crew) you only have two options: the vent in the ceiling can be open or closed. This means your cabin can either be uncomfortably warm or you can bundle up in blankets while you sleep and hope you don't wake up to find that one of your toes managed to poke out the side of your down-comforter and now, after succumbing to frostbite, has broken off and is rolling around back and forth on the floor somewhere as the ship lists with the waves. More importantly, the thermostat was a clear indication that we had an air filter, which on a cruise ship is more valuable to a crew member than a wooly mammoth–sized hair dryer would have been to the Shackleton expedition.

"I'll see what I can do," Arjun said. "Maybe there's a room with a bigger bed we can find for you two."

"That would be so nice," Gertie said. "We're here for two months, and…the bed is a bit small for the both of us. But I'm sure we can make it work."

We can make it work, I thought. I looked at the closet that was against one side of the wall. It was almost large enough to fit Gertie's scrunchie collection. I looked under the bed, where all my stuff was going. *Yeah, we'll make it work.* We had to stay positive. In ship-life we knew we couldn't let the little things drag us down.

Besides, we had a thermostat, and a *porthole*. This was no life in the bilge tank with the other crew members.

"I'll do my best," Arjun said.

Gertie said thanks. We told him how happy we were to be back on the ship. And we were. Both of us. Now that we were aboard, I was happy to be back on cruise control. Sure the small bed was a bit of a setback, but we'd batten down the hatches, unfurl the jib, and get this voyage under way.

"And hey," Arjun said. "Welcome aboard. We're very happy to have you both on the ship. Please, if you ever need anything, or ever need anyone to talk to, please, come and talk to me. I know that ship life can get hard sometimes, and I'm always here if you need anyone or any help." It was one of the most heartfelt welcomes that I had ever heard from a fellow crew member of a higher rank, and we felt Arjun meant it.

We wheeled our luggage into our room, which took up the two square feet of free space in the cabin. After Gertie closed the door, both of us ran up to the porthole window. We had a clear view of the Port of Miami in all of its concrete glory. Nonetheless, we were thrilled to get a glimpse outside of our own crew cabin for the first time in more than five years of working on ships. Our room was just above the waterline, and so the view put us at eye level with the feet of the passengers and crew members still scrambling around the port.

"Okay," Gertie said. "Let's get dressed for the gallery now. I want to have time to be up on the lido deck for sail away."

"Perfect."

I threw my suitcase onto the bed and pulled out my suit and my black bowtie. I was back on cruise control. As I dressed into my formal wear, I thought about those words: cruise control. Even the phrase itself is a pairing of positive and negative, and this is exactly what ship life is like. On the one hand, we were about to cruise through the sea, and sail far from the shores of our comparably mundane land-lives, yet this move to ship life was an exchange, one that required us to give up a great deal of control over our lives.

Before I stepped onto the ship, I worked from home and had made my own schedule. I could wear sweatpants and an old, comfy T-shirt all day if I wanted to. I would wake up every morning and have the freedom to work on whatever I pleased. My only responsibility was to make sure that my mug was always full of steaming snickerdoodle coffee, and that I didn't miss my work deadlines.

I sat on the edge of our tiny bed, with our porthole casting a circular ray of light across the room, which was made exceptionally dramatic by the dust that swirled around our cabin. Those days of making my own schedule and wearing sweatpants were over (well, at least for the next two months or so). I was putting on my cruise ship sea-monkey suit again, and now my life would be dictated by *ship time.*

Welcome to ship life. Welcome to cruise control. Please hand over your freedom to the Indian security guard at the gangway.

The phone in our cabin rang.

"Hey!" a voice barked from the receiver. It was Alex Ashebury, the art director who'd be training us for the next few weeks.

I tried to get in a response. "Hi, we just got—"

"Great. Look. You need to go back to the crew office to pick up your nametags. Grab a bite to eat real quick, and then meet me in the gallery ASAP. I'm ready to get you two on the floor. We got a lot to go over. How's thirty minutes sound?"

"See you then."

"Great!" *Click.*

I looked out the porthole window. I heard the deep, thundering sound of the cruise ship's horn, the final all-aboard warning. It was so loud that it sent a rumbling vibration through the walls of our cabin. The sound of the horn triggered five years of ship-life memories, which rushed over me like a tidal wave. Through the porthole I could see the pier workers in blue suits, ready to loosen the ship's mooring lines. Land life was about to drift away.

The voice of an Italian man blared from the speaker in the ceiling of our cabin. "Attention all-ah crew member. Attention all-ah crew member-ah. Please report-ah to your muster station for the crew-ah drill-ah."

I looked at the single lifejacket that was tucked into a tiny gap between the top of the wardrobe and the ceiling. *Only one lifejacket?*

We'd get this sorted out immediately. The Costa Concordia disaster was fresh on our minds when we walked aboard the ship for our art contract. The disaster reminded us that ship life was more than just beautiful beaches and piña coladas; ship life is also a treacherous sea voyage, one where you'd best have your life vest ready.

But I didn't have to worry about that right now. For the first time in my life, I didn't have to go to the boat drill. *This is going to be the cruise ship contract of my dreams.*

The ship sounded its horn again. I felt as if I had been

called back home, and it felt better than ever. It was like seeing an old pal after many years, the kind of friend that can make you laugh like no one else; the kind of friend that makes you more comfortable than anyone else. It was like embracing an old lover, one that you just never could forget. I had been in love with ship life once, and I knew I could fall in love again.

I looked at Gertie. She was wearing a blue and white dress with a repeating pattern of tiny anchors and ship's wheels, and her dark brown hair was curled in tight spirals, her nails glossy pink.

"I have a surprise," she said.

"I like surprises." *Sexy pirate costume?*

She walked over to her luggage and pulled out a small box. She opened the lid and, with a ceremonial flourish of her hands, whipped out an auctioneer's gavel, except this was no ordinary gavel. Apart from the gold rings around both ends of the mallet, the gavel was painted bright pink. She lifted the mallet up, and slammed it against the desk. "*Sold*!" she said.

"Sold indeed!" I replied.

It was the best thing I had ever seen, because it was just what we needed to make a billion bucks out here—a gimmick. We had decided that Gertie would run the auctions, and that I would sell art on the showroom. She would appeal more to the crowd, and I was a better salesperson one on one. We would split our commission fifty-fifty and share the other duties of the job. When I saw that pink gavel slam down on the desk, I felt us two pirates might actually find some treasure buried aboard one of these cruise ships, after all.

We walked down the hallway toward the open deck. I heard the thrusters ignite. I felt the ship begin to drift away from the port. We ran up four flights of stairs to a breezeway on deck five. The bright Florida sun sent sparkles across the surface of the sea. A warm ocean wind blew across the breezeway. We looked out over the ocean as the ship turned its bow seaward, and then we sailed toward the point on the horizon where the water melds into the sky in a misty, blue haze.

We were sailing home, back to the sea, back to our first true love.

CHAPTER FIVE

HOW TO BECOME AN ART EXPERT.

On our art contract, Gertie and I had plenty to look forward to. We had two seven-day cruises that sailed around the Caribbean, stopping in the sunny ports of St. Kitts, San Juan, and our first stop—beautiful St. Martin.

But what excited us most was that in two weeks we were scheduled to leave the port of Miami with our bow pointed east, and then sail through more than four thousand miles of ocean. The ship would battle the sea for eight days straight, cross the Atlantic Ocean, and finally approach the Port of Southampton in England, where we would see a speck of land on the horizon with a permanent rain cloud hovering over it, and smell the sea breeze mingled with the distant scents of steak-and-ale pie, Marmite, and West End showgirls.

However, at this moment, we were looking forward to learning what our job as art auctioneers would be like, and it turned out to be nothing like we expected.

Gertie and I jogged down the I-95, and after getting thoroughly lost in a maze of turns, shortcuts, and endless hallways that all looked the same, we finally found the crew office again, where we were given our nametags. Mine read: JOSHUA KINSER, ART EXPERT, USA.

I was now an official art expert. See! It said it right there on the nametag. With the added air of authority after becoming official art experts, and feeling a little bit like Frank

Abagnale, Jr. from the movie *Catch Me If You Can*, we took the stairs up to deck five. As we walked, I thought about how nothing had changed on the cruise ships since the last time I'd found myself walking through ship life.

The I-95 was bustling with crew members from all over the world. Forklifts were racing down the main corridor with stacks of luggage and threatening to smash anyone's toes that stood in their way. That unmistakable smell of the cruise ship still remained the same after all these years, that unique bouquet of fresh paint, body odor, and hair gel mingled with the lovely and subtle aroma of trash compacter, bilge water, and Banana Mountain.

We walked through the hallways and saw the same cast of characters that had always been on cruise ships. There were the musicians dressed in all black, a group of dancers wearing black tights and with their hair in buns, a middle-aged magician who looked bored out of his mind because he only had to work twice a week, the young men in blue jumpsuits that did all kinds of labor on the ship from greasing the winches to scrubbing the decks. There were the Italian officers with jet-black hair slicked back with olive oil, who smelled like a combination of spaghetti sauce, too much Old Spice aftershave, and the brass polish they used to shine their gleaming spotting scopes, which are primarily employed to examine the dancers who sunbathed on the crew deck in thongs. (I will never believe that it is coincidence that the crew deck on most ships is conveniently located directly in front of the bridge.)

We saw the Russian and Romanian casino dealers, the Indian cooks were there, too, looking more well-nourished than everyone else on the ship. There were the Jamaican bartenders and the core of the crew—the Filipinos. And if you've never befriended a Filipino, then you are truly missing out because they are some of the most kindhearted and generous people on the planet. They also make up the bulk of the crew on most cruise ships, many of them working in the housekeeping department. The interesting thing about Filipinos on the cruise ship is that you never know who is involved with the Filipino mafia and who is on the outside of the operation, so you must tread lightly, be observant. The goal here is to identify who's on the inside. We'll leave it at that for now.

To those who have never worked on a cruise ship, this is all probably starting to sound a bit culturally segregated. Well, that's because for the most part it is, but don't ask me why. All I know is that if you happen to be Filipino, chances are you will end up working in the housekeeping department or as a waiter. If you're Indian, you can very well count on spending your ship life by the X-ray machine at the gangway as a security guard, or plan on becoming an expert at carving ice sculptures and prepping baked Alaska as a member of the kitchen staff. If you're lucky enough to be Italian, you have a chance at being an officer or even a captain on the high seas. I'm not saying this is fair. Ship-life isn't fair, I know. This is just what I've observed.

We walked through the bustling crowd of internationals, all rushing around the ship to make sure everything was shipshape, and that every need of the two thousand passengers was always met. Everything seemed new and exciting again, but pretty much the same as when I had left, like going back to school and roaming around the halls again a few years after you've graduated.

We climbed the stairs to deck five and walked into the passenger area for the first time. Through the large windows that lined the promenade, we could see the foamy sea as it whipped off the hull of the ship. We had just left port, and so most of the passengers were doing one of three things: getting settled into their spacious staterooms, complaining to the customer service crew members, or searching for the buffet or another ice cream cone (one with colored sprinkles, please), which I'm not knocking at all. The first thing I do when I get on a cruise ship as a passenger is find the ice cream machine, and then I go straight to the kitchen and bribe an Indian cook for a few piping-hot chocolate lava cakes.

And perhaps you should highlight that last sentence so you remember to engage in shameless bribery on your next cruise. It's amazing how much ten bucks can buy when you finally find *Vijay Patel's Secret and Magical Cruise Ship Trading Post*—something that definitely exists on every cruise ship. You just have to know where to look. It's not hard to find. Just follow the smell of spicy curries, patchouli, chai tea, and thick mustache. This aromatic path to culinary Shangri La will never lead you astray.

We traveled through the threshold that separates the crew area from the passenger area, which is a transformative moment for any crew member. It's similar to the experience of someone who has been suffering from years of chronic back pain and then suddenly undergoes a successful back surgery. They knew they were in pain. They had been dealing with it for years, but they just never realized the extent of that pain until it went away.

We stepped through the doorway. The ship was everything we could ever want from a luxury cruise liner, minus Leonardo DiCaprio for Gertie and Kate Winslet for me, please. It was sparkling, dazzling: wood-paneled walls fit for a billiard room, more metal railing than a Supermax prison, oversized porthole windows that stretched from floor to ceiling, an ice cream machine around every corner, gastrointestinal viruses patiently lurking upon every door handle, bingo card, and shuffleboard cue. The smell of teakwood polish, recently purchased tropical shirts, and brand new seasickness patches filled the air.

The promenade looked as if the cruise company had taken an entire coastal block of St. Martin, complete with palm trees and a charming pastel-colored marketplace (but had the foresight to kick out all of the relentless hair-braiders and mangy island dogs), and then used a massive crane to plop the whole thing down, right in the middle of the cruise ship. This cruise line, which we will call Festivus, certainly had it together.

Yet, for the crew, the beauty of the cruise ship passenger area is always a bittersweet thing. The ship's splendor and elegance is a constant daily reminder of what ship life *could* be—a reminder, perhaps, of what ship life *should* be for the crew. Every day, we drift through that portal that takes us from the minor leagues right up to the majors, and it's wonderful as long as you're in that major league dugout.

However, at the end of the day, we always get a call from our team manager who says, "I'm sorry, but we're sending you back to AA. We already made the deal. You're now playing ball with a team out of Newark, New Jersey, *The Rusty Bunks*. Their mascot is a bowl of curry holding a mop for swabbing the decks."

Every night, crew members must leave the fantasy world

of the passenger area behind. They leave Oz, where everything is in color, and go back to crummy old black-and-white Kansas where the place looks like a tornado ripped through town and stripped it of everything that could possibly be considered "non-essential". It makes us feel as if we're not good enough, not good enough for ice cream cones with sprinkles and pizza parlors and snazzy nightclubs and brass railings and fine art and big porthole windows and shuffleboard on the breezeway.

Yet, this isolation from the good life up on lido deck does give us something to strive for. It makes us strive to save up enough money so that we can get the hell off cruise ships, find a better paying job where we're treated with more respect, and then come back to cruise as a passenger, or do what Gertie and I did and get promoted to officers as art auctioneers where the pay is quite good.

In ship life, the passengers are the haves, and the crew members are most certainly the have-nots. So I would like to propose a way to bridge this gap. You may not know this, but you, all you passengers. You have a great power. You have the power to keep a crew member in the wonderful fantasyland of the passenger area and delay the call to the minor leagues for several hours each evening, because you have the ability to invite a crew member to dinner in the passenger dining room.

Not all cruise lines allow this, but some permit crew members to dine in the guest dining room if they are specifically invited by a passenger. You can start your mission of generosity by talking to the maître d'. He'll know the rules. Make up a story about how your room steward or, shall we say, showband drummer or art auctioneer really made your cruise experience special. A cruise ship is all politics. The decision will probably be made based on how well the crew member is liked by management. And, again, you'd be amazed at what a bribe to the right person can get you on a cruise ship.

I was only invited to the dining room once by a guest. For some reason, the beautiful dancers often had lobster tail breath and chocolate melting cake burps—even the ones who weren't dating officers. So passengers, now you know, and in the wise words of Uncle Ben from one of those Spiderman movies, "With great power comes great responsibility." Use your power wisely. Use it for the greater good. The more lobster breath and chocolate melting cake burps among the crew the merrier!

Back on the cruise ship, we walked down the promenade, past a row of gift shops where I spotted an inflatable cruise ship that I really wanted and a coffee mug that said "I'm on Cruise Control" that I absolutely had to have.

Then we stopped. I looked at Gertie. She had this sparkle in her eyes. I think we both knew we could work this place like a fox on a turkey ranch. If anyone could make a million bucks in a cruise ship art gallery, it was us two.

Gertie kissed me on the cheek. "You ready?"

I straightened my jacket. "I'm ready."

We turned the corner and walked into the art gallery. Except it wasn't much of a gallery. It was a hallway, and at the end was the theater where the showband played—my old home for five years, back when I played in the band as a drummer.

It felt strange to be an outsider now. Had I really moved up? I wasn't so sure.

Passengers were shuffling around us. Many of them looked completely lost, still trying to get their bearings. For most people, a cruise ship can be as difficult to navigate as a ten-acre corn maze. I was surprised to see that many of the paintings that filled the gallery looked, I don't know, not as nice as I'd expected, I guess. As we took our first stroll through the hallway/art gallery, I noticed several paintings by famous artists. There were drawings (scribblings, really) by Picasso that looked very similar to some of the doodles Gertie had drawn on restaurant napkins while we were waiting to catch our flight.

We passed a collection of Salvador Dalis, the artist famous for his surreal paintings of melting clocks and other subject matter that is perfect for Pink Floyd album covers. There were several high-priced Dali originals among them—nothing recognizable, but originals nonetheless. I spotted a wall of Kinkades—paintings of idyllic log cabins nestled among swirling curls of fog and beautiful snow-capped mountains. A large collection of Wylands were displayed down the hall. Most of the gallery was filled with artwork by artists that I'd never heard of—and from the looks of some of the paintings, perhaps for good reason.

I really liked some of the artwork, but keep in mind that this is coming from someone who would throw away at least ninety percent of the paintings worth more than a million dollars that I've seen on *Antique Roadshow* without giving them a second thought.

At the end of the hallway, right in the middle so that not a single passenger could miss it, was an oil painting at least eight feet tall and nearly five feet wide. After a month on board the ship, I still couldn't have told you what the painting was supposed to resemble. It looked like a beached whale. Later I'd find out it was priced at over one hundred thousand dollars. When I heard this, I nearly sprayed the cheap champagne I was drinking all over the art auctioneer's face.

It never sold. Big surprise.

However, next to that travesty on canvas, was something that caught my eye: a rather large painting of water lilies. We walked closer, and the wide, swathing, unmistakable strokes of a pallet knife took shape. I looked down at the corner of the painting and then pointed at the name for Gertie to see—Renoir.

I heard a voice from behind me. "It's not the famous one. This is his great-grandson or something. We still sell them all the time, though. They *are* quite nice."

I turned around to see Alex Ashebury writing something down on a clipboard. He had changed into a dark blue sport coat with gold buttons and matching slacks, and a gray silk tie wrapped in a way so the knot protruded, silver cuff-links, and high-polish brown shoes. He was what women would consider a great-looking guy. During conversations with a hiring manager at Seven Seas Art Adventures, we were given a bit of background on Alex, something like:

1) He had reached legendary salesman status after selling over a million dollars' worth of art in one seven-day cruise. His commission was, oh, a mere ninety thousand dollars. Not bad for a week's pay, and we were told that selling over a million dollars' worth of art isn't as hard as you might think. Sometimes art auctioneers luck out and find themselves on a ship with a crew of Arab art collectors from Abu Dhabi, or a boatload of Chinese real estate moguls, or a herd of high-rolling oil babies from Texas. Plus, we had enough artwork

priced over one hundred grand to fill an entire catalog. That's only ten strikes of the gavel at one auction.

2) He was somewhat difficult to work with. But hey, who isn't sometimes?

3) He had an obsession with reorganizing the art gallery, and had a strange habit of, without any clear reasoning or warning, changing his approach to selling art. We were told that in order to survive a contract with Alex, we would have to learn to "Go with the flow."

Overall, we chose to look on the bright side. We were getting a cut of the commissions, so we were thrilled to be on board with a top seller. We all just needed to get along, and to sell as much art as possible. Simple.

In theory.

Alex looked us both over and then quite coldly said, "Did you two remember that it was formal night?"

I looked at my jacket. "Well, you said that—"

Alex walked toward a sprawling desk that was nestled into a little carpeted alcove where the art team schmoozed and conducted business, which mostly meant pouring champagne and trying to convince people they couldn't live without another painting of a cruise ship. Alex sat down behind the desk, folded his hands into a power-steeple, and then motioned for us to have a seat across from him on the couch.

I sank into the couch, and as if on cue, a Latin band on the floor above us started playing "Conciencia." Alex rolled his eyes.

"Who's the band?" I asked.

"I don't know. Same old stuff. These cruise ships can't find any good musicians."

Alex seemed as if he was in need of a vacation, badly.

This band didn't sound like the same old stuff to me. This wasn't Barnacle Bob and the Riff Raff Flim Flams with special guests Flotsam and Jetsam, like you find on many cruise ships.

The band had the perfect name for a group such as themselves who played a mix of salsa and Motown tunes—The Nacho Supremes.

"I think they sound *great,*" I said.

"You would. This is your first night. Wait until two weeks from now, when you're on the verge of making a sale, and you have to nearly scream to the customer just so you can be heard over *"Vámanos P'al Monte"* for the hundredth time. Then, come back and tell me how you feel about your friends in the band." I could feel his blood pressure rising from across the desk. I knew how he felt. I understood how the monotony of ship life can take its toll on a person.

Alex put his hand on his forehead and said, "I need a drink. Yes. Let's start this right. Let's toast. Hey, there's a bar at the end of the hallway, right on the other side of this wall. Here's my charge card. Go get us three appletinis. Doubles. Please. ¡Vámanos!"

I got up and danced my way to the bar. Maybe if I positioned the desk just right, I'd be able to see the drummer from my chair while I was doing our paperwork. I found the bar. It was in a large room with a stage against the back wall. An olive-skinned, heavyset bartender with thin, balding hair was polishing wine glasses. His nametag: BARIS CAKMAK, BARTENDER, TURKEY. I was the only person in the room, and judging by the look on the bartender' face, I figured the bar had been that empty the entire night. On a cruise ship, the best bar to work in is the crew bar. Everybody tips, and it's always busy. This guy had pulled the short straw and ended up in one of the many bars on the ship that passengers seldom visit.

I ordered three appletinis, one of them a double for Alex.

"How's ship life?" I asked.

"Look at this," he said as he grabbed a clutch of martini glasses. "It's like this all the time. Worst bar on ship. They put *best* bartender in worst bar on ship. Go figure. *Eck.*"

"How long have you been on ships?" I asked.

"This is my tenth year. And this is my *last* contract. I've been here six months, and I'm ready to go home. I sign off in Hamburg, thank God." His gaze drifted off, as if he were lost in a dream. "Hamburg," he repeated, longing for the shore of Germany. Then he came back to me. "After this, I never want to see another cruise ship for the rest of my life."

Hamburg was where we would start dry dock. It was a big sign-off. More than half the crew was going home or being transferred to a different ship. I knew that this situation was going to make the ship a pretty unfriendly place. When a crew member is only a few weeks away from signing off, they aren't interested in making friends. They've already signed off in their minds. They're already home.

I gave Baris the charge card that had "Seven Seas Art Adventures" printed on the front. "What will you do on land?"

"I'm opening my own bar in Turkey. On the coast. In Kusadasi. I've been saving for ten years. And now I've finally found the place I want. I want to be back with my family. My wife. My two daughters."

Most crew members had big dreams. When I talked with my shipmates, I'd realize that they all had these unique motivations that pulled them through every stormy day of ship life. Many were out at sea to save money so they could break out on their own. Some just wanted to provide for their families or buy a better motor scooter, but everyone wanted something. And I learned that you could tell a great deal about a person just based on what it was that they were searching for. Their desires often revealed their values.

I signed for a big tip. After all, we were putting drinks on the company account.

"We're right around the corner," I said, "and by the looks of Alex, we'll be ordering drinks regularly."

"Great," Baris said flatly, and then gave me a wry smile. "Now I have *one* customer, and they're crew. At least you tip well. Thanks."

I hoped to become good friends with Baris. It might be nice to make friends with someone who was about to own a bar in Kusadasi. Friends all over the world—just another perk of being a cruise ship crew member. I gathered the appletinis and carried them toward the art desk.

"Welcome aboard," Baris said as I walked away.

I said thanks. Yeah, this was Baris's last contract. Yeah right.

CHAPTER SIX

THE POWER OF DOING NOTHING.

I walked back into the art gallery clutching the trio of appletinis. Alex was shuffling through a shelving system stuffed with binders and stacks of paper, pulling out bundles that were stapled together. Gertie stood next to him, collecting the paper that he tossed onto the desk.

She turned to me and smiled. "Boat drinks! Yay!"

Alex threw about ten more bundles onto the desk. "I think that's it. These are artist bios. About fifty of them. Homework for you tonight. You need to know everything about these artists. Develop a spiel on each one. Write down five points for each artist, things you think will sell their paintings, and memorize them." And then he added emphatically, "We're going to sell every piece of artwork in this gallery on *this* cruise. A toast."

Alex picked up his neon green appletini. He lifted his glass high, and we followed his lead. Our glasses clinked together. "To making it freakin' rain on this boat."

It felt extremely odd to be drinking martinis in a passenger area while on the job. When I was a musician, if I would have been seen drinking martinis at one of my gigs in the passenger area, I probably would have been fired on the spot. No questions asked. No plane ticket home, just a not-so-gentle nudge off the gangplank. I told Alex how strange it felt.

Alex formed his hands into a power steeple again, and then turned serious. "Look, you two need to get that stuff out of your head…immediately. You are vendors now. You're not employees. You are officers. You are not crew members anymore. You are art auctioneers. You aren't musicians and social hosts any longer. You need to lose that low-ranking mentality right now. You need to throw it overboard and watch it sink. You can't let these managers and officers and the others out here push you around. They'll try, but you have to push back. You're here to sell art. You're here to make the cruise line money. You're an officer, and you have privileges. Most of these officers and managers out here are only going to give you the privileges you demand, the privileges you fight for. Don't be a pushover. You have to tell *them* what privileges you have, because if you ask them, they will treat you like a subordinate, like a crew member. They will tell you that you don't have any privileges, and then they will tell you to find a mop and start swabbing the decks. Do you understand what I'm saying? We're not freakin' deck swabbers."

Alex inhaled more of his appletini. "Especially these M&R managers. I hate even saying their name out loud."

"Who are the M&R managers?" Gertie asked.

"Marketing and revenue. They oversee all of the shops and vendors. They are your worst nightmare, and they are the ones who are going to try to make the rules for you to follow, but listen to me. Hear me loud and clear. You have to know your rights, and you have to draw a line in the sand. They are not your superiors. They are your partners, and you have to treat them as they are supposed to be treated, as an equal, or they will walk all over you and suck every single bit of fun right out of this job and right out of your ship life. We are allowed to drink appletinis. We are art auctioneers. We are not in the housekeeping department."

Alex took a slow deep breath. His shoulders sank. Then he leaned in toward us, and lowered his voice. "First lesson. Take a look at the guy who just walked into the gallery." Alex pointed quickly behind us. Gertie and I turned around. There was a man looking at the Renoir. He had on the typical golf attire: multicolored plaid shorts, red polo. I could smell the putting green from across the gallery.

We turned back around and looked at Alex. He was sitting up straight now, with his hands behind his head, and a smug grin.

"Okay? Well, what do you think?"

"About what?" Gertie asked.

"About him," Alex said.

"What about him?" Gertie asked.

"You are an art salesman. Your most powerful asset is the ability to accurately assess everyone that walks into this gallery."

"Okay," I said. "He's a middle-aged golfer who might want to buy that Renoir."

"Wrong. Gertie?"

"We should go and talk to him," Gertie said.

"Wrong. Wrong-wrong-wrong. What is it we're looking for, out here on the high seas? Money," Alex said. "We're looking for money. And you two need to find out where it's hiding on this ship. Do you think we should go and talk to Jack Nicklaus over there?"

"Yes," we both said, nodding.

"Wrong. Let me tell you a little secret. The first things you look at when someone walks into this gallery are their shoes."

Gertie and I turned around and looked at the guy at the

Renoir. He was wearing leather sandals and ankle-high socks.

Alex continued, "He's wearing Birkenstocks. Freakin' Birkenstocks. The next thing you look at is how expensive their watch is."

We turned around again. It was a big, square, plastic calculator watch.

"And if he passes those two sections of your test, then you look at the passenger's clothes. This guy doesn't even match. He's wearing plaid shorts with purple and yellow stripes, a red polo that's stretched out at the bottom and slightly faded around the collar. This guy thinks that the men's department at Walmart is an upscale clothing store. People with money always dress well on the first day of the cruise. They want to give the other people on board a good first impression. And they always match. Rich people always freakin' match."

"We could still talk to him," I said. "Who knows, maybe he'll buy a print or something. You can't tell everything from the way a person dresses."

Alex looked at me as if I had just told him that his contract was going to be extended for another three months, and that he would have to start helping out with the passenger boat drills in his spare time.

"No," Alex said. "Look, I know this is going to sound counterintuitive, but you only have so much time to talk with passengers. You only have so much time to sell art. There are over two thousand people on this ship. Most of them will never buy a single thing in our gallery. It's your job to decide who is worth your time. We could go talk to Mr. Socks-and-Sandals, sure. But while we're occupied with the Goodwill polo on the yellow-brick road to selling a twenty-dollar

Kinkade print, Bill Gates could be standing next to one of those original Wylands in the grip of an impulse-buy fever, thinking about how perfect that coral reef would look hanging on the wall in his penthouse at the Hilton Waikiki." Alex took a deep breath, and then finished off the remaining puddle of appletini, shaking the glass to get the last drops off the edge.

Alex continued, "My point is that you have to be wise about what passengers you spend time with. *This*…this is the difference between a thirty thousand–dollar cruise and a million-dollar cruise. I know, because I've sold a million dollars' worth of art on a single cruise." He paused to allow us to give him an approving reaction, which we did, and then he took a quick breath with his nose, and continued, "But here's the real heart of the matter. Let's say a woman walks into the gallery. Impeccably dressed. Gucci purse. More diamonds than a South African mine. Jimmy Choo heels. Do you talk to her?"

"Does she match?" I asked.

"Match-dot-com," Alex says.

"Then yes. I go and talk to her."

"You would think so. But you're wrong. Ha!" Alex pointed his finger in the air. "This is where it gets weird. You ignore her. You don't even look at her."

"Why?" Gertie asked.

"Exactly," Alex said. Then he leaned back in his chair and put his hands behind his head. "Because she is thinking: *why hasn't he noticed me?* And that's what you always need to be thinking. Why? Why is she dressing like that? Why is she in the gallery? Why does she collect art? And then *boom*! You realize what it is. And in that answer is the key to the golden city of sales. The answer is that she wants to impress people.

She wants to impress you. And *you* have to be unimpressed. You are a high-caliber art dealer. You see people write million-dollar checks every day. You cannot be impressed and dazzled by a pair of Louis Vuittons. If you act impressed, then passengers will see that you are putting them above you, but they need to be your equals. You have to act as if you are on their level. If you don't, they won't trust you. And trust is at the heart of every sale you make. So this is what you do. You sit here at the desk and look busy. Shuffle papers. Play solitaire. My favorite—drink appletinis and get some of my paperwork done. But whatever you do, don't talk to them. Make them come to you. Make them tell you what they want. And when they ask you questions, be slightly rude. Be short with them. Make them want to get your attention. Make them want to impress you. Make them feel that you don't believe they have the money to buy this fine art in the gallery. And show them that the only thing that will impress you is if they buy something very, very, *very* expensive."

Alex may have had a chunk of driftwood where his heart was supposed to be, but there was no denying it—the guy was probably an art-sales genius.

"I've been in this business for more than ten years," he said. "And I'm just starting to realize that this game is ninety percent psychological. The other ten percent—*luck*."

"So, we just sit here and do nothing?" Gertie asked.

"Sometimes there's great power in doing nothing. And in this case, doing nothing is better than doing something. The people who were never going to buy anything—they are going to leave. If someone wants to spend hundreds of thousands of dollars on a piece of art, they know it, and they will ask you about the paintings in the gallery. You see, doing nothing *is* doing something in this case."

"Got it," I said. To be honest it sounded like a bunch of mumbo-jumbo psychobabble to me, but I was curious. Could this really sell art? It sounded so brass-balled crazy that I thought it might actually work.

"But we still need to be prepared. I need you to know your stuff, do your homework, and be ready when Bill Gates comes in and asks you questions about that Picasso over there. We still need to do marketing, send out letters, run the auctions."

Alex turned to his left and looked at a pair of paintings in the gallery: pastel beach scenes with kids playing in the sand. Below the paintings was a small side table, and sitting right in the center of a table was an upside-down ice cream cone that a passenger had dropped right on the glass top. Streams of chocolate and vanilla ice cream flowed from the cone like thin milky rivers. A steady milk waterfall dripped over the side of the table and into a quickly expanding pond of dairy on the floor. Alex's face went red. He looked more frustrated than a passenger who just watched their passport get sucked into a cruise ship toilet—the only toilets on the planet that are apparently powered by jet engines on reverse.

Alex stood up, shaking his head. "Passengers."

I thought he was going to walk to the bathroom and grab some paper towels. Instead he grabbed the ship phone that was attached to the wall behind his desk and pushed four numbers. "Rashek…Yes, I need you to come down here. Someone left another ice cream cone in the gallery…and I want to change the art around…and adjust some lights…Hurry, please. *Click*."

Alex sat back down and watched the ice cream drip onto

the floor.

"I can clean that—" Gertie said.

"No," Alex said. "The art steward is on his way. It's his job. You need to meet him anyway. He's responsible for getting the gallery and auctions set up. He moves the art, and if you need to get something out of the art locker, he'll get it for you. Great guy, but you have to stay on top of your art steward if you want them to work."

Alex continued, "Now, let's get down to business. We have an auction tomorrow. Your first. I want one of you to try to sell something from the podium. Also, the M&R manager wants to meet you tomorrow. We'll make a trip to his office, and I'll try my best to keep from murdering him while we're there. I don't like to utter his name in the gallery, for fear that he may appear, but I'll make an exception just this once. His name is Angel. That should be, um, fun."

Someone walked through the gallery and caught my attention. He was tall and lanky, prematurely balding, and had the skin tone of someone who spends most of the daylight hours playing video games down in the Mariana Trench. He was wearing all black and was holding a black folder embossed with gold lettering—a folder I instantly recognized. When he got close enough, I could read his nametag: PETER VERSNINSKI, MUSICIAN, USA.

"That's Peter," Alex said. "Everybody calls him Squid."

"Hey, are you performing tonight?" I asked.

"Seven and Nine," Squid said.

I had to see this. I had only seen the showband from the audience once.

As soon as Squid was gone, a young Indian man, maybe in his thirties, walked into the gallery. He had on khakis and a blue Festivus Cruise Lines polo-style shirt. His hair was neatly combed over to one side, and he had a mustache like Richard Pryor, so thick it made me want to try to rip it off just to check if it was real. He was smiling, but it was this half-grin, and the half that was grinning looked forced.

"You must be the new art associates," he said in a thick Indian accent, his head bobbing back and forth as if it were attached to a spring. (I love this about Indian people. They're like happy, kind-hearted, mustachioed bobble heads, and I don't mean this in a demeaning, American-snobbery sort of way. They are also among the most important people to befriend on a cruise ship, because most of the cooks on a ship are Indian, and that means they have access to all of the good [edible] food on board. If you don't want to eat the food in the crew mess—and I assure you that you do not—then you need to make friends with the Indians. That thing about *Vijay Patel's Secret and Magical Cruise Ship Trading Post* applies to crew members as much as passengers on some ships.)

"Yes, we are," Gertie said. We both stood up and introduced ourselves.

His nametag: *RASHEK BADAMI, ART STEWARD, INDIA*. Rashek said something, but I didn't hear a single word. I was lost in a daydream about all of the south Asian delicacies that could be ours if only Rashek would be nice enough to let us into his secret world and allow us access to the Indian black market of cruise ship eateries. I was dreaming of barbecued curry shrimp kebabs, spicy fried zucchini, butter-dipped lobster claws, milky-sweet chai tea, steaming nan bread, and much more.

Gertie offered to help clean up the ice cream cone again, but Alex waved us off. "Rashek is going to give you a tour of the gallery. And if you like, later tonight he can show you around the ship. I would do it myself, but I have a table-tennis tournament in the crew bar to go to. Can I help you with anything else? You two all settled into your cabin?"

That reminded me, and so I hesitantly spoke up, "Actually, there is one thing we could use some help with." Alex began shuffling papers and unplugging his computer, but I went ahead anyway. "They've put us in a room with a single bed."

"For the both of you? Is it one of those extra-large bottom bunks?"

"No, it's a small single bed. We won't fit on it unless we both sleep on our sides. We love the room. Love the porthole. But do you think we could get moved into a room with a bed that's big enough for the both of us?"

"I would say that I *can't* believe this, but I do," Alex said. "Same old cruise ship bullshit. You have to fight this. It's the only way you'll get what you deserve. I told them there were two new crew members coming on board." Alex went on for a few more minutes about the importance of fighting for your privileges, and when he finally finished and left, we both felt like there was a chance that something might be done to resolve our bed problem.

Rashek showed us around the gallery. He could name the title of every single painting, the price of all the artwork, and he had the artists' bios memorized. As he showed us around the gallery, he was very passionate about his job *and* about the art. He took us to the back of the room, to what looked like the back wall. Then he reached into his pocket and pulled out a key ring that had as many keys as a prison warden's. He gave us a mischievous grin and raised his eyebrows a couple of times. "What do you see behind me?"

I looked at the wall. It was made from that faux wood paneling that you found on almost every cruise ship at that time. I looked at Gertie.

She shrugged. "A wall. I see a wall."

I nodded in agreement.

Rashek laughed and jingled his dungeon-master key ring. "I love this part. When I was just a child in Mumbai, I used to pretend there was a secret door in my house, and that it could take me somewhere magical. I think of this every time I open this door." Rashek's bobbling head was enough to nearly hypnotize me as I listened, like the gentle swaying of a snake charmer's flute that sends a venomous cobra into a spellbinding trance as it rises from a dusty, woven basket. His voice had this wonderful singsong quality. He would start his sentences at a very high pitch, and then descend in tone until he reached the end, then return again to that high pitch for his next statement.

I never realized how monotone Americans often are when they talk until I worked on a cruise ship and became friends with some of the Indians on the crew. They are masters of conversation, on how to use tone and pitch in speech to captivate the listener, and it all comes natural to them—it is a melodious voice, woven into their native tongue. A beautiful, flowing, musical sound.

Rashek turned to the wall and inserted one of his five hundred keys into a tiny keyhole. I heard a click, and then a panel in the wall opened. "Our secret door."

The door opened to a narrow room, shelving crammed with paintings.

Rashek turned to us. "Welcome…to the vault."

I was rather surprised at the quality of our vault. I remembered the first time that I saw an "art vault" on a cruise ship. It was not a vault. It was not the type of place to keep, oh I don't know, half-a-million dollars' worth of art. A vault has walls made of steel two-feet thick that require plastic explosives and a massive diamond-tipped drill to penetrate. A vault has one of those big hinged-doors with the wheel-thingy that you have to turn just right to hit the combination lock, a complex climate control system that regulates temperature and humidity, state-of-the-art cameras, and one of those cool alarm systems that uses lasers and mirrors to form a web of impenetrable triggers that require the flexibility of a female cruise ship dancer to get past. A vault has a team of security guards that wear flak jackets and AK-47s and escort you in and out of said vault.

The first vault I saw on a cruise ship was not a vault. It was a dusty room that was definitely too warm and humid for artwork. It was a room that was protected by walls made of fake wood paneling that could be penetrated by any four-year-old with a good grip and a spork. It was a room with a keyhole that could be picked by anyone with access to a box of paperclips and an IQ only slightly higher than a bucket of cruise-ship paint.

And that, my friends, was the perfect illustration of priorities on a cruise ship. The management on a cruise liner will choose to spend four thousand dollars on a cappuccino machine for the Italian officers on the bridge, and then build a rack system in an unused broom closet and tell the art vendors to enjoy their "vault". I can imagine the scene when an M&R manager first presented the new vault to the art auctioneer. The M&R manager is waving his hands back and forth like a magician, *See! It has a secret door. No one will ever know it's even here.*

No wonder paintings had been stolen in the past. But this vault seemed suitably secure. No four-year-old with a good grip and a spork could penetrate this vault. The kid would have to be at least six or seven.

"Are all the vaults like this?" I asked Rashek.

His head popped up from a stack of paintings. He smiled and said in his melodic, descending-pitch way, "Oh no. This is one of the nicest ones in the fleet. They are usually much worse. Much smaller. And usually they are in the crew area, in which case we have to haul paintings across the entire ship and up elevators every time we have to change the gallery around."

Rashek was very knowledgeable about the artwork and how the art job worked, and I began to wonder why we were being trained by a lower-ranking guy who knew so much more than us about the artwork and the art assistant job? Why wouldn't they just hire Rashek to be the art assistant? Why wouldn't they give *him* the chance to be an art auctioneer?

"How long have you been working as an art mover?" I asked.

"This will be my sixth year."

"And each contract is nine months?" I asked.

"Yes. But I'm going to be an art assistant. If I do well this contract, they said they will make me an art assistant on my next ship."

"That's wonderful," Gertie said. "Congratulations."

"I am very excited about it," Rashek said. "This would be a very big raise. And no more changing the gallery around. More money. Less work. I like it." Rashek moved his eyebrows up and down again.

"How often do you have to change the gallery?" I asked.

"Every auctioneer is different. Alex…" Rashek's shoulders sank, and he took a deep breath. "Alex, he sometimes changes the gallery three times in one day. I don't understand it. It's so much work, and I don't think it helps sell any more art than if we were to keep the same paintings up for the entire day. People will see something in the morning and then come back to see it again, but then it's in the vault, and I have to go and get it for them. It's too much work for one person, especially when it's an auction day. But anyway, have you seen the rest of the ship yet?"

"No, we plan on exploring it tonight," Gertie said.

"How about I show you around? Are you going to the crew party later? The theme is 'Dress like a superhero'. I'm going as Rama Chandra."

"We're going," Gertie said before I could say no.

On every contract I've ever worked, there was always someone who took me under their wing and showed me the ropes of the ship, helped me get wired in to the particular brand of ship life found on that particular ship. I had passed the favor along to other *greenhorns* in the past. It was clear that, for this contract, Rashek would be our guide.

What I really wanted to know was which Indian chef I had to bribe and how much I had to pay for a tray of curried lobster tail coupled with a syrup-drizzled platter of *gulab jamun* for dessert. I decided to ask Rashek when I thought the time was right.

I turned around to see Alex poking his head into the vault. "Hey, Rashek. I'm glad I caught you. I want to change the gallery around. Let's move the Wylands and all the

Kinkades back into the vault and put all the pop art along the front wall. Nothing but pop art for the afternoon. I think this is a pop art kind of crowd." Then Alex was gone again.

I turned around and saw Rashek's enthusiasm drain away.

"Okay," Rashek said. "Let's meet up in a few hours. I'll show you around."

We agreed, and I was more certain than ever that we were going to make a million bucks. But it wasn't going to take a million bucks to make *us* happy out here on this sea voyage of a lifetime. I knew we'd be happy if we only made a *half million* or so.

CHAPTER SEVEN

A SHIP-MILK MUSTACHE AND THE SPECTACULAR ROBOT BAND.

I walked into our cabin and was instantly mesmerized again by that odd thing called sunlight shining into our crew quarters. We spent a few hours staring out the porthole as the sea glided past, and then got to looking over some of the artists' bios, picking out points about each artist to memorize.

We heard a knock on the door. I opened it to find Rashek standing in the hallway.

"Ready to tour the ship?" he asked, his head bouncing from side to side.

Rashek led the way on our adventure through the delightful maze of tan tunnels, the bright and blinking fluorescent lighting, and the delightful garbage smells of the crew area. Our first stop was the crew mess, a place that makes Chinese street vendors look like potential James Beard Award winners. Nothing had changed in the two years since I had last stepped aboard a cruise ship. We walked down the buffet line, past the barbecued lizard tonsils and the Jamaican jerk chicken that had bones only found in the spines of Saint-somewhere iguanas. I felt as if I had been transported to the set of one of those cooking shows where contestants make edible dishes from bizarre combinations of ingredients like salted caramel, a bag of Funyuns, and two Mylar balloons that had washed up on the California coast (and the sand and seaweed must be incorporated into the hot-fudge-and-lutfisk soufflé for dessert).

Then I made my way down the well-worn path in the crew mess floor to the most popular entrée choice on the crew mess menu—my old pal, the big tray of white rice. My old, reliable friend—Rice Mountain.

There was a line for the rice, with crew member after crew member grabbing the big metal spoon and building small rice mountains on their plates. The crew members gathered around the tables that filled the long, narrow mess hall and talked in their many different languages. Empty boxes of cereal were scattered on tabletops littered with rice. There were bushels of bent forks (not a straight one among them), and stacks of multicolored plastic cups more suitable for the cafeteria at a children's daycare. In the air was that unique smell of curried narwhal mixed with the scent of body odor, steaming coffee made from concentrated syrup as bitter as a Jerusalem Artichoke, and that indescribable pheromone that can only be produced as a result of years of pent-up sexual frustration, absolute exhaustion, and the unwavering subordination you experience during a life at sea. I was back in the arms of the angel that guarded the cruise ship food and doled out the leftovers to crew members, but it was an angel that would never leave me hungry—and an angel that never charged me a dime—and so I was happy to be back. Besides, I hadn't put a single flake of corn cereal or white rice in my mouth since I left the ship, and so I was prepared to explore those shores once again, no matter how barren of vitamins and taste they were.

Then, through the chaos of the crew mess, I spotted something in the back of the room. It was as if a light from heaven shone down through the low-hanging ceiling of the mess hall. There, in a single beam of glory, a lone silver-clad machine was illuminated—the ship-milk machine. My jaw dropped, and I felt a little pile of drool collect in the corner of my mouth. I had not suckled the nipple of the ship-milk cow in two years, and I was overcome with a desire unlike anything since I first saw Jessica Rabbit say the line, "I'm not bad. I'm just drawn that way," back when I was eight-years old.

At that moment there was no Gertie; there was no Rashek; there were no crew members in that room. It was just me and the ship-milk machine. And nothing was going to stand in my way. I grabbed one of the slightly translucent, blue-colored ship cups that were covered with gashes and scrapes and were rumored to be indestructible. Then I walked to the back of the room and filled my cup to the absolute brim with the glorious ship-milk. I tilted the cup back, and thus entered ship-milk heaven. Mootopia.

I finished the cup and filled it up again. *This is going to be great.* The ship-milk machine was just twenty steps from my cabin, and in my cabin I had a fridge where I could hoard ship-milk and boxes of corn cereal like everybody else.

Since working on ships, I've done some research and found that this same adoration for milk is also found on aircraft carriers, fishing boats, cargo ships, and anywhere else you find large groups of people battling the high seas. My theory is that since crew members spend so much time inside the ship and don't get enough sunlight, they develop a vitamin D deficiency, and so they crave milk. It's just an idea, and I really don't know. I just know that everyone loves the ship milk, and it always runs out, so crew members have to get it when they can.

"Can we go, now that you've had your ship-milk?" Gertie said, shaking her head. She knew exactly how I felt about ship-milk, but she didn't exactly share my love of the stuff.

"Onward," I said, and wiped my mouth.

Rashek led us back into the dimly lit maze, and we climbed up a few flights of stairs. Everyone that we passed in the hallway was saying hello to him. Then again, this is just the way it is on cruise ships. Everyone is constantly greeting each other. It is part of the cruise ship culture, and a constant message in our training: smile and say hello to everyone you meet. A crew member never realizes how much smiling and greeting they have become conditioned to until they find themselves back on land after their contract has ended. They are in a shopping mall somewhere in small-town America, and they find themselves saying hello to everyone that walks by, as if they're the star politician at a political rally. Crew members only stop saying hello to everyone they see when they get punched in the face after trying to shake a stranger's hand at a gas station. It takes a bit of time, or a good strong punch in the face, for crew members to readjust to life on land sometimes.

Rashek took us to a door that read: *PASSENGER AREA*. He opened it, and we walked back into the sunlight—back into the world of crystal chandeliers, fresh food, teak wood floors, and color, back into the land of Oz.

We were standing in the stairwell right outside the art gallery, which had been changed into the pop-art extravaganza that Alex had ordered. We walked through the gallery and into the theater. The cast was in the middle of a practice run for a production show called *New Orleans Musical Beignet*. The title of the show didn't make any sense to me, but hey, this is a cruise ship we're talking about. Not much makes sense in cruise-liner land.

The theater was dark and cold. The curtain was drawn. It appeared as if we had arrived right before the rehearsal began. We took a seat in the back where we wouldn't disrupt the cast.

Suddenly, the curtain opened and blue lights flashed on stage. The backdrop and set resembled a Bourbon Street bar. The showband was set up over in the corner of the fake tavern. The band played a slow blues number, "Stormy Sunday" or "Light Blue Suede Shoes" or something—just another classic song the cruise line had paid a songwriter to rework so they wouldn't have to pay any royalties to the original songwriters. The whole band was dressed up in red-and-white striped vests and those flat-topped straw hats with red, white, and blue hat-bands that you see players in Dixieland bands wearing.

The trumpet player was moving his horn around, but he wasn't moving his fingers. The clarinet player was doing the same thing. Even the drummer was moving his sticks up and down without touching the drumheads. The musicians looked as mechanical as the Country Bear Jamboree band at Disneyworld or Munch's Make-Believe Band at Chuck E. Cheese. I bounced up and down, trying to contain my laughter.

Gertie shot me a look to get me to stop, but then my laughter made her start laughing too. "What is it?" she asked.

"Look at the band," I said.

"What? I don't see anything."

Rashek was leaning over too, trying to hear why I was laughing.

"They're not playing," I said. "The band isn't actually playing. It's all fake. They finally did it. It's all *fake*."

You see, what most people don't realize is that for a while now, the showbands for the production shows were "enhanced" with backing tracks. That is to say that the sound guys would play prerecorded tracks along with the band. This has enabled the cruise ship companies to slowly reduce the size of the bands and, probably, gauge how much the band member reduction affected the audience members' enjoyment of the show. Once in a while, there were sections of the production shows that I performed in where the band was just faking it, where all the music that was coming through the speakers was prerecorded and the showband just had to act as if they were playing. This was usually limited to short sections of the shows where the band had to perform some sort of dance routine on stage.

Even back then, everyone in the showband had feared that the day might come where the band did nothing but act as if they were playing their instruments. I know there are some cruise lines that still value live music and have their musicians playing completely live in the production shows. This particular company, which we call Festivus, did have quite a bit of live music in many of their production shows, but this particular section was completely faked. They looked like a showband of robots, and they didn't appear to be having much fun, which is understandable. The last thing a musician wants to do is spend forty thousand dollars on a music education at Berkley, and then go work on a cruise ship and be the animatronic backup band for Liver Lips McGrowl and his Country Bear Jamboree. This was just one more step closer to the showband being replaced by robots.

The band finished their introductory number, and then the singers and dancers walked on stage. We could feel the ship gently rocking back and forth. The band "played" a fast swing number, and the dancers jumped into an energetic jazz dance routine. The male dancers were spinning the girls around, sliding them between their legs, throwing them in the air, and I was taken back to a time when I was in the band.

When you live and work on a ship, the crew becomes your family. For a musician, that family includes the other members of the band, and your extended family is everyone else in the cast. So when I went to see the band play again, it was as if I was watching my old family from a distance, and it was a family that I was no longer a part of. All I wanted to do was jump back on those drums, go back in time. But I was an art auctioneer now. *How in the world did I become an art auctioneer?*

Gertie leaned over and snapped me out of my daydream. "Hey, let's go to the crew bar."

CHAPTER EIGHT

THE SQUID HAS A FOX, AND THE RETURN OF THE SHIP GOGGLES.

Rashek was like a mole. He had lived in this network of undersea tunnels for so long, he intuitively knew the quickest route to anywhere in his dusty, dimly lit burrow. The crew bar was in the back of the cruise ship neighborhood, all the way at the aft of the ship. To someone who has never worked on a cruise ship, walking from one end of the ship to the other sounds as if it would be a pretty easy task. *Au contraire, mon frère*. Oh, how I wish it were so. This is the perspective of the blissfully unaware passenger who has the luxury of simply moseying down the promenade and drifting joyfully from the pizza parlor at the front of the ship to the ice cream machine and burger grill at the back. Not so easy for a crew member.

When crew members are not working, we are not allowed to just wander around in the passenger area. Now, as officers, snooty as it may sound, Gertie and I had the privilege of walking through the passenger area. However, Rashek was not an officer, and so we had to go back to the burrow and navigate through the tunnels of the crew area. This would have been pretty simple if the navigational path of the crew area didn't constantly shift depending on the day and time. This is all thanks to 1) turnaround day and 2) the cruise ship crew member's mortal enemy—the watertight door.

Turnaround day is the day when the cruise ship returns to its home port to pick up a new herd of passengers. Their luggage is often filled with clean tropical shirts, tubs of sunscreen, and mouth wash bottles that have been emptied, cleaned, and then refilled with tasty rum in an attempt to escape the clutches of the dreaded ten-dollar rum punch that is found lurking aboard every cruise ship sailing the seven seas.

On turnaround day, it's out with the old (the stunned passengers who just got a glance at their bill before being shuffled off the ship) and in with the new (the smiling innocents who are delighted to find Filipino waiters passing out rum punch on the lido deck in exchange for a little charge to their passenger stateroom that is only about as costly as a mortgage payment in San Francisco). And on a ship that has more than two thousand passengers, at least four-thousand pieces of luggage must be moved from every stateroom to the port terminal, and vice versa. That's a barge-load of luggage transportation. The cruise ship companies don't want passengers to see this chaotic event. So, each piece of luggage is maneuvered through the crew area in big metal cages attached to forklifts. On turnaround day, all the main thoroughfares for foot traffic on the ship are pretty much off limits to crew members, and as a result, crew members must navigate through a tangled maze of crew-cabin corridors and back-alley stairwells to get anywhere on the ship.

But turnaround day is a predictable event, one that can be expected and therefore anticipated and planned around. However, watertight doors (metal doors that are found below the waterline of a cruise ship that can be closed in the event of a hull puncture to prevent the ship from sinking) are closed and tested at entirely random times, for the most part. This makes them quite maddening. Imagine living in a corn maze.

On one end of the corn maze is the door to your house, and at the other end is the door to your office. Each day you have to navigate through the maze to get to work. It's somewhat inconvenient, but eventually you memorize your way through your maze of maize.

Here's the fun part: now imagine that there's a little masochistic man who lives in a little glass box way up above your corn maze. Let's say he's a little Italian man who wears a white uniform with three yellow stripes on his shoulder boards. In his little glass box, he has these buttons he can push that cause big metal doors to close at random places in your corn maze, which drives you banana cakes every morning when you try to find your way to the office.

Today was our first day on this new ship, and it was a turnaround day. As if it couldn't get any worse for two people trying to learn their way around the ship, watertight doors had been randomly closed at nearly every turn. Luckily, we had Rashek as our guide, and Rashek wasn't just a wonderful ship mole with a compass implanted in his brilliant brain. He was an angel who kept us from spending our entire first day lost in the labyrinth of the crew area. So when the three of us finally made it to the crew bar, feeling like a team of lab rats, I figured the least I could do was buy Rashek a drink.

The crew bar was a large room, pool table to one side, table-tennis setup on the other, and a cluster of tables and chairs that were mostly empty except for a few Indian men who were gathered around a video game console and a big screen TV, playing Grand Theft Auto.

The man behind the bar had a big smile. His nametag: *GOODLUCK BAILEY, BARTENDER, JAMAICA.* I stepped up to the bar and ordered three rum and Tings.

Goodluck laughed. "What you know 'bout rum and Ting, mon?"

"We've spent some time in the islands," Gertie said.

Goodluck smiled and poured the rum. "Oh, we got a pretty island girl on de ship."

And so the competition began. Gertie and I could have been in the corner of the crew bar making out, and she could have had a large tattoo on her arm that read *I LOVE THE GUY I'M KISSING,* with a picture of my face below it, and some Italian officer would walk up to her, tap her on the shoulder, and say, "Ah-Bella donna, let-ah me buy-ah you ah-drink-ah." My experience dealing with other foreign men on cruise ships is like the United States' experience with their border with Mexico—once you let your guard down, you have an immigration problem, and once they find a nice hole they can slip through, they go and tell all their friends about it.

You may think I'm being harsh, but there's an easy test you can do to find out if the guy your girlfriend is talking to on the cruise ship is a jerk.

Step 1: Ask yourself the simple question, "Am I on a cruise ship?"

Step 2: If the answer is yes, then he is most likely a jerk.

I'm fascinated by statistics, and through extensive record keeping and complex calculations, I have determined that there is a positive correlation between cruise ships and jerks. Data proves that the rate at which you come into contact with a jerk increases exponentially the closer you get to a cruise ship.

I wasn't worried about Gertie. Perhaps I should have been. At the time I trusted her. I thought we were in this together. *Yeah, a real team.* But I definitely didn't trust

Goodluck or the penguins up on the bridge who had more magical charms than a Native American shaman.

We took our drinks and clinked our glasses together. I took a sip of the rum and Ting drink and felt my toes sink just a bit deeper into the imaginary Caribbean sand. My mind turned its attention to Saint Martin. We would be there in just a few days. The ship's engine was humming through the room and gently rattling the wine glasses and bottles of liquor behind the bar. The hull was singing its nautical song as we sailed through the ocean. Our anchor was up, and our bearings were dialed in on an island where the women were topless, the air was warm, the water was blue, the sunsets were bold, and the rum and Tings were cold. I didn't think life could get any better.

"That'll be tree" Goodluck said. "Tree (*three*) dollars, mon."

And just like that, my life got better. I'd been looking forward to this day again for a long time. The crew bar will spoil a person. There is no better example of sticker shock than when a crew member gets a bar tab from a bar on land after he has been out at sea for six months. *One hundred and what? Are you freakin' kidding me?*

It was nice to be back in the land of cheap booze. A cruise ship crew bar is the ocean's Dollar Store for drinkers. Beers, one dollar. Mixed drinks, one dollar. Top shelf or doubles, one fifty.

At least, those were the prices at this crew bar.

Gertie gave Goodluck a ten-dollar bill. We had decided before we got on the ship that we were going to be the queen and king of tipping. We had learned a long time ago that the only way to get a drink in the crew bar when it's packed is to be the people that always tipped well. It's part of what you do to get the ship wired.

For now, I viewed ship life again through a pair of rum and Ting–colored glasses, and suddenly I had my doubts about my former opinions of ship life. I looked across the room and took a deep breath and then noticed something.

I turned to Goodluck. "Hey, there's no smoke in here. Where are all the smokers?"

"De smoking section outside, mon. Out de door." Goodluck pointed to the back of the room.

We walked outside, immediately blinded by bright light. We were looking at the back of the ship. There was another bar in the middle of the room. Tables and chairs filled most of the remaining space. At the back of the room, running the entire length of the deck, there was an opening where we could see the ship's wake cutting through the ocean toward the horizon, as if we were viewing the sea in widescreen. Barstools were lined up against the ship's stern. We could sit and have a drink, gaze out over the sea, and watch the world slip away in the frothy wake.

I knew where I was going to be sitting whenever I had the chance, especially when the sea was calm and the moon was full and the stars were shining in the night sky above.

I looked around the room. There were a few tables to the right where a group of Italian officers were gathered, drinking Stella Artois and generating a column of smoke that was thick enough to send smoke signals back to the Port of Miami. Groups of Filipinos and Indians were smoking and drinking while they waited for karaoke and the table tennis tournament to begin at the crew party. We took a seat at the back of the room and enjoyed the sea view.

An ocean breeze was blowing into the crew bar through the opening in front of us. We could smell the wonderful, salty air. The room hummed with the sound of the propellers, and pulsed with the vibration of the engine. I loved cruise ships once again—the movement, the action, the sound of the ship and the sea, the view of the ocean stretching to the horizon.

And then I looked at Gertie. She looked happier than I had seen her in months. The breeze was warm, and the sun was shining on her face. She smiled, and I felt we had made the right decision.

The sea had brought us together. We had met on a cruise ship, in the crew bar, nearly three years earlier. The ship we were on when we met was sailing from Sydney. We had cruised around Australia, then crossed the Tasman Sea and sailed around New Zealand, exploring the gorgeous fjords and visiting postcard towns like Christchurch before the earthquake hit in 2010. From there we sailed into Asia, visiting China, Japan, South Korea and other ports of call.

Back at the Festivus crew bar, Squid walked in with a few other members of the cast and some of the other musicians in Liver Lip Mcgrowl's robot showband. Behind the animatronic band members was a flock of female dancers, one of the prettiest bird species found in the cruise ship wilderness. The dancers were wearing the unofficial uniform of cruise ship *twirlies*—hair pulled back in a bun, black tights, ballet flats for shoes, loose shirts, and a cheerful radiance of bubbly enthusiasm only equal to a golden retriever that has developed an addiction to double-shot espressos. I thought of Lisa, of course.

Across the room, a woman walked toward the group of

musicians. It was obvious she was Russian. She met all the prerequisites: tall, slim, beautiful, a love of 1980's America fashion. She was wearing a tight, colorful T-shirt with Cheburashka (the Russian version of Mickey Mouse) on the front, and thigh-high black boots over stone-washed jeans that could have been worn in a Rick Astley video back in 1987.

Most of the guys in the bar watched as she walked across the room. Gertie caught me looking, and she just shook her head and then gave me the look that made it clear I was in the doghouse. Guys: we can be such knuckleheads sometimes.

The Russian girl was exotic and foreign, and she dressed in that brazenly sexy way that only Eastern-Blockers seem to have the guts for. She walked in a beeline, straight to the musicians. Then she leaned over and kissed Squid right on his lips. Now squid wasn't exactly a Calvin Klein underwear model. And the Squid had a fox. I couldn't believe it—but then I remembered where we were. This wasn't real life. No, in real life Squid would probably never catch a fox. But this was ship life, an alternate reality where a crew member's dating options are drastically reduced to whatever two thousand people happen to be aboard the ship that they are assigned to.

An interesting phenomenon occurs when you're put into an environment where you generally only see the same one thousand or so crew members for six months. You realize that beauty is relative.

After a crew member spends six months with the same shipmates, anyone who is breathing and has properly functioning sex organs is considered datable. This is the phenomenon that crew members call *ship goggles,* because it's similar to what happens to a passenger after they've spent the entire afternoon at Carlos and Charlie's in Cozumel playing the flip-cup drinking game with tequila shots. After five months on a ship, a guy with a face that has all the handsome qualities of a blobfish will get as much attention from beautiful women as the Beatles did back in 1964.

A crew member knows that they've been wearing thick (and badly fogged-up) ship goggles once they get their sea legs squarely set back on land. They go out for the first time, to a mall or a club or a big restaurant, and they look around. Suddenly, they're surrounded by all of these people who are their own age. Suddenly the dating pool just increased by say, about four hundred million people—the entire population of the United States. Suddenly, they actually have *something* in common with nearly everyone around them. They think, *Wow, when did everyone get so damn good looking?*

We watched Squid kiss Svetlana Sosexyhotkova, and then we turned our attention back to the sea. A big orange sun was dipping behind the ocean, casting gold-colored sparkles across the water's surface. The crew bar DJ played his normal rotation of all the eastern-Europe dance hits from 1990 that I had never heard of, and crew members began to arrive for the "Dress like a Superhero" crew party. A warm sunset breeze began to flow into the ship.

In that moment, I realized that the ship had given us so much. We were buoyed by a great sense of hope. If this ship, this beastly hunk of metal, could float out here at sea, then so could we. We could make it. The ship gave us direction in our life too. We had taken that big step and followed our hearts back to ship life. We didn't just stay roped up to the dock on land. We had untied and headed out into the open waters.

Maybe we were bored. Maybe we were crazy. Maybe we

were young and looking for adventure. Maybe we truly believed that the ship that stays tied to the dock might as well be lost at sea.

It didn't matter now. We were moving forward. We were headed to Saint Martin, and we couldn't wait to sit in the sun and put our toes in the sand. But before any of that we had to run our first art auction. We would put Gertie's bright pink gavel to the test.

We hurried back to our crew quarters where a circular beam of moonlight was shining into our cabin. Sea spray splashed against the porthole. We climbed into our tiny bed, tossing and turning, trying to discover a position where one of our elbows wouldn't dig into the other's back.

Eventually, we gave up trying and settled for horizontal. We were both lying on our sides. I was squashed between Gertie and the hull of the ship, and I could hear the waves splashing against the side, could feel them pounding onto the ship's hull.

I began to drift into a half-sleep, that state of mind when your imagination runs wild, that moment right before you fall asleep when you used to see monsters in your closet as a kid. I imagined the cruise ship being slowly pulled apart. First, the bridge was ripped from the top of the vessel and was thrown into the sea. Then the lido deck was torn from the top of our cruise liner and hurled into the ocean. The hull buckled. Big metal rivets snapped out of place. Wide panels of steel sheared off into the waves.

Piece by piece, the ship was dismantled, until there was nothing left but Gertie and me. The two of us were laying side by side, her arms around me. We were gliding just a few feet from the ocean's surface, racing across and above the surface of the sea.

Then I drifted back to reality. The cabin rocked gently back and forth, like a massive metal crib. The engine hummed like the amplified motor of an old bassinet mobile. The walls of the crew cabin creaked and groaned. The song of the sea began to sing us to sleep. Together, we sailed upon the ocean, and our eyes drifted to a close.

It felt wonderful to be back, back where our room would rock us to sleep, back where nothing was safe on our bedroom shelves unless it was Super-Glued to the surface.

Our first day back on board had ended, and now we had to face our first big test. Auction day.

CHAPTER NINE

GERTIE AND HER PINK SECRET WEAPON.

It was judgment day, so naturally Gertie wanted to make sure her nails looked cute. She painted them pink and put on matching lipstick. She slipped on a little pink dress cut low in the front and a bit lower in the back. Then she pulled out a small shoebox from underneath the bed, opened it, and lifted out a pair of four-inch heels—bright pink, of course. She opened one of the desk drawers and grabbed her pink gavel, holding it up next to one of her heels, a perfect match.

I told Gertie she was a genius, and then I put on my best black suit. Guys have it easy. We've had pretty much the same fashion for the past three hundred years, ever since puffy shirts and powdered wigs went out of style. I had brought one of those short-bristled brushes onto the ship with me, so I could brush the dust and lent from my jacket shoulders and front. I liked doing it. It made me feel as though I was in an episode of *Downton Abbey*.

I put a big blob of gel in my hair, and we both looked ship-shape.

When we walked through the CREW ONLY door and into the art gallery, the place was already full of passengers. We had two hours until our first auction. Alex was sitting at his desk, ignoring everyone in the art gallery, working through stacks of paperwork and tapping the keys of a calculator.

"Good morning, Alex," Gertie said.

Alex didn't look up from his computer. "I've been thinking. How are you two planning on tackling the auction duties?"

"Well," Gertie said, holding up her pink gavel, "We've decided that I'll be the auctioneer, and he'll focus on one-on-one sales in the gallery."

Alex pointed at her gavel. "Cute. I'll let you give pinky a try today."

"What do you want us to do now?" Gertie asked.

"Nothing. Ignore the passengers. Make they come to us. Remember what I said. The ruder you are, the more art you're going to sell. Don't be impressed with anything the passengers do. Make them impress you by buying something in the gallery."

Back in the art gallery, Rashek walked up smiling. "Is there anything I can do for you before the auction starts?"

"Yes, let's trade out the Wyland paintings for some of the Dalis," Alex said.

Rashek's smile faltered but quickly returned.

"Gertie," Alex said. "Will you help him?"

As soon as Gertie was out of the gallery, Alex leaned toward me from across the desk. "So, how exactly do you two plan to split your earnings?"

"Fifty-fifty. Right down the middle."

"Why would you do that?" Alex said.

"We're a team," I replied.

Alex shrugged. "You should be making the lion's share."

Whether I liked it or not, Alex was our ticket to freedom. He was our ticket to the big leagues. We had to pass through his bush-league before we could be out at sea on our own as an art auctioneer team. The last thing we needed to do was to make enemies with Alex.

"I like Rashek," I said, hoping to change the subject. "He really knows the art. Great with passengers. He said he hopes to be an art associate on his next contract. That's a good move."

Alex laughed. "That's never going to happen."

"Why?"

"Because he's Indian trash."

Well, let's just say that was the point that I stopped being a fan of Alex Ashebury. No, I didn't like the cut of his jib, not one bit. However, to be fair, I had heard this term quite a bit on ships, and it was never directed toward one particular nationality. It seemed there was always someone who wanted to look down on the foreigners. I had heard Indian trash before, and also euro-trash, American trash, Filipino trash, Russian trash, and so on. Why do so many people seem to harbor the need to look down on other people who are different from them? But perhaps Alex didn't really mean what he was saying. Perhaps he was just repeating the things he had heard so many times on the ship. I wanted to give him the benefit of the doubt.

"Rashek said that he'd be an art associate on his next contract."

"Carrots. Chasing freakin' carrots. We dangle them. He chases. We get what we want, the hardest worker on the seven seas. It's simple. Sometimes it's hard to know who the rabbit is. Sometimes it's you. This time, it's Rashek. Rabbits and carrots. It's a way of life out here. You can tell yourself that you'll never start chasing them, but you're wrong. I'm chasing them. Why? Sometimes I get a nibble."

I heard a voice from behind me. "Excuse me."

I turned around to see an older man in a green polo shirt and tan slacks. He was thin, a face like a hawk, and a strong accent that sounded as if he came from one of the Scandinavian countries—Norway, perhaps. I glanced at his watch. Rolex. His shoes were scuff-less fancy leather.

Then I felt a little sick. Was I turning into Alex? *Noooooooo!* I've never been one to judge people based on how much money they made, and I wasn't going to start now.

Alex punched a few more numbers into his calculator then lowered his head, letting his glasses slide down the bridge of his nose. He peered over top of the tortoise shell frame. "How can I help?" he said in a tone like, *"Why are you bothering me, you cold-hearted prig? Can't you see I'm in the middle of trying to kill my calculator?"*

I was looking forward to seeing Alex's theory in action; his hypothetical thesis titled *The Positive Correlation Between Being an Asshole and Selling Art on a Cruise Ship*. Call me Skeptic McSkepticson, but I didn't buy it. I hoped to approach selling art in a different way once we were out on our own.

I had a different perspective of the job, I guess. I felt every passenger in the gallery was looking for something, and it was my job to help them find that special piece of art they loved, a painting that enhanced their life in some way, or perhaps an artwork they felt was a good investment.

I felt the job was a way to bring a person a bit of happiness. I didn't want to be rude to passengers. They had paid a great deal of money just to be on the cruise. I was never going to use Alex's tactic, no matter how much tried to convince me of his "Theory of Irritability".

Back in the art gallery, the passenger pointed at a painting on the wall. "I'm interested in the Craftman original.

Could you tell me more about it?"

Alex didn't look up. He grabbed a clipboard and handed it to me. "He'll help you."

And just like that, I was thrown into the world of fine art sales. I grabbed the clipboard, which held a stack of paper that listed every piece of art that we had on the ship, and included a detailed list of their prices and retail values. We walked over to the Craftman, a very nice watercolor of Big Ben with the River Thames reflecting the stars and moon above. I recited as much of the spiel about the artist as I could remember.

The passenger looked as if he wasn't listening to a word I said. "How much is it?" the Scandinavian asked.

"We have our auction in just about three hours from now, but I can tell you the starting bid." I flipped through the clipboard papers and found the Craftman painting. "The starting bid for this original is four thousand four hundred dollars. Would you like us to make sure to bring it up to the auction block?"

He looked at my clipboard. "What's that column of numbers there?"

"That's retail price. What this painting might sell for on land."

"How much is retail?"

I looked back at the listing. "Seven nine."

"That's over three thousand more," the man scoffed.

"It's a great deal," I said, felling like a used car salesman.

"Here's a question," the man said. "Why would your company sell this painting for four thousand out here, when they could sell it, allegedly, for nearly eight thousand on land?"

I had just encountered every salesman's greatest fear: the

critical thinker. I remembered what Alex had said about why we can offer such low prices and then recited something close to the company line, feeling like a complete shill. "Here on the cruise ship, we have much lower overhead than land galleries. We also buy in bulk and have relationships with artists, and..." *Blah, blah, blah.*

The Scandinavian smelled my fishy logic as if it were a plate of pickled herring at a Norwegian breakfast table. "Hmmm," he said and then he pulled his chin in, creating folds in his neck, and squinted—the fighting stance of the critical-thinker bird.

I asked him again if he'd like us to bring the painting up for auction.

"Sure," the man with an attuned sense for surreptitious aquatic-life said, and then he walked away.

I took a stroll around the art gallery. I guess it was the opposite of a victory lap—a defeat lap, perhaps. I looked at each painting as I walked, looking for small characteristics that stood out to me, anything I could use as a good selling point. However, I kept thinking about what the pickled-herring man had said. Maybe the numbers *were* fudged a little. There was no way I would ever know, no way I could know. But perhaps he was right.

I came to a group of paintings, a trio of numbered-and-signed limited-edition prints of colorful sailboats racing to the finish line of a tropical regatta: sweeping seascapes, pretty boat lines, and full canvas sails. I'd seen these paintings before, many different times throughout the five years that I'd worked on ships. I always loved them. I bent down and took a closer look at the numbers on the paintings. They were from a collection of eighty prints. This seemed to indicate that each paper print was only produced eighty times, making them "limited editions".

I took another look at the group of paintings. I had seen these exact "limited edition" prints on nearly every ship I'd ever worked on. That meant that these prints were possibly for sale on every cruise ship on the seven seas. How was it possible that fewer than eighty of these sailboat prints had been sold in the past five years? It didn't seem *impossible*, but it certainly seemed *improbable*.

I did the math. There are more than two hundred and fifty cruise ships in the world. Carnival alone owns more than eighty cruise ships. (I am not implying that I worked for Carnival). I felt at least one hundred of these ships had art programs on board.

I quickly calculated—five years was how many months? (Sixty.) The average cruise length was seven days. That meant that, after subtracting for dry docks and repairs, one cruise ship would probably take about two hundred cruises over a five-year period. If around one hundred cruise ships had an art program on board, that meant that one of the sailboat limited-edition prints that I was looking at could have been offered for sale on a whopping two hundred thousand cruises. And there were, allegedly, only eighty of them available.

But I had only seen the painting on about ten different ships. Even if the painting was only offered on those ten ships (which seems highly improbable), over the five-year period, the painting would have been available on around two thousand cruises without selling out.

No, this didn't seem right at all.

Across the gallery, Alex was sitting behind the desk.

"Alex," I said, "how long have you been selling these

sailboat paintings, these limited editions?"

"I don't know, at least seven years. I'm not sure."

"And how many did you sell last cruise?"

"I think two or three. They're regular sellers. Only four hundred dollars each, though, so I don't bother with them too much. If someone's interested, I tell them they can buy them at the auction."

"How many of those have you sold since you started working as an art auctioneer?"

"I don't know. At least fifty, maybe."

His response only brought up more questions. Could those limited-edition prints actually be not-so-limited prints? And who regulates the art industry? Is it left to individual local agencies such as New York City's Department of Consumer Affairs? Or do we rely on such vague market watchdogs as the United States Center for Bioethics and Human Dignity (yes, this is a real agency) to oversee our art transactions?

And the bigger question is: Who regulates and oversees art transactions when they occur in international waters? Are international waters simply a cesspool of watered-down regulation, murky backwater loopholes, and swashbuckling lawlessness where all integrity has run aground and modern day art-pirates use cannonball-sized lies to stealthily swindle an armada of unsuspecting cruise ship passengers?

The usual answer to questions like this is often the same—the market will regulate itself. Now, I appreciate people who believe in libertarian ideals; I hold many myself. However, from what I've seen, if any part of the cruise industry were left to self-regulation, it would self-regulate about as well as a school of sharks let loose at a Red Cross blood drive. However, the libertarians would say that after the sharks consumed all the available blood, self-correction would inevitably occur, which is a rather good argument.

At any rate, I have no distinct allegations or any definitive answers. I'm still trying to find them myself. All I have are hunches and observations. Yet, I began digging a bit, looking for answers when I was still working as an art hawker. I had to turn no further than the *New York Times* to find a few things that made me feel a bit uncomfortable.

In January, 2013, the *New York Times* published the article, aptly titled, "As Art Values Rise, So Do Concerns About Market's Oversight." After reading the first sentence, which describes the New York art market as a place that "allows opaque transactions and has few outside monitors", I felt that my hunches may have been correct. The article goes on to paint a picture of a seedy art world where auctioneers engage in sleazy practices such as "chandelier bidding", a bit of art market theatrics where the auctioneers pretend to spot bids in the room when in fact they are pointing at nothing but the light fixtures and exit signs. Fine-art auctions are described as venues where the value of artwork is most likely inflated, and where the operators largely lack both credibility and transparency.

In the article, the quote by James R. Hedges IV (an early leader in the hedge funds industry) may have best summed up the state of the art world's credibility when he said, "The art world feels like the private equity market of the '80s and the hedge funds of the '90s. It's got practically no oversight or regulation."

And this article was reporting on the art market in *New York City*. Imagine what the art market may be like out in international waters.

Another *New York Times* article, published in 2008, is titled, "Art Auctions on Cruise Ships Lead to Anger, Accusations and Lawsuits". The article gives a detailed account of several passengers who believed that the retail values of the Picasso prints they had purchased on cruise ships had been grossly inflated by the cruise ship art auctioneers by as much as twenty thousand dollars. Other passengers believed that the Dali prints they purchased were downright forgeries, citing the deluge of fake Salvador Dali artworks that flooded the art market in the 1970s as a potential source.

Near the end of the article, a detective with the Los Angeles Police Department goes on the record, saying that they often get complaints about art auctions on cruise ships, but that there is nothing they can really do about it because—yep, you probably guessed it—the art auctions take place out in that Bermuda Triangle where laws seem to go missing, otherwise known as international waters. The police detective said that passengers who believe they've been bamboozled by unscrupulous art brokers should go and talk to the FBI, as if the FBI is going to spend time chasing Dali-duplicating sea snakes to the ends of the Earth.

All of this information has only left me with more unanswered questions. Those sailboat paintings—are they really limited editions? Limited editions of what? Is the art market so unregulated that artists could lawfully manufacture eighty limited edition 12x12-inch prints, and then once they are sold out, fire up the printers again, but this time print eighty 12.1x12.1-inch prints? How many editions of the limited editions are there, really? It all starts to sound as if the limited editions are about as hard to find as a Southern guy who loves to drink beer at a NASCAR race.

However, at the time, I didn't know any of this. I just had a SDLR hunch, something didn't look right. I walked back to the art desk. Gertie and Rashek were talking and laughing. I asked them where Alex went. They pointed over to the side of the gallery. I looked over and saw Alex talking with the Scandinavian hawk, Mr. Pickled Herring himself. After a few minutes, Alex walked back over to the desk and grabbed me on the shoulder.

"You see?" he said. "You just have to be a little rude."

"What happened?" I asked.

"I let him impress me…with a silent bid at the auction. No one else will bid on that painting. It's sold. You and Gertie just made your first commission on a four thousand dollar painting. You,"—he pointed to me—"just learned the value of being rude."

I still didn't believe him. However, as the weeks rolled by, and I observed Alex's cold-shoulder tactics in action, I had to admit that his approach was supported by rather high sales numbers.

Years later, I was sitting in my car. I had just pulled into my driveway when a news story came on the radio. The story was about a report published in the *Journal of Consumer Research* which found that rude salespeople actually boost sales in luxury brands. The research discovered that "customers had an increased desire to buy luxury goods after being treated rudely." And the ruder the salespeople were, "the higher the desire customers had to buy the posh items." Though, according to Daren Dhal, one of the co-authors of the study, "You've got to be the right kind of snob in the right kind of store for the effect to work."

Alex apparently had the perfect amount of snobbery, and the cruise ship art gallery must have been the right kind of store, because Alex was the stuck-up sales king, and he didn't need to conduct any research to know that sex isn't the only thing that sells. Sometimes, being a jerk can work just as well.

Back in the art gallery, Alex smiled. "Why don't you two grab a bite to eat and take a half-hour break or so? Then meet me back here, and we'll head over to the M&R manager's office before the auction starts. He wants to meet you two." Alex paused and then sang the song from The Wizard of Oz, "We're off to see the wizard..."

I asked him what he meant.

"You'll see," he said. "You'll see."

CHAPTER TEN

WHO'S THE BOSS?

When we walked into our crew cabin, we saw that our bed hadn't been made, which we found quite unusual. The thin, blue blanket—which was so worn I suspected it may have been a personal effect from a passenger aboard the *Mayflower*—was exactly how we left it, crumpled in a messy heap at the foot of our tiny bed. Our dirty clothes were still strewn about the room. Our trash bin still contained the empty Ting bottles, as well as the welcome-aboard packets we had been given when we joined the ship the day before—always the first thing that cruise ship crew members throw away. And there wasn't a towel animal or little tasty chocolate mint anywhere in the room.

How could this be? Where on the seven seas was our room steward?

In the past, it had been like magic. I would board whatever cruise ship I was assigned to, and like a genie in a bottle, a kind-hearted, friendly, and often Filipino room-steward would materialize. Where did he come from? Don't ask me. One minute he wasn't there; the next minute—beam me up, Scotty—"Mr. Bayani Binaohan Pinagpala at your service." Without fail, he would learn my schedule, and while I was out of the cabin, he would make my bed and fold my clothes and change the bin and clean the bathroom and bring new rolls of toilet paper, and if he was really good, sometimes he'd even clean the shower once or twice a month. In return,

I'd pay him the going *crew* rate for a room steward on a cruise ship at that time—two dollars a day. (Don't make that face. I always tipped well. Always.)

I never had to ask for a steward, and well, I guess I had become a tad spoiled. So when I walked into our crew cabin and found it looking as though someone had stuffed a cork in the magic room-steward genie bottle and then tossed it out to sea, I felt as if I might have walked into a dream. Was I supposed to make my own bed and clean my own room?

Was I a child? No, I was an officer, dagnabbit. Was this a room that was attached to a keel and a motor? Yes, this was a cruise ship, and cruise ship officers as well as most crew members had friendly room-steward people that cleaned up after them. What had this ship world come to?

"Maybe Arjun can help us," Gertie said.

Yes, Arjun, the HR director. I opened the door, and there he was, across the hall, working on something behind his desk.

"Arjun, do you know where we could get a room steward?" I asked.

"We don't assign room stewards for crew on this ship. However, this might be your lucky day," Arjun said and smiled, the snow leopard returning. "A crew member joined the ship yesterday, and he asked me about crew-steward opportunities. Do you want his cabin number?"

I said yes, probably looking as desperate as a passenger who discovers the ship has run out of ice cream cones for the rest of the cruise. Arjun pulled out a little slip of paper from the top drawer of his desk. "Eight-three-zero-seven. Ronald's his name. Nice guy. I know him from a previous contract."

I said thanks, closed the door, and called Ronald

immediately. The voice on the other line wasn't Filipino but Jamaican, perhaps. I told him we needed a room steward, and after negotiating for a bit we settled on five dollars a day, since there were two of us in the room. This was fifty cents more per person, per day than I was used to paying, which amounted to a whopping seven extra dollars a week. (Hey, that's no chump change in crew dollars.) *For that price, this guy better be good.*

A few minutes later, Ronald knocked on our door. He was a tall black man with close-shaved hair and a cheerful, infectious smile. I remembered what Arjun had said: this was only Ronald's second day on board. Of course he was still smiling. In his left hand he held a spray bottle, and in the right, an old, battered-looking vacuum cleaner. Behind him was a cart of linens, trash bags, and cleaning supplies.

"You need a room steward," Ronald said with a thick accent.

I waved him into our cabin.

"Where you from?" I asked.

"Haiti. Port-au-Prince. De capital."

Most crew members on a cruise ship have an interesting story, and I often enjoyed learning about other people's lives. I felt I just had to ask the right questions. It seemed that most people didn't end up working on cruise ships on a whim. There were often complex circumstances, sometimes an intriguing blend of war, disaster, or poverty, that lead people to sail off into the deep blue sea. I've come to realize that there are many people in this world who, if they didn't have cruise ships, wouldn't have much for a home and not much of a family at all.

I wanted to ask Ronald about his life, but we needed to

go and meet with the M&R manager—"the Wizard of Oz", as Alex called him.

Gertie put thirty-five dollars on the desk, his pay for the first week. We would give him a tip at the end of the week, and a large one if he did a good job. We were one step closer to getting our ship fully wired, and it felt wonderful.

The next step to getting the ship wired was finding Mr. Lucky Lucky on the ship. You see, on a cruise ship, you can get lucky, or you can get *lucky lucky*.

And the first step to getting *lucky lucky* is to make friends with the guy that operates the trash incinerator. Go down to deck zero. Turn right. Go past the crew office, and then just follow your nose. Follow the scent of rotting vegetables, day-old chocolate melting cake, and burning plastic. It'll never lead you astray. Turn right into the little room that smells about as good as the Great Pacific Garbage Patch—yes, the room with the conveyor belt filled with garbage and the massive metal bins of sorted plastics, glass, metals, food, and paper products. Somewhere in that maze of flotsam, you'll find a man diligently working his daily twelve-hour shift among the stinky rubbish. That's one of your best friends on the ship. Or at least he should be, if you want to get *lucky lucky*.

Introduce yourself. Laugh at his jokes. Compliment his gelled hair and rubber gloves. Bring him gifts of air fresheners for his office, the little dangling ones that smell like coconuts and pineapples and are shaped like palm trees. Take him out to dinner at the crew mess, on you. Buy him drinks in the crew bar. Sing karaoke duets alongside him to Brittany Spears' "Hit Me Baby One More Time" at crew parties. You know, wine and dine him. Do whatever it takes. Just make sure and become his *paisano*. Because the trash man isn't just the trash man. He lives a double life. He's a cruise ship double agent. Mr. Lucky Lucky.

He runs a small but remarkable store, right out of his crew cabin. And inside, you will find a constantly rotating inventory: new bottles of suntan lotion, cruise ship key chains, unopened bottles of rum, woven sun hats, a trash bin filled to the brim with sunglasses, T-shirts, bow ties, silk ties, suit jackets, pricey Cuban cigars still preserved in plastic cases, packs of cigarettes, and lighters, lighters, lighters of every size and color.

In his store, he hawks the abandoned, the left-behinds, the thrown away bits and bobs that are tossed in stateroom trashcans once the cruise comes to an end. It all goes somewhere. It all goes to the trash incinerator. It all glides down the conveyor belt and passes directly in front of Mr. Lucky Lucky on its last voyage in this cruise ship world. And *he* has the whole trash world in his hands. Sometimes he plucks these unwanted items from their fiery fate and gives them a life anew, a life on the shelves of the Lucky Lucky store, where crew members can browse the rows of the unwanted vacation remnants.

But why do they call him Mr. Lucky Lucky? Why is it called the Lucky Lucky store? Because every time a room steward finds another pair of sunglasses in the trash; every time a bartender discovers another lighter that has been forgotten at his cruise ship saloon; every time the trash man finds another Cuban cigar drifting toward the flames and plucks it out of the heap of rotting ice cream cones with sprinkles, they have all dug out a nugget of cruise ship gold, and they all say the same thing, "Lucky, lucky! Lucky, lucky!"

Back on our ship, Ronald said, "Okay, Boss, I'll clean de room. It will be perfect. I'm a hard worker. You have nothing to worry about, Boss. If there is anything you need, you let me know. Okay, Boss?"

Ronald came from a different world. Call it a cultural divide, or maybe he thought it would help him get a bigger tip if he played the part of a subordinate. Whatever the case, he wanted to call me "boss".

"I work for you," Ronald said. "You're de boss. Whatever you need. Anything. I find it on ship for you. Okay, Boss?"

"We could use some tissues," Gertie said.

"I can get you tissues," Ronald said. "You are lucky. On my last ship, there was no tissue paper anywhere. This ship—it has tissue paper. Very good. It's happening all across de fleet. The company is no longer supplying tissue paper to the crew. They put locks on all the tissue paper storerooms. It will probably happen here. Crew members had to buy it themselves or get it from the Filipinos."

I figured there was a good chance that it wasn't the company doing this at all, but more likely a project started by something crew members call the "Filipino mafia", a group of often-Filipino crew members who operate the underground black market on cruise ships.

I know it sounds like the stuff of fantasy, but there are a lot of shadowy things that happen beneath the surface of the sea when no one is looking. It's hard for management to keep an eye on all the strange things lurking out on the high seas. You can have the most experienced watchmen in the world on a cruise ship, but sometimes you still run into a giant iceberg, sometimes full speed ahead.

But the Filipino mafia was of no concern to Gertie and me. Not yet, anyway. They didn't come into our lives until much later in our contract, so let's not delve too deep below the waterline just yet.

I told Ronald thanks.

"Okay, Boss," he said. "You have nothing to worry about. I'll take care of you two. Everything will be perfect, Boss."

CHAPTER ELEVEN

WE'RE OFF TO SEE THE WIZARD, THE WONDERFUL WIZARD OF ODD.

There was no yellow brick road, just a tan network of hallways and stairwells that led to the crew office door.

When we walked into the crew office, Alex was sitting at a computer, printing an invoice for the Craftman painting he had sold. "Well, let's go to the M&R manager's office and—"

And then the M&R manager popped out of the wall. Yes, I know it sounds bizarre. It was bizarre. He popped right out of the wall.

In the middle of the wall was door that was separated into two parts so that the top half of the door can swing open while leaving the bottom half in place, a dutch door. This door in the back wall was like a secret passage that connected the crew office to the M&R manager's office—also known among the crew on this ship as "the portal to hell".

So you can imagine my reaction when the wall suddenly opened, and a stubble-faced man poked his head into the room, and said, "Why hello! You must be the new art auctioneers," and then giggled a bit.

Alex was spot on. I did indeed feel as if I was in that scene in the *Wizard of Oz,* where Dorothy and the gang knock on the gate to the Emerald City and that midget in the green suit, the one with the handlebar mustache, pops out of the hole in the wall and asks, "Who rang that bell?"

The man who popped out of our wall was no midget. He

was tall and thin, a long face and hooked nose. He looked like a turtle…or Pete Townsend from The Who, whichever you prefer. There was a little tuft of grey hair in the front of his otherwise bald head, which looked as if a shriveled weed had somehow sprouted in the dry cracks of the Mohave Desert.

He greeted us with a smile, but it was the kind of smile that just didn't match the look in his eyes. Somehow it was off, as if he had learned to smile from an instruction manual, the type with poorly drawn illustrations that failed to show how to do it properly. He was wearing a white short-sleeved button-up with three stripes on the shoulder boards, and white pants that were as tight as the trousers you would've found in Rod Stewart's walk-in closet back in 1979.

We had only been on the ship for two days, but we had already heard some of the nicknames that crew members had for this guy. Usually, you can tell how much someone is liked by the number of nicknames they have. Even if they're teasing names, like Chubbs or Squid. However, in this case, the nicknames made it clear that he was possibly the most unpopular cruise ship officer to ever sip a cappuccino. Ronald simply called him "the boogie man". Alex called him "the wizard". One of the dancers who didn't know his real name just referred to him as "that guy that made me cry in the crew laundry that one day".

Gertie and I ended up calling him "Captain Coprolite".

Goodluck, the Jamaican bartender, called him—"ghost". I asked him why. Goodluck said it was because the guy was as white as a bed sheet—a passenger bed sheet, not a crew member's—and because his heart was dead. At the time, I'd thought that description was a tad too rude, much too harsh.

This was, of course, the beginning of our contract.

He may have been called a lot of names, but most importantly, he was our manager, the marketing and revenue manager, and so we were determined to be respectful and polite and get along well with the wizard.

We introduced ourselves and he looked at me. "That jacket's too tight. Make sure to keep it buttoned." He smiled in his odd mechanical way, and then added, "Let's meet at the wine bar after the auction…so I can meet you properly. And always feel free to stop by if you have any problems. I have an…open door policy."

I could hear the drum hits in my head (*duh dum shoop*). He pulled himself back through the hole in the wall and then closed the top half of his creepy Dutch door.

Alex tugged at my jacket, which until then I had thought fit rather nicely, maybe a European cut, but a nice fit.

We followed Alex out of the office and onto the promenade.

"So what exactly does the M&R manager do all day?" I asked as we walked toward the art gallery.

"The funny thing is," Alex said, "not once has he, or any other M&R manager that I've worked with, ever done anything related to marketing or anything that has helped us increase our revenue on the cruise ship."

"So what does he do?" Gertie asked.

"He walks around and looks for things to report to upper management. I've dealt with a lot of these managers. They're all the same. They're scared. They know their position became obsolete years ago, so they've decided to act like security guards for the crew, hoping that upper management will find this as a good reason to keep them on board. They need to validate their position, and they do it by writing up the spa girls for wearing too much makeup, or by going on witch hunts for crew members who don't have their suit jacket buttoned, or searching for people who aren't wearing their nametags in the crew mess. I give it two years, and they'll be gone. And I'll be glad when they are. The clock is ticking."

I decided then and there that I was going to do everything I could do to try to get along with Captain Coprolite. Maybe he wasn't such a bad guy.

We walked into the gallery where a crowd of passengers were waiting for us. The auction was scheduled to start in less than half an hour.

Outside the windows, little palm tree–lined islands began to take shape on the horizon. For me, this meant we were getting closer to a cold piña colada and relaxing on a Caribbean beach, which happened to be two of my three greatest pleasures in life at that time. My third occurred whenever I heard the passenger boat-drill announcement, and then I'd open the door to my officer's cabin, kick my feet up on my desk, and wave to my crew member friends as they walked to the boat drill that I no longer had to participate in, which for me was like a slice of cruise-ship heaven on Earth.

I don't care what anybody says. There's no better feeling in this world than climbing the workplace ladder and finally reaching a higher position in life where you get paid *more* for doing *less*. Just ask any member of Congress. They'll tell you the same thing.

About thirty or so people wandered around the art gallery, most of them feigning interest in the paintings to cover up their real reason for being there—free champagne.

Yes, there is nothing that cruise ship passengers love more than free stuff. I've seen passengers resort to fisticuffs over life-vest shaped lapel pins being passed out on the lido deck. And in case you're not in the know, if you're on a cruise ship right now and you're looking for some free booze, look no further than an art auction at sea.

However, be forewarned: Nowhere is the adage "You get what you pay for" more true than on a modern-day cruise ship. If you're someone with the remarkable ability to taste the difference between a glass of Evian and the water drained from a fish tank, then your palate is probably too refined for the bargain bubbly served at most art auctions at sea. You won't find names like Vueve Clicquot or Perrier-Jouet on the champagne bottles being served at these high-seas art sales, but you will find top-shelf brands that you may recognize, with names such as Duck Nipple or Bilgetank Saveur. Believe me, we art auctioneers take great pride in the esteemed quality of the free champagne we serve at auctions. We always search out the best bubbly available on Walmart's *bottom* shelf, trying to find those rare sparkling wines that have all the qualities that residents of the Champagne-Ardenne region look for in the water they use in their bidets.

The room was full of energy, and I was ready to start popping champagne open and let loose the torrent of alcohol, something that often makes people do things they regret the next day—which was exactly what we would need to get people to buy some of the art that we had for sale.

When Gertie walked into the gallery, a stampede of passengers ran up to her like a herd of gray-haired buffalo charging toward the last saltlick in the West. Gertie was immediately snatched up by one of the unwieldy bison, who was happy to ask her to do anything that required her to bend over and check the price of each and every painting in the gallery. The buffalo apparently had bad eyes, cataracts he said.

I was left on my own, and I found Alex at his desk. I asked him if I should start pouring the champagne.

"Not yet. We have to pass out the cards."

Alex reached into his jacket pocket and pulled out a stack of little white cards that read: *ONE FREE GLASS OF CHAMPAGNE*. He handed them to me. "Walk around the room and pass these out. Give each person *one*."

"One?" I asked then made a face like a passenger who had just tasted the coffee on board for the first time.

"Think about it," Alex said. "We don't want the kind of passengers at our auction who are here just so they can get a free glass of champagne. Do you think anyone with real money cares about free champagne?"

I did that telltale sign of lying, where I said no but nodded yes. I didn't think a passenger's financial situation had any correlation to them liking free stuff, but I did see Alex's point. We were after the real high-rollers on the ship, not the type of people who might be lured to a flea market by the promise of half-priced corn dogs. We wanted Rose from the *Titanic*, but Jack could stay down with the other corn dog eaters in third class.

To be honest, I completely lost interest in what Alex was saying, and so I began daydreaming as Alex continued talking about the merits of exclusion. I imagined how many passengers *would* show up to the auction if we started offering free corn dogs instead of champagne. After all, the auctions did take place midafternoon, perfect timing for a passenger's sixth mealtime. I imagined myself in one of those red-and white-striped carney outfits with the flat-topped hat. I was holding a big paper-cone megaphone and shouting, "Get your free corn dogs! Free corn dogs here! Get your free corn dogs!" as a mob of passengers came rushing down the promenade, all huffing and puffing.

I came out of my daze as Alex handed me a clipboard with the art prices tacked to it. A woman walked up who was wearing more gold chains than Mr. T (at the height of his fame). She called Alex "dumpling", and then asked about "a gaggle of sculptures over there in the corner." Alex shooed me away.

I started passing out cards, but I wasn't having much luck. I wondered if I'd get a better response if I was rude to the passengers while doing it, as in "Here, take this free glass of champagne, you jerk. I don't care if you like it or not," but I decided not to test Alex's Theory of Irritability at that time.

The crowd in the gallery grew, and before long I was standing in the middle of a swirling throng of *bona fide* art prospectors who could actually name a painting in the Louvre other than the Mona Lisa (which was more than I could do at the time). They were mixed in with the larger assortment of hagglers and buy-nothing browsers who were just looking for something "beachy", which actually translated to, "could I have another glass of champagne, please?"

Alex was running around, answering questions with the energy of the lead singer in a ska band, acting something like the male version of Gwen Stefani. Occasionally he'd stop to turn on the cordless microphone he was carrying to announce, "Auction starts in fifteen minutes!" Five minutes later: "Auction starts in fourteen minutes!" Five minutes later: "Auction starts in thirteen minutes!" And so on.

Finally, nearly forty-five minutes later, Rashek showed up

with a cart of dusty champagne bottles that looked as if they had been rescued from the rubble of the Mt. Vesuvius eruption, and we started popping and pouring. Alex was standing by the side of the stage, and he called Gertie and me over to the side of the stage. "Okay," he said, about out of breath from his amazing feats of salesmanship and looking as if he had as much adrenaline running through his veins as Alex Bumgartner did when he jumped back to Earth from space. "This is what I want you two to do. I want *you* on the right side of the stage, and I want Gertie on the other. Every time you see a bid go up, I want you both to clap real loud, point to the person bidding, and then call out their bid number. Got it?"

We nodded.

He continued, "I'm going to bring out the big stuff first and see if we get any action. Then Gertie can give it a go on one of the Craftman originals. I want to see what her pink gavel can *really* do."

We nodded again, and Alex ran onto the stage. He began talking to the crowd, first giving them a rundown of the auction rules, which lasted more than fifteen minutes and was about as interesting as a cruise-ship lecturer giving a presentation on the history of mooring ropes. Once half the people in the crowd were nearly asleep, and the other half were deeply disgruntled about the fact that they were only going to be served one glass of champagne, Alex felt he had the crowd right where he wanted them: right in the palm of whoever would be running the purser's desk where passengers could lodge complaints. So he was ready to start the auction.

Alex didn't do that rambling, fast-talking, auction speak

that I used to make fun of when I was a kid. You know, the type of auction bid calling that sounds like Porky Pig just had a stroke. *Im-n-a-Im-n-a-100-HERE-Im-n-a-Im-n-a-200-THERE.* No, Alex explained that *his* auction would be quite the classy affair.

Alex brought the first painting on stage and the bids started going up. Gertie and I clapped like Alex had told us to do, looking like two handicapped seals on each side of the stage.

We didn't sell any of the more expensive paintings, but we did sell a boatload of the three and four hundred dollar artworks. I'd thought that it would take an act of divine intervention to sell a few thousand dollars' worth of art at these auctions, but by the time Alex left the stage, wiping sweat from his forehead and giving us a wink, he had sold nearly twenty-five thousand dollars' worth of art. I wondered what we would've sold if we had given the passengers another glass or two of Duck Nipple champagne. The crayon drawing I made of my pet frog George when I was a kid, which was little more than a green blob with two uneven puncture holes that served as George's eyes, may have fetched thousands.

Alex gave Gertie a quick introduction, which left me remembering what my first music mentor said to me about working with divas on stage. His advice was, "The first thing you do at a gig is walk outside and look at whoever's name is lit up in lights outside the theater. That's the person that hired you. Don't ever, ever sound better than that person. If you do, you'll find yourself in the unemployment line."

But there was no hope here. Gertie wasn't happy with just being *in* the show; she had to *be* the show. The center of attention? No, the epicenter of all contemplation. She couldn't help it. It was her nature.

Gertie stepped onto stage holding her little wooden rectangle box. She walked up to the podium, opened it, and pulled out her bright pink gavel.

There was a little applause and Gertie took a deep breath. She gave a rather impressive presentation of a fifty-dollar watercolor print for her first try.

We were both hoping to find more treasure out at sea than Captain Hector Barbosa and his little creepy monkey in *Pirates of the Caribbean*. She waved her gavel around like a magic wand as she described the various merits of the print of a young girl playing in the sand on the beach, which included such unstoppable sales pitches as "It would look pretty good in a condo, don't you think?" and "Awww, isn't she cute? Doesn't she remind you of your own granddaughter?"

She opened the floor for bidding, and wouldn't you know, two or three hands popped up. I clapped, continuing my handicapped seal routine, while Gertie got her first shot at bid calling. She called the bids like Alex, but she put her own sophisticated spin on it, something like, "Um…okay, fifty, and um… sixty there…" and so on. She didn't miss a beat, as solid as the Phil Collins drum fill for "In the Air Tonight."

The gavel came down. *Pop!* "Sold!" Gertie said.

The audience clapped, and just like that we had earned our first commission, which was probably about fifty cents. Our art career had officially begun.

Alex was standing on the side of the stage, and he looked about as impressed as my goldfish looks when I tell her that I just finished writing another book. *So what? Feed me more flakes, you knucklehead.*

Alex went back on stage and brought the last piece of art up for bid. It was a blob of a sculpture that was supposedly made from brass. It looked like something you might end up with after you melted a saxophone down and then dumped the molten metal into a random prairie dog hole where it could cool into a mostly round shape. The starting bid was forty-five thousand dollars.

Everyone in the room looked down at their hands to make sure there were no involuntary muscle movements that could somehow be perceived as a bid.

After Alex announced the close of the auction, a group of buffalos immediately herded around Gertie again, the young salt lick in the pink dress. Many of them wanted to see her gavel, the pink secret weapon, up close.

By default, I was delegated to fielding complaints about the insufficient flow of champagne. I kindly informed the grumblers to take their grievances to the pursers at the customer service desk, which is precisely what every crew member says in response to everything that they don't want to deal with. This is also one of the many reasons why pursers have so much love for the art department on a cruise ship.

With the help of a crew of mostly-Filipino crew members that Alex had hired, we moved the enormous amount of art back into the "high-tech" art vaults. After the cleaning was done, Alex led us to the rather fancy wine bar on the promenade near the front of the ship. The lighting was low, and lining the back wall were three large porthole windows. I could see the sun just starting to set. In the distance, the islands of St. Kitts and Nevis rose out of the sea like the backs of two lone green sea serpents. Above them, a golden sky faded to a dark blue and the stars began to shine in the evening light. Yesterday, the ocean was dark blue. Now, the sea was a light shade of turquoise, the dreamy color of water where bright tropical fish and pirate-ship wrecks are found just below the surface.

In the corner of the room, right in front of one of the porthole windows, Angel, the M&R manager, aka "the wizard", was saying good-bye to a group of officers. Angel had a glass of wine that was about the size of a goldfish bowl. We sat down, and Alex ordered drinks for the rest of us.

"How'd the auction go?" Angel asked, and then leaned in. "How much?"

"About twenty-five thousand."

"Meh."

Twenty-five thousand will only get you a "Meh"?

Alex gulped down his small glass of wine as soon as it was set down on the table. "You need me for anything else?" Alex asked.

"No," Angel said. "But you and Gertie—you two stay behind."

Alex left. "I thought the auction went…okay," he said.

"You were there?" Gertie asked.

"In the back of the room. Checking on how things went." He looked at me. "You were slouching. And you both need to remember to smile. Make sure you pull those shoulders back."

He was right. I was a *sloucher,* guilty as charged. An X-ray of my spine would closely resemble an upside-down letter J. And maybe we *could* smile a bit more. We agreed, and then he waved us away, saying he had someone else to meet.

Across the promenade was a little cafe with free coffee, so we popped in and poured a couple of to-go cups. When we walked out, Angel was standing in the middle of the promenade. He put his hand in line with his eyes, and called us over with one finger. "What is that?" he asked.

"Coffee," Gertie said.

"You can't just walk around the ship with coffees. If I see you doing that again, I'll have to write you up."

Gertie summoned her peace-keeping forces to action. "Okay," she said cheerfully, with a smile—the same way she handled pretty much every situation in life, which seemed to work quite well.

However, I could tell Gertie was frustrated. We had been in a relationship long enough that I knew every subtle facial expression she had. And I think you can understand our frustration. Just moments earlier, we'd been sitting in the wine bar…drinking wine. At that very moment, every passenger that walked by the wine bar could see cruise ship officers sitting in the bar, laughing their purple-teethed heads off. Now Angel was threatening to write us up for walking three feet away from said wine bar and pouring ourselves a cup of coffee.

We walked away and threw our coffees in the garbage.

As we strolled down the promenade, we could hear The Nacho Supremes playing their salsa version of the Motown hit "My Girl", which they called *"Mi Chica"*, (*Mi Chica…Hablando de…Mi Chica*). We spent the next few hours out on the breezeway, watching the sun sink behind the sea, listening to the Latin band, and letting their rhythms "get us", just like Gloria Estefan said they would. I watched the sea turn into a reflection of stars, daydreaming about tying Angel to the ship's anchor and throwing him overboard as soon as the sun went down.

Ahhh, ship life. You're the only life for me.

CHAPTER TWELVE

PEOPLE, CAN I GET A REDEMPTION?

We were awakened by what sounded like the ship being attacked by a Somali pirate with a big-ass machine gun, but it turned out that it was just the anchor being lowered. That was when we discovered that we were in the prized location on the ship where the only thing separating our crew cabin from the anchor-chain winch was a half-inch thick wall that just happened to reverberate and loudly hum at the exact pitch of said anchor chain. I sat straight up in bed. It was my old pal: the ship life anchor-chain alarm clock. *Good morning!* I noticed that the ship wasn't bobbing around as much as usual. I figured we must have finally reached St. Martin.

I was extremely grateful to have survived another night of sleeping beside Gertie in our coffin-sized bed. You see, Gertie was prone to a strange form of sleep "walking" where she would flail her arms and legs around, and then sit up in bed and look at me as if she was awake, and then say something nonsensical, like, "Where's my frosty magnet?" or "Have you seen my plastic pony?"

She never remembered any of it the next day, and she adamantly denied that these episodes ever occurred. But I assure you that it was a terrifying experience to sleep in such close proximity to someone who at any moment might kick me in the lower back without warning because they had as much control over their nervous system as a golden retriever puppy that's dreaming about running through a field of

Milkbones.

When I climbed out of bed, I immediately realized that I needed a herd of massage therapists and chiropractors to cure whatever had happened to me while I was sleeping on my side all night in that tiny bed. The size of the bed allowed me about as much room as one of those boxes that magicians put you in before they saw you in half. I attempted to straighten my body, only to hear more popping than when you put an entire bag of pop rocks in your mouth at once.

I looked out our porthole window. I could see a long concrete pier with three other cruise ships roped up. The pier was poking out into the Caribbean Sea, which was a fantastic light blue that I thought only existed in those fake ponds at mini-golf places in Myrtle Beach, South Carolina.

The night before, we had received news from people back in the mountains of North Carolina that a big snow storm was blowing through town. They were looking at three straight days of snow-globe weather. I imagined our friends in Asheville in their flannel shirts and beards, out in their nearly vertical driveways shoveling snow.

The only things *we* would be shoveling today were conch fritters and pińa coladas into our mouths. Gertie was getting into a skimpy bikini made from as much fabric as you might find in a top-hat made for a horsefly. We both decided that the mountains of North Carolina in the winter were best suited for the bears.

We almost made it off the ship before we ran into Alex—who, before I could grab my fake mustache and pretend to be a passenger, decided to say something like, "Great, well, I'll just come along with you guys." This, I suspect, is the only way that most bosses ever get invited anywhere.

Since the ship was anchored offshore, we had to take a tender to port, which is always a bit of a worrisome undertaking ever since I saw one stranded at sea for more than two hours. So, with mixed feelings and at least a two hours' supply of granola bars, enough water bottles for a marathon drink station, and EPIRBs for Gertie and me, we boarded the tender. She told me she loved me, and I said the same, just in case that was our last chance.

There is nothing quite like feeling the Caribbean sun hitting your face for the first time, especially during a month when you know that the highlight of your neighbor's life is watching the icicles melt from his mailbox. We walked down the palm tree–lined concrete path that, for some odd reason, had been built just inches from the island beltway-road on St. Martin. If you're not careful, you can be decapitated by the side-view mirror of a speeding truck carrying a payload of coconuts. We thankfully made it to the beach unscathed...and, by the looks of the packed shoreline, so had every other passenger on the *four* cruise ships in port. We haggled for a trio of beach loungers with a man who could have passed as a member of Bob Marley and The Wailers, and then found a spot in the sun just inches from where the Caribbean Sea, as warm as bath water, rolled onto shore.

I put my toes in the sand, let the surf roll up to my ankles, and watched the waves as they were pulled back out to sea. Like every other topless beach I have ever been to, I was thoroughly disappointed with the quality of boobies, mostly because most of said boobies were on men. However, that didn't matter much at all really, we were here for the sun and the surf and the warm sea air. We were here to do nothing but work on our tans.

St. Martin beach is about as perfect as it gets. There are waiters who roam the coastline and are willing to retrieve a never-ending stream of ice cold buckets of Carib, tall dewy piña coladas, and our favorite at the time—large glasses of rum and Ting.

When our drinks arrived, Alex proposed a toast. We lifted our glasses. "To the both of you. I think you'll make excellent art auctioneers. You've got talent. I mean it. The both of you. You'll go far in this business."

I didn't know Alex had those kinds of compliments in him. However, over the next few months, the man would surprise us time and time again. Not only with encouragement, but with his inspirational attitude, the extremely motivating type of self-help droning that can only be accomplished by watching too many episodes of *The Oprah Winfrey Show*.

Our glasses clinked together, and I took a long, slow sip as the palm fronds swayed around us and the waves rolled onto shore. We had arrived in paradise.

Gertie stood up and walked to the water and dipped beneath the surface of the salty sea.

Alex looked down at his drink and swirled the ice cubes around, making them clink against his glass. "You know, I've been under a lot of stress. The ship, you know. Ship life."

He laughed and then took a deep breath. I didn't know quite what to say, but I knew exactly what he meant about the stress of ship life and what that can do to a person.

He continued, "I saw the way you two looked at me when I said Rashek was Indian trash—and well, I don't really think that. I just say things sometimes. I don't know. I'm just really stressed out. I've been on this ship for nearly four months. Too long. I'm ready for a break. I need a vacation from..."—he looked around at the beach—"from this vacation."

I told him I knew how he felt. I shared the story of how I had turned into a sea donkey too once. It was a few years back when I tried to stay out at sea for eight months straight. I became pretty *dark.* It was a rough time, and I found myself getting irritated over really little things.

We talked about how ship life can do strange things to crew members, how many a good man has been lost out at sea. Alex might have fallen overboard, but he knew how to reach for the lifeline and pull himself back on board.

I was glad to hear that Alex had come around. I reminded myself that we had only known Alex for just a few days. Yes, he had been an obnoxious scallywag at times, but that didn't mean that was who he *really* was—you know, deep down in his rum-and-Ting-soaked heart. He was human, and so by nature, he wasn't perfect. Neither was I, of course. I'd had more than my share of frustrating days in ship life. *Everyone deserves a second chance.* Besides, I was really starting to like him, that dirty seadog son of a gun.

I watched Gertie walk back out of the sea, all glistening with salty beads of Caribbean water. I leaned the beach lounger as far back as it could go. A mangy island dog, apparently inspired by some of the locals to grow its own clumpy mess of dreadlocks, came up and nuzzled itself next to me. I fed him one of my granola bars, which seemed to make him very happy. Then I leaned back in the lounger and fell asleep to the sound of waves washing onto shore and the wind rustling through the palms. I dreamt that Gertie and I were on a fantastic adventure aboard a giant, gleaming ship that took us to exotic islands all around the world. Then I woke up to find out that it all was true.

Our lives continued for the next few weeks in this predictable fast-paced pattern of art peddling and bid calling, from which we would occasionally be granted shore leave. We sailed from one golden-coasted island to the next, all of them infested with iguanas as well as locals asking us to ride in their taxis or buy their cigars. We usually plopped down on some beach where we were guaranteed access to a limitless supply of Red Stripe beer and hair-braiding professionals, people who knew no boundaries in their inventiveness when trying to persuade us to take on the hairstyles of Snoop Dog or Stevie Wonder. Unfortunately, Gertie never let them give her *cornrows*.

We continued to sell what Gertie and I thought was an astounding amount of art. However, this amount always left Alex and the M&R manager looking about as excited as a cruise ship crew member who finally gets on *Wheel of Fortune* only to win nothing but a cruise to Jamaica. *Gee, Pat. I just can't wait to see Ocho Rios one more time, you jerk.*

Even though we were taking in at least sixty-thousand dollars in sales per cruise, our commission was very small. That didn't matter much. Gertie and I were looking forward. We were excited about getting assigned to our own ship where we could work on our own. Once that happened, even if we only sold as much art as we were selling now, our commission would be around two thousand dollars a cruise. Even more enticing was the fact that these sales were considered low to Alex. Gertie and I would have been happy with half as much.

The day finally arrived for our big crossing, the day that passengers boarded the ship and we set sail from Miami with our bow pointed straight to Southampton, England. That morning, we walked into Alex's office and found him looking rather depressed.

"What's wrong?" Gertie asked.

"We're not going to make a dime on this cruise. These people are here for the ferry ride. They don't want to buy any art. You never do well on a crossing. Do you know how much tickets are for a crossing cruise? Some people only paid three hundred dollars for this cruise! We're in the cheap seats now, partners."

He was right. Alex was pretty much always right when it came to matters in the gallery. We sold some art, but not much. Yet, I learned a very valuable lesson, one that I will share with you here. If you're the type of person who is always looking for a great deal on a cruise—in other words, a person who has a pulse and does not have agoraphobia—then you need to mark your calendars for the dates that the cruise ships sail across the pond and journey from America to Europe, or vice versa.

Even after five years of working on cruise ships, I had no idea how good of a deal these cruises were. They cost much less than the vast majority of plane tickets from the US to England, and you get all the perks of being on a cruise ship: the food, the shows, the norovirus. That's the plus side. The downside—well, you have to be on a cruise ship for around ten straight days, often aboard a ship that's sailing in the same seas used in the film *The Perfect Storm*.

The worst part, however, is the cabin fever. No, a ten-day

long crossing on a cruise ship produces something far worse than cabin fever. It produces what experienced cruise ship doctors call a ship-berth breakdown.

Most of us have probably had the experience of going a bit bananas after spending too much time at home, but nothing compares to what happens to a person when they haven't seen a spit of land for more than seven days straight. Passengers begin to get a crazed look in their eyes, like a seagull that's part of a flock of birds where all the other birds are much better than him at getting the bits of bread that beachgoers throw into the air, and therefore he spends his life without ever tasting the wonders of stale baguette and resents the other seagulls mightily.

Nonetheless, the crossing cruises are one of the cheapest cruises on the blue highway, and I highly recommend climbing aboard if you have the chance, have exceptional balance, have a reasonably sound mind, and have a willingness to accept the fact that when the ice cream runs out there will be absolutely no more ice cream cones until you get to Southampton. I know, life is hard for passengers sometimes.

After ten days of sailing through waves so big we thought the ship may just break in half, our last day at sea finally arrived. Off in the distance, we could see the coast of England, that wonderful land of chaps and blokes (and apparently a high number of uncles named Bob) who bloody well know what *real* and *proper* football is (not this daft American bollocks with pads and helmets)—a place where cookies are biscuits and biscuits are scones, and where Freddie Mercury is thought to have had a jolly good set of teeth.

The three of us went out to the bow to watch the ship sail into port. I was ready to do more than kiss the ground—I wanted to eat a pile of dirt, to make it a part of me once again. After that, I wanted to find the nearest steak-and-ale pie as quick as possible. The quality of food in the crew area had really taken a turn for the worse as of late, which I hadn't thought was actually possible. Any more turns for the worse, and we would have been scraping the barnacles off the hull of the ship.

We still had coffee, though. I guess concentrated coffee syrup never really goes bad.

Gertie's hair fluttered in the wind. The sky was a steely gray, and the clouds looked as though they had taken out a winter lease over the English port, which they probably had. The days of warm winds and cold piña coladas were long behind us now it seemed. From this point forward we thought it would be hooded sweatshirts, wool socks, and thick lip balms that worked wonders on cold sores for us. A chilly wind blew over the bow of the ship as we pulled into port, and the cruise ship sounded its deep and thundering horn, again and again.

We were celebrating the great triumph of completing our magnificent ocean escapade, rejoicing with the loud and rumbling might of the cruise ship's roar. *Whooummmmmmph! Whooummmmmmph! Whooummmmmmph! Whooummmmmmph!* We pulled into harbor, and the old metal girl that had served us so well on our deep sea adventure was tied up to the dock. Her engines were finally shut down, and she was given a chance to rest in that calm wharf, a tranquil refuge from the stormy seas that she had battled so bravely.

There was still one more leg of our journey before we

reached what is known as dry dock. We still had to sail through the English Channel, into the North Sea, and then up the Elbe River to Hamburg, Germany, a two-day voyage. To our extreme joy, this was going to be a two-day cruise *without* passengers. Yes, this was the end of the line for our beloved, tropical shirt–wearing, chocolate melting cake–devouring, conga line-dancing, ten-meal-a-day eating friends. And we do love you.

You had to have a special pass to go on this next leg of the journey. You had to know what it was like to eat white rice for three meals a day. You had to know how it felt to realize that your most prized possessions in your crew quarters were an air freshener and a remarkably revealing Batman costume that you were just itching to wear at the next crew party. Yes, you had to be one of the special few who dare to leave all of their friends and family behind to go live in a place where the hull of a ship is referred to as "home sweet home". You had to be one of the brave men and women who throw caution to the wind and sign up to work aboard a sailing city where you may or may not have the opportunity to see sunlight for days at a time. You had to be a member of the special society of people who are willing to live closer to a bilge tank than should probably be legal.

If you wanted to keep sailing from Southampton, you had to show your crew member ID.

So I was quite surprised when I saw a rather large group of individuals waiting for the ship on the Southampton dock. There had to be about three hundred people, most of them men with burly characteristics like muscles, beards, cigarettes, and the kind of face that you usually find on pleasant places such as "Most Wanted" posters. They looked like a mob of

Vikings who were about to invade cruise liner land. Maybe we were picking up a crew of convicts to be transferred from a facility in Southampton to a prison in Germany, or perhaps we had stumbled across a very lost group of Harley Davidson enthusiasts who took an exceptionally wrong turn somewhere back in Ipswich.

"Who are *they*?" I asked, sounding like a child who's spotted a pair of Jehovah Witnesses walking up to his door for the first time.

"Contractors," Alex said. "*Bloody* contractors."

CHAPTER THIRTEEN

IF IT LOOKS LIKE DRY DOCK, AND IF IT SOUNDS LIKE DRY DOCK, RUN AWAY. RUN AWAY FROM THE DOCK.

If you've never had the opportunity to experience dry dock on a cruise ship, you're really missing something, something that you'll want to really miss every other time you are given the opportunity to experience it.

The contractor Vikings didn't wait until we reached Hamburg to start their invasion of our once pleasant cruise ship country. No, dry dock started the moment the contractors got on board, and it started with a bang, and then a buzz, and a saw, and a pow, and then was followed with a series of clicks, pings, pangs, booms, and thumps. And the noise never stopped. A pair of earplugs became my best friends during that two-day sail to Hamburg, during which time I felt as if I was living inside of a jackhammer.

Gertie and I had hoped to spend the two-day cruise relaxing on the lido deck sipping rum punch and mojitos from all the silly funnel-shaped passenger glasses that we never got to use. We'd had a busy schedule planned, which mostly included trips down the water slide and a hybrid of shuffleboard and beer pong that we had invented in the crew bar one night and were itching to try out. We were determined to discover what it was really like to cruise as passengers.

Instead, Alex told us we needed to get out of our lido-deck loungers and stop lying around like a pair of island lizards. He told us to put on a pair of gloves, a boiler suit, and a sturdy pair of safety glasses, and then help the rest of the crew cover the art gallery in plastic.

Yes, the first phase of dry dock was to get the ship looking as though it had been suddenly purchased by an old woman who cared less about what her house looked like and more about whether someone might lose control of the ketchup bottle and send a rogue dab of tomato sauce hurling toward her antique furniture. It was captain's orders: every square inch of carpeting and furniture had to be covered in plastic, which would shield valuables from all the dust and woodchips and sparks that would soon be found in nearly every room of the cruise ship.

Dry dock is fascinating, and it's a nice place to visit, but I really wish I wouldn't have had to live there. I had been through dry dock before. I knew there would be long periods of time, sometimes entire days, where all the water on the ship was shut off. The air conditioning system would often be inoperable too, leaving the ship either sweltering or frigid, depending on the outside temperature where your dry dock took place.

In our case, since the ship was in Germany in early spring, the ship would be about as cold as a glacial core sample. The Internet would be down for days at a time. There would be no television service, and we would have to live and eat with contractors, who often had manners similar to a pack of rabid wolves.

Did I mention the noise?

We didn't sleep for two nights, which was only slightly worse than the quality of shut-eye we were already getting.

The entire crew was talking about nothing but Hamburg. It became a sort of catchphrase, a buzzword. A single mention of Hamburg would create a sense of hope and happiness whenever it was uttered. We would pass someone in the hall, and we would say, "Hamburg!" and the other person would reply, "Hamburg!" It was all that needed to be said, because it was all that any of us were thinking about. It was our flag, our zeitgeist. Hamburg meant freedom. It meant a chance to dine on decent foods such as schnitzel, chewy pretzels with spicy mustard, and grilled bratwurst with tangy sauerkraut. It meant the chance to get a stout German beer in a big etched stein.

But most of all, for most of the crew, Hamburg meant prostitutes. There is a red-light district there, the Reeperbahn, that a lot of our shipmates were quite interested in visiting. Many crew members believed that the Reeperbahn was where they'd finally find that perfect present, the loveliest of all souvenirs that sailors can bring back to their wives from their adventurous days at sea: herpes and gonorrhea.

Gertie and I disembarked from the ship as soon as we roped up in Hamburg. We walked along the Elbe, a river of cold rushing water. We found a little shop that had cappuccinos, and we settled into a couple of chairs that gave us a view of the riverbank. It was a spot where we could nestle into a little portico that would block us from the icy winds that were blowing down the waterway. We huddled there and talked over our options. We *owned* the next ten days. They were ours to do what we pleased.

We talked at length about all the things we could do, all the places we could go. Then we decided to do what any two sane people with valid passports and a pocket full of cash who found themselves in Germany while it was still cold would do: we boarded the next flight to Paris.

What I remember about the city of lights is all like a dream. We arrived on the first day of spring. The locals claimed it was the first day that it hadn't been cold and rainy in months. Puddles were drying along the Champs Elysees. Flowers were blooming around the Eiffel Tower. The entire city had been washed clean by the long rainy winter. The sky was the color of a blue bird. It was warm in the sun, but still cool enough to wear a scarf and try our best to look like a proper pair of Parisians.

I remember a full moon rising over the sparkling city as we watched from the steps of Sacre Coeur. Banana and Nutella crêpes along the Seine. Drinking champagne and seeing the Eiffel tower glitter for the first time. Breathing the sweet fresh air in Luxembourg Gardens, and feeling more free than I had since I boarded the cruise ship several weeks earlier. Eating plate after plate of the most delicious *steak-frites,* beef bourguignon, and other things I can't pronounce properly.

In a flash, our Paris playtime was over. We stumbled back to the ship, wearing berets, our burps smelling like French wine and *jambon et fromage* baguettes.

Alex was waiting for us in his office. "I have some…news," he said. "We're being transferred."

"Where?" Gertie asked, sounding shocked.

"To the *MS Barnacle.*"

"What's it like? Where's it sailing to? When do we leave?" Gertie fired off questions as if they were bullets from a shipboard rifle.

"It's sailing around the Mediterranean. Barcelona is the home port. Cruises to Italy, France, Greece, Spain, Croatia. All over the Med. Good stuff. Some of the best cruises."

"That's wonderful," I said.

However, something on Alex's face said it just wasn't so. I was thrilled at the idea of being transferred to a ship in the Med. We had loved Paris. I couldn't wait to get back to the land of inexpensive good wine and croissants. And the Greek Isles, the coast of Italy—all just icing on the rum cake.

"It's a big transfer," Alex said. "Many of the crew members from this ship are going there all at once. Us and"—he looked down—"Angel. The M&R manager is going too."

We didn't let this little bit of bad news throw a spanner in *our* good times. No, we stayed positive. We could handle this.

"But there's something else," Alex said. "I've heard that it's not a very good ship. I heard it's a *dark* ship."

I had been on ships of darkness before. There were always a few of them floating around in the fleet. It's a well-known phenomenon in the cruise ship world. No one really knows how it happens, and no one really knows how to destroy them, but everyone knows that they are floating out there like little pesky black holes on the deep blue sea.

"Are you sure?" I asked.

"That's what I've heard. I guess we'll see."

I wanted to go back on a ship of darkness about as badly as a bride wants to hear the song "Love Stinks" played at her wedding.

Nonetheless, the ship gods had called our number. In two days' time, we would be on a plane headed for Barcelona, headed back to a place that I never thought I would return to again—a ship of darkness

PART THREE

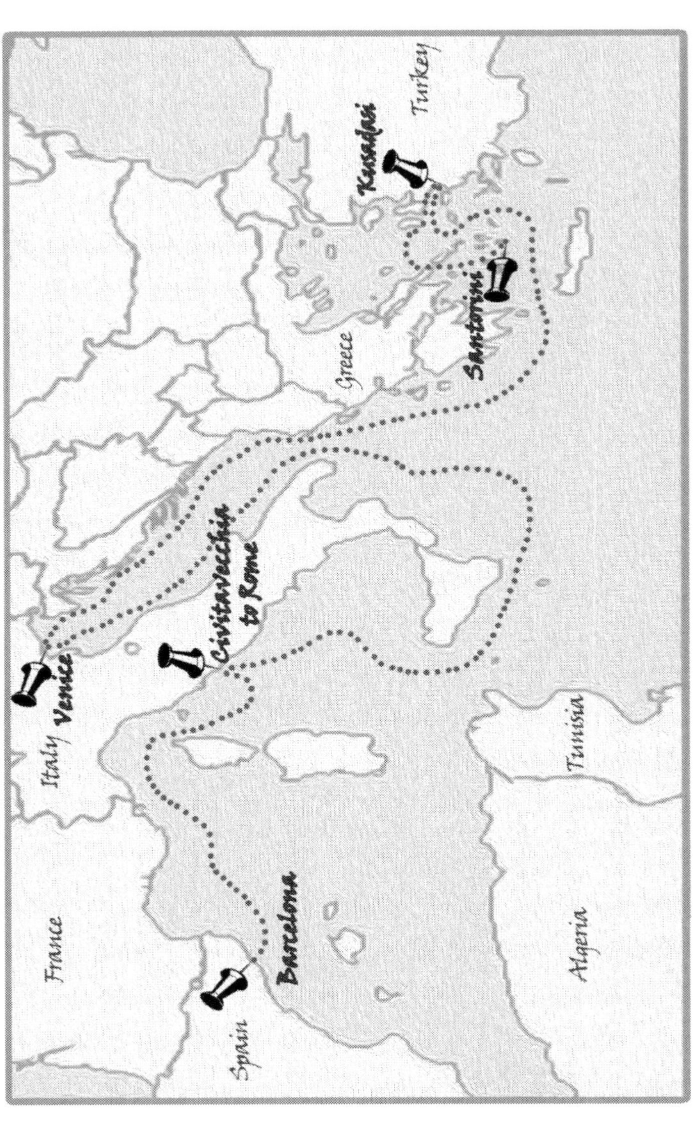
Venice
Civitavecchia to Rome
Kusadasi
Santorini
Barcelona
Italy
France
Spain
Greece
Turkey
Tunisia
Algeria

CHAPTER ONE

A Couple of Pirates with a Dream

There were naked people in the room with us. We were Americans, and so naturally we found this quite strange.

Gertie and I were in Germany—Hamburg. We were enjoying our last night of freedom before we were thrown back into ship life, a life on deck Z. Our vacation from our cruise ship vacation was coming to an end. Tomorrow we would board a plane at Hamburg International and fly to Spain—Barcelona—where we would walk up that rickety gangway one more time, and once again climb aboard the big cruise liner: home sweet sea-bound home for the next two months.

I sat in the humid sauna of the Hamburg hotel and tried not to catch a glimpse of the nude strangers sitting next to me. What I could see in my peripheral vision was quite enough, thank you. Enough for me to immediately develop a powerful phobia of the invisible but devilishly persistent forces of gravity.

I glanced at Gertie, rather perky and young, and I suddenly had the epiphany that, at that very moment, every bit of our firm skin was being relentlessly pulled down toward the center of the Earth. At the time, I didn't realize just how *true* that was.

At the time, I didn't know that omens sometimes like to hang out in German saunas.

I closed my eyes. My mind drifted back to the sea, and I

wondered what our life would be like once we walked aboard the *MS Barnacle,* our next assignment as a pair of art auctioneers in the cruise-ship art gallery. We really didn't know much about our new home.

Some of the crew members on our last ship had just come from the *Barnacle,* and they made the cruise liner sound about as charming as a 17th century French prison.

I imagined Gertie and myself standing at the end of the long concrete pier, waiting for our new ship to pull into port. I saw us standing in the rain, a thick fog swirling just off the Barcelona coast, dark and cold waves splashing against the dock. In the distance I heard the loud, bellowing blast of the cruise ship horn, which eerily echoed around the Spanish seaport. Then we get the first glimpse of our new home, the *MS Barnacle,* as it drifts from the swirling fog.

When our former crew members described the *MS Barnacle* to us, they called it a ship of darkness. You, reader, may have the tendency to dismiss this claim as a figment of my imagination—which I readily admit has a remarkable bent for exaggeration—but you should not fall into this dismissive trap. A ship of darkness is no laughing matter at all. These ships are as real as the intestinal viruses that patiently lurk on lido-deck railings, and they have about the same effect on the body and a much more sinister power over most seafarer's minds. Crew members consider them the Bermuda Triangles of happiness, health, and sanity for those too weak to resist their mysterious powers.

I knew they were real. I had lived on a ship of darkness once before. I had battled the violent sea beneath her shadowy sails. I had walked through its narrow, darkened halls, and stood at the bow of the black seadog of a ship.

And now, we were told, we were about to return to a ship of darkness once again.

The waiting was the hardest part. We didn't know what kind of living conditions we were going to be subjected to for the next two months. But for now, our plans were simple: let the steamy heat of the sauna in our Hamburg hotel wash our concerns and worries away in the sweat that dripped from our bodies.

But I had been having a hard time relaxing ever since those two Germans had walked into the sauna with us, pulled their towels from their bodies, and showed us their birthday suits.

Since my parents lived through the seventies, I had been raised with a healthy fear of the scandalous things that often occur in European saunas. Gertie looked at me with an expression that I had seen many times before—the distinct face that passengers make when they first come aboard a cruise ship with big, cheerful smiles and then are told that their Caribbean cruise may be compromised just a tad due to a little thing described as a "bit of engine trouble, which has also severely damaged the power, toilet, and air conditioning systems on the ship."

So we did what any sensible Americans would do. We quickly stood up, clutched our towels close to our bodies, and waddled out of there as fast as we could. Once safely on the other side of the foggy glass door, Gertie turned to me, let out a deep sigh of relief, and said, "Weird."

I wiped the sweat from my forehead. "Yes, definitely weird." Then I realized that Gertie and I had better get used to a culture clash with the Europeans, because we were about to spend the next two months sailing around the Mediterranean, trying to convince suspicious passengers and savvy art collectors to take a short break from their carefree cruise and purchase millions of dollars' worth of art while aboard our ship.

It was no easy task that we had before us. We had found that out while aboard our last ship. In my opinion, the difficulty in selling art aboard cruise ships was the inventory. Much of the artwork that we were trying to sell had as much artistic value as the paint splatters left on the drop-cloths that crew members use when they paint the ship rails.

Back in the Hamburg hotel, we gathered our belongings and a few hours later we were walking the streets of Hamburg, searching for an authentic German bistro where we could enjoy one last genuine bratwurst and a farewell pretzel—chewy with a side of spicy mustard, please.

We retreated from the cold and blustery German spring weather and took shelter inside a small café that had an oversized pretzel etched into the storefront window. The name of the place was something like Schnitzel, Sauerkraut, and Spatzle. Perfect. We nestled into a little table near a heater vent that blew a constant stream of toasty air over our toes. The table was near the front of the restaurant, where we could enjoy our last meal as people with a normal degree of freedom while watching the sun set behind the Elbe River—a river that was swiftly flowing out toward the ocean, just like us.

Gertie ordered stein-sized mugs of Weizenbier, the German wheat beer I had fallen in love with ever since we roped up in Hamburg. A waitress brought us a basket of warm pumpernickel bread. Gertie put a slice on her plate but just picked around the edges.

"What's wrong?" I asked. If Gertie wasn't guzzling that beer faster than a frat boy at a toga party, then something was definitely wrong, my friends.

"Nothing," she said.

"I can tell something's bothering you."

Gertie looked out the window toward the setting sun. The gray, swirling water of the Elbe was illuminated like a golden ribbon winding through the center of the old, picturesque city. The sun shining through the window brightened her face. "I don't know. I guess I'm a little worried. Who knows what this ship's going to be like?"

I agreed. Every cruise ship has its own unique culture, its own often-nonsensical set of rules, its own crew of "interesting" officers, as well as its own below-deck power struggles that are often all too easy to become entangled in if you don't navigate the stormy waters of the crew area with the sailor skills of Lord Nelson.

The waitress arrived with our beers. Gertie smiled and lifted her glass. "Cheers. To a new adventure."

We drank, and when the beer came down, her apprehension was gone, which didn't surprise me. Gertie was often the optimist between us, sometimes detrimentally so. We could be facing certain death, and she would have said something like, *"Don't worry. We'll probably come back as dolphins. It'll be fun."*

Gertie tore off a nub of bread. "They said the ship was one of the oldest in the fleet."

The *MS Barnacle* was decidedly not the flagship of Festivus Cruise Lines, but this wasn't the first old ship that we'd climbed aboard and lived to tell the sea-tale about. We knew that living on an old ship required a great deal of patience, an open mind, and a decent supply of buckets for bailing water. We knew what we were signing up for—or, rather, what we had been told to do. In any case, we understood that joining a new crew is always a gamble and that sometimes you're just dealt a bad hand. We had been on new, beautiful, absolutely grand ships. But this time, we were probably about to climb on a ship where the most valuable thing on board was the phone number for Sea Tow.

Gertie took a deep breath—one of those *I'm going to have to accept my fate* type of breaths. Then she forced a smile. "We'll be fine."

That was the spirit, Gertie. That was the Gertie that always kept a positive attitude.

I took a sip of the crisp German beer. "Yeah, we'll be fine. And hey, it's just a ship. It's just ship life. As long as we remember that it's not real, it can't get to us. It's just a fantasy. It's not real life. It's ship life."

Gertie perked up. "And think of all the incredible ports that we'll be sailing to. Barcelona. Cannes. Venice. Kusadasi." With each port she named, the twinkle in her eyes would shine just a bit brighter. She sped up, as if her words were being fired from fast-loading naval artillery. "And we'll be going to Rome. Dubrovnik. Naples. Livorno. Provence. *Santorini*."

The roll-call of ports sounded like the bucket list of a romantically involved couple that loved nothing more than ripe olives, fresh pizza, postcard-perfect beaches, the world's greatest wines, beautiful dark-haired women, and an endless supply of men who still believe that it's fashionable to wear Speedos to outdoor social gatherings.

"I can finally ride the donkeys in Santorini," she said,

holding her beer mug in the air. *Cheers to the donkeys of Santorini!* "We're going to Greece. The Greek Isles. I've always wanted to do that. Don't you want to ride the donkeys?"

To be honest, I had never heard of these apparently famous donkeys of Santorini, but I smiled and nodded anyway. *Just smile and nod, boys. Just smile and nod.* "Yes, let's ride the donkeys," I said and lifted my beer too. The last light of the Hamburg night dimmed to a soft purple glow. The Elbe River began to sparkle with the reflection of stars. "To the donkeys of Santorini."

"To the donkeys," Gertie said. "May we live to tell the tale."

I wasn't quite sure what she meant by that last bit, but I nodded again and took a big sip of the Weizenbier. Looking back on it all now, I realize that omens also like to relax in German pretzel parlors.

We may have been headed to a so-called ship of darkness, but that didn't mean we had to accept our fates without a fight. Besides, maybe the ship wouldn't be so bad, after all. Maybe it had changed. Maybe we could make a difference, a positive difference, and turn that ship around. We had faced challenges before. We had encountered some pretty rough seas over the years.

We knew that even if you fall overboard and find yourself all alone on a great big, scary ocean, it doesn't mean that all is lost. We knew that sometimes you are saved at the very last minute, right when you are about to give up, right before you let yourself drift down into the dark depths of the unforgiving sea.

We vowed right then and there that we would be the beacons of positive light that would shine throughout the ship of darkness and bring a sea change to the crew-member culture aboard that lost vessel. We had heard the calls of the forgotten sailor's souls from across the deep blue sea, and we were going to climb aboard that depressed ship and answer their SOS pleas as boldly and as fearlessly as we knew how.

And with us we would bring the lifesaving first-aid kit that every forlorn crew member aboard a ship of darkness needs: a red satchel filled with positive attitudes and optimistic outlooks, a sturdy hand-powered bilge pump, a couple of gas masks hooked up to oxygen tanks, diving gear in case we suddenly found ourselves with an unexpected reef in our crew quarters, a lifetime supply of coconut and pineapple-scented air fresheners to mask the smell of our crew cabin, a warm wool blanket for when the ship thermostat gets stuck on the setting labeled "ice cream freezer", a thin sheet for when said air conditioning system breaks down, horse tranquilizers to be used when the ship is placed under "Red Alert", the obligatory bottle of habanero hot sauce to mask the otherwise unpalatable foods that are served in the crew mess, our very own industrial-grade life raft just in case we decide to jump ship or to use before the ship finally gives up and settles into its final resting place somewhere around the Mariana Trench, and a highly experienced maritime lawyer that specializes in overtime violations and workplace living-condition grievances.

Ship of darkness, ship of shmarkness. It might be dark now, but wait until we get through with it. We'll have that suicidal crew singing "Anchors Away" as fast as a cruise ship doctor can say, "Yes, you have norovirus. Definitely norovirus." And then we'll go to Santorini and ride our donkeys straight into the sunset—a big, orange, Greek sunset.

And we'll laugh our entire way around the world, leaving a big foamy wake of unforgettable memories trailing behind our old, junky cruise ship.

Just a couple of pirates with a dream.

Just a couple of kids who did *not* know the difference between optimism and wishful thinking.

CHAPTER TWO

Gertie Gets Her Popes in a Row

"It's pronounced *Bar-the-lona,*" Gertie said as we sat in the industrial-gray terminal at Hamburg International. I was watching, through the floor-to-ceiling windows, as several rain-streaked planes took off into cloud-filled skies.

I took a sip of my cappuccino: frothy in an oversized mug. For me, the prospect of traveling to countries where cappuccino preparation is considered an art form on par with Michelangelo's *David* was one of the most thrilling perks of our upcoming Mediterranean itinerary.

"*Bar-the-lona*?" I asked. "I'm not saying it that way. That's like when Americans talk about Spanish countries and, out of nowhere, adopt a Spanish accent just to say the country's name. It sounds ridiculous."

"But that's what it's *really* called." Gertie said and put out her hands to emphasize the point.

She was wearing a fashionable red sweater with a low-hanging neck, valentine-red nails, matching lipstick, a travel-bug twinkle in her eyes. We were always most comfortable on the move; fickle nomads ready to pack up the tent as soon as we felt the first cool breeze blow through the valley. We had gypsy genes and vagabond blood running somewhere deep in our seadog souls. Two restless hearts searching the sea for the next adventure, the next ramble.

I laughed. "*Bar-the-lona*. Nope."

Gertie shook her head. "Ughhh." She looked out the

window. "I want to see the pope."

"Okay?" I said. Her mind seemed to work in a way where completely unrelated subjects were somehow connected. "In *Bar-the-lona?*"

"See. That's not so hard. Now you don't sound so American. We should blend in. Like locals. We'll have more fun that way."

"Sorry. Barcelona."

Gertie rolled her eyes. "No. In Rome. You're impossible. The pope. In Rome." She reached into her purse, pulled out a small pink notebook, and quickly flipped it open with the conviction of someone with the one thing I hate most in this life—a plan. I was a fly-by-the-seat of my pants kind of guy. The quintessential just-wing-it type of fellow. Gertie, well—she didn't *just* have her ducks in a row; she had her ducks performing a choreographed dance routine, like those performed at football games where the ducks, when viewed from an aerial perspective, spell out clever words like "quack" and "fowl ball". She had the birthdate of her future first child already marked on her calendar. Her burps were on a schedule. *Oh, it's 10:27…burp.*

The moment we found out what our cruise-ship-port itinerary for the next two months would be, I saw the hamster wheel turning in her head. I looked at the first page in her notebook: the word *ROME* scribbled at the top followed by a numbered list of things to do that continued onto the next page, the handwriting getting smaller and smaller as it neared the bottom.

"What's that?" I asked, looking down at Gertie's notebook, even though I knew the answer.

"Our schedule," she said all chipper and bright.

"Hmm. What if I planned out a few of our ports?"

"If you planned our port days, we'd spend our only day in Provence sleeping in our crew cabin."

She was right. I loved to explore ports, but I found ship life to be somewhat exhausting after a month or so. And whenever I imagined making the extra effort to get off the ship and explore the ports, sometimes I just wasn't up for that. Cruise ship crew members call the boring ports *sleeper ports* or just *sleepers.* The lingo is also used to describe ports that crew members have already been to a million times. A conversation might go like this:

Crew member A: I've never been to Ocho Rios. What's it like?

Crew member B: Oh, it's a *sleeper.*

After three or four months on board, I'm usually either dying to get off the ship whenever I can, or I just want to use my time in port as a chance to get some decent shuteye. When the cruise ship is in port, the ship is the quietest. In fact, port time (apart from the day when the ship is in its home port) is really the only time that the ship is quiet at all. Most of the crew members are either sleeping because the passengers are gone—and therefore their workload is at its lightest—or are off the ship themselves. The ship engine is turned off. The ship isn't rocking. Waves aren't slapping against the hull, which often compromises a crew member's ability to sleep by sounding as soothing as a Chinese gong being struck with a rubber mallet by someone with the upper body strength of a mixed martial arts fighter.

Back in the airport terminal, I thought about what Gertie had said. I swirled a biscotti in my cappuccino. "Yeah, I guess you're right. I enjoy more down time than you. But can we compromise? You know, not stay on-the-go all the time." I envisioned us enjoying lazy breakfasts and slow European-style lunches at seaside cafes that overlooked a rocky coast where the sun-washed Mediterranean splashed into a cloudless sky, or at little bistros where we could enjoy views of picturesque piazzas and old-world architecture while sheltered from the sun beneath bright-red Peroni parasols.

She picked up a pen and pointed to the long list in her notebook in a *now, let's get down to business* sort of way. "We only have a few hours in each port. We should make the most of it, but yes, I'll compromise. So. Rome. The pope. I looked it up, and you won't believe how lucky we are."

"We're going to get to ride in the pope mobile?" I said.

Gertie smirked, and then pointed back to the first item on her Rome schedule: one word, *POPE*. "No. Did you know that the pope gives his papal address on Wednesdays?"

The only thing I knew about the pope was that he wore a funny hat and that he spoke way more Latin than anyone else I knew. I shook my head.

Gertie continued, "And guess when we'll be in Rome? On a Wednesday. We'll get to see the pope give his papal address. At the Vatican."

"Really?" Now that was really something. Gertie and me and the pope. All in the same room. Who would have thought? "And it all lines up perfectly?" I asked.

"Well, I wouldn't say *perfect*. It's going to be tough. The ship actually docks in Civitavecchia, which is about an hour's drive from Rome. I did some research. We can take the rail and get there about as fast and for less money. But the pope will give his address at ten in the morning. We'll probably be able to get off the ship at eight, but we'll have to really book it to make it to the Vatican on time."

"An early start. We'll make it," I said. "All aboard the pope mobile."

"And that's the start of our Rome day. Next we'll go to the Vatican—probably two hours would be good..." Gertie fired off an entire guidebook full of must-see attractions that most tourists would plan to visit over a three-month-long hiatus in Italy. I zoned out somewhere around the Trevi fountain. My big plans for a languid lunch of lasagna and Lazio wine at Piazza Navona had burned up in a big cloud of Gertie's overambitious smoke. But hey, I wasn't complaining. I had the best kind of tour guide in all of Italy: one that's free, knows how to navigate the transit system, and might let you kiss her after the tour is over if you play your cards right. No, I didn't have anything to complain about.

I looked out over the wet runway and sank into my chair as Gertie continued to spout off her never-ending to-do list for Rome. I could hear the other people around us speaking German: a woman trying to teach her son how to speak softly in the airport, a middle-aged man and his wife arguing, an old German woman talking on her cell phone and laughing in a soft, strained way. It might sound strange, but most of what I had experienced in my life that featured the German language had been in Hollywood films about World War II. Every time I found myself out in Germany where I could hear the language, I felt as though I was walking around in *Schindler's List* or *Life is Beautiful* or something. I expected to see Steven Spielberg around every corner. That always left me feeling rather unsettled, thinking about all the tragedy that had taken place in the country just years earlier—a war that members of my family had fought in.

I enjoyed my time in Germany, but I was ready to move on, ready to go somewhere with architects that valued beauty a bit more than function, a place where the locals always chose wine over beer. I wanted to go to countries where you found more Piaggio scooters and disgruntled donkeys than Mercedes and Volkswagen taxis, travel to coastal European villages where Gertie could get out of her sweater and back into the bikini that she preferred. Gertie and I just didn't fit in with the German culture. Germany didn't have a single decent beach and we always looked rather out of place drinking piña coladas and Mai Tais on the Elbe. Not to mention that we couldn't find a decent rum and Ting anywhere in the place. No, we were ready to sail to sunnier shores. We were ready to hang out for a while at Club Med.

"Do you think the money will be better?" I asked.

Gertie looked up from her notebook. "You haven't been listening to me, have you?"

"The Trevi Fountain. The Vatican. Piazza Navona. Of course I have."

Gertie scanned over her list: the fact-checker at work. "Piazza Navona isn't on my list. Besides, the Trevi Fountain was way back at the beginning."

"I can't keep all the piazzas and pizzas and leaning towers of Pisa straight. You know how I am with foreign languages. Remember the time I pointed to a menu in Paris and said 'I want this one' only to have the waiter inform me that I was pointing to the gratuity statement at the bottom of the menu?"

Gertie laughed and then caught herself. "I know you weren't listening."

"So what do you think? Do you think we'll make more

money?"

"Where?"

"On the ship. In the art gallery. Remember? We're not here for a vacation with the pope. We're here to work as art auctioneers on the cruise ship."

"Right. Umm, yeah, I think so. I hadn't really thought about it before you mentioned it, but yeah, that would seem right. The cruises are more expensive in the Med, and so the passengers might have a little more extra money to spend on art. Alex will know. We'll ask him once we get on board."

"Ahhh. Just the mention of his name makes me feel like I have paperwork I need to finish." Alex Ashebury: art salesman extraordinaire, the head honcho of the art gallery for the next two months aboard the *MS Barnacle*.

We had gotten off on the wrong peg-leg at first, but after a while we really started to like Alex. Not as a ship-life friend per se, but more in the way you learn to like the algae-eating slug in your fish tank back home: He's not your favorite sea creature in your little, fake aquatic environment, but you grow to appreciate his better qualities and quickly realize just how much you really depended on the grimy fellow, even though he is a slimy, scum-sucking sea slug who leaves a trail of mucus behind him wherever he goes. No, all joking aside. We eventually loved the guy, that salty seadog son of a gun.

"Two months," Gertie said. "We just have to get through these next two months, and then…" She gazed out over the tarmac and stared into the distance as if she was lost in a utopian daydream, as if she were spinning through visions of a golden world. "And then we'll be out on our own."

I still didn't believe it. I was the *I'll-believe-it-when-I-see-it* type of guy. And nowhere is skepticism more appropriate than on a cruise ship. I don't even get excited about our next port until I step foot on dry land. Why the pessimism, you ask? I'll give you three reasons: the *Carnival Triumph,* the *Costa Concordia,* and a little lesser-known ship—the *White Star Titanic.* That last one was full of optimistic people who said the ship was unsinkable. Sometimes it pays to be a pessimist. Sometimes good old-fashioned optimism can cost you your life. The pessimists were the ones who walked out on the *Titanic's* top deck sometime around two a.m. and took one look at the big chunk of iceberg slowly melting near the bow of the cruise liner and thought, *"We're all going to effing die."* The pessimists were the first ones in the lifeboats. They were the survivors. Maybe that's why there are more pessimistic people in the world. Because optimists die first. Pessimism is deep in our genes because it was passed on to us by the legions of pessimists who lived long enough to procreate.

"Yeah," I said. "We'll see."

Gertie shook her head. "You're always such a pessimist. You have to visualize success. You need to make a dream board. You need to think positively."

"You can't think facts away." I said, and I knew I was opening a can of worms, but to be honest, I kind of felt like fishing.

"If we believe that we're going to make it, then it will happen," she said. "We have to believe it." She put her hands in front of her face and then spread them apart in the same way that a magician does when he says *abracadabra.*

"We believed—completely believed—that we would be art directors by now, and that we'd be out on our own at this point too. That's what the company told us when we first took this job. I believed it. You put it on your dream board. We both visualized it. Now, we're about to board a plane for a two-month contract on the *MS Barnacle.* And we're still only art associates. Do you think they're just dangling a carrot?"

Gertie looked out the window, rain streaking down the thick glass panes, a steel-gray sky, wind whistling somewhere out on the tarmac. "But this is for the best. This happened for a reason. Everything happens for a reason," she said.

At the time, Gertie could have been the poster child for Dr. Norman Vincent Peale's book, *The Power of Positive Thinking.* I wanted to believe her. I really wanted to believe it—and at the time, I did, with all my cappuccino-soaked-heart.

CHAPTER THREE

The Fighter Pilot and the End of a Cold War

We needed a taxi from the *Bar-the-lona* airport. Luckily, once again, Gertie was prepared. She had done her homework and learned that the taxi drivers often try to overcharge Americans for fare to the cruise terminal. The guidebook she had bought in Hamburg said the trip should cost around twenty-five euros. Most of the cabbies were asking sixty. A few drivers just drove off when they realized we were savvy, but we finally found one who agreed on a fair price.

Our driver raced through the Spanish hills at speeds that ensured instant death if the vehicle came into contact with anything other than air. We tried to make conversation along the way. Gertie asked the cabbie where the best bars were in *Bar-the-lona*. He replied, "*Ceviche*? Um, *compras*?"

So we decided to just enjoy the scenery. The taxi climbed a steep, scrubby hill that looked exactly like the dry, shrubby slopes of California. When we reached the top of the mountain and crested the peak, we could see the cruise ship terminal below us, extending out from the base of the mountain all the way to the Spanish coast. Several behemoth-sized cruise liners were roped up at the docks. The blue of the Mediterranean Sea stretched out to the horizon.

The driver darted down the hillside and brought the taxi to a halt in front of the cruise port. I was hit with a wave of heat as I stepped out of the cab. Gertie tipped the driver generously after he didn't try to pull some shenanigan in front of the cruise port like trying to charge us an extra ten euro for each piece of luggage, which seems to be an international tradition for taxi drivers who are used to dealing with typically wealthy cruise ship passengers.

We wheeled our luggage up to the terminal and told the Indian security guard that we were *Barnacle* sign-ons. A few minutes later, a cruise ship officer finally found the time between a busy schedule of sunbathing on the crew deck in a Speedo and sipping cappuccino on the bridge to come down to the cruise terminal and escort the newbie crew members onto the ship. I assumed the officer would be an Italian, because 99.99999999 percent of them are. But the fellow who walked up to the security station, dressed in an all-white uniform with yellow stripes on his shoulder boards, was a young Filipino kid: short, squat, black hair, gelled fohawk, aviator glasses, big biceps, looking like an Asian fighter pilot straight out of *Top Gun*. He didn't smile when he saw us. No, he was too cool, too macho for that sort of thing, the kind of guy who believed that enthusiasm was a weakness.

"New art auctioneers?" he asked flatly from the other side of the X-ray machine.

Gertie waved. "Yeah, that's us."

"Bags through the X-ray. I'll meet you at the gangway." Top Gun turned around and walked away. *Welcome to the Barnacle. Please leave your hospitality at the gangplank.*

I nearly pulled all the muscles in my back while trying to lift Gertie's luggage onto the conveyor belt, which was about as heavy as a prop used in one of those *World's Strongest Man* competitions. The Indian security guard, keeping in custom with others of his fun-loving ilk, had the healthy appearance and cheerful personality of a wax sculpture.

We wheeled our bags back into the heat and then walked down the concrete pier, towering ships on both sides, a canyon of cruise ship hulls. I could hear the clacking of Gertie's red high heels echoing off the tunnel of cruise liners. Gertie insisted on wearing high heels. Gertie always tried to look her best for ships.

I put a hand up to my forehead to shield the sun. Our new home came into view. "She's pretty small," I said.

The *MS Barnacle* looked to be about half the size of our last ship, but other than that, it really didn't look so bad. A little paint here and there, a good scrubbing, and the old girl would look as good as new.

Her ropes, tied to the rusting bollards at the edge of the dock, creaked and stretched. The bright white sun-washed hull gleamed in the morning light. Every shade of blue graded the turquoise water from shore to sea. The salt-drenched air was as thick and hot as a summer-hurricane rain in the Deep South.

"I like the smaller ships," Gertie said. "Our first ship was small. The crew was so fun. Everybody knew each other. Fewer passengers. Less work. It was very relaxed." She scanned the length of the vessel. "Well, relaxed as far as cruise ships go."

I knew what she meant. Back then, I was in the band, and she was a social host. She hosted bingo games in the promenade lounge and drank with passengers, getting as sloppy as a sailor on shore leave. She would occasionally show up on our showband stage to perform in one of the social host acts. For this she'd always be dressed in a fairly-sexy croupier's outfit to perform a ridiculous skit for a thousand or so passengers who were dozing in and out of their food comas. The skit required me to do a drum roll when the male cruise director—a guy with a remarkably hairy chest, a bushy mustache, and a belly that closely resembled a rum barrel—came prancing on stage in a ballerina's tutu and then mooned the audience. This was precisely when I needed to hit my largest, loudest drum-set cymbal for the big finish. Timing was everything in this type of sophisticated show. *And folks, that's what you call working on a cruise ship for a living. There's no business like show business.*

Geez, those were the good old days. We didn't make much money back then, but at least we still had fingernails that weren't all chewed off and digestive systems that were ulcer-free. It was a trade-off. Everything was a trade-off in ship life. Now we were art auctioneers who were sailing on a promised-sea of dollar bills, but the art job was quickly becoming more of a drag than what happens when you suck a dolphin into the cruise ship thrusters, and our stress levels were climbing to heights that were probably equal to that crazy-looking guy in Edvard Munch's painting called *The Scream.*

Back at the *MS Barnacle,* we dragged our luggage up to the edge of the crew gangway. The metal stairway to ship-life groaned as the cruise liner rolled ever-so-slightly in the harbor tide. Gertie and I stepped aside to allow a stream of disembarking crew members off the ship, their pale and sleepy faces leaning into the Barcelona (sorry, bar-the-lona) sunlight like a stampeding herd of milkweeds stretching for a dapple of sun in an otherwise darkened forest. Their exhausted expressions flowered into smiles as they stepped ashore, blinking at the bright light, as if they were Neanderthals emerging from their musty cavern dens after a long, gloomy winter of lovely cave living.

At the end of the line was a notably busty, dark-haired, tan-skinned, luscious sea creature: long legs like a great blue heron, short skirt, white button-up that was obviously custom tailored to draw the eyes from her tiny waist to the unbuttoned front, where one would discover wonderfully compressed and boosted breasts that were big enough to double as life rafts in the event of a maritime disaster, the floral-stitched edges of a lacy bra teasing sailors like a sea siren from the island of Capri. Her mating call of stilettos clanked against the metal gangplank, and it was paired with a walk like a runway model who never got enough attention as a child, a pouty face that made me finally understand what all of those Barry White songs were about, and two yellow stripes on her shoulders that left no doubt about whether she knew how to take control of a ship in distress.

The Bathsheba of the seven seas, a shipwreck waiting to happen.

As the cruise-vessel vixen trotted by, Gertie (always the consummate friendly) flashed a welcoming smile and a kindly wave. The busty beauty looked at Gertie, arched one expertly tweezed eyebrow, and then made an expression like cruise ship passengers make when they discover that we don't bring ice cream machines and colored sprinkles to the passenger lifeboat drill.

Gertie's waving slowed and then stopped altogether. While her hand drifted back down to her side, Gertie said in her distinctly catty way, "Did you see the way that b**** looked at me? I'll rip her face off."

"My, my, my," I said. "I guess you don't welcome a little onboard competition, do you?"

Gertie squinted: small distrusting eyes. "Competition, huh?"

I had unwittingly walked to the end of the pirate-ship plank. Sharks were circling below. Gertie had her sword drawn. I might as well have just walked off the edge. I wasn't in the doghouse. Worse. I was in the seadog house, a house that bobbed in an ocean filled with great white sharks, and I had just chummed the waters.

Maybe I could talk her down. "Well," I began in a high-pitched voice, "I mean, come on. She was kind of a decent-looking woman." Calling the double-D delight a decent-looking bird was like calling Marylin Monroe a toadfish. I felt Gertie's pirate sword poke at my ribs.

"So, you're saying that a *'decent-looking woman'* is competition for *me?* I saw the way you looked at her."

Logic: A man's best friend, but a couple's worst nightmare.

She was right. I had looked at the gal as if it was 1912 again and her breasts were the last lifeboat on the *Titanic. Rose, I'll never let go.* Sometimes I could be such a monkey-jacket wearing, hornswoggling, seadog scamp. Who knew how long I'd be in the brig this time?

I just lowered and shook my head. I heard Gertie's high heels clanking up the gangway, leaving me behind as she boarded the *MS Barnacle.*

I looked past Gertie and saw Top Gun standing at the top of the gangway, waving at me in a *Hurry up; I don't have all day* sort of way.

I could hear the siren's song once again, drifting into port on the *Bar-the-lona* waves. Her voice was clear and soothing, and she sang her seductive song:

Back in your cruise ship days
You used to dance on the decks
You laughed on the water
You sailed with the sun

Go where the current does push
Sail where the ocean does pull
Back in your cruise ship days
You had a life filled with fun

Back in your cruise ship days
You had islands in your eyes
You had oceans on your mind
You and your crew bar chums

It's just a cruise ship dream
It's just a fantasy
It's not reality
Those ships at sea

It will be better than before
You'll find yourself on ship and shore
Reclaim your life of port and starboard
Now in your cruise ship days

I pulled our bags up the *Barnacle's* gangway and into the darkened alcove of the cruise ship security station. Top Gun said something to the Indian security guard, who waved us through the threshold and onto the I-95, the long hallway stretching the length of the ship.

We walked about ten steps, and then Top Gun put out his hand. "Wait here."

Hurry up and wait. Welcome to ship life.

Top Gun disappeared behind a door down the hallway.

I thought about how sometimes when I walk into a place, the smell triggers strong associations and memories. Whenever I go inside an old Florida beach house anywhere along the Gulf of Mexico that hasn't been remodeled since the 1970s, one with wicker furniture and green shag carpet, bead-board ceiling, salt air–soaked walls—a beach retreat where a lifetime of blue crab and shrimp has been boiled and where swimsuits and towels have hung on the balcony to dry for decades—I get overwhelmed by memories of my childhood. I had a similar experience when I smelled the inside of the *MS Barnacle* for the first time, except the memories weren't exactly what I would call 'fond'. It smelled like an old big-box grocery store built in the sixties with blinky fluorescent lighting and thin, clapboard walls where milk was spilled and had soured somewhere around aisle nine.

A few minutes later, Top Gun popped out into the hallway and waved at us to hurry up. "Leave your bags outside," he said. The sign on the door: *CREW OFFICE.*

We walked in, and Gertie made another attempt at a smile and a wave to the woman who was working behind the counter. Nothing. "Hello," Gertie said cheerfully, trying again. The woman kept her head down, typing away on her keyboard, as expressionless as a jellyfish. Gertie gave me a side glance, and then shrugged.

The computers in the room looked rather outdated, like something that could still connect to Netscape. I looked around for floppy discs. The machines appeared as if they had just enough memory and processing power to run a video game with the high-tech graphics of *The Oregon Trail.* Her computer was R2D2 to C3PO. No, it was worse—Q1C1 at best. I hoped that the art department delegated a little more to their IT budget. I had forgotten how to operate DOS after we sold our Tandy 1000 back in 1989.

The woman behind the keyboard (blue suit jacket, narrow face, stub nose, shadowed cheeks, straight black hair, pale as a Greenland native in the middle of winter) lifted a small, tan-colored envelope with the numbers *0604* scribbled on it. I could see that a different set of numbers had been written on the envelope and then scratched out. "These are your room keys," the woman said mechanically in a Russian accent that had as much warmth as a cruise ship ice sculpture. She almost set the packet down on the partition that separated us from the seemingly animatronic crew of office workers on the other side, but then she picked it back up and looked at the numbers again. She fiddled with her mouse and tapped a few more times on her keyboard as if she were double checking, squinting at the computer screen. Then she tilted her head quickly to one side, in a dismissive way, and set the envelope back on the counter and slid it toward us. "You are on this floor. Take a right out the door. Go past elevator. Turn right into second doorway. zero-six-zero-four. Here are your velcome"—welcome—"aboard packets."

"Thanks," Gertie said.

"Next," the woman called out like a slaughterhouse foreman.

We walked out onto the I-95 and found Top Gun pacing. "Ah, great. Head to your rooms and get your luggage inside. Petryk and Natalievsky will swing by for the handover." He stormed down the hallway as if he were running late for a pressing appointment on the flight deck.

I called after him. "Who's Petryk?"

He turned around, back stepping. "Old art director."

He turned back around and blended into the crowd of crew members. I called after him again. "Where's Alex?"

I saw some hands shoot up out of the crowd as Top Gun dodged a forklift that was zipping down the corridor, beeping loudly as it zoomed through the crowd, parting the crew members like Moses on the Red Sea. The forklift was carrying Banana Mountain down the I-95. *Oh, it's banana mountain! I can't wait to pick fruit from your fertile mountain slopes once again. Come back banana mountain!* Top Gun didn't turn around. He just shrugged and kept walking toward his next shipboard duty. Banana Mountain drove off into the Red Sea of seafarers, never to be seen again…until next turn-around day, of course…and every turn-around day after that…for all of eternity. No one can stop Banana Mountain. No one.

And no one can stop ship time either. Not even Top Gun. Today was turn-around day, the busiest port day of the itinerary, when the ship is in home port, resupplying, refueling, swapping passengers, exchanging luggage. The clock was ticking. Every one of our crewmates were scrambling to get their checklists ticked off so they could escape out into the coastal sun and taste a salty bit of freedom in Spain for a moment.

The bustling crew members that zigged and zagged down the I-95 and trickled into every tributary hallway made the ship hum with a chaotic buzz, as if we had creeped inside the dark dusty tunnels of a fire-ant hill right when some sadistic, chubby-cheeked kid turned on a garden hose and poured a thick, cold, glassy stream of water right down into the colony mound that made all the ants go nuts as they scrambled for survival. We were in the heart of the beehive, and the queen had just been plucked from her throne. The worker bees were going bonkers like we had never seen before.

We fought our way to our new crew cabin, passing entire groups of crew members with glazed-over eyes and the mindless focus of sleepwalkers.

"This is it," Gertie said and opened a door, just off the I-95. We took a right turn into a short stub of a hallway with a door at the other end. *Wait. We are standing in the middle of the ship. This isn't good. Plus, we're on deck zero. But we are officers?* I looked to my left and saw a door with the numbers spelled out in little stickers, the kind you find on cheap mailboxes in the suburbs. The silver and black numbers were peeling at the edges—*0604*.

Gertie shuffled through the envelope and pulled out a keycard. She took a breath and lifted her eyebrows one time, and then shoved the card into the door. "Well, the moment of truth."

At the top of the door handle, a light flashed red and then green. I heard a click. She turned the handle and swung the door open.

At the back of the room, we found our worst nightmare: a wall. Right where our beautiful porthole window had been on our last ship—the little round window that let the beautiful sunlight pour into our lives like a fountain of pure gold—now we saw nothing but a barren, solid, tan, dirty, old wall that was probably about as clean as the gangway handrails at the end of embarkation day. I thought back to the time when we could look out our porthole window and see the ocean, the beautiful and shimmering ocean. Back to when we could watch those sunny Caribbean islands with honey-colored coasts of rock and beach sail past, and cruise by those vibrant island villages that looked as if they were towns that only sold bright-colored paint. Against the back wall was a bunk bed, both bunks as narrow as the coffin-sized bed on our last ship.

Gertie turned to me, and said in a chipper tone, "Not exactly what I was hoping for, but I'm sure we can spruce it up a bit. It'll feel like home in no time."

Gertie: the Mary Poppins of ship life. Just a spoonful of sugar and a bit of elbow grease, and she'd have the wreckage of the *Queen Anne's Revenge* in shipshape.

Just when I was about to inspect the cabin further, I heard a distinctly Russian voice from behind me. "Helloooo."

Gertie and I turned around to find a pair of very happy-looking people waving at us. It was Petryk (short, thin, peach fuzz mustache, spiked dark hair, black suit and tie) and Natalievsky (tall, model thin, dirty-blond curls, big-eyed kitten on the front of her T-shirt, stone-washed jeans, gray flats, blue eyes with sea-foam green specks).

Petryk poked his Ruski head into the crew cabin. "So, this is your new home? What do you think?"

I thought the cabin looked like the kind of place where we were likely to find roaches the size of luxury SUVs and rodents that were sometimes employed on Hollywood sets as stunt doubles for buffalos in cowboy flicks, but I knew it would be a waste of air. Petryk was on his way out. He didn't care about what kind of room we ended up with.

You may think I sound too cynical right now, but nowhere in life are people more in touch with their inner *what's-in-it-for-me* selves than in ship life. On a ship at sea, self-interest isn't a matter of selfishness; it's simply the fabric of survival.

Gertie was looking at a sprawling patch of rust on the wall near the metal trim around the "bathroom" door, the bathroom being a tad larger than the one on the airplane that we flew aboard to get to the cruise ship. "It's not as nice as the room on our last ship."

I peeked into the bathroom. It looked as if I would have the luxury of a half-inch of space between my kneecap and the shower curtain when sitting on the toilet. As a matter of convenience, I could use the sink as an armrest.

Nothing new, really. Just another crew cabin head.

Petryk shrugged. "You hungry? Let's go to the passenger buffet on lido deck and finish the handover."

With our luggage locked in our quarters, we followed Petryk as he raced through the cramped, chaotic, mono-color labyrinth of the crew area. We fought to keep up with Petryk who worked his way through the subsurface maze like a lab rat with an eidetic memory that possesses the skills of a championship boxer: bobbing and weaving, darting and ducking, a fancy-footwork machine. I sprinted up a set of stairs; the stairwell ship-hull white.

Petryk looked as if he was leaning into the wind and rain of a fierce squall. His eyes were as bright as a lighthouse beacon, his face as determined as an Admiral at the Battle of Trafalgar. Why so fast? Why so eager?

Of course; of course! Petryk wasn't marching to the buffet line. No, Petryk was marching home.

We popped through a doorway, the door marked *PASSENGER AREA*. We walked into a new world: light, bright light, dark blues, exquisite stitched fabrics of reds and golds, long wooden bar tops with brass ship-clocks on top that had every component of their gyroscopic machinery polished to a high sheen, teak floors, marble tiles, glass elevators, porthole windows big enough to walk through if the glass were removed, the blue-green sea sparkling to the horizon, tuxedo-clad waiters balancing trays topped with a pyramid of stacked glasses of rum punch and piña coladas and Mai Tais with paper umbrellas, carpets with a repeating pattern of compasses and life preservers, white-gloved servants in black-tailed coats with towel-animal rabbits on gleaming silver platters, clean air, fresh air, crystal air, color, color, *COLOR*.

Another flight of stairs brought us out into the sun. We burst onto the lido deck: smiles and sunlight and blue sky ceilings, wide-brimmed hats and white linen shirts with coconut shell buttons, thin sundresses with designs of pineapples and palm trees flapping in the spring breeze, bikinis and breasts and plastic-surgery lips, children laughing and spinning down spiraling slides, blobs of passengers splashing in pools and pools and more blue pissed-in pools, a volcanic eruption of tropical shirts and sunglasses and sunburns that stretched to the square of the stern, flexi-plastic straws and milky puddles of ice cream cone drippings, deck swabbers and winch greasers in blue boiler suits, tan-skinned busboys with gray tubs of pizza bones and burger bits and gravy-splashed ceramics.

Just another day in paradise. Just another deck to scrub in a crew member's life of lido-deck luxury.

The sundeck was a circus. I expected to find, just farther up the ship, crew members on stilts dressed as Blackbeard and Captain Cook. On the starboard I heard a Filipino band playing "Help Me, Rhonda" (sung as "Help Me, Londa").

Petryk darted into the shade of the passenger-buffet dining room, The Compass, which must have been a reference to the fact that the buffet line would guide you straight to the shores of diabetes and obesity. But the food was great. There were hillsides of peanut butter-and-raisin cookies, full hindquarters of roast *beast,* an entire room devoted to ice cream and sprinkles, six varieties of green tea for starters on the drinks. I grabbed a plate and ogled at the overwhelming variety of food, feeling as if I were looking into a pantry at Buckingham Palace, and then I did what any sensible American would do: I grabbed a cheeseburger and a hot dog and piled on as many french fries as would fit on my plastic dish.

We sat down at a table. Petryk dipped a piece of pizza into a splotch of sour cream. *Very Ruski.* "Don't get used to this," he said.

"Why?" I asked.

"Because you never get to eat up here."

Gertie picked a fry from her plate and dipped it in ketchup. She was a good old *American Girl*—she even had the dolls back home to prove it. They were stuffed in a drawer with American flag bathing suits and Daisy Duke–sized shorts with little illustrations of apple pies on them. "But we could eat at the passenger buffet on our last ship," she said.

I realized at that moment that we had turned into the very people that I loathed. We were *last shippers,* those irritating crew members who always talked about their last ship. "On my last ship we had ice cream machines in the lifeboats. On my last ship there was this one crew cabin with really clean air. On my last ship. On my last ship."

But there was no turning back. Once a last shipper, always a last shipper.

Petryk took a chomp from his sour cream-dipped slice of pepperoni and mushroom. There was a dab of sour cream in the corner of his mouth. "Well, this isn't your last ship, babe," he said. "And you won't be eating up here…at all." He said it with the finality of a captain's order to abandon ship after all the lifeboats have already sailed off *without* the crew.

Gertie arched her brows. "Then why are we up here if it's against the rules?"

"Because I don't give a shit," Petryk said. "This is my last day, and they can kiss my ass. I've had to put up with this crazy management for nine months. *Nine freakin' months!*" He thrust a finger in the air and waggled it around for a moment. His eyes went all crazy and big, like a possum right before he's run over by a sports car going ninety miles an hour.

I knew that look. It was the look of the wild sea donkey, the crazy beast that crew members sometimes turn into when they've been out on the cruise ships for too long. Natalievsky, who hadn't said a word since we met her, reached over and put her hand on his forearm and smiled, which seemed to have a calming effect on Petryk. She looked at us, and I could see worry in her eyes. "We are so ready for our, um, how do you say?" She looked at Petryk, "*otpusk.*"

"Vacation," Petryk said. "We are veady"—ready—"for the holiday."

"Is it really that bad?" I asked.

Natalievsky laughed. "You have no idea. We were—"

Petryk thrust out his hand to stop Natalievsky from speaking. "*Enough.*"

Natalievsky looked as if she curled into a little, cute ball, putting her hands in her lap and looking down at her beet soup with a cold dab of sour cream drifting around on top.

Petryk continued, "This has been very difficult ship. The worst ship I have ever worked on in my life. Did you know? Crew members. They jump overboard few weeks ago. *Two* of them." When he said the word *two*, his eyes went all wild again, like a weird twitch, a shock of electric current to his shuddering, edgy brain. He put up his fingers so we could count them. One. Two. One finger for each sailor lost at sea.

"Why?" Gertie asked.

"Huh." It was more of a short, breathy laugh, Petryk's way of saying that he thought the question was stupid. He picked up a packet of crackers, and when he tried to open them, they split open too fast. The crackers burst into crumbs and were scattered all over the table. He had cracker dust all over his hands. "Because this ship like hell." Then he rubbed his hands together, like he was washing his hands clean. "But it's *your* ship now."

I realized that my lips were pressed together tight. The muscles in my lower back were all scrunched up. I tried to relax. "Did they live?"

"Who?" Petryk asked.

Had he already forgotten about the crew members who jumped overboard? "The crew members who jumped," I said.

"We were out in middle of ocean. We found one. The other one? I don't think so. But we heard nothing else from captain. No why crew member did it. No where he went. We never see him again. Sent home, we guess. Back to Philippines or India or wherever."

We sat in silence for a moment. Gertie and I had lost our appetites. Gertie sipped on her cold soda. I took a sip of hot tea.

Gertie finally broke the silence. "So what rules should we know about?"

This may sound like a silly question. Yes, we had just come from a cruise ship. We should know what the rules are, right? But when it comes to cruise line rules, each ship has its own set of official and *unofficial* rules.

Petryk laughed. "*Rules*. They change every day. I don't even know anymore. My advice: try to avoid management all the time. Keep a, um, how do you say in American? *Nizki profil*. Um. Small profile. Yes. You keep the small profile."

"There's a new M&R manager coming aboard, you know," I said, hoping that might make things better. Our last M&R manager, Angel, would join the *Barnacle* today, too. Angel was difficult, but we didn't have any crew members jumping overboard on our last ship, so maybe that was an improvement on the current bleak management team we were apparently about to deal with.

Petryk shrugged. "No. No. M&R one of best. Maybe only good one. But he's gone. Who do you have coming to ship? Do you know?"

"A man named Angel."

Natalievski put her hand over her mouth and giggled like a Japanese girl in a cartoon skit, as if she was afraid to let her laughter out into the open air.

Petryk sighed. "Oh my, *bozhestvo,*" he said.

Natalievski let a single word trickle out her mouth, "*Bezumny*."

Petryk looked at Natalievski and laughed. "*Glovy Drakona*." Then he looked back at us. "Angel. I know him. He is worst. He is *bezumny*. That man is insane."

CHAPTER FOUR

Next Stop, Dodge City!

Petryk didn't give us a handover; he gave us a shove-off. Then he waved and ran for the gangway, disappearing into the bright Barcelona sunlight forever. Before they left, Natalievski looked worried for us, but she didn't say anything about it. I guess Petryk would have stopped her if she tried. After we ate what we were told would be our last meal of our contract from the passenger buffet, we cruised back down to our cabin, getting lost along the way and ending up in the trash compacter room a few times before realizing we were going in circles. We finally stumbled upon the right hallway and found our little, grimy door with the peeling mailbox stickers on it—*0604*. There was a pink Post-It note hanging on the door handle.

Meet me at the crew office. Can you freakin' believe this?
—Alex

No, Alex. We can't. We didn't even open the door to our room. We just turned around and headed back down the I-95, weaving past the forklifts and swarms of crew members, passing another Banana Mountain. Then we saw Alex standing in front of the crew office door.

When he saw us, he put his hands up in the air as if to say: *Why me*? "Can…you…*believe*…this?" he said.

"What?" I asked.

"These rooms. Wait—don't tell me there's a penthouse

suite behind that door to 0604. You won't believe what they have me in. No. No. No! Just *no*."

"Where's your room?" I asked.

"Just down the I-95. Starboard."

"Porthole?" Gertie asked.

"Yeah, but it is *not* the art director's cabin."

When I heard Alex say that, a million questions ran through my head. I chose just a few. "How do you know that it's not the art director's cabin? What does that even mean? Can't they just put us in whatever cabin they want?"

"Again! You're thinking like a crew member. We are officers. We are vendors. We are not crew members. I know the art director that was here before me. I know that she was in a passenger cabin. And I know that a *passenger* cabin is the art director's cabin on this ship."

Gertie put her hand out. "Wait. You're saying that on some ships, art directors get guest cabins? Like, in a passenger area?"

"Yes, on some ships in this fleet this is the case. Real guest cabins. Look, I'm not living in the shithole they put me in."

"You should see what they have *us* in," Gertie said.

Alex shook his head. "We're getting shafted. Somewhere there's a couple of girls, and they're the girlfriends of some high-ranking officer or the captain or someone, and they're living in the rooms that our company is paying for."

"Hold on," I said. "Seven Seas Art is paying for our rooms on these ships?"

"Yes and no. Seven Seas is sending the checks. But the truth is that *we* are paying for them, by working our butts off and making these ships millions of dollars every quarter. And then they're going to try and pull some switcheroo nonsense! I don't think so. Not while I'm art director on this ship. They might be able to pull this with some greenhorn *FNG,"*—(effing new guy, in cruise ship lingo)—"but not with Alex Ashebury."

I knew from experience that Alex was really mad when he talked about himself in third person.

"What do you want us to do?" Gertie asked.

Alex pressed his lips together and started to nod. He pointed at us. "I want you to see if you can find out who is living in our designated rooms and where those rooms are located. I'll work on the crew office and the HR"—(human resources)—"director on board. Like I said before, you have to fight for everything on these cruise ships. You lay down for a second, and management and crew and even passengers will walk all over you."

Gertie perked up. "So you think we'll get moved to a new cabin?"

"Yes. And I know something else. If they don't move me, then I'm jumping ship. You might be taking over sooner than you think. I'm not putting up with this kind of BS. I've been working in this business way too long to get shafted like this."

Alex started to walk away and then turned around. "Let's meet in the art gallery in thirty minutes. Deck five. Port side."

We headed back down the I-95 toward our crew cabin. We were a few hours from sail away, and the foot traffic in the main hallway had died down a bit.

Gertie pointed down the hallway. "Look at this guy."

She was pointing to a Jamaican man who must have been in his forties (graying short-cropped hair, very thin, as tall as a basketball player, room steward uniform, huge smile, shining white teeth between large puffy lips). He was still fifty feet or so down the hallway but he stuck out because of his height, his unique air of happiness, and one other thing—his extremely loud singing. We could hear it clearly over the clamor of the forklifts and the chatter of the other crew members.

As he walked by, he waved and smiled. "How every-ting? Everything be irie, mon."

Seeing him among the other tired crewmates aboard the ship was like finding a life raft after you've been drifting for a few weeks in a stormy ocean. You could almost touch his positivity.

I had seen this before on dark ships. The singers. There's always one or two of them. You'll find them in vacant stairwells in some out-of-the-way nook down below the waterline. Every night they'll be there, in their own private refuge from ship life, just singing at the top of their lungs, letting their voices reverberate in their secluded little echo chamber, listening to the beauty of their voices rising and spiraling up the drafty staircase, climbing all the way up to the top deck where the officers and rich people live. Their voices travel from the dark depths of the ship's hull and drift all the way up and up and up into the upper echelon, like a dream, a fantasy of something they themselves may never see while they are awake in that ship life. And these singers bring their melodies with them wherever they go: at the crew bar, they sing on the dance floor; on the crew deck, they sing out to the sea; and below the waterline in the maze of hallways, they sing to the crew. It's as if their singing somehow protects them from the gloom of the ship, as if it's a type of musical force field that repels the darkness.

"Do you think that helps?" Gertie asked as we turned the corner into our hallway.

"What? Singing? I think it helps. But I'm a musician. I think music always helps."

"We need to do that on this contract."

"Sing?"

"Not sing exactly, but make sure we stay positive. No matter what's happening around us."

"Yes, I agree. 100 percent." I put the keycard in the door and watched the light turn green.

"That's the key to staying positive on one of these ships of darkness, isn't it?" Gertie asked as we walked into our room. "No matter how dark it gets in our ship life, we need to think positively in here"—she pointed to her head—"and feel hopeful in here." She pointed to her heart. I thought it was cute and absolutely right.

Our room smelled like absolute crap, as if the Kraken had wandered in while we were gone and taken a dump on both of our bunk beds and then smoked an entire pack of cigarettes before it left the room.

Gertie put her hand over her mouth. "Oh no, it stinks in here."

I propped the door open with one of our suitcases. "Let's see what we're working with here." I opened the bathroom door. I felt as if I had opened the door to the sewage treatment facility on an aircraft carrier. "Well, that doesn't help." I shut the door. But there was another smell coming from somewhere near my feet. "Does it smell a bit musty in here, too? A bit moldy, maybe?"

"Definitely," Gertie said. She began sniffing around like a

trusty hound dog on the hunt for its favorite bone. "I think it's coming from the carpet."

"But the carpet looks brand new."

"It does, but look at this." Gertie pointed to a corner of the room. "It looks like the carpet is a different color over here." She bent down and looked closer, and then she grabbed a corner of the carpet and lifted it up. "Really? Are you kidding me?"

She dropped the carpet, then did that thing that people sometimes do when they're totally grossed out where they make their arms look like the arms on a T-rex and shape their hands into duck bills. Then she made a face like passengers do when they discover how many passengers on the previous cruise contracted a cyclospora parasite from the same spinach salad they just ate at their early dinner seating. Then she kind of danced around the room for a bit, a type of running in place reserved for times when she was as repulsed as possible—like the time she realized she had contracted cyclospora after eating leftover spinach from the passenger dining room.

"What is it?" I asked. Had she found a roach riding a rat at the cruise ship's annual Infestation Rodeo under there? Or maybe a slice of baked Alaska that a crew member had smuggled from the passenger buffet and stashed under the carpet, then forgot about when he heard an announcement for the passenger boat drill.

She stuck out her tongue. "It's old carpet. Underneath."

I walked over and took a look for myself. She was right. The carpet we were standing on was new, but it had just been thrown on top of the old carpet underneath. This layered carpet sandwich of dark, damp filth was just the kind of place that every hopelessly-romantic bacteria dreams about. This was mildew-colony nirvana, a parasite paradise. But it was our own little slice of parasite paradise. *Awww, how cute.*

Cruise ships: a wonderful place to live, work, and grow, as long as you're a mold spore or an intestinal virus.

"Maybe we can get HR to change it out," I said.

I was feeling a tad hot in the room, so I looked around for the thermostat. What a fool. Of course there was no thermostat. This wasn't an officer's cabin. We were below the waterline again. We were down in the bilge tank with all the other scallywags. "Is it hot in here to you?" I asked.

Gertie was starting to sweat. She looked around the room for a place to sit down. Atop each bunk was a bundle of crumpled bed sheets that clearly hadn't been washed, perhaps for an entire contract. Personal hygiene isn't exactly a sailor's strong suit. Some crew members that I've worked with smell as if they take showers under faucets that produce a liquid mixture of sweat, onion juice, and french fry grease. She sat down in the single chair in front of the desk that was against one of the walls. We would definitely be cleaning the entire room with bleach wipes, the crew member standard for day one on a new ship.

"Let's turn up the thermostat," Gertie said.

"There is no thermostat."

We both knew what this meant. No thermostat equaled no air filter. I looked up at the air vent, a circular protrusion in the ceiling with a small lever attached to it that is supposed to allow crew members to adjust the amount of cold airflow coming out of the vent, but instead has about the same varying degree of options as an on/off switch—that is, when the lever hasn't already rusted off all together.

I was intimately familiar with these holes in the ceiling. I had spent so much time living in crew quarters that were about as comfortable to live in and as well-appointed as a wooden rum barrel, that I considered myself a highly accomplished air vent technician. To be fair, though, every crew member should be awarded an honorary degree in air-vent rigging after mastering the art of adjustments required to produce the perfect amount of airflow from these dodgy air-duct devices. It usually required the highly technical process of removing the air vent's cover and stuffing the vent with just the right amount of air fresheners and fabric softener sheets until you have achieved the perfect amount of air flow to keep your crew cabin at the desired temperature. This doubled as an effective way to mask the stench of your ship berth by making it smell like a very busy laundry facility.

I went to work immediately. I tried to adjust the lever. It wouldn't budge. So I did what any cruise ship air-vent technician worth his salt would do: I ripped the air vent cover off and looked inside. It was just as I suspected. No air filter. Just a filthy hole in the ceiling. But then I saw something else, covering the inside of the air duct and the underside of the air vent cover. I ran my finger inside the air duct and inspected it closer.

"What is it?" Gertie asked. "Is it dust?"

"No. Worse. It's soot." If Gertie was the Mary Poppins of ship life, then I was Bert as the chimney sweep. I could hear the "Chim-chim-eny" song playing in my head as I stuck the cover back on.

I sat down on the edge of the bed. Gertie slowly sat down beside me. One minute we were up in the penthouse, and now we were back down in the cruise ship ghetto. The roller coaster of ship life. The problem is that if you ride too long, it'll make you feel sick.

"Positive," Gertie said. "Think positive." She pointed toward her head again. I knew she was right. Then I had an idea. I bet if I stuffed a copy of Norman Vincent Peale's book, *The Power of Positive Thinking,* in the air vent, it would make our room the perfect temperature. I was positive—positive it couldn't get any worse.

Then the air system coughed a few times and turned on.

I felt a blast of air erupt out of our air hole. It made Gertie's hair flutter in the wind as if she was in a 1980's music video. She moved her nose like a rabbit, sniffing the air. "That smells awful."

I sniffed the air too. We were a couple of rabbits on the edge of a crew bunk. Mixed in with the blast of air—the comfortable temperature of an arctic breeze in December—was a steady stream of cigarette smoke.

"That explains where all the soot came from," Gertie said.

I let my head drop down a bit. We were going to need two or three Dr. Norman Vincent Peale books for this type of air vent. The power of *really* positive thinking, powerful enough to block the air flow entirely. I didn't think it could get any worse.

Just then I heard a sound that was similar to the cry of a dying cat, followed by the noise that a dump truck with bad shocks makes when it hits a pothole going sixty miles an hour. It came from somewhere in our hallway.

"What the heck was that?" I said. I looked out our open door and saw a crew member in a casino-dealer tux walk by.

Gertie looked puzzled. "I think that was the door to the hallway."

We listened as the casino dealer walked down the hall,

his footsteps reverberated and were amplified by the hollow, metal walls. When he reached the door at the opposite end of the hall, we heard the dying cat noise and then the dump truck hitting the pothole again.

It happened again. *Dying cat...dump truck hits the pothole...tap, tap, tap...crew member walks by our doorway...tap, tap, tap, tap...dying cat...dump truck hits the pothole.*

I realized this was probably going to happen at all hours, day and night. I was a light sleeper, so I probably wouldn't be getting much sleep in this crew cabin. My shoulders sank. There was absolutely no way it could get any worse.

Then we heard a very loud sound coming from the side wall—the wall right at the head of our bunks, right where we would be laying our heads at night. It sounded like one of those big speaker systems that you find in cars driven by people who have no appreciation for something called music, speaker systems that are built for one thing only—window-shattering bass. We heard it again, *BOOM,* and this time it was followed by loud high-pitched taps, like a hammer striking the head of a railroad spike.

Were we living in a time machine that had transported us back to the old railroad days of the Westward Expansion?

Then the *BOOM, TAP, TAP, TAP, BOOM, TAP, TAP, TAP* became progressively quieter as it drifted down the wall and continued to drift all the way down the side of the ship. Gertie and I looked at each other. I put out my hands and shrugged.

I followed her out into the hallway, then through the dead cat door to the I-95. I looked down the hall and solved "the mystery of the railroad ghost".

I watched as a crew member strolled down the I-95, banging his fist as hard as he could onto the metal railing that ran down the side of the hallway wall—*BOOM*—and then, with one finger, tapped a gold ring against the metal rail two or three times (*TAP, TAP, TAP*).

The metal rail that crew members were using as a hallway instrument was attached to the other side of our crew cabin.

Maybe he's the only one who would do such an inconsiderate thing. Doesn't he realize that someone is trying to live—or, God forbid, sleep—on the other side of this wall that the rail is attached to?

Then we heard it again, as if the ghost train chugged down the old, dusty tracks from behind us: *CHOO-CHOO, CHOO-CHOO*. Another crew member played the metal rail, as loudly as an African djembe at a hippie drum circle, as he walked down the hall. We weren't living at some small, quiet, friendly stop along the cruise ship railroad as we had hoped. No, we were on the wrong side of the tracks in cruise liner land, and this was the railway to insomnia.

Gertie froze in her tracks—or on the tracks, like a damsel in distress that's paralyzed by fear in the bright light of an oncoming train, one foot wedged between the railroad ties that just won't come loose. "We have to get a new room."

"We will," I said. "Alex is working on it as we speak. I'm sure of it. Let's just stay positive, remember."

Her words just kind of squeaked out. "Positive. Think positive. Be positive. It might be time to start singing."

I wanted to start singing, too. I heard the song in my head. It was set to the melody of "I've Been Working on the Railroad":

I've been working on the cruise ship

All the live long day
I've been working on the cruise ship
Just to pass the ship time away, HEY!

Can't you hear the ship-whistle blowing?
Rise so early in the morn'
Can't you hear the captain shouting?
*I-ah Accidentally-ah fell-ah into the lifeboat-ah**

*A Costa Concordia reference. The captain of the ship claimed that he accidentally fell into a lifeboat as a way to explain why he abandoned his ship long before all of the passengers and crew were safely evacuated.

My watch alarm went off. It was time to meet Alex in the art gallery and get this art-show on the sea. We may have had the worst crew cabin ever—at least ever since those French galley-type rowing ships went out of style—but we weren't there to spend our time lounging in luxury in a stateroom fit for King Henry VIII. We were there to see the Med, to have fun, work hard, sell a ton of art, and to make a boatload of money along the way. It was time to start popping some Duck Nipple champagne and to start taking long walks down art peddler's lane.

I was positive. I could see the light at the end of the tunnel. Or was that the headlight of an oncoming train? *SMACK!*

CHAPTER FIVE

Champagne and Sea Hawks

Alex was sitting behind his new desk, looking quite pleased with himself as he talked on the ship phone. He twirled the spiraled telephone cord with one finger, the way a school girl twirls her hair. His feet were kicked up on top of the desk, further evidence of his happy-days bravado. *Maybe he has some good news for us.* The art gallery desk was in front of an oversized porthole with a postcard view of the Mediterranean Sea as we sailed toward Civitavecchia, our port to Rome and the pope.

The gallery wasn't much of a gallery at all: a narrow hallway where we could hang art on both walls, and a few partitions for extra art-display space. The *Barnacle's* gallery was a quarter size of the one on our last ship. This seemed like a less-than-ideal storefront from which to sell high-priced artworks.

However, there was a plus side: once again, the art gallery was located in a high traffic area. The main theater was forward from our starboard gallery. Aft was a souvenir shop, also starboard. Are you confused yet? Don't worry. You'll get your sea legs before we're done.

I knew that our lives were about to revolve around the boom and bust schedule of the foot traffic that passed through our gallery, which would mostly occur whenever a show in the main theater was about to start and then resume again an hour later when the show ended. This was exactly how it was on our last ship, where most of the time we stood around twiddling our thumbs, not a single passenger anywhere near the gallery. Then the theater doors would swing open, and a herd of fifteen hundred people wearing seasickness patches would stampede toward the lunch buffet on the other end of the ship. Lucky for us, our gallery happened to stand between the ravenously starving passengers who hadn't eaten in two hours and their grilled hot dogs, hamburgers, pizza, french fries, and that awful-tasting fruit punch and lemonade that you find on every cruise ship in the world.

The art gallery would be an absolute madhouse for a half hour, Gertie and I acting like young floor brokers in the throes of a bull market trading day on the New York Stock Exchange. Alex would throw out his hooked lines as the colorful and meaty school of passenger fish swam down our narrow canal on the way to their favorite feeding reefs. Few took his bait, but once in a while, one of the weaker fish in the school, straggling far behind the sparkling shoal, would get snagged by the one lure that historically no sailor can possibly resist: free alcohol.

His catch of the day would swim in a sea of free Duck Nipple champagne until they were properly glassy eyed, slurring, and flopping around on the deck. Alex had a very special and scientific way of knowing when it was the right time to pull back hard on his fishing rod and get that hook sunk deep into their cheek. He would show them a certain painting on the wall that closely resembled a framed stain. The painting looked as if a passenger accidentally splattered their chocolate ice cream cone during a particularly violent list on a transatlantic crossing. When he showed the passenger the stain-resembling painting, and the passenger replied something like: "Oh no, no—that's not art at all," then he would order another bottle of Duck Nipple and stop the art tour right there since none of the other art in the gallery was much better. But once he showed them the stain painting and their reaction was something along the lines of: "Yes, I've always wanted to acquire an impressionistic interpretation of an aerial view of the Canary Islands." That's when he knew that he had hooked that most desirable aquatic species of the sea—the sucker fish. And that was precisely when he would gently reel them in, pull them to shore, grab them by the gills, and swiftly filet them of a small portion of their expendable income.

But he was a conservationist in the cruise ship art gallery world, a conservationist who understood how to operate an economically sustainable offshore fishery. And so he was a responsible catch-and-release angler. He wanted to survive in the shark-infested art-world waters, and so he would do the sensible thing: once he had a legible signature on his invoice, he tossed the sucker fish back into the Gulf Stream where they were free to swim back to the shoal and thus continue their fight for survival. They would continue along their journey and eventually procreate, which would populate our art gallery waters with more beautiful sucker fish minnows who would one day return to the sea, occupy our sailing vessels, and thus continue the cycle of oceanic life that we art auctioneer fishermen and women so desperately depend on. The whole web of life of the cruise ship art world is really a remarkably beautiful thing once you see it from this compassionate perspective.

After our catch-of-the-days were unhooked and thrown back into the art gallery ocean, the gallery would become quiet for a few hours, like a north Florida reef right after the BP oil spill (not a fan, BP). The gallery would be a dead zone until the newlywed game was over or until the ventriloquist magician/ukulele comedian show let out. Then, once again, our gallery would be a blustering swarm of migrating passenger fish who were just trying to navigate the Gulf Stream as fast and safely as possible. These passenger fish would look absolutely terrified by the presence of another species of sea creature that was wearing a name tag and lurking on the edge of their warm-water highway, trying to lure them from the school with a glass of very cheap-looking bubbly and a fishy look in their eyes.

It's a stressful way to live, but no one ever said the life of a fisherman or woman was an easy sea to sail. We knew what we were in for when we signed up. We had seen *The Perfect Storm* and *Deadliest Catch.*

Then again, I bet those guys on *Deadliest Catch* had better crew cabins than we did.

Back in the art gallery, I saw Alex put down his phone. Gertie was looking at a *nature morte* of a life preserver with some block and tackle, the type of painting that art appraisers at Christie's auction house have nightmares about.

"This gallery is tiny," she said.

I heard Alex Ashebury's voice from behind me. "It's not the size of the worm. It's how you wiggle it."

He looked genuinely happy, but in a medicated sort of way. "We're going to sell every freakin' piece of art in this gallery. Today!" Yes, he was definitely medicated. *I'll have the little blue pills that Alex is devouring, please.*

Gertie asked, "Any news about our room?"

"Well," Alex said, still smiling, "it doesn't look good. I

just got off the phone with someone in the crew office. You're going to have to stay where you are."

Gertie looked as if she was about to hit him over the head with the dreadful still-life painting. "Alex, our room is disgusting. There's no way that—"

Alex put out his hand, and calmly said, "I'm sorry, but the crew office doesn't have anywhere else to put you. You're only here for a short amount of time; you'll just have to deal with it."

"*Deal* with it?" she asked. "An hour ago, you were telling us to fight this thing tooth and nail, and now you're saying that we should just lie down and *deal with it.* What happened?"

Alex kept his cool. "Look, I'm as unhappy about this as you are, but there's nothing we can do. We have to learn to pick the right battles if we're ever going to win the war."

This didn't sound like much of a war to me. This sounded like an outright surrender, and Gertie and I were the only two casualties on the battlefield. Since I felt entirely uncomfortable with the prospect of letting a perfectly good conflict pass me by without somehow getting involved, I had to speak up. "But these aren't our rooms."

Alex shook his head. "0604 is your room now. There is honestly nothing I can do. Trust me. I did *everything* I could."

I didn't trust Alex as far as a toddler could throw the ship's anchor. "But where are our rooms?" I asked.

Alex squinted. "What do you mean?"

"You said that someone else on this ship must be sleeping in the rooms that are assigned to the art auctioneers. I don't think we should have to live—"

Alex put his hand out again. This time he had the fingers

of his right hand curled into a loose and nonthreatening fist, his thumb lightly resting on top, just as Bill Clinton did when he talked at presidential debates. Alex had summoned his inner politician. I assumed that he was about to start lying.

He spoke softly, diplomatically, like a friend who is trying to talk his buddy into using a different type of lure on a fishing trip. "Now look. Let's be reasonable here. We don't need to make any waves. There are a lot of politics going on here, and the last thing we need to do is make waves with the cruise company. No waves. That's our goal. If we do that, we'll have nothing but smooth sailing."

This smelled as fishy as a cruise-ship kitchen on lobster night. "So what are you going to do?" I asked.

Alex took a step closer to both of us. "I'm not going to make any waves." Then he tapped me on the chest with his Bill Clinton thumb. "And neither are you."

Gertie's attitude had progressed from bludgeoning-with-still-life to clubbing-with-heavy-brass-statue-of-a-dolphin. This was absolutely out of character for her, which is a testament to how dire the prospect of living in that crew cabin was for Gertie. I understood her feelings completely.

"I thought you were going to sign off if they didn't give you a new room?" Gertie asked.

Just then the doors to the theater swung open and a swarm of sucker fish swam out toward us. Alex reached into his jacket pocket and pulled out a stack of business cards that read *ONE FREE GLASS OF CHAMPAGNE*. He tapped me on the chest with them, and then handed each of us a stack of our own. "No waves. Pass these out. Let them know about the auction tomorrow. Two o'clock. After this, I'll show you our office downstairs."

Alex shuffled away toward the throng of passengers, making them walk around him if they wanted to get by. He passed out champagne cards so fast that he looked like an octopus in a suit—an octopus with the hookup for free champagne.

Gertie and I stood to the side, up against the wall of art, looking like two of those creepy paintings that you find in a haunted mansion on *Scooby Doo,* the kind of painting that follows you with its eyes as you walk by. I'd try to hand out one of the cards, and the group of passengers would instantly disperse, as if they were a bait-ball of minnows that were swirling and spinning through the ocean. I was the pelican diving into the sea. Whenever I spotted the densely packed bait-ball of fish passing by, I'd stick my hand out, trying to give away a card, and the bait ball would disperse, the fish swimming away in every direction. Once they walked past, the bait ball would come back together, into its tight little circular huddle, and swim off toward the gift shop.

But hey, the pelican catches something once in a while, but it wasn't easy. The last thing a passenger wanted to do while on vacation was to take some type of paperwork from a man in a suit. That's what they were trying to escape from on land.

Soon the chaos of the post-theater rush was over, and the gallery was quiet again. Alex took us over to his desk. He sat down and put his hands on top, power steeple style. "Okay, we need to talk. This is a new ship, and I can already tell that we need a new approach. Let's wake these people up. I need you to be hawks in this gallery. Aggressive birds of prey. Osprey. Sea eagles. Sea hawks."

We had heard this about Alex, heard that he liked to

change his style. But this was a total one eighty. On our last ship, we had been told to ignore passengers. To be rude. Remember Alex's *Theory of Irritability* that had surprisingly worked so well? Now, after all that hard work of training us and molding us into the little rude art auctioneers that he wanted us to be, how could he just throw the whole approach out the porthole?

But I knew that Alex had experience on his side. He saw something that I didn't. However, I was no hawk. It wasn't my style. And Gertie was no high-pressure saleswoman either. It wouldn't work for us. So I just did what I always did with Alex, just smile and nod. I wasn't going to be some used car salesman–type of art pusher with a slick smile. I was just going to be myself. Be honest. I felt I'd sell more art that way anyhow.

Alex kept talking. "I want you stopping every passenger that walks through here. Tell them about the auction. Show them a painting. Tell them how great of a deal the art is on board. Give them a champagne card. Pour them a glass of Duck Nipple. Just don't let a person leave here without a fight. Got it?"

We both nodded our heads.

"Good. Hawks. Sea hawks. Now let's go to the back office, you two sea hawks."

We followed Alex through the cruise ship maze, two fledgling, baby sea hawks waddling behind the alpha bird of an art-peddling flock.

CHAPTER SIX

1912 with a Plastic Flamingo

As we walked down the promenade, I heard the engine rumbling and felt the ship battling the waves of the Mediterranean Sea. The *MS Barnacle* was on its way.

I tried to shift into cruise control, tried to feel like everything was now on autopilot, but that button on the end of my imaginary gear shifter must have been broken, because I felt rather uneasy. We were now cruising into uncharted territory as we sailed aboard an alleged ship of darkness. I swallowed my discomfort and forged ahead, hopefully toward a happily-ever-after ending—preferably one where I didn't have to rescue Gertie from the arms of a fire-breathing sea dragon, or vice versa, before we got to the last chapter.

Alex stopped at the atrium, a spiraling vertical tunnel of glass elevators, marble staircases, and chrome railings. I peered upward to see passengers leaning over the rails and looking down on us from the five or so decks stacked above.

Alex pointed toward a stage on our deck, the stage next to the atrium bar. A man on stage was wearing a black suit with a bright-red bow tie, the kind that looked as if it was purchased at a magician's shop and could squirt water across a dinner table. He had a face like a politician at a fundraiser barbecue: sunburned chubby cheeks, plastic smile, greasy forehead, slicked-back thinning hair, a money twinkle in his eyes. "That's the cruise director, the CD," Alex said.

I listened to the CD explain excitedly how the passenger's shipboard charge cards worked. He sounded like a carney announcing the two-headed woman at the county fair: "It's very simple. You're on vacation! You're not here to budget! Budgeting is boring! This is Festivus Cruise Lines! These are the Festival ships! You buy whatever you want. Anything! And just put it on this card, and don't worry about it. I mean, you're on vacation! Buy what you want. We'll take care of it." Then he moved the microphone away from his face and added softly, "when we bill you at the end of the cruise."

That got a big laugh from the crowd, who had already succumbed to the unique consumer-zombie virus that can only be contracted after drinking two whole servings of rum punch from plastic cruise ship smokestack–shaped cups.

Which brings me to an all-important question: Where do these cruise ship companies find these cruise directors? They dance, they sing, they're comedians, they possess a magical power to make you laugh while you unwittingly fork over thousands of dollars of the coveted vacation fund that you were saving for a future trip to Disney World—the same vacation fund that your wife wouldn't let you use to bail your only son out of jail but now after only two margaritas she feels entirely justified using to buy a whole sack full of "I *HEART* Festivus" key chains. So, given cruise director's supernatural powers over us lesser passenger and crew member beings, we must come to the very scientific and reasonable explanation that cruise directors are aliens and should not be entirely trusted.

Passengers should perhaps treat cruise directors like beautiful sea sirens: don't look them in the eyes, or you will fall hopelessly under their spell. They are spectacular sea creatures, ones that remind us all that vaudeville isn't dead. Vaudeville is alive, going strong, and thriving in the soul of every money-giddy cruise director on the seven seas.

I looked the cruise director in the eye and felt an unexplainable urge to reach into my pocket and hand him a ten-dollar bill. "He looks like a nice chap," I said.

Alex smirked. "Dr. Jekyll and Mr. Hyde more like it. I've worked with him before. Frankell Shinster. Charm of a Japanese game show host. IQ of a hamster. Daily alcohol consumption equal to a Jimmy Buffet concert." He squinted and shook his head. "It's so strange. To think that when he wants to, he can act so nice. But when he's with the crew..."

Alex shrugged and walked on down the atrium, his two sea hawk chicks in tow. We reached a door that was tucked into a little alcove next to the atrium bar. He motioned toward the door as a doorman at Buckingham Palace would flourish to introduce the Queen of England for tea time. "Welcome to our office," he said.

When we walked inside, I felt as if I was stepping into a narrow alleyway that had been converted into the headquarters of a newspaper bureau, one that had been hit exceptionally hard by the Great Recession of 2008 and now teetered perilously on the brink of bankruptcy. The copy machine looked like the same one people used to photocopy their butts back in high school—and high school had been nearly two decades ago, for me.

The place was pretty much empty, except for a few other crew members tapping furiously on keyboards as if their productivity quota was closely monitored by a North Korean dictator.

Gertie forced a smile. "This will work," she said toward

the other two crew members whose backs were to us as they worked on their computers. "Is this where we can design our fliers and print the 'free champagne' cards?"

That kind of statement was meant to announce to the other crew members in the office that we were new kids on the block. Gertie was hoping that someone in the office would turn around and say hi, but the other crew members just kept tapping away.

Alex tried to get our shipmates' attention, too. "Nice to meet you. We're the new art team on board." One of the crew members raised his hand and then quickly put it back on his keyboard. I wouldn't want to have *my* back to Gertie at that moment. This was the type of situation where the police report would read: "He never saw it coming. One minute, the guy was typing a positive-spin press release about the whale the cruise ship bludgeoned in the Mediterranean Sea, and the next minute he was underneath the copy machine, flattened to about the thickness of a crêpe."

Gertie was a very nice girl, but she didn't like being ignored. And to think that she had spent so much of her valuable time curling her hair and painting her nails and picking out the perfect Lilly Pulitzer dress, the one with the design of tiny octopi and fishing hooks, and now no one was even giving her the attention she so rightfully deserved. It was downright rude.

Gertie rolled her eyes. Suddenly the door burst open, and in rushed the cruise director, Frankell Shinster.

Gertie smiled and put out her hand, "Hi, we're the—"

Shinster grunted and walked into a small office that was off to the side of the room. He pushed the door closed behind him. Alex gave us the *I told you so* look.

Alex smiled. "Welcome aboard."

I nearly pooped my pants when the back wall opened up and Angel, the M&R manager from our last ship, popped out of the wall again. He *got* me every time. He just stood there and smiled at us, as he hung out of the top of the Dutch door that had been built into the wall between our office and his. "We're Off to See the Wizard" played in my head.

I had never noticed it until now, but Angel looked more like a plastic pink flamingo than anyone else I had ever met (tiny dark eyes, hooked beak, craning neck, pink sunburned face, completely hollow on the inside).

He smiled, proud of his wall-popping entrance. "Hey, you guys. Auction tomorrow?"

Alex nodded. "Two o'clock."

"Good. All settled in?"

I thought perhaps Angel could help us with our room problem. "Yes, but we do have—" I said.

"Good." Angel looked me up and down. "Still wearing that jacket, huh? What's with those buttons? And that jacket *really* is too small."

I looked down at the buttons on my suit jacket.

Angel smiled and looked at all three of us one at a time. "And hey…watch those hands!" Then he pulled the top part of his Dutch door shut and left us looking at the wall again.

"What a strange man," Alex said quietly.

"Yes," I said. "And what do you think he meant about watching our hands?"

Alex shrugged. "Who knows?" Then Alex gathered us into a tight huddle. He lowered his voice. "Look. Here's the plan. We need to try and work together to keep Angel happy. We need to get him on our side. From the beginning. Just be nice to the guy. Do what he says. Soon we'll have him in our pocket. Is he a bit strange? Yes. Have we all heard crazy stories about the way he treats crew members? Yes. But listen, he has *power* over us in this ship life. Let's get that power out from *over* us and get it working *with* us. We need him on our side, not working against us. Just do what he says. Humor him if you have to. Look at this like a game. The Game of Ship Life.

"And let me tell you this: I know that Angel can be a gift sent from heaven if you have him on your side, but if he turns against you, he's a sea monster."

Gertie and I nodded our heads.

"If we don't make any waves, we'll have smooth sailing from here on out," Alex said then pointed at us. "No waves…Not even a ripple."

We both nodded again.

Alex relaxed. "You two hungry?"

"Starving," I said.

"Let's go check out the crew mess. See what type of goodies they have for us aboard the *MS Barnacle*."

Goodies? I realized Alex was being as optimistic as one of the watchmen aboard the *Titanic: "Relax. Don't be such a worrywart. It's just a little iceberg. We'll be fine."*

CHAPTER SEVEN

No Chicken Noodle For You

Gertie and I stood in front of the crew mess buffet line, our bodies illuminated by the glow of the orange heat lamps, like a couple of hobos warming our hands over a barrel-drum fire. The food had a vagrant quality too. I grabbed the big metal spoon that was stuck into some lumpy UFO (unidentifiable food object) and gave the curry a few stirs, hoping this would help me locate some piece of meat that would be useful in classifying the species that we were being served. I couldn't tell if it was bait squid curry or a blowfish quill stew, so I abandoned the spoon and walked to the next metal serving-tray down the line.

I glanced over at Gertie, who appeared to be foraging under the heat lamps as well. Maybe she had found something edible in the crew mess forest. She looked at the buffet line with the kind of face you make when you're stopped at a red light and you look over at the car next to you and see the person inside eating a booger.

I read the label on the little white card above the next tray: *JERK CHICKEN*. I would have had to use a detailed diagram in the *Grey's Anatomy of Chicken* textbook in order to correctly identify what part of the chicken was being served. This was not the kind of conventional cut that you'd find in your local chicken shop back home.

Six months later, I finally discovered what Festivus Cruise Lines was feeding us in their special "jerk chicken" recipe. I was cutting up one of those pre-cooked rotisserie chickens that you can get for around five bucks at grocery stores in the United States. I had used a cleaver to hack off a drumstick from the breast. I stopped and pointed at the little knuckle-type joint that is located just past the drumstick—a messy cluster of bone, chewy cartilage, gristly fat, and slimy chicken skin—and said, "That's it. Ha, ha! I found you at last, you greasy devil!"

Back in the crew mess, I still had an empty plate. I walked down the buffet line and carefully calculated my delicious dinner options, and gradually came to the conclusion that I would only eat the food on that buffet if everything else on the cruise ship had already been consumed—and that included the other passengers and crew members. I found Gertie filling a bowl with ship's milk as if she was going to serve an alley cat out back. When I saw her grab a box of raisin and bran cereal, I decided to follow suit. We were only a few weeks into our ship-life card game, and we were already folding.

Usually crew members made a predictable progression through the food options in the crew mess. At first they will eat anything. Then one day they wake up and find themselves unexplainably gagging every time they're within a forty-foot radius of the crew mess. Then they go a few months eating nothing but heaping salads drenched in the cruise ship's "house dressing", which tastes like nothing more than watered-down mayonnaise with a bit of concentrated coffee syrup thrown in for coloring and Italian-officer-cigarette ash for a thickener.

After crew members contract some type of cyclospora virus from contaminated vegetables that were brought on board while the ship was roped up in Thailand, they reach the inevitable point where they'd rather snorkel with Jaws and his offspring than see another cruise ship vegetable. This is the moment where they become dangerously desperate and eventually succumb to a culinary life consuming nothing but oranges and the spicy lentil curry called dhal.

The crew buffet downward-spiral continues when crew members find themselves barely surviving off of generic boxed cereals with names like "Puffy Bites" and "Choco Balls"—names that suggest that the manufacturer was unable to get legal permission to use words such as "chocolate" and "wheat" in the cereal titles because the products contain so few natural ingredients.

As I stood filling a bowl with ship's milk—which I was very excited about, might I add—I realized that Gertie and I had entered a crew-buffet Black Hole. We were *already* eating boxed cereal. We had boarded the starship *Enterprise* and had zapped into warp speed, thus bypassing all the appropriate food-planets along our regularly scheduled crew-buffet adventure. We had landed at the end of the line, in a galaxy far, far away.

But where would we go from here? I had never passed this point. We were going where no crew member had gone before.

Captain's Log. Stardate 0604. Aboard the MS Barnacle—also known as the Ship of Darkness.

Today we drifted into a deep space territory on the outer edges of the cruise ship universe, nearly sickened by the sight of the crew mess buffet line. We resorted to desperate, desperate measures and ate boxed cereal on our first day. Boxed cereal! I almost asked Scotty to beam me up, but I resisted the temptation and sailed onward, into the dark unknown.

Gertie asked me why they would feed us this kind of garbage, and I said, "Damn it Gertie, I'm an art auctioneer, not a cruise ship cook." She didn't get the joke because she has never watched a single episode of Star Trek *or* Big Bang Theory *in her entire life.*

We seem to be in the midst of an outright disaster which leads me to fear that we are being fed by Klingons who are hell-bent on destroying our crew through a slow program of dysentery and scurvy.

I don't know where we will sail from here, but wherever our journey takes us, I will face the jerk chicken on the buffet line bravely, boldly, and with a pinched nose.

I followed Gertie to the back of the busy crew mess, to a table that was up against a wall with a small porthole window where we could watch our first sunset sink into the Mediterranean Sea. Gertie carefully laid her tray and bowl of ship's milk on the table without spilling a drop, which is quite a difficult task when the ship is rolling in the waves.

She sat down at the table and pulled her hands in, like two little kitten paws, and smiled. "Meow."

I guess it was appropriate since we *were* being fed like animals.

I had just sat down too when I heard a voice from behind me. "Hey!"

I turned around and saw an old friend from a previous contract where I had worked with a completely different cruise line company that we'll call Kingdom Cruise Lines. He was a musician from Poland, a fellow drummer, who played in one of the lounge bands on board. I wasn't exactly surprised to see him. It is a small ship-world, after all.

The saying goes, "The grass is always greener on the other side." Well, in ship life, "The sea is always bluer on the other ship." Crew members are constantly on a never-ending sea quest for better pay, better food, better ports, better crew cabins, better looking crew members, and more shipboard privileges. The crew member pool is often filled with the same swimmers. We're all one big, mostly happy albeit highly dysfunctional cruise-ship family.

After six years working on ships, I could probably be plopped down on any random ship out at sea right now, and I'd know at least one person on board, and they'd probably still be complaining about how they were about to jump ship and sign on with a different company because—yep, you guessed it—ship life was much better "on my last ship". I made friends with my Polish percussion pal back in my early cruise-ship days, yet I couldn't remember his name. But I'm a man, and men have funny memories. For example, you could tell a man that he will be drawn and quartered if he leaves the toilet seat up one more time, and he still won't be able to remember to put it in the proper position that will save his wife from falling down the watery rabbit hole. However—and here is the salient point—right before the executioners whip the horses that will rip him to pieces, he'll be able to recite from memory every single statistic associated with the 1972 Miami Dolphins football team. You know, the one that Don Shula coached, the only team to have a perfect season in the history of the NFL?

I glanced at his name tag, hoping not to give myself away: *BARTEK BROVINSKY, MUSICIAN, POLAND.*

There was a girl sitting next to him. Very pretty. A thin and petite brunette. Pale skin. Librarian glasses. Serious smile. Name tag: *JULSKI FINNICK, MUSICIAN, POLAND.* Bartek introduced her as the piano player in his band. They were in the lounge lizard business, something I had done on my first contract aboard cruise ships, and I had fond memories from those days with Star Man and Gary.

We moved our "food" over to his table. "So, how are things here on the *Barnacle*?" I asked.

If we had been in a Warner Brother's cartoon we would have seen steam coming out of his ears. Maybe one of those little gray clouds would have swung above him and started raining on his bald head. "This is the worst ship we have ever been on. *The* worst."

"Worst contract," Julski said.

Gertie gave a sympathetic look and then shoveled cereal in her mouth.

I asked them what was so bad about the ship.

Bartek took a deep breath in a *Where do I even start?* sort of way. "This is dark ship." He was shaking his head. "Management crazy. The food is not eatable. Our cabins—we get no sleep. I am done with this. Not good life."

"With this ship? Or working on cruise ships all together?"

"No. With ship life. I am done."

Julski chimed in, "Yes. Done with ship life. This is *last* contract."

"They are working us too hard," Bartek added. "Five hours a day. This mandatory performance schedule." He clucked his tongue and shook his head. "How can they expect us to sing and play music for five hours a day? With only one day off a week. My voice will be gone forever after six months of this. My hands will be ruined after few years of this kind of playing. And then what will we do? Work at grocery store in Poland?"

I had been hearing about this mandatory five-hours-per-day musician-performance schedule for years now. The whole thing came about after some pencil-pushing accountant became the CEO of one of the big cruise lines. I guess he decided that the cruise companies weren't getting enough productivity out of their musicians. The guy must have valued creative minds about as much as a high-fashion model values a wart that just popped up on her face out of nowhere. He must have known as much about playing live music as a DJ hired for a wedding reception. It was as if the president of the cruise line pulled the number out of a hat: *"Five hours. That sounds about right. What do you think, Cletus?"* (Cletus being his goldfish.)

Singing and strumming a guitar on a cruise ship for five hours a day, six days a week, might sound like a pretty cushy job to some of you, but the voice and hands have their physical limitations, not to mention the AMBD (acute musician boredom disorder) that inevitably sets in after a cruise ship musician performs on the lido deck for the thousandth time in one month. At that point, a passenger requesting "The Electric Slide" again is enough to drive some cruise ship musicians to throw their guitar amplifier in the lido deck pool while it's still plugged in.

A word of advice to passengers: Don't walk up to the cruise ship band and request "Margaritaville," "Brown-Eyed Girl," "The Cupid Shuffle," "The Electric Slide," "Mustang Sally," or "Sweet Home Alabama." I don't care if the band's lead singer is wearing a Jimmy Buffet shirt and talking about how he's from Mobile, the band does *not* want to play these songs for you. They'd rather undergo a lobotomy than play "The Electric Slide" one more time. If you must ask them to play one of these tunes, write your request on a hundred-dollar bill that is attached to the back of a 1969 Les Paul Deluxe Goldtop. Then and only then should you be able to sleep with a clear conscience at night.

Bartek continued, "And we're playing to no one. Most of the time, there isn't a single person in lounge. We are good band. But with all the things that go on aboard ship, no one is going to come and listen to us for five hours a day. We beg with management to lighten schedule. But no. Today, five hours in lounge. Tomorrow, five hours in lounge. Every single day,"—he pointed his finger in the air—"five hours in lounge. I feel like jumping overboard."

Then his eyes went all sea-donkey crazy. He used two fingers to make his hand look like a man walking on the edge of the crew mess table. Then his hand-man jumped off the edge of the tabletop. "*Wheeeeeeeee!*"

Bartek had already gone *dark*. I knew it when I saw it. I had been there before, too—playing jazz sets in the cigar bar for no one, performing Dixieland concerts in the atrium for two passengers who were fifteen feet away in the casino and mindlessly pulling the one-armed bandits, performing jazz tunes for people who wouldn't have noticed us even if we were Miles Davis with Weather Report as his backup band. Cruise ship passengers wanted Bob Marley, not Bob Mintzer (who I think is great. Love your playing, Mr. Bob). Two months of performing concerts where you have a reception from the audience that's about as welcoming as Lee Harvey

Oswald's reaction to JFK when he passed by the Texas School Book Repository is enough to bore a dark hole in the soul of almost any musician.

"How much longer is your contract?" I asked.

Bartek looked as if he smelled something rotting. "Two months. And then no more cruise ships. This is my *last* contract." He leaned across the table. "Why do you think so many new crew members signed on today? Because so many people on this ship request transfer." He let that hang in the air for a minute. His eyes got as big as mine when I first saw what was being served on the *Barnacle's* crew buffet line. "We had two crew members jump overboard a few weeks ago." Bartek looked around, as if he was afraid someone might be listening to what he was saying.

"We heard," I said quietly.

"And someone else left ship last week. Do you know where we sail from?"

"No."

"Dubai." Bartek said this very matter-of-factly, in a *case-closed* sort of way.

I didn't follow what he was saying and I squinted.

"You haven't heard about it?" he asked

Gertie put down her spoon. "About what?"

"The coronavirus."

"No," she said. "We haven't heard. Was this in Dubai?"

"Yes. It started in the Middle East somewhere and eventually spread to people in Dubai. Four or five people in that country had died while it was our home port. Then we sail back to Med two weeks ago. We had dancer on board who became very sick during relocation cruise. Started coughing all the time. Then he stop working. Then he went home. I've heard that he is in hospital now, but other dancers on board say doctors don't know what's wrong with him."

"Do you think it could be coronavirus?"

Bartek shrugged. "I heard on news yesterday that they confirm first case of virus in Italy."

A guy walked into the crew mess that I recognized. He was lanky, tall, as pale as the thin strip of skin beneath a cruise-ship showgirl's thong. It was Squid, the showband guy from our last contract.

I asked if Squid wanted to eat with us and he walked over and sat at our table. I asked him what he thought of the food.

"I expect it to be like this." He said. "We work on a cruise ship, not at the French Laundry."

He began disassembling a chunk of chicken cartilage from the bone to get to the delicate strip of meat that was hiding somewhere in there. He looked incredibly focused and rather unhappy, like a surgeon who had drawn the short-straw and was now performing the liver transplant on a high-powered-lawyer patient who specialized in medical malpractice.

Squid looked at Gertie. "Can I ask you a question?" he said.

"Sure," Gertie said.

Squid chewed on some chicken gristle. "From a female perspective, if you act excited to see another man whom you have not seen in several months, does this mean that you're attracted to him?"

"Hmm, is this hypothetical?"

"Sure," he said.

"Well, hypothetically, how excited did she get?"

"Like a passenger who just won the hairy chest contest."

"And was this hypothetical other man attractive?"

"On a scale of one to ten, I would say, soap opera leading man good-looking."

"Hmm. I'd say, hypothetically, her reaction doesn't mean that she's physically attracted to the guy. Maybe they were just good friends."

Squid pressed his lips together and blinked. "Friends. Hmph."

"Is everything okay?" Gertie asked.

"It's just hypothetical." Squid said, and then went back to operating on his chicken knuckle.

I had to ask him. "Is Svetlana on board?" I was referring to his girlfriend from our last ship, the real fox, the hot Russian bird that many of the other crew members called Svetlana Sosexyhotkova. The squid had a fox.

Squid didn't look up. "Yep. Seems like almost everyone from the *MS Universe* was transferred here."

Gertie leaned in. As a female cruise ship crew member, she had learned to do many things well, two of them being: 1) how to successfully apply makeup during a squall in the South China Sea, and 2) how to smell drama in the salty cruise ship air. "So who's this soap opera guy?" she asked, seeming a bit too interested in this mystery sailor for my pirate blood.

"That was hypothetical," Squid said.

Gertie's shoulders sank. There was no gossip treasure in this possibly shipwrecked relationship. At least not yet. Though, I felt sure that Gertie would keep her American submersible-sonar pinging, always searching for secret soviet vessels, as if we were back in the good old Cold War days.

I turned back to Bartek, the sea donkey who had been

quietly nursing a cup of hot tea. "Is there a slop chest on board?" I asked. The slop chest is the crew store on cruise ships, usually tucked away in some small room down below the waterline or found as an extension of the crew bar. The term "slop chest" is commonly used to refer to stores found aboard merchant ships where crew members can purchase goods and charge the price of items against their pay. In fact, this odd, esoteric term has been used as far back as the early 1800s, as in "Argh, get me some grog from the slop chest, you scallywag scum bucket, or I'll make you walk the plank." You'll also hear the term used aboard military vessels around the world.

Needless to say, the term is about as far from appetizing as one could come up with to describe the place where crew members go to buy snacks and supplies. And to the cruise company's credit, this is one of the few places on a cruise ship where the prices are not *grossly* inflated. The prices are often quite reasonable, just a bit higher than what you might find in a convenience store in the US.

It's also the last resort for crew members who have reached the end of their crew mess food options. Once a crew member has grown tired of box cereals, they start putting together meals from foods they can purchase in the slop chest, meals that look as if they could be found on the type of menu that middle–school–aged children dream about: two candy bars for breakfast, a bag of potato chips and a sack full of sweet-and-sour gummy worms for lunch, two cups of microwavable sea creature–flavored noodles for dinner with a couple of ice cream sandwiches for dessert. So, if you're a doctor that specializes in treating gout, obesity, or diabetes, open up a chain of clinics in every cruise ship port-town you can find. Cater to crew members and you'll never run short of patients.

I knew Gertie and I were on the fast track to the slop chest. We'd be able to live off of boxed cereals and ship's milk for one month—two, tops. Then we'd have to resort to smuggling food back on board from ports and buying supplies in the slop.

Bartek took a sip of tea while he thought about my question, smiling the whole time. It was a sea donkey smile, a bit villainous, a tad sadistic—the way that someone smiles at you who has already taken Advanced Organic Chemistry while you are telling them how excited you are about taking the course.

Bartek lowered his tea mug. "Why don't I show you?" he said.

Gertie turned to Squid. "Let me know if you have any more hypothetical questions."

Squid nodded, and we followed Bartek to a larger section of the crew mess, just past a small partition that separated the officer's mess from the crew member's dining hall. In the officer's mess, we had nicer tables and a smaller buffet line, but the food selection and the overall feeling that you were eating dinner in a 1982 hospital cafeteria was about the same. The major difference being that the crew mess was much more crowded and a bit louder, in the way that a jet engine is a bit louder than a library. I had seen very nice officer's mess halls on other ships. Unfortunately, we were not aboard one of those ships. Bartek took us to the back of the crew mess—where we found a small room filled with shelves, nearly all of them empty.

Near the door there was a small bin that was half-filled

with noodle cups. I looked at the Styrofoam cartons inside: *PRAWN-LIME MICROWAVABLE NOODLES.* I tried the small fridge and found a few cans of dark brown soda, the writing on the bottles in Arabic. There were a few essentials: soap, dental floss, toothpaste, also labeled in Arabic.

Bartek was still smiling. "The crossing from Dubai took fourteen days," he said. "The slop chest has looked like this for two weeks. We keep asking when we're going to get another shipment, but nothing has happened. I don't understand it."

As we stood in the dusty, nearly empty room, crew members kept walking up and poking their heads into the slop chest, most of them uttering some type of curse word, shaking their heads, and then walking away, rather unhappy to find their beloved slop chest so barren.

I opened the door to the cooler and took out one of the Arabic sodas. I looked at Bartek. "You know you've hit a new low in your life when you get emotional about the lack of candy bars and potato chips in your life," I said.

"Come and talk to me after you've been eating in the crew mess for two more months."

He was right. Gertie was digging around in the microwaveable noodle box, searching desperately for a chicken- or beef-flavored carton that maybe just maybe had been overlooked by the two thousand crew members who rummaged through the box, searching for the same thing every day. I rummaged through the bin too. I mean, who knows? Someone *could* have overlooked it.

"It's no use," Bartek said. "They're all prawn lime. Trust me. I've been through that box a million times."

I felt it was exactly that type of self-fulfilling-prophecy

negativism that turned Bartek into a sea donkey in the first place. We kept digging. We only abandoned our search after we were confident that we had looked over each carton three or four times, and even then it didn't feel right to walk away from the bin without checking one more time.

There's something strange about those microwavable noodles. Crew members can reach the point where they'd rather eat tree bark than another cruise ship filet mignon that the cooks whip up once in a while (Interpretation: when too few passengers selected filet mignon at dinner on "Surf and Turf" night), but crew members never seem to grow tired of their microwavable noodles.

We said good-bye to Bartek for the evening and headed back toward our lovely crew cabin. Before we plunged down below the waterline, we stopped on a breezeway and watched the full moon race alongside our ship as we sailed through the Mediterranean Sea. We could see inky blotches of land in the distance that would rise up in tall dark masses of hills and mountains, the occasional glow of some far off home that was perched on a coastal Italian mountainside, while the moon shone its silvery light across it all. It was very romantic.

Gertie turned to me, never one to miss an opportunity for romance on the high seas. I looked into her big brown eyes, and she leaned toward my ear and whispered, "I really thought that we were going to find a chicken-flavored noodle cup in that box."

"I know. I did too. Chicken is the best," I said, whispering romantically too.

"You know, we'll be in Rome in two days."

"Just two more sleeps."

"We're going to see the pope. Can you believe it?"

"The pope is quite a bucket-list event," I said, holding her close.

"Do you think they'll have chicken-flavored noodles in Rome?" she asked. "I really want some, now that we've been talking about them so much."

"We can only hope. So, do you have our Rome itinerary all planned out?"

"Oh, yes," she said enthusiastically. "We have to catch the train no later than nine thirty a.m. Then we have to get off at…" Her voice just drifted away like a cruise-ship napkin that is blown overboard. She kept talking, but I didn't hear a single word.

I had finally learned to tune her out completely, a real milestone in our rather dreamy shipboard romance.

CHAPTER EIGHT

The Lorax and the Monster in the Drain

I woke up the next morning clutching the top edge of my thin blue blanket. The bed sheet was damp with sweat. Before we had tucked into our separate bunk beds for a wonderful night of constantly-interrupted sleep, the air conditioning system had kicked on and coughed a few times. Then apparently a party ensued where all the little gnomes that lived in the cruise ship air ducts got together for a night of cigarette smoking, stopping occasionally to open and close the dying-cat and dump-truck-hitting-a-pothole door. Next, they would run down the hallway so they could keep us awake with their hammering and tapping on the I-95-railroad handrails. And apparently, the smoking area for the party in our air duct was located right near the hole in our ceiling, which caused all the gnome smoke to blow directly into our cabin.

Silly cruise ship gnomes. They can be such jerks sometimes.

In the middle of the night, I got up and closed the vent. Our crew cabin grew hot without the cool smoke-filled air blasting into the room. That's when we realized what our double-layered carpet actually smelled like.

Remember the carpet? The sandwiched, damp floor-covering that probably harbored bacteria large enough to be legally recognized as suitable candidates for admission into Ivy League schools.

We were torn. We could keep cool and breathe air that was about the quality you would find if you stuck your mouth around the tip of a paper mill smokestack back in 1965, or we could live in a room that smelled like the carpet from the *Titanic* after it had been pulled up from the bottom of the ocean and then forgotten in a dryer that was never turned on by some absentminded maritime archeologist. Robert Ballard: *"Okay, who forgot to start the dryer with the* Titanic *carpet from the Grand Ballroom in it again? Billy, was that you? I swear. One day, I'm going to build robots named Alvin to replace all of you knuckleheads."*

As you can imagine, this wasn't exactly the type of situation we expected to find ourselves in as the mid-ranking officers that we supposedly were. Something had gone terribly wrong aboard this vessel, and one night of sleeping in this unpleasant crew cabin was enough to motivate me to get out there and try to find out how to fix it. The place to start? The Human Resources (HR) director. This was a person with the power to turn our ship life around.

I told Gertie that I'd talk to the HR director about getting us a different room.

"Didn't you think it was strange when Alex asked us not to fight management about our rooms?" she said. "After everything Alex said. It was a complete one-eighty."

I felt there was more to the story here too. There was something hinky going on at Churchill Downs, something rotten in the state of Denmark.

"Ask the HR director what room Alex is living in," she said.

"You think that's why he changed his tune?" I asked.

"I think there's at least a chance that Alex got what he wanted, and now he doesn't want us making any waves."

I didn't doubt that he'd do that to us. After all, this was a cruise ship, a place where you find more backstabbers than at Marcus Brutus' Birthday party in 44 BC. But Alex must have known that we'd find out eventually.

"Do you think we'll actually be able to get into the room that's rightfully ours, the room that Festivus designated as an art team cabin?" Gertie asked.

"Truthfully, no, but we should try. Maybe we can at least get something better than this."

I walked to the crew office and, once again, found the most depressed-looking group of people ever assembled in one room since the movie *Old Yeller* was last shown in theaters.

They gave me the name of the HR director and told me that his office was just around the corner. I was told he had an "open-door policy", which probably meant absolutely nothing. Most of the open-door policies I had encountered on cruise ships existed so that crew members could exit as quickly as possible when the officers told them to leave. As I walked to the HR office, I thought about crew cabin politics.

Real estate is the most valuable commodity in cruise liner land, and nowhere else aboard a ship is the political battle more heated than in the war for crew cabins. Those who control the crew real-estate market aren't willing to give up their properties for a few measly hundred-dollar bills. We had to put down larger chips than that of we wanted to get in the game, and a *Monopoly game,* my friends, ship life is.

It's no coincidence that the worst property on the Monopoly game-board is that turd-colored square, Mediterranean Avenue. We might have been living in a turd-colored, turd-smelling square on Mediterranean Avenue, but we had faith that if we maneuvered around this board just right, we could end up with something as golden as St. James Place maybe. No way for Boardwalk or Park Place. That was dreamy passenger-type stuff; staterooms with back walls that were nothing but ocean views, and room stewards who called you names like "Your Highness" and "Your Majesty" upon request.

Mediocrity is all that a crew member can hope for in this ship life. Average is the goal, the tropical port of call in crew members' dreams. We just wanted your average clean air, your average one layer of carpet (preferably dry, but not a deal breaker), an average bathroom that smelled better than a New York subway, and an average porthole window with an average amount of sunlight pouring in. Was that too much to ask? Can I get a *witness*, people?

On past ships, sometimes I'd luck out and be assigned a wonderful cabin. Unfortunately, this was often not the case. This time, we had been assigned a crew cabin that was worse than some of the shacks you'd find on the bad side of town in a Dickens novel, but we couldn't just outsource a new room. A cruise ship is a classic zero-sum game. For every winner, there's an inherent loser, because you can't just pull a new crew cabin out of the sea. They're not making any more real estate aboard the ships.

Gertie and I felt we needed to do two things here: 1) find something of value that we could offer, and 2) make a good impression with the people who had the power to help us. Power—that was our biggest problem. Getting a good crew cabin often came down to three things: sex, politics, and power. Sometimes money, if there was someone you could pay-off.

Just like life on land, your position in ship life often came down to one basic principle: It's all about who you know. And on a ship, it's often all about who you're sleeping with. Rank is relative in ship life. A crew member who finds themselves in the position of being on top of an officer every night might as well have three yellow stripes stitched onto their shoulder boards, and this applies to men and women. Hey, no one ever said that ship life was fair.

But what was *our* position in ship life? We were members of a fairly autonomous department that had no one under us (except our art steward) and everyone on the ship above us. We didn't oversee or have access to any valuable shipboard commodities except the Duck Nipple champagne storage cabinet, and all crew members would rather drink Corexit-laced sea water during the BP oil spill (not a fan, BP) than drink the bubbly that we had on tap. We also weren't the gatekeepers to any valuable cruise-ship privileges.

We were nobodies in this ship life, but we did have charm and a few other things that always spoke louder than even the most charismatic and persuasive negotiator. We had a legally binding contract that clearly stated that we were entitled to an officer's cabin, and a little blue book that is every cruise ship crew member's very best friend: The International Labor Organization's Handbook of Seafarer's Rights. Those were our secret weapons though, only to be used in moments of mutually assured destruction after all other avenues of diplomacy had been abandoned. Once we pulled out *those* cards, we wouldn't be making many friends with the management aboard the ship, and we wanted to avoid having maritime tariffs used against us, aka taking away our shipboard privileges. We wanted to avoid naval warfare at nearly any cost.

The HR director was sitting behind a small wooden desk with a ship's wheel clock on top. He was a healthily plump and friendly looking man, face like a walrus, a push-broom mustache, frayed eyebrows, bald head as shiny as a young Navy recruit's shoes, thick-rimmed glasses that could double as an effective form of birth control. If you took away the glasses, the man looked very much like the Lorax, the Dr. Seuss character, and in a good way. Give him a tree stump and a bit of yellow hair around the waist, and he would have been a perfect match.

His name tag: *ALFRED SUMTERFORT, HR DIRECTOR, USA*.

I knocked on his door—which was open, might I add.

He looked up from a stack of paperwork. "Come in. How can I help you?"

I sat down and explained our situation, and from the moment I said *cigarette smoke* he began nodding his head in agreement. This was unusual for a cruise ship officer. I was used to dealing with Italians on cruise ships, and in my experience, Italian officers enjoyed hearing an American complaining about cigarette smoke about as much as drinking a glass of wine made with grapes grown in Tijuana, or as much as drinking a cup of American coffee. *I-ah only drink-ah cappuccino-ah.* Yet, here was Alfred, leaning back and listening, looking as if he agreed. A breath of fresh sea air.

"Don't worry about a thing. I'm going to do my best to get this straightened out."

"Do you think you can get us a new room?" I asked.

"I'll try my best, and I think I can," he said.

I asked if he knew where Alex's room was located, but he didn't know.

However, maybe the tides had turned. Maybe St. Francis of Paola, the patron saint of seafarers, was looking down on Gertie and me, after all.

As I walked out of his office, Alfred Sumterfort smiled. He gave me a pat on the back. *What a guy.*

What a politician, who probably sat down, pushed up his glasses, thought about our crew cabin plight one last time, and then immediately turned on his computer, rolled up his sleeves, and dug right into an exhilarating game of *Minecraft*.

I walked back to the scene of the crime, room 0604, to find Gertie unpacking her luggage and effectively "commandeering by imminent female domain" all of the available storage space in our tiny crew quarters. The room looked as if a hurricane had ripped through a seaside women's-clothing boutique and the resulting tidal surge had caused a massive drift of high heels, sundresses, hair products, nautical-themed bikinis, and maritime-motif panties to wash up on shore. Gertie pointed to two thin drawers underneath the bunk bed. Each drawer was almost large enough to hold a box of crackers. Then she pointed to the armoire against the wall. There was a small sliver of space in the wardrobe that miraculously wasn't filled yet with girly suit-jackets and sweaters with sailboats knitted on the front.

Gertie smiled. "I saved you some space. Love you." Then she looked at the hillside tangle of flotsam and jetsam and put a finger to her lips. "Now where do you think I could put my shoes?"

I wanted to suggest the shipboard garbage incinerator, or perhaps the Mediterranean Sea, but I decided I'd rather sleep in my own bed that night instead of out on the breezeway in one of the cruise ship loungers—a place I had grown rather familiar with through the years as a result of living with women in ten-by-ten crew cabins, and by the fact that I had a big mouth that was pretty much like the air vent in our crew quarters—it wasn't connected to any sort of effective filter. The lounger on the breezeway was my go-to seadog house, and I was sure Gertie would send me out into the cold, salty air before this contract was over. Something about the smell of foot sweat that her mountain of high heels had brought into our room, made me feel rather certain of that.

I decided to keep my mouth shut this time. Gertie possessed a remarkable sense of humor, but her humor wasn't quite elastic enough to stretch into jokes about her heels, clothes, hair, nails, body-mass index, eating habits, mother, father, siblings, hair stylist, port activity decisions, her favorite football team (the Seminoles), her drinking, her love of Italian men, or her love of donuts and chocolate and especially chocolate donuts. These no-go zones are also known by all intelligent men as "the big four". That was *four*, right?

I suddenly felt rather cramped. The walls felt as if they were closing in on us just a little. At least Gilligan had an entire island when he was shipwrecked. I didn't know if I could survive a whole season of this show. But I did the right thing. I just smiled, nodded, and said, "Wherever you want your shoes to go is fine with me." *Good doggie. Now, roll over and pay me alimony for the rest of your life. That a boy!*

"So what did he say?" Gertie asked.

I filled her in on the details.

"See," she said, "we just have to think positive, and everything will work out just fine." Then she looked down at Mount High Heel that rose up before her like a multicolored volcano of leather, straps, and buckles, and said, "I think the toilet drain has something living in it. It keeps making this weird groaning noise, and then it kind of burps, and then it smells really bad in here."

Great news. Our bathroom drain farts because there is a particularly gassy sea monster living inside of it. I'd seen worse on ships, drains that were like Old Faithful at Yellowstone National Park. They erupted and flooded the surrounding area on a fairly predictable schedule that coincided with every time a passenger got a towel animal lodged in their toilet—which is on the fifteen of every hour aboard a cruise ship, in case you want to be around to see the old girl blow her top.

"We have the auction in a few hours," she added, as if this could somehow be distorted into a message of good news.

"Maybe the monster in our drain would like to buy a giclée on canvas," I said.

"I already asked him. He said he was just here for the free champagne. But maybe he'll buy a lithograph. Why don't you go and see."

CHAPTER NINE

The Champagne Charlatans Strike Again

We sold a boatload of art at our first auction aboard the *MS Barnacle*. Thanks in no small part to Gertie's magic pink-colored gavel, and thanks in large part to Alex's auction-house wizardry. Things were looking up. Then again, up is about the only place you *can* look when you're living below the waterline.

During the auction, Alex had posted me at my honorary position as the official hand-clapper every time someone raised their bid card, so I was able to revive my vaudevillian-esque "handicapped seal" routine again. After the auction was over, I picked up the raffle tickets and discarded "free champagne" cards that people had left behind on the tables, and then we moved back to the gallery to start our long day selling art there.

Alex posted us like sentinels guarding the gate of a medieval castle, Gertie at the north entrance, me at the southern gateway. Then he told us to circle the perimeter. We looked like two vultures that had been caught in a thermal vortex of hot air when I found two passengers in my sea-hawk sights. They were a young couple wearing matching bright yellow shirts, in the way that some passengers do so that they don't lose each other in the shipboard crowds. They were browsing in the gift shop next door.

Once they walked close enough to my perch, I swooped down and caught them while they were looking at a painting in the gallery.

"Looking for anything in particular?" I asked.

They were a young couple, seemingly in their early thirties, and they were as pale as the snow drifts that our neighbors back in the mountains of North Carolina were probably shoveling as they cursed our names while thinking about all the fun we were having in the Mediterranean sun.

The girl (athletic build, turned-up nose, face like a porcelain doll, mousy shoulder-length hair, rum punch breath, sunscreen odor) leaned in toward the oil painting. "No. Just browsing. But this *is* very nice."

That was my cue. "Would you two like a glass of champagne?"

The woman turned to her husband and smiled in a coy way, as passengers do who had read the *Cruising World* article titled, "How to Get Free Booze on Your Next Cruise".

"What do you think, Buster? Should we have a glass?" she said.

"Sure, Chloe. Why not?"

Their acting was so wooden I figured they'd float away if I threw them overboard. They looked as if they were about to drop onto the carpet and start rolling around laughing. This wasn't the first time I had encountered champagne con artists. There were a few on every cruise. They were easy to spot. They walked into the gallery every night after dinner and talked about how interested they were in every piece of art I showed them even though they looked as if they had about as much money as a barefoot college student eating dinner at a free Hare Krishna vegetarian buffet. I knew champagne hustlers when I saw them, and Buster and Chloe were two certified *bam-booze-elers*.

But truth be told, even though Alex hated it, I fed into this type of freeloader behavior. Call me a sucker, but I had a soft spot deep in my heart for passengers who had the guts to search out the free stuff in life. I love free stuff, so they felt like family to me, the type of people who will spend thirty dollars in gas driving around the rich neighborhoods to see if anyone left a ten dollar piece of furniture out on the curb.

And I think more art auctioneers should feel this way. These passengers are why crew members have jobs in the first place. They pay a lot of money to go on a cruise, and even though my main priority on board the *MS Barnacle* was to sell art, I never lost sight of the fact that I had a real opportunity to dramatically improve the experience of a passenger's cruise. So let the passengers drink their free Duck Nipple champagne, you hornswoggling skinflints. And while I know that what I'm about to say may cause a flood of e-mails from cruise ship art auctioneers, I don't care. If you're on a cruise right now, go find the art gallery and wander around until you see them break out the bubbly, and then ask them for a glass. You deserve it. If you start to feel guilty, don't. But if you still do, remember that none of those crew members would be there without that huge chunk of income you forked over for your all-access pass aboard the sailing buffet. So, cheers to all the passengers who know how swindle free booze. Free drinks in the art gallery for everyone, on me!

I scampered over to our portable ice cart that we had commandeered for the art gallery from the cruise ship's main kitchen—which on the cruise ship black market runs about a twenty-dollar bribe—and poured two glasses of Duck Nipple.

"How was dinner?" I asked.

Chloe's eyes lit up. "It was wonderful. Lobster. Filet.

Chocolate melting cake. Just perfect. Buster ate two plates."

She put her hand on her chin and cocked her head to the side. *Oh, no, here it comes.*

After five years on cruise ships I had developed a sixth sense for stupid questions. There was nothing supernatural about it per se; I had simply developed a highly technical and scientific way to determine when I was about to be asked a stupid question. Here is how crew members can apply this groundbreaking science that I discovered to their own cruise ship contract experience: 1) Ask yourself the following question: "Am I talking to a passenger?" If the answer is yes, then you know you are about to be asked a stupid question in precisely T-minus ten seconds.

I saw that curious twinkle in Chloe's eyes, a twinkle that always made my stomach turn. "So," she asked, "do crew members eat the same food that we eat?"

I wanted to tell her that for lunch we had the option between a white pasty substance labeled *SHE CRAB SOUP* that looked as if the only crab parts it contained were the pulverized shells of horseshoe crab, or a gooey dark-brown curry that closely resembled something I saw in a documentary once where the host was scraping some sludge off an Alaskan beach right after the Exxon Valdez had decided to prematurely eject its cargo all over the coast of Prince William Sound. The temptation to explain to passengers exactly what ship life is like is certainly enticing.

However, I had learned that honest answers were a type of gateway drug to more stupid questions, and I had grown tired of opening that particular can of giant sea-worms quite some time ago, like around the second day I had been aboard a cruise ship as a crew member. So, I just nodded and smiled and said my standard answer to stupid question #45.1, which is: "We mostly eat what we catch while fishing from the back of the crew deck at night." And then I smiled and asked them where they were from.

"Canada," Buster said. "We're your maple syrup friends to the north."

"Is this your first cruise?" I asked, but I felt I already knew the answer to that question. Champagne con artists were always veteran or, at the very least, return cruisers. It takes a few cruises to build up the confidence to put together a good cruise ship heist.

Buster lifted his glass, swallowed the entire flute of Duck Nipple in one gulp, and then said, "Nah, we're pros. We'll actually be on this ship for a few cruises."

"How many?"

"Four weeks."

This isn't common, but it's not unheard of. In fact, Gertie and I had worked on a cruise ship that sailed all over Asia, a different itinerary every week. There were passengers that stayed aboard that ship for two or three months straight.

Chloe and Buster were my favorite type of passengers; they made you feel like some things in ship life were *not* disposable. You see, long-term passengers, like long-term friends on land, give crew members a sense of stability and community in their otherwise unstable lives which are lived in a shipboard neighborhood where the faces change every week or so.

Chloe pulled a walkie-talkie out of her back pocket and pushed the talk button. I heard a beep come from Busters trousers. He pulled out his own bright yellow walkie-talkie that had a piece of tan duct tape plastered on the front that read *BUSTER.* He gave Chloe a mischievous grin and pushed his button. *BEEP.* "Captain Buster to Head Deck-Swabber Chloe."

BEEP. "Arghhh, This is Captain Chloe speaking. If ye call me a deck swabber one more time, you'll be walkin' the plank, you filthy sea biscuit."

BEEP. "Captain Chloe, do you think this biscuit-eater would bring us another glass of champagne if we asked him in a nice pirate way?"

Now that was not a stupid question. "I'd be happy to, you filthy freebooters," I said, and then brought them two flutes filled flat, right to the point of overflow. We walked around the gallery for a while, and I had more laughs than I ever expected to find aboard the *Barnacle.* When they left the gallery, they were weaving down the promenade as if we were sailing in waters as rough as the Tasman Sea. Duck Nipple will do that to a band of merry pirates. I could hear their walkie-talkies beeping all the way to the end of the promenade. I was glad to have them aboard; they were a beam of brightness on this ship of darkness. I was willing to take in the sunshine wherever I could find it.

I walked over to Alex. He was shuffling papers on his desk—the invoices from our sales at the last art auction. He didn't look up. "They're not going to buy anything," Alex said.

I liked Chloe and Buster. They were my ticket to making the time pass more quickly during these dreadfully dull gallery hours. I could spend the night passing out "free champagne" cards and staring at a giclée on canvas of a rowboat tied up in a Venetian harbor that actually gave me seasickness, or I could spend my evenings laughing with

Chloe and Buster while serving them bottomless glasses of champagne, all while learning how to talk like a pirate. And if other passengers came into the gallery who might buy something, I'd help them find what they were looking for. I wasn't trying to get out of working, just trying to work hard and have fun too. It's not impossible to do both at once, even though your boss may think otherwise.

I shrugged. "You never know. I think they might come from money."

"You think?" Alex asked.

"I do."

"Hmph. You've got a lot to learn, kid. And go easy on the champagne next time. We don't want management cracking down on us."

"Why would they care? Isn't champagne one of our best tools to sell art? Who's going to buy this stuff if we can't numb a passenger's critical thinking skills with a few gallons of alcohol?"

"Like I said, you got a lot to learn. Think outside the box. See the big picture. How do cruise ships make most of their revenue? Alcohol sales. For every glass of champagne we give away, the cruise company is losing the chance to sell one more rum punch that costs as much as front-row box seats in Yankee Stadium during the World Series."

Alex was right. Everyone had a rooster in the shipboard-cockfight for onboard revenue.

I heard Gertie from behind me, "They seemed fun," she said.

"They'll be back," Alex said. "Right after dinner tomorrow." He frowned. "Champagne charlatans, Gertie. Two champagne charlatans." Then he swiftly stood up, dropped his pen on the desk, and looked at his watch. The sun was just starting to reach for the sea and cast a deep orange glow through the porthole window. Outside, sailing by, I could see the Italian coast of Corsica: rolling dark-green hillsides and soft-lit clusters of low-rise stucco villages. It had been less than two days, and I was already starting to drool when I thought of the kind of shore leave Gertie and I were going to have while strolling down the gaslight-lined cobblestone streets of sleepy, Italian portside towns. I wanted to breathe the fresh cologne-drenched air, and continue my search for the perfect pizza. I was ready for Rome.

"It's six o'clock," Alex said. "We have a two-hour break. Have you seen the crew bar?" Alex asked this in the way that a husband asks his wife if she saw their itemized bill at the end of their fourteen-day cruise. *Have you seen this bill? How did we drink seventy-two piña coladas over fourteen days?*

Alex asked us if we felt like getting a drink. We assumed the question was rhetorical. Crew members are like drunkard seagulls. If you want to quickly attract a swarm of yapping seafarers, don't throw stale breadcrumbs in the air, just toss cans of Stella Artois into the sky, and a flock of cruise ship crew members will appear out of nowhere.

CHAPTER TEN

Big Joe's Place

The crew bar was an odd L-shaped room. The bar area was in the narrow, cramped section in the bottom part of the "L" which was about ten feet long: counter height stools against the bar top, two tables against the back wall, a tiny space to stand that also served as the only foot-traffic thoroughfare for crew members. It was a claustrophobic's nightmare. Houdini: *I never had panic attacks until I stepped into the* MS Barnacle's *crew bar.*

And this was the only bar on the cruise ship that served the entire crew of about two-thousand-plus internationals who loved beer more than their grandmother. I didn't recognize the bartender (in his fifties, short with a smug smile, pudgy, a dark tan that when combined with his shaved head and extra thick eyebrows gave him a decidedly Mr. Potato Head appearance). Name tag: *BIG JOE, BARTENDER, INDIA.*

This seemed revealing. Maybe he had connections. You often don't get a nickname like "Big Joe" on a cruise ship unless you're an insider.

Big Joe stuck out his fist for a fist bump. "Charunjeevi Damamdora."

Crew members rarely shake hands. They are intimately familiar with the wide variety of wonderful viruses that habitually colonize on human hands and cruise ship door handles. Hand shaking, the gateway to norovirus, is avoided at all costs.

Then again, many of these crew members who refuse to shake hands are the same ones willing to have sex and exchange gallons of various bodily fluids with any other crew member on board as long as they meet their sky-high standards of possessing a pulse and having four limbs. (The limbs are optional. A plus, but not a deal breaker.)

Gertie and I introduced ourselves to Big Joe. Gertie always made a particularly wholehearted effort to get on a first-name basis with all crew bartenders since they were the ones that had the power to add a splash or two of extra rum to her punch. So Gertie didn't try to conceal the fact that Big Joe was going to be her new shipboard BFF when she slid a twenty-dollar bill across the bar in exchange for a single vodka cranberry, which in cruise ship currency cost about one dollar fifty cents USD for top shelf. I was also frugal about everything in life, except when it came to bribing the crew bartender.

There are two things in life that are worth splurging on: a babysitter without a criminal record, and anything that results in me not having to wait in line for a drink at a cruise-ship crew party. Big Joe looked at the twenty-dollar bill that Gertie had put down at the bar and then winked. "Thank you," he said in his sing-song Indian accent. He slipped the twenty into his pocket, and we slipped Big Joe into ours. Two symbiotic species fighting for survival in the remote back country of the wild cruise ship jungle.

Alex was motioning for us to follow him. He led us past the bar into a longer but equally narrow room. There was a pool table in the middle of the place that reminded me of the singer named Prince. It *was* a pool table, but because of its current condition, we would be forced to refer to it as "the table formerly known as a pool table". The felt had been ripped from the surface and bunched up in a pile on top, revealing a severely cracked slab of slate underneath. A few of the leather pockets had been ripped, and they were lying on top of the table, as well.

"Is this the only pool table in the crew area?" I asked.

Alex looked puzzled. "Is this the first time you two have been to the crew bar on the *MS Barnacle?"*

"Yeah."

In a British accent, Alex said, "Well, allow me to introduce you to…the crew bar" Then he put out his hand in a regal flourish as if he were a servant introducing King Henry VIII. "And this, Your Highness and Her Majesty, is the beautiful crew bar pool table. It may not be suitable for a jolly good game of billiards, but it makes an excellent place to rest your evening cocktails, because it does *not* matter if they spill when the ship hits a rogue wave. It also makes a delightful spot to sleep if your crew cabin is located in a place on the ship where sleep is absolutely impossible."

"How long has it been like this?" I asked.

Alex lost the British accent. "Someone said two months."

I wasn't surprised. Cruise ships, like the military, adhered to the same protocol maxim: SNAFU, Situation Normal, All Effed Up. This was at least the case in the crew area. The *passenger* area? Absolutely not. A cruise ship captain would "sound-ah the alarm-ah" the moment the ice cream machine temperature dropped to the point where the chocolate-vanilla swirl was, in the words of one passenger, "a bit too mushy". However, when the only cappuccino machine living in the crew area coughs up its milk frother and then suddenly lapses into a coma, the dedicated cruise ship cappuccino-machine repairmen might as well etch *OUT OF ORDER* into the machine's metal casing instead of hanging a temporary sign, because that will be the last time any crew member aboard that ship will ever sip a cup of coffee that tastes better than winch oil mixed with pine pitch.

If you think I'm exaggerating, wait until you read about "Pizza Night" aboard our wonderful *MS Barnacle.*

No one was hanging around the pool table. However, there were about fifty crew members crammed into an area at the end of the room, which was separated from the "game room" by a half open sliding glass door. A steady cloud of cigarette smoke drifted toward us from the other room.

I pointed toward the open glass door. "Where's the nonsmoking section?"

Alex laughed. "You're standing in it."

We followed Alex over to the glass door.

Gertie grabbed the handle. "Can we close it?"

She pulled the door shut and slid the latch down, but when she let go of the handle, the door just retracted back open and let out another storm cloud of swirling smoke. She shrugged. I gave it a try too, hoping I might be able to engineer a better result, but the door was on a spring, and the latch was busted.

When I looked up from fiddling with the door, I noticed that quite a few of the crew members in the smoking room were glaring at us. Their scowls reminded me that smokers tend to be remarkably offended by people who attempt to shield themselves from cigarette smoke, in the same way that a plumber would be offended if you told him that you thought it was disgusting that someone worked in shit all day. It's as if smokers somehow take personal offense to the fact that you wish to live a healthier lifestyle than them. *Hey, if breathing carbon monoxide, arsenic, benzene, formaldehyde, and vinyl chloride among a whole slew of other known carcinogens is good enough for me, then it should be good enough for you, too, you stuck-up goody-two-shoes a-hole. I mean, who in their right mind chooses to breathe oxygen over carbon monoxide and all that other great stuff? You're such a tool.*

But I get it. To each their own, right? Smokers should be able to do what they want with their life, and I respect that. I just don't want to be negatively affected by other people's unhealthy decisions. I think that's a fair and respectful balance in this situation.

I turned to Alex. "You worked on this ship before. Was this door like this back then?"

"Yeah, a lot of people have complained about it, but you know how it is. Usual cruise ship bullshit," Alex said then laughed and took a sip of his vodka cranberry.

"So where do crew members who don't smoke hang out?" Gertie asked.

"The crew deck."

I looked around for a door that might lead out to the crew deck, but then realized that we were portside, midship. There wasn't going to be any sort of deck attached to this crew bar. "Is the crew deck a breezeway?"

"No," Alex said. "It's on the other end of the ship."

"Forward?"

"Yeah, and crew members smoke out there, too, but once in a while, you can find a spot with some fresh air…if the wind is blowing just right and there aren't too many crew members out there."

Our crew bar might as well have been a world away from

the crew deck. The only way we could have a drink out in the open air was if we smuggled our drinks through the crew area and brought them out to the crew deck, which was a highly risky move and absolutely against the rules.

But rules, shmules. Sometimes it's better to be a pirate than to join the Navy, if you know what I'm saying.

And no pirate worth his salt is going to let a few pesky cruise ship rules get between him and his barrel of rum. We were pirates, back in those days. We played by our own set of rebel rules. We flew our own Jolly Roger flag.

And once you go black flag, you never go back.

I was even prepared to become a moonshine smuggler if circumstances required it. I already had a small backpack that was dedicated to the purpose of covert OSOs (onboard smuggling operations), which often turned into SOSs (save our souls) after we were caught by the Indian security guards aboard the cruise ship. We lived in a shipboard ecosystem where a third offense of chicken-fajita smuggling was adequate grounds for dismissal from the cruise ship fleet. It was food smuggling rules like these that made crew members feel the heavy weight of subordination. It was enough to make us feel as if we were back in high school, and nobody but the cheerleaders, quarterbacks, and homecoming queens want to go back to high school.

Back in the crew bar, Alex was ready for another drink. We walked past the ratty pool table again. It looked as if some of the Filipino crew members were using it as the boxing ring for illegal cock fights in the middle of the night—the kind of cock fights where people bet on morbidly muscular roosters that wear razor blades on the back of their legs, can bench press entire chicken coops, and have intimidating names like

Jack the Sickle-Feather Ripper, Jamaican Jerk Chicken, and The Beak Freak, the kind of cock fights that are only found in the unruly rural backwaters of places like Columbia, Nicaragua, cruise ships, and Louisiana.

We were about to turn the corner and walk toward the bar, when Alex stopped and pointed toward a door. "This is the Internet room."

There was a small placard on the door: *CREW INTERNET CAFÉ.*

Oh, how lovely that sounds. A crew Internet café. It sounded like the kind of place where you could relax into the sublime comfort of a plush sofa and sip frothy cappuccinos while nibbling on a cinnamon-swirl scone.

Alex opened the door to the Internet café. There were about ten computers in the room, most of them occupied by crew members who were typing so furiously I thought their life savings might be at stake if they didn't get done with their e-mail to their wives back in India in the next five minutes. (This is pretty much true since cruise ship companies generally charge crew members the going rate of a Starbuck's mocha latte for every ten minutes of shipboard internet use.)

"I figured you might want to know where this is, since we don't get Internet in our rooms on this ship."

Bummer number forty-nine.

Alex continued, "This ship is also a bit strange in the way it calculates the cost for crew members to use the Internet. I can't quite figure it out, but to simplify, the Internet costs different amounts at different times of the day."

"Seriously?" Gertie asked.

"Yeah, it's strange. I think it's twelve cents a minute from one to six in the morning—you know, when everyone is sleeping. Then it costs about twenty-six cents a minute at all other times of the day, but it seems to change all the time. One time I used it on a Saturday night, and I was charged forty-five cents a minute."

It sounded crazy, but I believed it. The only thing that cruise ship companies weren't historically chintzy about, as far as the crew was concerned, was alcohol, which had never made a lick of sense to me. Why would cruise ship companies encourage their crew members to drink alcohol aboard ships around the globe?

It may be easy for people to just shrug off the condition of the crew bar and say, *Hey, what's the big deal? There are other places for crew members to spend their time on the ship, right?* And yes there are, but there are very few, especially for people of lower rank than Gertie and me. We were officers and so we could stroll around in passenger areas. Once in a while, if we had permission, we could even eat in the onboard restaurants if we were willing to pay the exorbitant prices for a decent meal at sea. But most crew members could be fired if they were seen sauntering along the promenade when they weren't working. On cruise ships, crew members should be seen and not heard, and when they aren't working they shouldn't be seen, either. So for most crew members, there are only a few places to go when they clock-out at the end of the day: the crew bar, the crew deck, the crew library, the crew mess, and a few quiet breezeways in crew areas. And the crew bar isn't just our neighborhood pub—it's the only pub in town, the only pub at sea.

You can imagine what it does to a crew's morale when they work every day in the passenger area, among all the greatest luxuries that money can buy, and then take the crew train back to the wrong side of the tracks. They walk into their neighborhood pub for a drink after a hard day's work and find the place looking like a bar on Bourbon Street right after Hurricane Katrina ripped through town, minus the fun Mardi Gras decorations, neon lights, and those swirling daiquiri machines that put me in a hypnotic trance that causes me to buy a mudslide every time. I don't think the crew bar needs to look like a lido-deck poolside bar, but the crew bar on the *MS Barnacle* was the worst crew bar I had ever seen in Ship Life–land.

Alex bought everyone a shot of Sambuca. Then Gertie and I made our way back toward our crew cabin, a bit disheartened by the state of our crew bar for the next few months, but determined not to let it get us down. It would take more than a rat-hole crew bar to sink our ship, then again a rat hole in a ship's hull probably would sink a ship if you didn't catch it soon enough.

CHAPTER ELEVEN

Everything Will Be Perfect, Boss

Gertie and I were walking down the I-95, toward our crew cabin, when Ronald, the Haitian room steward we had hired on our last contract, walked up. "Boss. Boss," he said.

It was nice to see another smiling, familiar face aboard our ship. So far most of the other crew members we met had seemed about as interested in making friends with two Americans as a Native American Cherokee would have been during the smallpox epidemic of 1738.

Ronald cut to the chase. He was a business-minded kind of guy. "Boss, do you need a room steward? I take *good* care of your cabin, boss."

I told him we'd like to hire him again.

"Same price?" Ronald asked, ready to bump fists and close the deal.

I bumped his fist. "Same price."

"When do you need me to come by, boss?"

Gertie interjected, "Do you have any time tonight?" She said, sounding desperate.

"Yes, I come by tonight, boss. I do *great* job. How is your cabin, boss?"

I wanted to tell him that we were afraid to use the toilet in fear of being pulled down the drain by the tentacle of a giant sea monster, but I didn't want him to change his mind about cleaning our room.

I shrugged. "Meh. It could use a good scrub down."

"Okay, I come by in just a few minutes. Is that okay with you, boss?"

Gertie was already nodding her head. She put out her hand and grabbed Ronald on the shoulder. "We need tissue paper. We can't find any on the ship."

Ronald shook his head. "I don't know, boss. You remember what I was saying on our last ship. I told you that I had heard the ship company had taken away all of the tissue paper supply for crew. Well, on this ship, we have to sign for tissue paper at the beginning of the day, and we're only given enough for us to refill our passenger staterooms. But, boss—" Ronald lowered his voice. "I'll find you tissue paper. Don't worry, boss. I know someone in Filipino mafia. I've heard they have tissue paper. I'll do good job, boss. I'll find you tissue paper. You can count on me, boss." Then he moved his hand quickly through the air, like a sword cutting the air. "Don't worry, boss. Everything will be perfect, boss. Okay?"

Gertie took a deep breath. "Okay…thanks."

"I'll knock on your cabin in a few minutes," Ronald said and then turned around and jogged down the hall. Ronald was a grade-A hustler. I could tell that he was climbing a steep hill. He was reaching for something, something better, and I hoped he would get it. I felt this way every time I met someone with that kind of determination, that kind of intensity. It was nice to see it then. It's nice to see it now when I meet someone who seems possessed by a dream, a dream from which they will wake up one day and find that, hopefully through pure willpower and self-discipline and intelligence alone, they have climbed from the outlands of the weak and ordinaries and pulled themselves into a bright future born of their very own fortitude and imagination.

Moments later, Ronald was knocking on our door. Gertie opened it and squealed. When she turned around, she was grinning and clutching a roll of tissue paper as if it were a winning lottery ticket.

Ronald propped the door open with a rubber door stopper and grabbed a few bottles of cleaning supplies from his housekeeping cart. "I told you. Don't worry, boss. I'll take care of everything, boss."

"I'm going to the gym while Ronald cleans our room," Gertie said as she grabbed her gym bag and walked out the door.

I thought back to when Gertie and I were on our last ship. I wanted to hear Ronald's story. Who was Ronald? How and why did he end up leaving Haiti? How did he end up here, today, cleaning my room as we sailed along the coast of Italy aboard this massive cruise liner? But first, there was a more pressing question I had to ask. "How'd you do it?"

"What, boss?" Ronald asked as he sprayed our bathroom mirror. Then he added, "This not an officer's room. How do you end up in dis room?"

"I don't know," I said. "We're working on it. But the tissue paper. Where'd you get it?"

"I have *paisanos*...with connections," he said and smiled mischievously.

"So how long have you been working on ships? How did you end up out here?"

"My father," Ronald said. "He's living in Miami. He married an American woman. He made a connection with the cruise lines and got me a job out here. See, boss?"

"Yeah, but why not just move to America and work there?"

"I have to save up enough money. Then I go to America. I'll live in Miami. Buy an apartment on the beach. Get a job. Done," He swiped the air again with his hand. He said it as if it would be so easy, a sentiment I heard time and time again from foreigners on ships who were trying to carve a way to America or England or Italy or France or anywhere other than the economically depressed and politically corrupt countries where they were living. "I never want to go back to Haiti. I have been working out here since February 2010. Ever since the earthquake."

I had forgotten about the earthquake that rocked Haiti back in January 2010, leveling cities across the island—a 7.0 magnitude that devastated the country.

"You were there? In the earthquake?"

"Yes. I felt something bad the night before," he said as he started scrubbing our sink. "I felt it in my stomach, boss. I couldn't sleep." He started scrubbing faster, harder. "I felt like God was telling me something, warning me that something bad was going to happen, and happen soon. I couldn't sleep. You know, boss, it is this job that kept me alive. It's the only reason I'm here today."

"You were in the earthquake?" I asked.

"I had to get my paperwork to join ship. I had saved for two years. Nothing is cheap in Haiti, except what we're paid for work. It took me two years to save the money to come here. And I finally had enough to get my paperwork on January 10th, 2010. I was inside de capital building—"

"In Port Au Prince?"

"Yes, PAP. I was inside the capital when the earthquake hit." He stopped scrubbing and walked out of the bathroom so that I could see his hands move as he acted out the experience. "It was like the whole building was picked up off the ground and then thrown back down. *BOOM!* God took care of me. I prayed to him." Ronald pointed a finger up toward the ceiling. And then he smiled, his eyes watering just enough for them to glisten, but he held back the tears. He shook his finger in the air. "I prayed. And God listened. I was there, in the capital building, boss, because there is still something for me to do here, because God wants me here, boss."

I nodded my head. "And what did you do after the earthquake?"

"I searched for days. I searched for my family and my friends. I found some of them, but most of them were gone. I never saw my best friend again. But I looked. I *looked. I did.*" He was almost pleading, begging me to agree that he had looked for his buddy. Then he stopped, and nodded his head, and said, "But that's what you do, boss. That's what you do when everyone else around you is hurt. That's what I did. I didn't even think about it. I just started digging. I just started searching. That's what you do, even if all I could do was move a few pieces of concrete that's what I did. If you can, you have to dig, because you might be the only one who can. You might be the only person that can help them, that can help your…your *friend*."

He was shaking his head and just staring right through me, looking into the void of his past that he wanted to change so much. He let out a deep breath.

It was quiet for a moment, and then he came back to me, to the ship life in which he was living. He smiled. "But that is life. And now I am here. And soon I will be living in Miami. But don't worry, boss. I'll take care of your room while I'm here, boss. Don't worry, boss. Everything will be perfect."

But I wasn't so sure. I had a feeling in my stomach too, as if something just wasn't quite right. I hardly slept that night, and by daybreak, once it was time to get up and see the pope at the Vatican, I had only had a few hours of sleep. I couldn't shake Ronald's story out of my head. That morning, we left Ronald's pay for the week on the dresser, wrote him a little note, and stuck it in the envelope: *DON'T WORRY, BOSS. EVERYTHING WILL BE PERFECT, BOSS.*

CHAPTER TWELVE

So The Pope, The Truth, Vijay Patel, And A Twerking Jamaican Girl All Walk Into The Slop Chest

We were running through the streets of Rome, and all I wanted was a pizza. I could smell them as we hurried down the cobblestone streets of the Italian capital, but there was no time for pie. Gertie wasn't a stop-and-smell-the-roses type of girl, unless those roses happened to be illustrations on a wine bottle label.

We had an important date with the pope and his papal posse, and Gertie was *not* going to be late. She had planned it all out, had all her popes in a row. She wore a special yellow dress, twisted her hair in big curls, and painted her fingernails all cutesy with pink polka dots over sea-foam green.

As we got closer to the Vatican, the crowds began to grow. Soon we had shuffled our way through the dense throngs and found ourselves on the outer edge of St. Peter's Square, which had been roped off and was already full of visitors waiting for the pope's Wednesday audience. We found a spot where we'd have a distant view of the pope. Massive television screens flanked the papal altar. The crowd was restless, giving the whole scene the feel of a World Series baseball game right before the home team's favorite batter came up to the plate. We were looking west, through the Coliseum-style columns that lined the oval-shaped border of the famous Vatican piazza.

I said the word, "Piazza." This was not good because it reminded me how badly I wanted pizza.

Gertie looked like a passenger at a shipboard Bingo game who was just one square away from winning the Grand Bingo Tournament at the end of the cruise, the one where they only win a plastic trophy and a T-shirt but get more excited about the prizes than the day they received their college diploma. Cruise ship bragging rights can do this to a person. Plans coming together can do this to a Gertie.

I turned to Gertie, "Do you think there's a good pizza place around here?"

The crowd started clapping wildly. Gertie pointed, "There he is. There's the pope." She turned to me and smiled. "We are in Italy, and we are seeing the pope." It was certainly a pinch-me on my Mitre hat kind of moment.

We were so far away from the pope that he looked like a small white dot against the backdrop of St. Peter's Basilica. Fortunately, the powers that be of the Catholic Church had actually considered us little people in the back rows already, and so we were able to watch the pope on the "Jumbotron" screen. His white robes fluttered in the spring wind.

I listened to him speak, the Italian language flowing like a gently winding river that speaks the poetic language of the heart and soul. I had no idea what he was saying. I do not speak Italian. In fact, I can barely understand what the Italian officers on the ships are saying when they are supposedly speaking English. *Can-ah you-ah hand-ah me-ah the cappuccino cup-ah.* What?

However, sometime later, long after my contract was over and I was back on land, I became curious. What did the pope say to all of us gathered on that hot spring day? What was his message? What did he say to Gertie and me that morning? I found a transcription. During that papal audience, the pope spoke about the tendency for people to believe that *Truth* is relative. The pope said something along the lines that we were "living in a time when people are extremely skeptical of Truth." He said that we were experiencing an era where many people had the inclination to consider absolutely *nothing* as definitive and to think that truth comes from consensus or from something we like. He went on to ask the questions, "Does the truth really exist? What is the truth? Can we know it? Can we find it?" Later he answered these questions, saying that "The truth is not grasped as a thing, the truth is encountered. It is not a possession; it is an encounter with a Person."

At the end of his speech, the pope blessed the audience—a blessing that was said to extend to all of the religious articles that anyone had brought with them. Then he reached into a small white cage that someone in the audience had given him and released two white doves. The doves flew into the air and soared over St. Peter's Square.

In that moment, I recognized the beauty of such a gathering. We gather often: as families, as friends, as enemies, in coffee shops, in Congress, in church, in concerts, aboard cruise ships. There was a sea of people that day, people who had poured into that Vatican square to hear the pope's message of peace and truth. Yet, at the very same time, all over the world—today possibly more than ever—people gather for the opposite reasons: to lie, to kill, to destroy, to control, to deceive, to manipulate, to commit acts of terror, to *exploit*.

That moment compelled me to question my own

intentions and the motivations of others around me. Why are we gathering? What am I trying to gather together? What are my intentions?

Most importantly, I look back on that moment and realize now that I too was struggling with some issues that were very similar to what the pope had spoken about in his papal address. Would my experience aboard the *MS Barnacle* be defined by my thoughts and perceptions of the ship and ship life itself? Or was there an absolute truth to what we were experiencing aboard the ship that would affect us regardless of how we perceived it? Could we change the future—our own futures—by simply willing a new and brighter future into existence? Or should we face the darkness that we perceived by challenging it and battling it and driving it back into the deepest and darkest fathoms of the sea?

Does the truth really exist? What is the truth? Can we know it? Can we find it?

I knew a few other questions that I wanted answered immediately: Does pizza really exist? Where is it? Can we find it? Can I eat it?

And we did.

We found our pizza at a small café that was tucked along the edge of St Peter's Square.

At first, Gertie resisted. "But it's not on our schedule," she whined. "We have to get into the Vatican before all the crowds start lining up after the papal address. Look at them." She pointed to the hordes of people and then pointed to the Vatican entrance. All the people were gravitating right toward the ticket booth at the front of the Holy City. "They're all going to the Vatican. Right now. And they're heading straight to the Sistine Chapel. If we don't go right now, we'll spend the rest of the day waiting in lines, and we won't be able to do half the things in the Vatican that we could have done. Trust me." She shook her list of plans in my face. "We don't have time for pizza. How could you be thinking about pizza when we are steps away from the Sistine Chapel?" It was a good question, but the answer was simple.

I took a deep breath. "Because when I'm hungry, I like pizza more than fine art." It was the truth. I only wanted to see the name Michelangelo if it was lit up in neon because it was the name of a Michelangelo's Pizza Shop. "I'll make it quick," I promised and then disappeared into the little café.

Minutes later, I came running out with two slices of pepperoni tucked into a wax-paper fold. I ate them as we waited in line to buy tickets to the Vatican. We had three hours before we needed to turn around and run back to the train that would take us back to port, back to our beloved *MS Barnacle*.

We rushed through the endless maze of statues, Roman relics, priceless paintings, and breathtaking views of the sprawling ancient city seen from small open windows with decorative wrought-iron frames. We dashed up and down staircases, pausing briefly to marvel at a huge storeroom filled with marble busts of ancient romans carved from the waist up. It was the most fantastic example of abs carved in stone that I had ever seen, which begged the question: Did everyone in ancient Rome have really great abs or did every person to ever have their likeness immortalized in marble demand that the sculptors portray them with washboard stomachs?

I think historians may have gotten things a bit wrong in the ancient history section. I don't think Socrates and Plato were running schools of classic philosophy; I believe they were actually conducting boot-camp style exercise classes. Socrates to his students: *Okay everybody; don't forget to grab one of the Ab-Buster machines on the way in. Nobody wants their statue to be pudgy. Or should I keep in step with my wildly popular Socratic Method and say: Does anyone really want their statue to be pudgy? Xodes, start the lire music. And make it upbeat. We've got to push, people! Let's go. And I and II and III and IV!*

The Vatican also left me with another profound impression: The Catholics may be the most successful *hoarders* of all time. If someone at the Vatican hasn't already called one of those hoarder reality-TV shows, then someone should definitely pick up the phone and do it, because they would be a shoo-in. I mean, who really needs four thousand ancient marble busts sitting around collecting dust? I promise you, if we looked hard enough, we'd find some random bishop and his cats buried under a pile of priceless oil paintings. You really want to put a dent in global poverty? I've got a few ideas. Let's start with—oh, I don't know—perhaps a little thing called a *garage sale.* The Vatican is like the ancient history version of the set of the 1970s sitcom called *Sanford and Sons.* It's really gotten out of control. Someone in their family really needs to put their foot down and gently tell them that "It's time to let go of some of your friends. I know they feel like real people to you, but they're not. They're just a collection of old Roman stamps."

But when we stepped inside the Sistine Chapel, it all made sense. The need for preservation. The gift of conservation. The beauty of the culture.

My jaw dropped. I slowly said, "Woooooowwwww."

And then a man in a red jacket, some type of Sistine Security Guard, told me to shut up. There would be no verbal fawning permitted while viewing Michelangelo's *Last Judgment*.

Soon afterward, we trotted out the other side of the Vatican and once again raced down the cobblestone streets, running to our ship mother before she sailed off without us. We climbed aboard with mere minutes to spare. As the ship sounded its all-aboard horn, we walked into the crew mess, badly needing to refuel after miles and miles of running around Rome. Inside we found nothing but the same chicken knuckles, wilted lettuce, and lentil curry dhal that we always found in the crew mess, so I poured a cup of ship's milk, grabbed a banana from the fertile slopes of Banana Mountain, and threw a few chicken knuckles on my tray.

It was midday. The crew mess was mostly empty except for a group of smiling Indians who were sitting around a large table in front of the portholes at the back of the room. The minute we turned the corner and saw the table of Indians, we were hit by a wall of delightful and entrancing culinary aromas. I stopped in my tracks.

Gertie and I found a small table in the back of the room, just a few tables down from the Indians. They smiled and said hello as we sat down with our food and ship's milk. I glanced over at the Indian table, and knew these were the people that I'd been searching for throughout our entire contract.

Covering every inch of tabletop were clusters of plates and platters. Atop each dish were collections of the kind of foods that cruise ship crew members dream about at night: curried lobster tails, spicy grilled shrimp wrapped in bacon, deep fried eggplant slices sprinkled with goat cheese and pepper shreds, layered stacks of expertly baked and slightly charred Indian-style flat bread, ripe tomato slices skewered between slabs of fresh mozzarella brushed with olive oil and basil bits, and the Indian desert of my deepest desires: golden fried gulab jamun drizzled in sugary syrup.

We had inadvertently stumbled into a cruise ship café of crew food nirvana.

And these Indians were not just ordinary crew members. These were not just ordinary Indian cooks. They were the gatekeepers to *Vijay Patel's Secret and Magical Cruise Ship Trading Post.*

This was a store with no easily discernable entrance, a club with no application. You had to bribe your way in, accept an unsolicited invitation, or have the good fortune to befriend a crew member in the inner circle of Indian cruise ship cooks—a crew member who, like a member of the mysterious Masons, could act as a sponsor and bring you aboard this scrumptious rickshaw-style food truck of the sea.

It was difficult to bring my spoon of raisin and bran cereal to my mouth with all of those scents of exotic spices and grilled meats and sun-kissed vegetables swirling around the crew mess. I felt like the household dog, one that's served a bowl of dusty dog food that smells like dried-up cornhusks and soybeans and then has to sit on the back porch and look through the window as he watches the human-half of his family eat a juicy steak dinner. Gertie and I were drooling, too.

Then something magical, perhaps divine, happened. To my surprise, one of the Indian cooks piled a plate high with tasty treats and walked over to our table. "Please," he said, "have some of our food."

Gertie took the plate in both hands and pulled it *toward* her as she said, "Oh, we couldn't. We just couldn't."

Gertie set the plate onto our table as the smiling Indian

cook continued, "In India it is tradition to share food with others. Always we share food," he said.

He smiled and gave us a slight nod of the head, a kind of Indian bow. He gestured, encouraging us to taste the gifts he had brought to our table. I grabbed a skewer of bacon wrapped shrimp. Who wouldn't go for the bacon first?

He continued, "This is the month of Purnima, Buddha's birthday. In this month, we try to bring happiness to others, especially to those who are less fortunate than us."

He nodded again. I had to agree with him. I hadn't realized just how deprived I had actually been until the grilled shrimp and salty bacon touched my lips.

We thanked him and the other Indians at the table again and again, and then continued with our feast that had appeared before us like manna from heaven. The gods of the sea were smiling on us once again. Neptune had risen from the turbulent waves and slain the crew-mess sea monster with his sparkling trident. It seemed as if old Saint Nicholas, the patron saint of boatmen, was there by our sides as we set sail along the Italian Seaboard, cruising south toward Naples and the Amalfi Coast.

It wasn't lost on us that Saint Nicholas had become the model for our modern-day Santa Claus, after he cultivated a reputation for secret gift giving. He'd been known to bestow remarkably generous gifts upon unsuspecting travelers, sailors in particular. Perhaps this feast was an unplanned celebration of the turning of our tide.

We finished our Indian spread, and walked into the larger crew mess hall. I immediately noticed some commotion from the back of the room. A large crowd was gathered around the door to the slop chest, the crew store that had been our one-stop shop for snacks and treats as long as the only things we wanted were prawn-lime noodles and odd-flavored Arabic sodas, which I wanted to drink about as badly as I wanted to contract a strange and incurable rash after riding a camel in Dubai.

"Let's see what's going on," Gertie said.

Just then, a pair of Jamaican women wearing housekeeping uniforms ran past us. One of them looked at me and said, "A new shipment, mon! A new shipment in the slop chest, mon! We be blessed. Everything be *irie* now!"

I ran into the slop chest, Gertie right behind me. The Jamaican girls, with huge grins, were standing beside me. The slop chest was full of all the best sweet and salty goodies: rows of fried potato chips, crate-sized boxes of candy bars, gummy creatures of every species, enough soda to bring tears to the eyes of young children, and in the corner of the room, looking as if a golden beam of sunlight was shining down on them from heaven above: chicken-flavored microwavable noodle cups.

For a moment, Gertie, the Jamaican girls, and I just stood still and stared at the stacks of junk food, as if we owed some debt of respect to whatever maritime marvel (man, woman, or supernatural being) had engineered this miraculous feat and delivered us from our misery, delivered us onto a ship with a storehouse of convenience store–quality garbage.

We observed a moment of silence, and then suddenly, as if someone had blown a whistle on the streets of Brazil to mark the start of a carnival street party, we all burst into a spontaneous, festive dance. The Jamaican girls were twerking. One of them raised their hands into the air and shouted, "Hallelujah! The slop chest be refilled! It's a miracle, mon!

Jah"—(God)—"bless!"

Gertie and I were twirling and clapping and dancing to the tune and rhythm of some unseen swing band. We grabbed handfuls of potato chip bags, fistfuls of candy pouches, bars upon bars of chocolate, bottles of fruit juices, and cans of sweet sodas. We left the slop chest, realizing that it said quite a lot about how low in life we must had fallen to dance at the delivery of sugary detritus that had about as much nutritional value as driftwood and shipwreck debris. But we felt blessed, blessed indeed.

We soared down the hallway toward our cabin, each carrying plastic bags, both of us as happy as two puckish pals with pillow cases on Halloween who went trick-or-treating with two masks each so they could revisit all of the homes that passed out the premium candies.

After turning onto the I-95, I heard a voice calling out from behind me. "I was hoping I'd run in to you." It was the Lorax look-alike, the HR director, Mr. Alfred Sumterfort—the chap with the bushy eyebrows and push-broom mustache. His breathing was labored from picking up his pace just a bit to catch up with us. "I have some good news."

Gertie was glowing. She cupped her hands. "About our cabin?"

Alfred took a deep breath. "Yes, about your cabin. I believe I may have found you a new room."

Gertie lifted her bag of slop chest flotsam into the air. "Yes!"

Alfred put out his hand. "Now, I can't make any promises," he said, successfully deflating our enthusiasm.

I felt as if I had just left port on a cruise ship and was dancing the conga at the sail-away party, and then the captain came over the loudspeaker to announce that the cruise was cancelled, the ship was turning around, and that all the passengers should probably just go back to work immediately, captain's orders. Alfred really knew how to fart in the bathtub right in the middle of a romantic candlelight soak, if you know what I mean.

Then he continued, "But I might be able to get you transferred into a more suitable living situation in a few weeks."

We thanked him. "When will you know for sure?" Gertie asked.

"Just hang tight where you are," he said in a very reassuring voice. "You'll be the first to know as soon as I hear anything."

Gertie looked as if she wanted to hug the old, cuddly Lorax. Suddenly, Alfred had saved the coastal forest from the cruise ship lumberjacks. Perhaps Gertie and I were actually going to live happily ever after aboard this stinky ship of darkness after all.

Alfred waddled away. "This is amazing. What just happened?" Gertie said.

"I know. It's as if everything just fell into place."

"Do you think it was the pope? Do you think we were blessed by the pope?"

"I don't know, but everything seems to be going our way." It was as if we were two newly hatched sea turtles who had been swimming for three days straight, battling the sharks and the vicious, relentless currents of a cold, heartless sea, and now we had finally reached the warm waters of the Gulf Stream and found a big, yellow patch of Sargassum weed drifting in the great expanse of blue, to rest our tiny flippers upon. And now I just hoped we could ride this current of good fortune all the way around the Mediterranean.

We walked by a hallway, and I stopped in my tracks. I put out my hand, causing my bag of junk food to swing. "Wait. Did you see that?" I whispered.

"See what?" Gertie replied in a low voice.

"Svetlana and…and someone else."

"Svetlana who?"

"Svetlana. Squid's Svetlana."

"With who?"

I backed up a little and poked my head down the hallway. Svetlana was standing in the hallway with a man, but this man wasn't a squid. There was no mistaking it—he must have been the soap-opera guy that Squid was worried about. Svetlana had her hand on his shoulder and she was leaning in toward him as if she wanted to kiss him, as if she were asking him to, but she had stopped just before their lips had touched, which seemed to stir an electric charge somewhere near the guy's zipper.

I poked my head back out. "That's definitely not Squid," I whispered.

"It's none of our business," Gertie said as we started to walk back down the hallway.

"Squid will be devastated," I said.

We walked on in silence. The reality was there. The truth was there. We had encountered it, and the truth now hung over us like a nearly cracked mast hangs over a crew that's battling a rough storm. Maybe things just weren't what they seemed to be out here on the old deep blue sea.

CHAPTER THIRTEEN

The Goose That Laid The Golden Duck Nipple, And The Positive Thinking Hamburger

Crew members lose track of time in ship life, and it had happened to Gertie and me. Weeks had passed since we had run toward the Vatican in Rome. Our ship life had washed into a blurry existence where we might as well have thrown the calendar overboard. We were now living a ship life where the days of the week no longer mattered. In our life, there were no weekends, just sea days and port days. And there were no holidays from this cruise vacation. There were only workdays and those rare days when we were in port and were actually permitted to get off the ship and explore the real world for a bit before having to climb back aboard for a half day of work. Our time off the ship in ports felt like pure bliss.

We had fallen into a ship life routine, but unfortunately this routine didn't include any quality sleep or much good food other than boxed cereal, ship's milk, bananas from Banana Mountain, and chicken knuckles for the most part. We had felt a few weeks prior that we were starting to sail on somewhat smooth seas, but the wind was taken out of our sails when the HR director never followed through. We were several weeks into the contract, and we were still living in 0604.

We were standing in the atrium, surrounded by art on easels that some auctioneer before us had spray painted gold. The gilded easel façades made us look as if we were faux art dealers, imposters, posers hiding behind a thin veneer of slickness and used car salesman–style pitches. Alex was trying something new: a morning auction. He had brought out metal canisters of coffee, cherry-filled danishes, and of course free alcohol, this time in the form of orange juice and champagne mimosas.

You know what they always say aboard cruise ships. *The early bird gets the tequila worm.*

Gertie walked up as I was pouring mimosas at a table tucked to the side of the atrium. She was wearing a little black dress, her hair pulled back, with a few strands hanging on each side of her face. Her dark makeup seemed an appropriate match for the mystery and sophistication of the Italian port that we were docking at later that day. "We aren't going to sell a thing," she said.

I agreed then handed a passenger a cup of coffee made from concentrated-coffee syrup.

"These people are half asleep," Gertie said. "You have to be awake to go shopping."

I thought this was a good thing. When your job is to sell the type of prints we were hawking, customers who were half asleep may have been an advantage.

Gertie put her clipboard down on the table and helped me pour coffee. "Okay," she said in her getting-down-to-business voice. "As soon as the auction is over, we're going to pack this art up as quickly as possible. I am *not* going to miss the sail into St. Mark's Square. I don't care if we have to pay someone else to pack up the rest of this stuff. I *will* watch us rope up in Venice."

I didn't argue with Gertie. After much negotiation, she had relented on Venice, allowing us to have a schedule-free experience there. I was thrilled at the prospect of being allowed to play it by ear. I didn't care what we did, as long as it involved pizza on the canal, lots of wine, a few tubs of gelato, and a night that ended with us running around the city wearing Venetian masks. The masks would also be helpful in blocking out any light and helping me fall asleep, which had mostly eluded me ever since we first walked up that gangway and stepped aboard the *MS Barnacle*.

However, this was not just another port among a string of stops along the amazingly beautiful Italian coast. No, this was the most special of all occasions that a crew member can encounter on a contract. Tonight was an *overnight*. Once we stepped off the ship, we wouldn't have to return for close to twenty-four hours. Overnights are rare in the cruise ship world these days, and I wasn't going to let it pass us by without grabbing it by the reins and milking the experience for everything it was worth.

And so, a few days earlier, I had cashed in my 401k and spent it on a shipboard Internet card so I could get online and rent us a hotel room in a Venetian bed-and-breakfast. I couldn't keep myself from smiling, as the visions of the floating city with lamp-lit canals and cobblestone alleyways filled my daydreams. I imagined us floating down a quiet canal, sipping wine in the candlelight as the water of the Grand Canal reflected the Rialto Bridge and the stars of the Mediterranean night. I could actually taste the fresh air pumping into the hotel's ventilation system. What a dream.

I was knocked out of my morning fantasy when Chloe and Buster, our passenger friends who were cruising with us for the next month, walked up and tapped me on the shoulder.

"Ah yes," I said in my best British-butler impression. I walked over to a small side table next to the coffee stand and grabbed two particular champagne glasses. On each glass was a Post-it note, their names written in my handwriting.

"We have a special treat for *you,*" Chloe blurted out, bursting with excitement.

"Do I get this special treat now, my lords?" I replied, keeping up with the butler act.

"Soon," Buster said. "It'll be great. You and Gertie will love it."

"We will be delighted I'm sure, my lords. Thank you for the kind gesture, whatever it may be." I bowed and then, as always, they scampered off once they had their free drinks in hand. They were very clever champagne charlatans. They knew not to overstay their welcome. As Frank Abagnale, Jr. said in his book *Catch Me If You Can*: "The fox who keeps to one den is the easiest caught by the terriers." The difference here was that we all knew they were cons, but they thought they were playing a game where they were still the deceivers.

Of course, Chloe and Buster drove Alex absolutely banana cakes. He would say, "How can you feel comfortable about letting them weasel around the gallery and drink our champagne when you know that they'll never buy anything?" He'd quiet down about it after a while, but then our friends would come back and get another glass of champagne and Alex would be all in a rage again about how I was wasting my time. Gertie and I would laugh about it, and somehow the pair of champagne charlatans always acted as a reliable stress reliever for Gertie and me. It gave us something to laugh about, and when you're out at sea for as long as we were, you always need someone to laugh with or something to laugh about. No one wants to turn into a sea donkey. Laughing helps keep you human when you're salt-necking it out on the cruise ships on a long contract.

Alex's voice boomed over the shipboard speaker system. "Good morning, ladies and gentlemen. Just a friendly reminder that our onboard auction will begin in fifteen minutes. Fifteen minutes!" There was no discernable reaction from the ten or so passengers lazily wandering around our makeshift atrium art gallery. The passengers looked tired. They might as well have been wearing footed pajamas as they sipped their bitter coffees and watered down mimosas.

And then it came without warning. At first I felt the ship lift up just a bit, and then our vessel jolted to the side in a rather violent list.

Everything went into slow motion—just like in the movies, but oddly enough not in horror movies, which this so closely resembled.

Several easels in the room tilted forward. People screamed around me. Gertie let out a high-pitched squeal that left me temporarily deaf in one ear. My eyes went to an original oil painting priced at more than fifty thousand dollars; its easel tottered on the front two golden-painted legs. A man was standing directly in front of the painting, and in the disorienting jerk of the ship, he had turned his head away from the painting behind him in an effort to brace himself against a faux-marble column of the atrium, the only thing that kept him from crumpling to the floor. The painting was rather large: four feet square, a messy palette knife impression of gondolas on the Grand Canal.

I ran toward the teetering canvas with outstretched arms. "Nooooooo!"

I could see Gertie running toward a painting to my left, catching it in midair before it smashed into a glass sculpture with a pointy top that looked as if it would have no problem ripping right through the pricey piece of art. As I ran toward the gondola painting, I watched in horror as rows and rows of paintings and prints came crashing down onto the high-gloss marble floors. I watched as the gondola painting slipped off its spray-painted perch. A corner of the heavy-looking wooden frame smashed into the back of the passenger's head, immediately producing a red, lumpy goose egg.

The painting crashed onto the floor. The passenger grabbed the back of his head. The frame separated from the canvas. A chunk of wood went spinning across the floor. The delicate pallet knife painting tipped over and landed painting side down onto the marble floor with an echoing *CRACK*.

Glasses smashed as a large portion of the coffee cups slipped off the table and sent a mosaic of ceramic bits splaying off in every direction. Easels and paintings tumbled and rolled around the atrium like square tires that were pushed down a hill. I heard the sound of a hundred metal easels clanging against one another and then falling onto the hard surface floor, sounding like an interstate pileup on a snowy, ice-slicked highway.

Time slowly returned to normal, but then I felt the ship lift a bit again and then roll to the other side as we drifted over whatever rogue wave, whale, or reef that we had just encountered on our way toward the port of Venice. The clumps and clusters of paintings and easels slid across the marble floor, screeching and scraping as they went.

The worst sound was that of the easels with paintings that had somehow, in some miraculous feat of balance, managed to stay upright. As the ship listed in the other direction, these easels scraped against the shiny floor, sounding like ten thousand fingers scraping down a Jumbotron-sized chalkboard—a sound that still sends shivers down my spine whenever I think of it today.

And then we were sailing smoothly once again.

Passengers began to chatter. I took a deep breath and looked around, the artwork carnage on the atrium battlefield not looking as bloody as I would have expected after the chaos that had ensued in the row of paintings and easels closest to me. Most of the paintings had survived the violent list. Most of them were still standing.

I looked over at the passenger who was rubbing the back of his head. *Oh geez,* I thought as I imagined myself taking the witness stand in a major maritime-injury lawsuit where the passenger walked into the courtroom with his head in a cast, three holes cut out: two for his eyes, and one for his mouth so he could give a sobbing testimony of the pain and suffering he had experienced as a result of the clumsy art expert who had failed to keep a gondola painting from smashing into his skull—an event that caused him loss of all memory and caused such disability that the man could only eat things that could pass through a straw and had lost the ability to work or do anything more difficult than to testify at the court hearing and, of course, sign and cash his huge settlement check. Lawyers call it "cruise and sue". Crew members hear about it all the time. We're told to never get on an elevator with a passenger because of all the sexual assault lawsuits that have arisen from such mistakes.

I put my hand out toward him. "Are you okay?"

He rubbed the back of his head. "Am I bleeding?"

Oh please God don't let there be blood. I looked at the back of his head. There was only a big, red lump, no blood. "No, just a bump," I said.

"What happened?"

"Well, it seems the ship hit a wave and—"

Alex swooped in with an Indian security guard. Alex glanced at the back of the man's head. "Sir, do you need any medical attention?"

The man looked a bit dazed, but then he smiled. "That was one heck of a list. Didn't see that one coming. No. I think I'm fine."

Alex looked at me. "Two bottles of Duck Nipple. Two of the prints that we give away at auctions. A handful of 'free champagne' cards. Now." He pointed toward our office that was just around the corner.

I raced to the little room and returned with a veritable gift basket of art-department goodies. I found the passenger signing some type of form that the Indian security guard had handed him.

Alex grabbed the bottles of champagne and handed them to the passenger. "It's your lucky day."

"Wow. Thanks!"

Alex continued, "And you and a guest can eat at the onboard steakhouse, on me. I'm very sorry this happened. If there is anything we can do, just let us know."

The man signed his name at the bottom of the form, certainly signing a statement that said he hadn't suffered any serious harm, and signing away any possibility of a lawsuit. And just like that, Alex was the naval diplomat that saved the fleet from a looming maritime war.

He was the best closer I had ever seen. He never skipped

a beat. As the passenger walked away, holding two dusty bottles of Duck Nipple valued at somewhere around half a million dollars each and a few prints of colorful sailboats racing toward a glowing sunset tucked under his arm, Alex turned on the cordless microphone in his hand. "Okay, ladies and gentlemen. Fifteen minutes to auction time. Fifteen minutes!" Then he called for our Indian art steward, the low-paid and low-ranking crew member that the art company had hired to help us organize the art auctions and gallery aboard the *MS Barnacle*. "Bashrek! I need you immediately! Bashrek, where are you?"

The sale was a flop, proving that morning flea market–style art auctions and barely averted maritime disasters just don't exactly put people in the mood to spend money. After the auction ended and the passengers slowly slipped away, Gertie and I, along with Bashrek and his team of hired hands, got down to the hard work of packing up the art circus and getting the show moved back into the art gallery. Gertie and I were carrying the damaged gondola painting to a wheeled cart that we used to push the paintings back to the showroom.

"We only have an hour before we're sailing past St. Mark's Square," she said. "We're leaving in forty-five minutes. I don't care how much of this is packed up or not. I'm not missing this." I agreed with her, and so we picked up our pace. Just as we loaded the very last painting onto one of the carts and watched Bashrek and his boys haul the eyesore out of the passenger area and toward a crew elevator, I heard Alex behind me. "Hey, there are a few more things that I need done before you two can get off the ship."

Gertie went red, but she bit her lip and asked, "What

exactly do you have in mind, because the—"

"I know you want to see the sail in. We all do. But this is important. I need this flier copied."

"How many?" I asked.

"Six hundred."

I turned to Gertie. "See. That's not so bad. We can get this done in ten or fifteen minutes. We'll make it."

Then Alex continued, "And folded…and stuffed in envelopes, then labeled with the room numbers on this list." He handed me a few pages of spreadsheet stapled together. "And then delivered to the crew office. Then put in the little cubbies in the mail room for housekeeping to deliver them."

Alex had come dangerously close to being thrown overboard that day.

"No problem," Gertie said. "We'll have it done immediately." Then she looked at me and smiled and gave me a quick nod, as if to say, *Don't worry. I've got a plan.* And a more brilliant plan hadn't been hatched since that Trojan horse doohickey.

As we walked back to our room, Gertie explained our course of action. "Okay, you know how Ronald is always saying he'll do anything he can to help?"

"Yeah," I said.

"Well, let's pay him to get this done. I'm not going to miss my sail into Venice."

It was brilliant, indeed. I called Ronald, and after a short negotiation, he agreed to do the whole ordeal for fifteen dollars, and then said, "Don't worry. Everything will be perfect, boss."

It was the beginning of a beautiful relationship between Ronald and us, the start of a covert operation that Gertie and I code-named Operation Ronald. Unbeknownst to Alex Ashebury, nearly every time he passed on a boatload of busy work to us—work that, by the way, was mostly his responsibility but which we could not gripe about if we ever wanted to see ourselves running our own ship—we would simply enact Operation Ronald, picking up our cabin phone and calling in the Haitian.

Alex must have thought we had the arms of octopi, the way we stuffed so many envelopes and still had the time and energy to explore so much of the ports. But no, we just had a trick up our sleeves. We were working the right way: By doing as little of the mindless busy work as possible and outsourcing the art department to Haiti.

But let's get real. Alex didn't care how we got the work done. He just didn't want to have to do it himself. He was the chap who was really working smart. He was outsourcing his job to Gertie and me.

We packed our bags and headed toward the bow of the cruise liner where we could watch the ship sail into port, the beginning of our Italian adventure that would end at a comfy hotel room, our cushy Venetian retreat. We were walking down a hallway in the *passenger* area, taking a shortcut to the crew deck, when we heard Alex's familiar voice echoing through the long, narrow, carpeted hall. The sound stopped us in our tracks.

"Do you hear that?" I asked.

"It's Alex," Gertie said. "I think it's coming from over here." She walked to a door at the end of the hallway, still in the passenger area. We had asked Alex where his room was located, but he was always evasive.

The voice was unmistakably Alex, and it sounded as if he

was on the phone, in the middle of a heated conversation with the front office. The door was slightly cracked; we both peeked into the room. I could see Alex in a bathrobe, sitting on the edge of a bed that was at least three times the size of our bunk beds combined. He had a silver room-service platter sitting next to him. On the platter, I could see a wonderfully juicy-looking hamburger with perfectly green lettuce flowing off the edges and a ripe red tomato slice that had been picked off and put to the side. In the back of the room, there was a sliding glass door that led out to his personal balcony. I could smell the fresh air, the type that only exists in cruise ship cabins that don't have sea monsters living in the toilet drains. There was a large dresser against the back wall and (can you believe it?) a *thermostat* right beside the door that was set to a perfectly comfy seventy-two.

"What a weasel," Gertie whispered. "I'm not surprised a bit. Look at him eating that hamburger. Room service! He's getting room service, and we're living in..."

Gertie and I walked away to the bow of the ship where we watched St. Mark's Square glide past and got our first delightful glimpse of the labyrinth of romantic canals that cut through Venice and the masterfully-constructed arched bridges that crossed them.

We stood on the bow, with the wind blowing and the sun hitting our cheeks.

"We have to stay positive," she said. "We can't allow negative thoughts to change our perspective of the ship."

I looked over the lagoon as we circled the small island of Venice, an island refuge for us from our own floating ship-life isle. The ship sailed slowly and effortlessly through the glassy waters of Laguna Veneta, which reflected the blue sky above—a sky dotted with small, puffy, white clouds, giving us the impression that we were sailing on air.

But no matter how much I would have liked to believe it, I could do no more than just *imagine* that we were sailing through the sky. Some facts just cannot be changed by will alone.

CHAPTER FOURTEEN

You Must-ah Have-ah A Pass-ah Port-ah

Gertie was holding the map, twisting it around. She held it upside down, then to the left, then to the right, then back where she started again. Gertie and I were lost; lost in a maze of tiny alleyways, look-alike canals, and narrow old-world streets with Italian names that all sounded the same to us. We had pulled out the map when we passed a storefront window for the third time and Gertie said, "Hey, that's weird. All the Venetian mask shops have the same ones in the window."

We had been walking around in circles for the past half hour, not getting any closer to our bed-and-breakfast retreat. So we did what any sensible Americans who were lost in Venice would do: we stopped for some lemon gelato, studied the map of Venice (which looked about as confusing to us as the instruction manual to CERN's Large Hadron Collider), and then continued to walk around in circles for another half hour like two lost puppies in an episode of *Milo and Otis* that had gone horribly wrong.

"I'm telling you," Gertie said at a beautiful arched bridge, "this is the same bridge we crossed a half hour ago."

Gertie was usually the type of person who seemed to have a compass inside her brain.

However, even with all of Gertie's navigational prowess, Venice had the both of us stumped. Finally an older, local man (mustache that curled on the ends, knitted sweater with a gondola stitched on the front) looked at our map. Gertie explained where we wanted to go by pointing to the name of the hotel, and then the old man mumbled something in Italian that sounded exactly like, "Pad-ah pad-ah bee-da, vee-da, lee-da," and then pointed to our left and sent us on our way. Minutes later, we were walking into the cramped lobby of the Venetian hotel that I had booked for us.

Gertie said, "See. I found it."

I nodded, but I knew it was luck. Pure luck.

A thin man in a silk bellhop uniform stood behind the lobby desk and confirmed our reservation. He looked exactly like a venetian puppet: a bulbous nose, dark slicked-back hair, the pallor of someone who just emerged from a wine cellar after refusing to leave their favorite bottle of wine all alone until it had properly matured. And of course he had the obligatory scarf looped around his neck. The French and the Italians: It can be two hundred degrees outside, and they will walk around in Speedos but still wrap scarves around their necks just to stay fashionable.

"Pass-ah ports-ah please-ah," he said in a bouncy rhythm that you might find in the lyrics of a polka ditty. He stuck out his hand.

Gertie smiled and rummaged through her purse. "We work on the cruise ship, and they keep our passports on board at all times, but we have our driver's licenses and our shipboard IDs, too."

The bellhop/lobby boy/scarf aficionado frowned and shook his head. "No, no, no. You must-ah have-ah a pass-ah port-ah."

Gertie looked as if she was about to punch Mr. Scarfy Pants right on his giant Italian nose. I tried to remember my lawyer's cell phone number so that I could call him before the police arrived and threw us in an Italian prison where we would be forced to live off a diet of the best wine I've ever had in my life and stale bits of garlic bread. All that sounded fine. But Gertie probably didn't want to spend the rest of her life in a prison where the uniform undoubtedly included a black-and-white striped scarf.

Gertie stuttered, "What? Wait. Passports? Why do you need our passports? Here are two IDs. Our pictures and names on both." She was shoving the IDs in his face, which shockingly didn't seem to be helping matters much.

"It is the law-ah. I'm-ah sorry. But we need-ah your pass-ah ports-ah, please-ah." I usually like to hear the words "pass-ah ports-ah please-ah". I always know that I have arrived in Italy or France, both countries I love with all my heart and have souvenir coffee mugs to prove it.

But this time, the words meant that our ship-life dreams were being flushed down the drain. Our dreams—of spending the night in a quiet room that was larger than the cab of a pickup truck, and of getting a good night's sleep breathing fresh air that was completely absent of cigarette smoke and sea monster farts—were being loaded onto a gondola and being sent down the Grand Canal, never to return again, and all because of some lousy law that required hotels in Italy to see travelers' passports before allowing them to check in.

"Wait," I said. "I've never heard of this. We've spent a lot of time traveling around Italy. I've never had to show my passport at a single hotel." I had him. *Ah hah!* Was he trying to scam us? Was the scarf-wearing ponce trying to swindle us out of our passports?

Mr. Scarfy Pants did that thing that Italians do and stuck his nose in the air, frowned, and looked right through us.

Then he said, "This is not Italy, *signore. This*...is Venice."

He stuck his finger toward us and then thrust it downward as if to punctuate the sentence with, "case closed."

They really thought they were something special there in Venice, but just because you live in a country with some of the best food and wine on the planet and on an Italian island that is too good for cars and has all kinds of unique and beautiful canals running through it and is unarguably one of the most romantic and artistic and gorgeous cities on Earth doesn't mean you're better than everyone else. Actually it does, but I thought he had let the whole thing go to his head just a bit, and nobody likes a show-off, even when they're right.

Gertie blew air out her nostrils. I made a "Pshhh" sound. None of this impressed Scarfy Pants very much.

"Come on," Gertie pleaded. She winked. She smiled.

"Can't you make an exception for us?" she said.

"No. It is against-ah the law-ah. No exceptions-ah."

My shoulders sank.

Gertie put out her hands. "I can't believe this."

We surrendered and headed for the door.

Then I put out my hand. "Wait." I took off my backpack and pulled out my laptop. "We had to send scans of our passports to the art company when they hired us," I said.

Gertie's eyes grew larger than a handful of Venetian pearls. I turned to Scarfy Pants, who looked disappointed that we hadn't left the premises yet. "We have scans of our passports."

He considered this for a moment, tapping his finger on the side of his giant beak. "Yes-ah, that will work-ah."

We high fived, very American, which didn't impress Scarfy Pants at all. He approved our passports, and we ran up the stairs.

Our room looked as if it had been decorated from the gewgaws and antique adornments that had fallen out of a Venetian dream: a few bits of Murano glassware on a shelf (probably cheap imitations, but let's not spoil the moment), delicate Burano lace draped over slender-legged end tables, frosted glass lampshades on patina-brass lampstands with skeleton-key style switches, light-green braided rope adorning the bottom edges of the intricately carved plaster-pressed crown molding, a claw foot tub and a cast iron sink with a brass lion's head spout where steaming water poured from the mouth of the roaring beast, a bed big enough for the two of us to lay on our backs without touching, and a glass rose-colored chandelier with an explosion of glowing lit blossoms.

Gertie opened the wood-framed casement window in the corner of the room. We could hear the sound of a distant accordion drifting down the narrow alleyway where pink and red bundles of bougainvillea flowed from window-box planters. We watched as a prickly-bearded man in a leather vest pushed a wooden handcart filled with ice and fish down the cobblestone street. The sound that drifted past our window was a soft sound, one that can only be made when water and wine and art and love and music and flowers and Italy all flow into one narrow alleyway and drift past the little Venetian window of two young lovers.

We opened a bottle of wine that Gertie, in a last-minute stroke of genius, had stuffed into her handbag. And it all made sense again. The stresses of ship life and the full-steam-ahead speed of a life at sea all sailed away on that sound, that languid pulse only found flowing through the canals of the Queen of the Adriatic, atop the bridges of the City of Water, and through the window in a Venetian spring.

That night, we watched the moon rise over the Grand Canal. An endless stream of wine corks floated past as we feasted on basil pizzas and Italian wines. In that moment, we reclaimed our love of ship life; we rediscovered the pure bliss of being port-hopping pirates with wine-stained teeth. But when you're a cruise ship crew member, the problem with leaving the ship is that it reminds you of everything that you miss about life on land, especially when you're living aboard a ship of darkness like the *MS Barnacle* that ropes up at the most beautiful ports in the world. These violent ups and downs are what cause crew members to develop a form of nauseating seasickness that derives from the undulating emotional experience of navigating through the rough ship-life waves. These waves lift them up all the way to the moon when they're in port and at the crest of the tsunami-sized surf, and then slam them into a rocky coast every time they climb back aboard their stinky ship. You see, the worst part about shore leave is leaving the shore, forcing yourself to walk back up the gangplank again to rejoin your crew. It's all enough to make you want to abandon ship. But nobody wants to abandon ship if they don't have to.

Or maybe the reason we didn't just say, "forget it", and stay in Venice and learn to play "When You Wish Upon a Star" on the accordion for tips and spend the rest of our short lives drinking wine and laughing and eating basil pizza with our feet hanging over the side of a gondola was something much deeper. Something deep like we couldn't abandon ship life because our stupid passports were still on board the cruise ship.

CHAPTER FIFTEEN

There's Always One Bad Rum-Filled Apple in the Bunch

We climbed back aboard the *MS Barnacle*, smelling of wine, lemon gelato, and all the Murano glass that we touched but couldn't afford to buy. We were very tired, having gotten lost on our way *out* of Venice, too.

My advice: Don't go into Venice without a GPS system, a sextant, a star chart, a life raft, and a highly-detailed map. Venice is more difficult to navigate than finding your way from the buffet line to your stateroom on the first day of your cruise aboard the *Symphony of the Seas* (the largest cruise ship in the world at the time). Everyone who has ever visited the city comes back with the disturbing experience of meeting cruise ship passengers dressed in tattered evening gowns and mud-stained tuxedos who are wearing "I Like Ike" buttons on their lapels because they have been wandering around the city of bridges since 1951. There's a good reason there are too many Venetian mask shops in Venice. They're all owned by cruise ship passengers who got lost in the city and were never able to find their way out. We were lucky to have made it out alive.

While jogging toward the crew mess, we passed by the atrium. Gertie tugged on my shirt-sleeve and made me stop to watch a comical routine that a group of cruise ship chefs and the maître d' were performing for the passengers who were just getting back on board. The show was like something out of a *Three Stooges* episode, and if you've ever cruised before, you've probably seen it. It's a standby cruise ship act called *The Rum Cake Disaster*. We watched as the head chef tried to orchestrate a rum cake cook-off. He selected guests from the audience, making sure to find passengers who were willing to drink a bit from the rum barrel. The head chef delivered instructions, while the maître d', whenever the chef's back was turned, took rum shots with the passengers and mischievously added shot after shot of rum to the same cake. At the end of the act, the head chef went down the line of freshly baked rum cakes, tasting each one, finally arriving at the rum cake that had about an entire bottle of rum added to it. The chef took a bite and then spit the cake out. Everyone in the audience howled with laughter.

Once the show ended, we shuffled into the crew area and made our way down to the crew mess. The place was packed. A line of crew members were wrapped around the room. Gertie and I glanced over the buffet line: more chicken knuckles, a clump of pasta noodles in olive oil, and a bowl of apples.

Gertie picked up an apple. "I've been craving some fresh fruit," she said, and then made a face like Robert Shaw made when Jaws attacked the *Orca*. Gertie squeezed the apple, showing me that it was as soft as a ripe peach. She turned the fruit over; it was completely brown on one side. We both dug through the basket of apples, but in this bunch, all the apples were bad.

Bartek, our friend in the lounge band, waved us into the buffet line, letting us cut in line.

"What's going on?" I asked.

"It's pizza night," he said.

I looked at a table that had been set up in the crew mess.

There were pita slices, a bowl of tomato sauce, pepperoni circles, a variety of other diced vegetables, and a few different types of cheeses.

"This looks great," I said.

He pointed over to the end of the table. "Well, don't get too excited. The toaster machine is broken." I looked at the industrial toaster at the end of the table, the type with the metal conveyer belt inside.

"So everyone is eating the pizza raw?" Gertie asked.

"Raw, not exactly. Cold, yes."

"How long has the toaster been down?" I asked

Bartek shrugged. "Ever since I got here. And that was about six months ago. Management claims that one of the crew members broke it, and so they don't feel they should fix things that crew members don't respect."

Sounded about right. Gertie and I weren't surprised.

After sitting down with our cold pita pizzas, we saw one of the Indian chefs from the rum cake show walk into the crew mess with one of the cakes. It was covered in a wonderful white frosting. He walked over to the buffet line and set it down and then walked out of the room. Most of the crew members in the room, including me, stood up and swarmed the cake as if we were a flock of ospreys circling the last trout in a high mountain lake. I cut a big slice for Gertie and me.

I sat down at our table, took a taste of the cake, and then immediately spit it out onto my plate. I heard forks hitting plates and then groans from the other crew members who had cut slices of the rum cake too. This was followed by what sounded like an extremely vulgar version of "It's a Small World After All": cursing in about every language of the world.

"What's wrong?" Gertie asked.

"This is the rum cake with the bottle of rum added to it."

"Why would they bring that into the crew mess?" she said.

Her question was rhetorical, of course. There were at least thirty rum cakes made at the "Rum Cake Disaster" show, and it says a lot that the only cake they brought into the crew mess was the one that was inedible. Maybe it was a joke. Maybe the chefs thought the cake was just as edible as everything else they served in the crew mess. I didn't care what the reasoning was. I slid the plate away from me, which smelled as bad as a rum-breathed pirate in a bakery. I had lost my appetite, and I wished we would have stayed in Venice.

But we were back on the *Barnacle*, and it was time to get back to work. Alex had scheduled gallery hours for the rest of our first night back on board, so we stopped by our cabin and changed into our formal wear. Cruise ship crew members: people who can go from shorts and sandals and five o'clock shadows to looking as if they are about to pick up their date for prom night, all in about the time that Superman can change into his superhero getup in a phone booth.

I stuffed my pockets full of "free champagne" cards on the way out the door. The cards had become an integral part of our art auctioneer uniforms. Alex expected us to have them on hand at all times, and he asked us to pass them out liberally.

After taking a set of stairs that led back into the passenger area, we walked toward an elevator with bushy, plastic plants on each side. There was also a bit of faux foliage behind us, against the glass-plated railing that helped guard passengers from falling to their deaths on the atrium floor five decks down. Surprisingly enough, I've never heard of this happening.

As we walked past the elevator, I recognized the couple that was stepping out. They had shown some interest in buying an original painting.

The husband stuck his hand out and waved us down. "Hey! Has that painting sold yet?"

"No, sir," Gertie replied. "We'd be happy to bring it out for you tonight, if you'd like to stop by the gallery."

Then, out of the corner of my eye, I noticed something quite strange. Angel, the M&R manager, was standing behind one of the plastic yucca trees by the glass railing behind us. I looked over and saw him staring right at us, as if he was a Russian spy in one of those low-budget films in the 1980s, where the Russki infiltrator disguises himself as an indoor plant and sneaks around eavesdropping on Top Secret conversations. I couldn't imagine why Angel was being such a knob, so I just ignored him.

The husband smiled. "That would be excellent."

I dug into my pocket and pulled out a "free champagne" card. "Here's a card to bring to the auction with you. A free glass of—"

Angel hopped out from behind the yucca tree and walked right up to me. "Excuse me. What do you think you're doing?"

Gertie rolled her eyes.

"I'm handing these passengers a card," I said. "For free champagne. They're interested in buying a piece of art."

"No, before that?"

"What?"

"You had your hand in your pocket."

"I was getting a—"

"I already warned you about your hands in your pockets," Angel said.

The passengers couldn't seem to believe what they were hearing—which, in fact, was nothing more than the reality of ship life for crew members on some ships. I didn't want to lose a sale over something like this, so I just ignored Angel for the moment and spoke directly to the passengers. "I'm sorry, but I've got to deal with this. We'll see you in the gallery tonight?"

As they walked back into the elevator, I pulled Angel to the side. "What are you talking about?"

"You're not allowed to have your hands in your pockets. This is absolutely against the rules. It makes you look very unprofessional."

Now, to be fair, I had heard this before. Every time I joined a cruise ship, I had to go through orientation training. Every company had a specific look that they wanted crew members to adhere to. There was always something that the current management team was targeting and trying to eradicate. On one ship, it was facial hair. If the management saw a stray hair sticking out of a mole on your neck, they'd send you to the staff captain. Three hairs, and you're out. In each training, there was always a bit about how crew members should never have their hands in their pockets, but no one ever enforced the rule. It was mostly a moot point. Crew members never had time to have their hands in their pockets because they were always working.

I had put my hands in my pocket to retrieve a card that might help us make a sale. And the irony wasn't lost on me that it was the *Marketing* and *Revenue* manager that was now reprimanding me for doing something that was *marketing* our products and which might actually generate some *revenue*.

Then I thought back to the day that Gertie and I first boarded the *MS Barnacle*. Angel had popped out of the wall like the guy in *The Wizard of Oz* at the gate to Emerald City, and said "Watch those hands!" Now I knew what he meant. He was targeting hands in pockets, and he was letting me know that I better not slip up. It was petty, but such is ship life.

Angel touched my jacket lapel. "And I've told you to get a new jacket. This one is way too small for you." He gave me a forced, mechanical smile. "If I catch you again with your hands in your pockets, I *will* write you up."

I could have been more diplomatic. I could have been more tactful. But I didn't have time for Angel's nonsense. I thought maybe Angel was just having a bad day, that he'd come to his senses tomorrow and start acting like a normal person. And Alex had warned us, had directed us from his experience (which I sincerely valued) when we first joined the fleet: "You are not crew members. You are vendors," he said. "You have to fight for what is rightfully yours in this ship life."

Gertie and I walked away. "How much time do we have before we need to be in the gallery?" she asked.

I looked at my watch. "Twenty minutes."

"Let's get a drink."

That sounded perfect. There was nothing that sounded better at that moment than a nice, cold, pacifying, pirate-sized rum punch. Except maybe demagnetizing all of Angel's crew-cabin keycards when he wasn't looking. That would have felt pretty good, too.

CHAPTER SIXTEEN

Big Joe and The Black Seadog

Big Joe was in the crew bar, and he poured us two rum and Tings. A squall had blown in after our ship left Venice, which made all the bottles clink behind the bar. Our highball glasses slid across the wooden slab as the ship rolled in the swelling seas. The walls creaked and groaned at the stress of the storm. Through the porthole windows that lined the back wall of the bar, I could see rain sliding down the round glass panes, smearing the dark-blue and foamy-white scene of the choppy waters that swirled and splashed and raged outside our ship. The rain was falling in gumdrop-sized globs that pinged against the metal hull like rubber bullets being shot from buccaneer muskets.

I felt as if I should have had a stubbly beard and a cigar hanging from my lip, and I should have walked into the bar and ordered a whisky on the rocks and talked to Big Joe about harpoon mechanics and our search for the great white whale. It was one of those nights, where the sea and the ship and the storm and the steely gray sky all converged to make a sailor feel like they were on a great adventure, that they were truly battling toward something good, through something treacherous, and into the very soul of what it means to be a seafarer and a courageous sailor out on the dark, mysterious sea.

Gertie and I sipped our cold grapefruit rums and kept our elbows on the bar to steady our balance aboard the swaying ship. A pair of talking heads on TV rattled off mindless chatter about the Middle East and the economic troubles back in the US. I had been cruising long enough now that as I watched the back-home news, I felt as if I was viewing a sitcom: a drama that unfolded every day, but a drama from which I felt very far removed. The feeling was similar to what Joseph Conrad said in *Heart of Darkness*: The ship had become our home, and the sea was now our country.

A wispy Indian man, one we had met in the crew bar after we were blessed by the pope and given the Indian feast, walked in and handed Big Joe a Styrofoam food box. It was a delivery. I could smell the concealed cruise-ship contraband: curried shrimp and grilled lobster tails. Joe clasped the to-go box between his hands and tucked it underneath the bar.

I asked, "What do you think about— "

Joe put out his hand and looked at the television. "I want to hear this."

Scrolling across the bottom of the screen was a wide, red banner that read: *BREAKING NEWS—CORONAVIRUS HITS FRANCE.* The news report went something like this:

France has had its first confirmed death in the quickly spreading coronavirus epidemic. Early reports have revealed that the man, a resident of France, had been traveling in Dubai and began noticing symptoms of the virus after he returned to France last week. The man was held in quarantine until his death earlier this morning. There have also been unconfirmed reports of three other coronavirus cases in the country. The French government is advising travelers and residents to take extra precautions when traveling in the country and is considering a ban on travel to Middle Eastern countries where the virus has been identified. In other news…

Big Joe picked up a glass and started polishing it with a

white rag. "This is why we bump fists."

I nodded. We were supposed to be in the gallery by now. Gertie called Alex to let him know we were running late. When she came back to the bar, she told me that Alex asked for one of us get to the gallery immediately. She volunteered to go back. I ordered an ice water.

Alex said we needed to get to the gallery as fast as we could, that he thought it was going to be a busy night. We felt it was too rough outside for passengers to be walking around the ship. Most passengers were never on board the cruise ship long enough to grow their sea legs. Whenever there was even the slightest swell, passengers stumbled around the promenade like drunk, one-eyed pirates with uneven peg legs. Most passengers were probably huddled under blankets, sucking on pieces of ice, and covering their bodies with as many seasickness patches as they could get their chocolate melting cake–stained hands on.

Alex had also deceived us about his cabin—the one that ended up being a stateroom in a passenger area with room service that would deliver limitless platters of hamburgers and french fries and chicken fajitas to his door at any hour, day or night. So we didn't mind being a few minutes late for work. It was the least we could do. *Cheers! To Alex and his scallywag ways!*

I paid for our previous round of drinks to close out the tab—three dollars and fifty cents. A cruise ship crew bar: The only place in the world where you can turn a ten-dollar bill into a lethal case of alcohol poisoning.

I looked at Joe. "Why do you think alcohol is so cheap for crew members on cruise ships?"

He looked up at the ceiling. "Because that's what they

decided it should cost. I don't know."

The ship swayed back and forth. A miniature ship's bell replica that Joe rung whenever he was tipped well swayed with the waves, lightly ringing out as we rolled with the sea.

"Yeah, but think about it," I said. "Everything else on the ship for crew members is expensive. They won't let us eat the good food that's served to passengers. They're greedy with the shipboard Internet access. They charge us if we want to eat in the passenger restaurants. They took away our toilet paper. They're even making a profit in the slop chest. But when it comes to alcohol, they practically give it away. It doesn't make sense. A candy bar in the slop chest is about the same price that we would pay in a convenience store back home. But beer is cheaper in the crew bar than anywhere in the world that I've ever been."

"Well, you know what I think?" Big Joe leaned over the bar. "I think it's because they want to numb crew members to what's really going on around them. I think that's why sailors have always loved the rum. It's because ship life is *not* easy."

Joe had a point, but I think everyone at the bar that day would have agreed that life on a modern cruise liner was much cushier than making the crossing in steerage aboard the *Mayflower*. However, the living conditions aboard even some of the most beautiful-looking cruise ships can be tough to deal with if you're living below the waterline.

Cruise ships are a lot like beautiful people: even the most gorgeous and charming blondes and the most handsome men with faces like Disney princes can turn out to be quite nasty on the inside, once you delve down deep enough beneath the surface and search through the lower decks of their deceptive façade.

What Big Joe was suggesting sounded a bit too conspiratorial for my blood, but it did make a lot of sense, and it did answer the question: Why are cruise ship companies so generous with their alcohol for the crew when they are so tightfisted with everything else? What if cruise ship companies were deliberately encouraging their crew members to drink alcohol so they would be numbed to the poor living conditions they are subjected to when aboard the ship? It didn't sound so farfetched and implausible to me. On some cruise ships, the company has even adopted a practice for the crew known as *cambusa*, where crew members can put in their alcohol and soda pop orders with their room stewards, and the alcohol will be delivered right to their crew cabin door.

Why *are* they going to such great lengths to encourage crew members to drink? And is this really the type of practice cruise ship *passengers* should tolerate? Who wants to cruise through shoal-laden waters aboard a ship with a crew that's half drunk most of the time? Crew member to passenger: *Hiccup. Ma'am, it seems as if the cruise ship—hiccup—has hit a reef, and now we are sinking. As part of the Festivus Cruise Line's crew, I think this would be a good time for you to take a shot of tequila with me, because we are all probably going to die. Hiccup. Hey, is that a lifeboat? Cool. There's no way—hiccup—that I could lower that thing right now. That takes, like, a lot of "coordinization" and stuff.*

"What do you think of this ship?" I asked.

He pressed his lips together as if he was trying to hold back a flood of words that wanted to come pouring out of his mouth. Then he shrugged and kept polishing his glasses. "It's a ship. I have my friends." He tapped on the Styrofoam box under the bar and smiled. "I have my bar. I don't pay attention to the ship life. It's like this virus. I know I'm going to be okay. I don't listen to what these people say. About people dying." He shook his head. "I look to all of the good things in my ship life. If I believe that I will be happy, then I will be happy no matter what is happening on the ship."

His words reminded me of the tall Jamaican man that we always saw singing as he walked around the crew area.

I leaned forward. "But this ship. It's the worst ship that I've ever been on."

"Yes," Big Joe said. "It's a dark ship. It's the darkest ship I have ever been on, too. Just look at this pool table. Look at the smoke blowing out of the broken door around the corner. These things come from the top. They say a lot about the type of captain and management that we have on this ship. And the whole feeling of a ship, the entire mood of the place comes from the top. It's like a mountain that we are living on. When it rains, when times are tough, this is when you realize what kind of stuff you have on top of the mountain, because it all trickles down to everyone that lives below, and eventually it gets into the sea and spreads all around the world."

"So don't you think that crew members should say something about this?" I asked. "Shouldn't we do something about it?"

"I'm not sure there is anything that can be done. I think we all just have to focus on what is good. We can't define our ship life by the darkness that we find aboard our ship. We have our ship life aboard the ship, but we also have our inner life. If we define our ship-life in this way, then we create a monster inside of *us*. And we feed this monster by focusing on it. You have to starve it. You have to choose to ignore the monster or you have to confront it. That's the only way to starve it, to kill it."

"But do you really believe that a person's reality is created by how he perceives the world around him?" I asked. "Do you really think that reality can be altered by what someone believes or by what someone wants reality to be?"

Big Joe popped off the cap on a Stella Artois and poured it into a tall, slender glass, filling the glass halfway. He slid the glass toward me. "I think in ship life, it's important to have *inner* peace despite all of the *outer* turmoil that we must endure aboard our ship. And I think that your *response* to the turmoil can alter your *approach* to living aboard the ship. If you respond to the ship life environment negatively, then your approach to ship life will be altered in a negative way too. This negative approach will affect your results, also in a negative way. And then if you react to the results negatively, the whole cycle starts spinning all over again, just like the propeller spinning outside our ship. Around and around. Fighting the current."

I took a sip of my water. "Inner peace despite all of ship life's outer turmoil. I like that."

I liked what Joe had to say, but I thought his propeller analogy could only cut so deep. "But then aren't you just choosing to ignore what is really happening?" *What if reality is harming you?*

"Well, when you can't change your ship life, then you have to focus on what is positive. You have to stop feeding the monster. You have to *stop* focusing on what is *happening* to you, and *start* focusing on what you are going to *do*. You have to keep executing, keep focusing, and keep sailing forward. You can't ever tie yourself to the wheel of a sinking ship."

"I agree with that," I said. "There's a big difference

between saying 'I won't live on this ship' and 'I haven't found a way to be happy on this ship yet.' It's important to know the difference. But do you really think that your perspective can alter your reality? Is it really a self-fulfilling prophecy type of thing? It seems to me that this ship *is* dark. So many crew members want to leave."

Big Joe leaned on the bar. "I had a girl in here yesterday. She was sitting right where you are sitting. And she was crying. She said she was leaving. She said one of her managers wouldn't stop harassing her, was writing her up for everything she was doing, always finding some way to turn the positive things that she was doing into something negative. I have learned in life that there *are* people who are sadistic. Ship life is no exception. There is evil in the world, and to ignore its existence is to turn your back on reality and to put yourself in harm's way."

I looked past the ripped-up pool table and out the porthole window, out into the storm that was raging outside our ship.

Joe continued, "Sometimes you have to make adjustments. Sometimes you have to assess your reality and do what is best for you. Sometimes you have to recognize when something evil is headed your way, or when you're sailing right into a storm that is just too massive for you to survive. It's okay to change course. It's okay to set a new bearing and head for safe harbor. And it's better to do it before you find your ship *in* the storm, because when the waves are high overhead and the currents are strong and the winds are ripping down your sails—that's when it's hardest to take control of the helm and turn your ship around before it capsizes and sinks to the bottom of the sea."

This reminded me of the morning that I stood out on the breezeway of a cruise ship as we sailed from Mexico to the port of Tampa in Florida. We were sailing through the Gulf of Mexico, and we had been forced to depart from Cozumel early because a hurricane was ripping its way through the Gulf toward the coast of Louisiana. If we had stayed on our plotted course, we would have sailed right into the eye of the hurricane. That morning, as the sun rose over the Gulf, I could see a swirling mass of black, dark clouds in the distance, spiraling toward the coast. I was looking into the eye of the storm that was about to destroy many lives, many homes, so much happiness.

Big Joe grabbed a glass and filled it to the middle with Stella Artois. "What do you see?" he said. "Is the glass half full or half empty?"

I rolled my eyes. I had heard the cliché too many times. But I played along. "I'm definitely a glass is half empty type of guy these days. I wasn't always like this, but I guess the ship has gotten the best of me." I laughed.

But Joe wasn't laughing. He put his hand on top of the glass. "Some people look at this glass and say it's half full. They are the crew members who hold a positive perspective. Some people look at this glass and say that the glass is half empty. Those are the crew members with a negative perspective."

He grabbed the glass and threw it in the trashcan. The glass shattered. "But sometimes," Joe said, "you just have to get a new glass."

CHAPTER SEVENTEEN

Operation Lobster Eyes

While traveling—whether we are jetting through the clouds or walking along the high mountain ridges of the Appalachian Trail or even sailing across the oceans on a cruise ship—we can discover truth. One truth is that there is always a middle. No matter how far you are flung out into the world, no matter how far you sail into the sea, you will always reach a point where you must either turn around and sail back home, or just keep sailing on toward the horizon. But even when you sail around the world, eventually you come right back to where you started.

There is always a middle, even when you are unaware that you have passed that point. When you live on a globe and exist in a life that is, at its very core, a circular journey, there is no way to escape from going anywhere but around and around and around.

This is true on a ship, and it is true in a crew member's ship life as well. Even though crew members may feel that they are sailing forward, racing and battling through a sea with their sails full of wind, they always reach a point where they are no longer going anywhere, but instead are simply returning home.

I didn't know it at the time. There was no way for me and Gertie to recognize it—sometimes awareness is as slippery to grasp as sea water being poured through your fingers—but it was about two weeks after I had that conversation with Big

Joe, during the storm as we sailed off the coast of Venice, that I now believe that Gertie and I had hit our middle. And we hit that middle point like the *Titanic* hit the iceberg, as if we had rammed our bows into a massive, cold barrier that was strong enough to sink what many believed to be unsinkable, solid enough to stop, dead in the water, a cruise liner that was racing full speed ahead.

This was about the time that we both began to feel sick. It started somewhere deep in our lungs and then spread upward until we were trying to cough it out, but it didn't want to leave. There was no way to know where our sickness had come from. There were so many possible causes, too many usual suspects in the cruise ship lineup: our layered carpet, the soot-filled air ducts, the smoke-swirled air conditioning, the broken and restless sleeps, the poor quality of food, the stress of long work hours, the pressure of ship life in general, and living in a crew cabin alongside that sea monster that was hanging out and farting in our bathroom drain.

Our sickness could have come from any of them, but there was one thing that always festered in the back of both our minds—the coronavirus.

Neither of us felt it was too absurd to believe there was a possibility that we could have contracted it. The *MS Barnacle* had just sailed from Dubai, where the epidemic started, right before we climbed aboard. There were reports of people dying from the virus in France, where we were sailing now. Some of the deaths had occurred in ports that we had visited and were continuing to visit. The news reports confirmed that it was difficult but not impossible to contract the virus from person-to-person contact, and reassured us that the virus usually only spread in "hospital-like environments, where people are found in dense concentrations." I had never heard a more perfect description of a cruise ship in all my life, except for the fact that a cruise ship is nowhere as clean as a hospital—especially down in the crew area, which as you know by now is often about as clean as a pile of seagull poop on the lido deck.

But we knew the chances were slim. We were young. We were healthy, and so we stayed positive. We put the idea aside, and decided that we had just caught a bad flu, a pesky cold that we just couldn't shake.

And the work didn't stop just because we were sick. A few weeks or so after I had that talk with Big Joe, I was standing in front of an original oil painting, my favorite in the room, a scene of the sun setting behind a field of red poppy blossoms. I was admiring the beauty of the painting. The strokes of the palette knife created a subtle motion in the painting, which brought the field of poppies to life. The flowers swayed in a light breeze.

Out of the corner of my eye, I saw Chloe and Buster walk into the gallery for their nightly bottle of Duck Nipple. I heard the burst of static coming from Chloe's walkie-talkie.

"Ground control to Major Tom."

Buster answered, "Your circuit's dead. I think there's something wrong."

I turned around. Chloe was dressed in full formal-night presentation, head to toe: an evening gown of silver sequins sparkling in the gallery lights, a flapper-style headband of golden beads, hair curled and shined, silver-sparkled ballet flats for dancing to the big band in the main theater lounge, a silver bracelet with ship anchor charms, diamonds in her ears and in her eyes. Buster was in a traditional black-and-white tux with silk bow tie and short, modern tails. He was holding a platter with a rounded plastic top. I could see a filet mignon and lobster tail with asparagus and baked potato through the hazy, tan plastic covering.

He bowed toward me and held the platter out on his fingertips. "For you and Gertie, *monsieur*."

"What is this?" I asked.

Buster stood back up and extended the platter toward me. "We've talked to some of the other crew members, and we heard how awful the food is down in the crew area, and so we thought we'd bring you a little something special from the dining room."

I was shocked. It was such a nice gesture, but then I poked my head into the main hallway of the gallery. Alex was sitting behind his desk. Gertie was showing a young man a pop art painting of a dog with a bone in its mouth that I thought had about as much artistic value as a hairball that a cat coughs up.

I was looking for Angel or anyone else in upper management. If I was caught with food from the dining room, I probably would have been fired. Festivus Cruise Lines was obsessed with keeping contraband cuisine out of the crew area. There is food everywhere in the passenger areas. And at most times of the day, there are more *types* of food on a cruise ship than the number of lifejackets aboard the ship, and much of it is delightfully mobile. Passengers can saunter past the buffet line and grab a quick sandwich or a stack of chocolate cookies to provide the quick burst of caloric energy they may need to fuel their exhausting journey from their stateroom to the lido deck pool. Most passengers are like modern day

Hansels and Gretels, leaving a trail of ice cream cone sprinkles and chocolate chip cookie crumbs behind them wherever they go, presumably so they can find their way back to their staterooms—which is fine by me, because after five years on cruise ships, I have grown exceptionally tired of telling passengers where their cabins are located.

However, crew areas fall under a very different set of shipboard rules, and the security guards enforce these food regulations as if they were one of the Ten Commandments. *Thou shalt not take unto thee any other foods than the foods that are offered unto thee from thy crew mess. Thou shalt not take thou foods out of thy crew mess.* These commandments are the most difficult edicts to observe in the crew-member bible, because crew members are literally surrounded by the highest quality of food that money can buy, yet they are rarely allowed access to any of it.

I looked at the platter of surf and turf that Buster was offering and immediately heard the theme music to *Mission Impossible* playing in my head. This would need to be a covert operation: Operation Lobster Eyes.

If any of you are on a cruise ship right now and you want to turn a crew member's ship life right around, bring them a to-go platter of passenger food from the dining room. They'll be like a puppy that you saved from the pound; they'll be your best friends until the day they die.

I quickly thanked Buster and Chloe and explained, "I know this may look rude, but if I'm going to take this food, I need to leave immediately and take it to my cabin, because we are not allowed to have food from the passenger dining room."

Buster nodded. I took the platter and slipped into the

crew area through a side door that led to a stairwell.

There was no way to hide the glorious platter of steak and lobster. I simply had to act confident and hold it out in front of me as if there was nothing wrong with it. It was a fake it till you make it type of thing, and I faked it all the way back to our crew cabin. Once safely inside, I let out a deep breath. Then I picked up the phone and called Gertie in the gallery to let her know what had happened.

Gertie walked in the room a few minutes later. We poured glasses of wine and savored every morsel of the succulent slices of grilled filet and butter-dipped lobster tail. It was the best meal we had eaten aboard the ship in months.

As I sat on the floor of our cabin eating our unexpected treat, I thought more about why the cruise companies choose to treat passenger cuisine as contraband. Were they simply concerned about rats and other vermin stowaways living and multiplying down below the waterline? Did they believe that crew members just couldn't be trusted with the responsibilities that come with bringing food into their crew cabins? None of these reasons made much sense. Crew members have formal cabin inspections every few weeks. Any food that is found to be improperly stored is grounds for disciplinary action, very similar to the way in which US Navy ships and military barracks operate. Also, crew members are free to buy all sorts of snacks and foods from the slop chest, and are allowed to bring foods aboard from ports as long as the food is packaged. Yet, on most cruise ships, it's as if there's a cruise ship iron curtain, an embargo against crew country. And these rules unfortunately lead crew members to stress about the implications of something as kindhearted and innocent as an offering of food from one passenger to two horribly fed crew members.

We walked back to the gallery to find Chloe and Buster wandering around the room, looking like two goldfish mindlessly swirling in a small glass bowl. These two friendly goldfish did not have any champagne in their hands. Alex looked as if he was ignoring them.

Gertie immediately hopped over to the champagne cart and poured two full glasses of Duck Nipple for our favorite cruise ship guests.

"So how is the cruise going?" I asked, and then winked. "Thank you. That was incredible."

Chloe lit up. "The cruise has been fantastic. Our rooms are so beautiful. The ports have been absolutely inspiring and so romantic." She pecked Buster on his cheek. In response he wiggled his eyebrows.

"Calm down, you cheeky monkey," Chloe said with a playful grin. "And the ship is so delightful. So gorgeous. So clean. So sparkling. It's just marvelous. It's all just marvelous."

"Well," Gertie said, "I'm glad you two are having such a wonderful time." she handed me a glass of champagne that she had poured and then grabbed one for herself. "To being above the waterline. To being on top." She looked at me and pressed her lips together. I could hear the touch of frustration and sadness in her voice.

Buster wiggled his eyebrows again. "Yes. Hear, hear," he said in an English accent and then looked at Chloe. "To being on top, my dear." He bumped Chloe with his elbow.

Chloe lifted her glass. "To the cruise life."

Gertie mimicked Buster. "Hear, hear."

We clinked glasses. Gertie and I took a long sip, and I felt the warmth of the champagne bubble up from my stomach and go straight to my head.

"Hey, are you guys all right?" Chloe asked.

"What do you mean?" I replied.

"Well, I've heard you both coughing a lot over the past few days. I just figured I'd ask."

"I think we picked up a bit of a cold," Gertie said. "I think we'll be fine. We—"

"Excuse me," Alex said from behind Chloe. "Gertie, could I talk to you two for a second?"

We followed Alex to his desk. He sat down and shaped his hands into a power steeple again. "There have been a few changes in ship policy that we need to go over, and I need you both to promise me that you won't get upset."

"Okay. What's up?" Gertie said apprehensively.

We couldn't make that kind of promise to Alex. We were both near the end of our anchor chains by this point. Nearly every day, the ship management was changing the rules to some aspect of our job. Most of the directives were coming straight from Angel, and word on the ship was that he was delivering the same frustrating demands to every department that he had jurisdiction over. One day he would tell us to start doing our paperwork for the gallery one way, then a few days later, he would change it back to the way it was, which would disrupt our entire system of invoicing all over again.

The last change Angel made had really affected our job in a negative way. Angel had told us about a week earlier that we were no longer allowed to hire fellow shipmates from other departments to help us with our art auctions.

The art auctioneers really needed an entire team of people for the auction to run smoothly and flow seamlessly. Hiring shipmates from other departments had always been common cruise ship practice. We needed them to help us set up the art and move it to the stage for the auction, and then to break it all down after the auction was over, which was an exceptionally labor-intensive task.

Crew members practically fought over the opportunity to work for the art auctioneers, because it was the best money they could make on the ship. We'd often pay them ten or fifteen dollars per hour of work, and this was the equivalent of striking gold on the cruise ship mountain.

All gold-mining operations were brought to a sudden halt when, seemingly on a whim, Angel had decided that we were no longer permitted to sublet labor from the rest of crew, making Angel the worst landlord in the history of Cruise shipville. As a result, our last auction was a maritime disaster. We just didn't have enough hands on deck. The event left Gertie and I exhausted from running around the gallery like passengers searching for lifejackets as the cruise ship is going down. We pleaded our case to Angel, but he just smiled as if he was enjoying the conflict and refused to budge.

Now, Alex was about to give us the details of the latest policy changes. He cleared his throat. "Okay, for starters, Angel is implementing *another* new rule. He says that starting next week, one person from each department must be on board the ship with the department cell phone at all times."

"When we're in port?" Gertie asked in a pleading tone.

Alex put out his hand to calm her. "Yes. When—"

I blurted, "But that's what port manning is for." For passengers, Angel's request may seem reasonable. And for most departments it would be easy enough to just assign the ship phone to whatever crew member from that department was on port manning at that time. (Port manning is the regulation that requires a certain percentage of crew members to be aboard the cruise ship at all times. When the ship is in port, some crew members are required to stay on board, to man the port.) But this was way more complicated for the art department. We were a department of three. This meant that if we rotated the phone and the duty of staying on board the ship each time we were in port, then Gertie and I would only be able to leave the ship together once every *three* ports.

Gertie asked, "Is this a fleet-wide directive?"

Alex looked down at his steepled hands. "I've asked around. So far it seems this is only happening on our ship."

I realized that there was another implication to the matter. Once Gertie and I took over the *MS Barnacle* from Alex, we would be a department of two. This meant that Gertie and I would never be able to get off the ship together at all.

"Wait. It gets better." Alex took a deep breath and looked me in the eye. "You two have to start doing passenger boat drills."

I felt as if I had been bludgeoned in the gut with a mast pole powered by a hundred Viking sailors. Take away my freedom to explore ports. Ban me from the passenger buffet. Whip me with braided stays and jib halyards, but don't—please don't—make me go and help conduct the passenger emergency boat drills. I'd rather spend the rest of my life drifting in the Bermuda Triangle aboard the most flimsy life raft ever made since Robert Redford got into that raft in *All Is Lost* than have to start helping with the passenger boat drills.

I could see the kids with ice cream cones screaming and yelling after I told them they couldn't bring food to the boat drill. I had visions of the rebellious passengers who attempted to cause an unmanageable mutiny on the ship after being told to "Please stand behind the line" on the breezeway for the millionth time. I just didn't want to go back to that life. I felt myself sinking back down to the depths of a lowly crew-class crew member.

"But we're officers," Gertie said.

"There's nothing I can do. I tried. I'm sorry."

I didn't want to say anything that I thought I might regret. "Is that all?"

"Yes," Alex said.

Gertie and I walked over to the edge of the hallway gallery and didn't say a word. As if on cue, Angel walked up and stopped in front of us. It seemed as if he had been listening to our conversation from down the hall. He had probably been watching us, hoping he would see us squirm just a bit.

Angel didn't say hello. He just smirked. "I guess you two haven't noticed the posters around the ship?"

"No. What posters?" Gertie asked.

"I have introduced a new campaign on the ship." He smiled. "To boost morale. To improve the appearance of our crew members. I've noticed a lot of slouching. You two are slouchers. I need you to stand up straight when you're in passenger areas. Stand tall." He smiled again. "Stand *proud* for Festivus Cruise Lines."

"Sure," Gertie said sarcastically. "Whatever."

Neither of us moved a muscle. But Angel didn't go away.

"Like this," he said as he put his hands behind his back, holding his right wrist with his left hand and arching his back, thrusting his chest out like a rooster that's searching for his mate. It looked absolutely unnatural and ridiculous. "Stand tall," he said. "For Festivus."

I mimicked him. Gertie did the same. Angel laughed and walked away. I clicked my heels together and saluted him. "Yes, sir."

The minute he turned the corner, we relaxed and went back to our ergonomically natural "slouching" position.

I walked over to Alex. "Do you mind if we take a little break?"

"No, go right ahead," he said and waved us off.

Gertie and I walked down to the crew mess. I wanted to grab a tall glass of ship's milk and pick a banana from Banana Mountain, which always seemed to cheer me up. We sat by one of the porthole windows in the crew mess, and watched the sea roll by. I just felt like looking outside of the ship. Imagining myself on the outside of this ship-life world for a moment. I needed a break from my ship-life reality. Gertie pointed to the back wall. "There's one of the posters."

I turned around. There were two posters hung at the back of the crew mess. The first one had a picture of a Filipino crew member. He was smiling and standing with his hands behind his back, his chest puffed up, as a passenger walked by and waved to him. At the top of the poster, in big red letters, were the words: *STAND TALL. STAND PROUD FOR FESTIVUS CRUISE LINES.* The other poster was an illustration of a giant smile, something like the Cheshire Cat. The smile was just floating in the room. And at the top of the poster: *REMEMBER TO SMILE. SMILE BIG FOR FESTIVUS CRUISE LINES!*

I looked around the room. I didn't see anyone smiling in the whole place. But no one cared if we smiled down here in the bilge tank, I guess.

CHAPTER EIGHTEEN

Don't Worry, The Lorax Will Make Everything Perfect, Boss

That night, as we were about to open the door to our cabin, I saw our neighbor walking toward her room. She was a Romanian girl: short, chubby, red hair pulled back in a ponytail, wearing a croupier tuxedo that smelled of stale cigars. Her mascara was slightly smeared from a long day of dealing cards in the casino.

I asked her, "Are you having trouble with your ventilation system? Is smoke coming into your cabin all the time?"

Her accent was thick, and her sentences were broken and abrupt. "Of course. I have smoke all nights. It is awful. Disgusting."

"Are you smoking in your cabin? Do you know if any of our neighbors are smoking in their cabins?"

"I have asked everyone. No one smoking. I complain to HR. Multiple times. Nothing done. No one care."

I had asked around our hallway too, and everyone said they were having the same problem. Smoke was streaming into their cabins at all hours of the day, sometimes all night long. I looked at the Romanian girl. "Why don't we all go see the HR director together?"

Her shoulders sank. "I am Romanian. No one care about me. I have no power to change anything in this ship. You are American. They listen to you. You might make change. Me? No." She shook her head.

"I think they'd listen to you just as much as they'd listen to me."

"No. You wrong. This cabin." She tapped on her door. "It is shit. I have tried to get moved, but no one care. I hate this ship. It is depressing. I would leave if I could. But once this contract finished, I done with this ship life. No one should have to live like this. This my last contract. But you should try to make change with these cabins. They might listen to you."

I told her I would try. However, I didn't agree with what she was saying. I felt she probably just didn't want to make any waves and suffer the consequences of trying to do the right thing. All crew members lived under the same maritime laws. We were all sailing under the same Panamanian flag. All crew members signed the same seafarer's agreement regardless of what country they came from.

Gertie put down her purse as we walked into our cabin. "What a day," she said.

There was a knock on our door, and I felt like ignoring it. I just wanted to lie down in my coffin-sized bunk bed and look at the back of my eyelids for a few hours. I wrestled myself to the door and found Ronald standing behind it with his cart of cleaning supplies. I rubbed the top of my head. "That's right. You're scheduled to come today."

"Do you need me to come later, boss? I can come tomorrow, boss."

"No. You're here. The room needs to be cleaned. Come in."

Gertie put her gym bag together and left me in the cabin with Ronald. I grabbed him a lime soda out of our tiny fridge that was nestled underneath the desk. He opened it, took a long drink, and then started spraying a cleaning solution around the bathroom.

"Ronald, how's your contract going?"

"Okay. But this ship. It's dark, boss."

"I know. It's a tough one."

"No. There's voodoo here, boss. I come from Haiti. I know it when I see it, boss. There's voodoo on this ship. But God will protect us if we ask him to. Just like he protected me in the earthquake. So I'm not worried, and you shouldn't be, either. You and Gertie—you'll be fine. Everything will be perfect, boss."

"Thanks, Ronald. But this ship, it's a hard ship to sail."

Ronald grabbed his lime soda and took a long drink. Then he smiled and started wiping down our mirrors. "Ship life is easy. It's all just how you look at it. But I have to be here. I don't have a choice. And when you don't have a choice, you just have to make the most out of whatever hand you're dealt, because that's your only choice. That's all you can do. But you and Gertie, why are you two here?"

"What do you mean?"

"You're Americans, boss. The only reason I'm here is so I can make the money I need to get to America. If I was an American, I'd never be here. You have so much opportunity. Why would you want to be *here*? Living like *this* if you don't have to?" He put his arms out to his side and looked around our cabin.

"We thought it would be fun, and we could make a lot of money if we stick it out. We want to travel. We thought it would be different. We were promised it would be different."

"One day I'll see you in Miami, boss. And we'll both be smiling. You'll see, boss. I'll be there. You'll be there too, boss."

I stood up from the edge of the bed. "I think you're right, Ronald. Everything's going to be fine."

"That's right, boss. Everything will be fine. Don't worry, boss. Everything will be perfect, boss."

"I'm going to step out for a few minutes, Ronald. Will you lock up if I'm not back before you're finished?"

"No problem, boss. I take care of everything, boss."

I walked out of the cabin and started jogging down the I-95. At first I didn't know exactly where I was going. I just felt like I needed to get out. I just needed to move. I headed for the crew elevators that would take me up to the crew deck. I made it to the crew office and then stopped. I turned left into the little hallway that led to the HR manager's office. I found our friend, the Lorax, sitting behind his computer tapping on the keys. He looked up and smiled when he saw me.

"Come in. Come in," he said as he waved me into the office. "What can I help you with?"

I decided to make one more plea to help us get a new cabin. I knew that he could make it happen. I explained to him that Gertie and I were starting to get sick. We both had coughs that we couldn't kick, mine worse than hers. I also told him about the Romanian girl in our hallway, and confirmed that no one else in the hallway was smoking. I ended with, "We have to get a new cabin as soon as possible, and something really should be done about this ventilation problem. It isn't right to have crew members living like this."

The Lorax leaned back in his desk chair, put his hands behind his head, and took a nice deep breath of the clean air that was pumping into his office. "Look, let me tell you something. We are on the same side. I have been trying to get these changes made for years. I know there is something very wrong with the ventilation system on this ship. I know that the door to the smoking section is broken, and I don't think it's right. I know how you feel." He stopped and looked out his door. He looked as if he was rethinking what he was telling me. Then he stood up and closed the door to his office. He sat back down at his desk and told me that the ventilation system was broken. He said there was a part that wasn't operating correctly.

"I've been trying to get the company to fix it, but…but they just don't want to spend the money," he said.

I wasn't surprised. I told him that I didn't feel it was right for crew members to live like that and that crew members didn't expect to find themselves in these kinds of living conditions when they signed up for a contract. I asked him to do something. Gertie and I wanted to work hard for the cruise company, and we weren't asking for much. We just needed healthy living conditions so we could do our job well and continue to do it for years to come.

I didn't see myself as David and Goliath or anything like that. I knew I wasn't any sort of hero, and I wasn't trying to be. I was just another crew member trying to get the cruise ship company to do right by the crew. There were many before me and many after me. I knew I was just one more cog in the machine, one more frustrated, coughing crew member in the long line of complaints that the friendly Lorax had to deal with.

"There's only so much I can do," he said. "I can't order this part. I can't fix the ventilation system myself. If I could, I would. But I will try to get you and Gertie into a different cabin, a better cabin. But you have to be patient. Just stay positive. Let it go. Just focus on the positive."

CHAPTER NINETEEN

Kusadasi And The Filipino Mafia

After a few months at sea, crew members are always searching for some kind of release. Some find it in the crew bar. Some find it when they're out traveling in ports. Some find it by blowing their tops and taking their frustrations out on fellow shipmates.

We were searching for one the day we docked in Kusadasi, Turkey. Gertie, of course, had plans. It was all written down in her little pink notebook. I didn't mind, though. There are worse things in the world to be controlled by than Gertie's little pink notebook. Weird cruise ship managers being among them.

It had been a week or so since I had talked with the Lorax, and we were still in cabin 0604, but hope springs eternal and all that. Our coughs had continued their downward spiral. I began to sound as if an octopus was stuck in my throat and just wouldn't come out. Each of us found ourselves wheezing quite a bit, often at night, mine worse than hers. We went to the ship doctor several times and he might as well have told us to "put de lime in de coconut" and then we'd feel better, because all they did was prescribe cough syrup and a few ibuprofens, which is the same thing that ship doctors prescribe whether you have a cold or your fingers are amputated by the lifeboat winch. We'd get off the ship and our symptoms would relax, and by the end of the day, we'd be breathing fairly normal again. Once we got back aboard, it would all start back up, and the coughing would build until the next time we walked down the gangway.

We were allergic to the MS Barnacle, but then again, anyone with a pair of lungs and a pulse would be allergic to that ship of darkness.

Gertie, of course, had a plan. She decided that we needed to go to a traditional Turkish bath. It would be just what the doctor ordered. We could sit in the rejuvenating steam, fill our lungs with fresh, clean air, sweat out our toxins and frustrations, and then get a relaxing massage.

I had never been to a Turkish bath. I knew nothing about them. Gertie however, had written it down in her notebook of plans and so she became rather fixated on it, similar to how she felt about seeing the pope a month or so earlier.

Angel hadn't implemented his ship-phone rule yet, so as soon as the ship docked in Kusadasi, Gertie was pulling me down the gangway and then jogging up a steep hillside that led to what she called, "The best Turkish bath in the world! I looked it up!" (She said this while she pointed to the itinerary in her notebook, of course.)

We coughed all the way up the hill, grateful to be off the ship, grateful to be on this incredible adventure in the Mediterranean. Even though things weren't exactly going our way, we never lost sight of how lucky we were to have the opportunity to travel the world while working on the cruise ship. We still felt blessed, by the pope in fact.

When we reached the top of the hill we had a wonderful view of the rocky, serpentine coast. I looked out to sea and across all the blue shades of the Mediterranean. We continued hiking down the winding road until we reached a beautiful domed building. In front, a mosaic-tiled pathway snaked up to a large wooden door.

We paid a small fortune at the front desk, Gertie insisting that we get the "All the Way" package, which I wasn't sure I liked the sound of at all. A thin Turkish man led us to the back of the building. He gave us each a robe and a small towel. We changed out of our clothes, and then walked into the steam room.

The benches in the steam room were made of marble and decorated with dark blue and sun-yellow tiles that swirled into a mosaic of waves and ships and sailors at sea. They curved around the edge of the circular room. The mosaic tile theme continued all the way up into the impressive dome, which depicted a man on the bow of a ship who was holding a spear, ready to pierce the scales of a massive sea dragon that was emerging from the waves. At the dome's center was a round skylight that allowed a single beam of bright sunlight to pierce through the steam and illuminate a large, round marble slab in the center of the room.

Several other cruise ship passengers were lying on the marble block having their bodies scrubbed with soapy sponges by healthy, plumpish Turkish men who had chest hair so thick it could have passed as a maritime forest. The beastly men wore large gold chains around their necks, some of them with gold charms of ship anchors, ship wheels, and crosses.

They called us over to the marble slab. A man said something incomprehensible to me and then pointed to the slab in front of him. I lay down and then felt the sponge attacking my back, which felt more like a Brillo pad than I had hoped. The soap foamed up around me. Then I felt a blast of cold water as the Turkish bath workers washed the soap off our bodies.

I watched as the Turkish man slapped Gertie on the back of the thigh and then pointed toward the door. As we walked out of the Turkish bath, I realized that we had just paid a rather excessive amount of money to be bathed, which left both of us feeling like absolute suckers. So my advice: Skip the Turkish baths and go to the beach or see some ancient ruins.

After we climbed back aboard the ship, feeling like half of our skin had been removed, I was walking down the I-95 when Bartek, our buddy from the lounge band, stopped me and said, "Hey, you should come and play music with us sometime in the store room."

I hadn't played music or touched a drumstick since we had first climbed aboard the cruise ship more than two months ago. This sounded perfect. Maybe I could pound away my ship-life frustrations with a pair of drumsticks and a few battered drumheads. I could be like one of the singers on the ship with their force-field of music to help keep the black seadog at bay. I asked Bartek where they rehearsed.

"There's an extra drum set on board," he said. "The Filipino mafia has it. They've got a whole bunch of music equipment. It's in the storeroom at the front of the ship where they stay. I'm cool with them. I'll show you where it is."

Bartek led me forward, down the I-95, until we got to the last stairwell at the front of the ship. As we descended down into the depths of the vessel, I could hear the waves crashing against the bow as the ship cut through the sea.

The Filipino mafia, or the FM, had been little more than a myth to me until this point. I had heard crew members mention them since the first day I stepped aboard a cruise ship more than five years earlier, but I always felt they were probably the stuff of legend, or at most, just a loosely knit group of crew members that conducted a petty amount of illegal activities aboard the ship such as selling cigarettes, alcohol, and sometimes dabbling in the more serious undertakings of running prostitution rings and gambling circuits. Aboard the *MS Barnacle,* the rumor was that the Filipino mafia was the organization responsible for the toilet paper shortage. The FM had the only tissue paper in cruise-liner land, which allowed them to perform a stunning act of alchemy at sea when they turned the toilet paper into gold by selling it on the cruise ship black market at a stunning profit. We didn't know how or why this type of activity was tolerated on cruise ships, but it didn't surprise us.

Bartek took me through a maze of stairwells and back-alley doorways that eventually led to an unlabeled door. I could hear muffled music and rowdy conversation on the other side. Bartek opened the door, and we walked into a storeroom that was filled to the ceiling with large rolls of carpet.

As we walked by the carpet, he said, "Do you remember that dancer that I told you about when you first got on the ship?"

"The one that got real sick and went home?" I asked.

"Yes. Well, I heard yesterday from some of the other dancers on board that he died."

"How?"

"They said even his parents don't know what caused it. He got real sick and had to leave the ship. A few weeks later. *Boom*. He's dead."

I could see smoke billowing out of a small room just on the other side of the rolls of carpet. We stepped in front of the doorway and found ten or fifteen Filipino crew members sitting around a card table, smoking cigarettes, slamming down cards, yelling as they played. There was a big screen TV on the back wall, and a couch against the side of the room where several Filipino women sat talking and laughing and drinking wine. Boxes of tissue paper and other contraband lined the walls. The Filipino crew members didn't even look up when we walked in.

Real estate is the most precious commodity aboard a cruise ship. How could these crew members have their own lounge? How could there be a second unofficial crew bar that most people on the ship knew nothing about? I had doubted the Filipino mafia really existed, but then I saw their face. Now I'm a believer.

We walked past the secret enclave, and then stepped into a smaller room with a drum set, a few tattered amplifiers, and a bent microphone stand with a cheap switch-on microphone attached. How could they have all of this music gear tucked away at the front of the ship like this? It was as if I had peeled back one more layer in the complex bulb of the ship-life onion, feeling I was still far from the core.

I sat down behind the drum set and grabbed a pair of splintered sticks. I tried to bang out a tune or two, but it was so badly tuned and in such disrepair that I soon gave up, lost heart, and put the sticks back down. I looked up to see a Filipino guy standing in the doorway.

"You drummer?" he asked.

"Yeah, I'm a drummer," I said in a discouraged voice.

"You fix drum set. You fix drums. Make sound better."

I thought about it for a second. The drum set was a shipwreck; actually I had snorkeled over shipwrecks in shallow Caribbean waters that were in better shape than this rust bucket.

I looked at the Filipino guy. "Yeah, I think I can fix it, but it'll cost you. You got any tissue paper?"

The guy just smiled, a big, happy Filipino smile. "Yeah, we got toilet paper. Plenty of toilet paper."

I told him that I'd try to make it back down there to fix the drum set as soon as I could, but I had to get back to the gallery, so I asked Bartek to lead me up to the surface. There was no way I would have been able to find my way out of the maze he had led me through on my own.

As we walked up the stairwell again, I thought about the dancer who had left the ship, never to return again.

We walked back into the light of the I-95, passing Banana Mountain as it was being transported by a forklift. *Oh, look! It's Banana Mountain!* Banana Mountain always seemed to brighten my day.

I was determined to stay positive. Just stay positive. Everything will be perfect, boss.

CHAPTER TWENTY

The Small Beautiful Bird and The Big Hungry Sharks

A week or so later, I was speed-walking down the I-95 with a fruit smoothie hidden under the front flap of my suit jacket, feeling completely ridiculous. After thirty-something years on planet Earth, I had risen to the respectable position of a cruise ship serf who was living under an unreasonable dictatorship that forced me into an embarrassing career of fruit-smoothie smuggling. But it was all for a good cause. Gertie wanted a fruit smoothie.

She was very sick at this point, didn't want to get out of bed. Perhaps she had contracted something from the food in the crew mess, possibly ingested some cyclospora that was tagging along aboard a piece of wilted spinach. Her respiratory issues were progressing along nicely too, as were mine, which had left us mostly unable to breathe without succumbing to a fit of coughs.

That morning, I asked Gertie if she wanted me to bring her anything to eat. She opened one eye and whispered, "Fruit smoothie," as if it were her last dying wish, in a voice that resembled Marlon Brando from *The Godfather*.

I knew exactly how she felt. Ever since we had climbed aboard the *MS Barnacle,* all we both had craved were heaps of fresh fruits and vegetables. It happens to most crew members, after a few months on board. At the beginning of a contract, I'd dream of tropical islands, scantily clad cruise ship showgirls splashing in the Caribbean waves, and quiet spots under palms to sit in hammocks and watch the sea roll ashore. Then suddenly, one day I'd start dreaming of organic farmers' markets and tropical islands with giant bright-orange carrots, beautiful sun-ripened tomatoes, and sweet-smelling strawberries splashing in seas of non-GMO spinach hummus. It was my body trying to tell me something—perhaps that I was slowly dying from malnutrition—and it happened to Gertie too. It probably happens to anyone who spends more than a few weeks eating the food in the crew mess.

If you're on a cruise ship right now, go and ask one of the crew members what they dreamt about last night. I'd be willing to bet a lifetime supply of seasickness patches that the answer will contain the following four things: sunlight, land, throwing their cruise-ship manager overboard, and a mound of fresh fruits and vegetables.

I walked into our crew cabin and stopped in front of the bunk bed. I was pretty sure Gertie was dead, because she was not taking this day-off opportunity to watch the shipboard movie all the way from start to finish, for the first time in her life—something that cruise ship crew members are never able to do because of their busy schedules. As a result, I believe I hold the world record for the amount of times that a person has watched the first forty minutes of *Titanic*—and yes, the James Cameron film about the worst cruise ship disaster in history is regularly shown on the cruise ship crew channel.

Gertie opened her eyes, and I revealed the tall, frosty glass of fruit puree that I had been hiding behind my jacket with the flourish of a cruise ship magician pulling a towel-animal rabbit out of a hat.

She tried to say the words again, "Fruit smoothie," but this time she just mouthed them and the words came out all breathy, like a slow leak in a bike tire. She sat up in bed, her hair a twisted mess atop her head, like a bird's nest built by an impatient, mentally-challenged sea hawk. "You know, there's a silver lining to getting sick," she whispered.

I had to hear this one. Gertie: able to find the bright spot in a black hole. "What's that?"

She stuck out her hand and grabbed the smoothie, then smiled. "I've lost five pounds in the last week. Being sick isn't so bad, after all."

She wasn't the only one who had lost weight. I was shedding pounds faster than a cruise ship passenger with norovirus. I encouraged her to go see the doctor.

"I don't want to be quarantined," she said. "We'll be in Santorini in a few days. I want to ride the donkeys, remember?"

I had forgotten about the donkeys. Gertie had talked about them when we were back in cold and rainy Hamburg, Germany. That seemed like a world away from our life now aboard the *MS Barnacle,* which was sailing down the warm, sunny, Mediterranean Coast. I hadn't seen someone so excited about a bunch of donkeys since one of my more deviant showband mates tried to get me to go see the donkey show in Mexico—and that's no kid-friendly adventure with Shrek that I'm talking about. If anyone on a cruise ship ever asks you if you want to see the donkey show while you're visiting a Mexican port, run away as fast as your little legs can run. No amount of tequila will allow you to un-see what you will see at the Mexican donkey show.

"Yes," I said. "Riding the donkeys in Santorini. I remember now."

Then I saw her face start to regain its natural glow, as if

something had stimulated her circulation for the first time in days. "I have it all planed out," she said as she picked up her little pink notebook that was tucked under her pillow. She flipped through a few pages. "First, we'll ride the donkeys up to the top of the hill. Then we'll go to the Ponta-Venetian Tower, which is a beautiful thirteenth century tower in this magnificent castle with..." Her voice just kind of melted away. I started daydreaming about cucumbers covered in tzatziki sauce, mounds of Kalamata olives, and piles of gyros dripping with lamb grease, thick slabs of red-red tomatoes, and endless triangles of honey-drizzled baklava dancing in unison as if they were a chorus line of flaky, sweet showgirls.

Then I blurted out, "I heard they have really great vegetables in Santorini. Let's make sure to eat at a nice restaurant at the top of the hill. After the donkeys, of course."

"You're right!" Gertie said as she scribbled something in her notebook. "I'll add wine, too. They have a special white wine in Santorini that I love. It's called Assyrtiko, after the grapes that are grown on the island."

"Yes. Donkeys, wine, and vegetables. Sounds perfect. I have to get back to the auction."

She kept writing in her notepad as I walked out the door, confirming the fact that nothing rejuvenated Gertie like a bit of planning and scheduling and the prospect of getting absolutely smashed drunk off of cheap Greek wine.

I jogged down the I-95 and looked out the oversized portholes. Greek isles sailed past. The sea sparkled and the hillsides were dotted with clusters of stucco-white and sea-blue colored homes with domed roofs. I walked to the aft lounge. A welcome desk had been set up in the center of the hallway that led into the room where our auction would take place. A young Asian woman with straight, ink-black, shoulder-length hair was sitting behind the desk. Alex stood behind her, showing her how to get passengers setup for the auction.

"Jing-Wei will be helping us today," he said. "I hired her."

"I thought we weren't allowed to hire anyone from outside departments anymore."

Alex shook his head. "Angel can go choke on a barnacle. You can help Jing-Wei. Make sure to give every guest a card for a free print when they come in. We're going to sell every painting in this room."

Alex walked away, and I sat down. Her name tag read: *JING-WEI MEI, HOUSEKEEPING, CHINA.*

She smiled shyly. "It mean small, beautiful bird."

"You're from China?" I asked. I had never met a crew member from China before. The world was changing. Maybe the Chinese economy had taken a turn for the worse, or there were more freedoms and mobility recently afforded to Chinese citizens, which made our planet feel as if it had grown a little smaller, once again.

"Yes, I from Guizhou region of China. My parents farmers. I find job on Internet. This my fifth day on ship."

"How do you like it?"

"I am very tired," she said. "I have no sleep in two days. I keep being told by crew members. Do this. Now you do that. I have no time to sleep."

I had seen this before. Crew members will sometimes pass their work on to the new kids on the block. Not knowing any better, people like Jing-Wei unwittingly fill up their schedule with the work that other shipmate slackers should be doing.

"If you need to go and sleep, then go. I can handle this."

She shook her head. "No. No. I want this job. This job pay more than any job on ship. This good opportunity for me. I send money back home to my family. I sleep after we done."

Ship life was often a microcosm of the world economy, allowing seafarers to lift the veneer and peek inside for a moment. Sometimes what we found underneath that veneer wasn't very pretty, but we were often humbled by the determination of the human spirit to rise above individual circumstances. I am grateful that cruise ships give many of these less-fortunate people in our world the opportunity to do that, to climb out of poverty, to escape warfare and conflict, to find a family again out on the deep blue sea.

I always loved to get a little peek into all the different cultures that crew members came from. We were all condensed together on our sailing city—a sailing city that at its heart flies every flag of every nation, and does so amazingly peacefully. In fact, if you want to find out how we can achieve peace in this world, just go on a cruise and observe the crew members. You'll discover pretty quickly that the best way to create world peace is to give every man and woman a job with adequate pay, an endless supply of food and water, a tolerable amount of living space, a government that is respected and properly functioning, cheap beer, and a place to watch the World Cup. Do all of this and you pretty much have peace on Earth. A cruise ship is quite a beautiful thing when you look at it with that perspective, don't you think?

Back on our ship, the passengers began flowing into the lounge. Each one of them asked about the free print that they had been told they would receive at the end of the auction. This was a bit unusual, but we had passed out free prints before, so I didn't think much about the extra attention the prints were getting.

Alex had hired the Chinese girl to help with the welcome desk, but he was unable to round up the crew of shipmates we needed to run the auction smoothly. Gertie was out on sick leave, so that left me, our Indian art steward named Bashrek, and a small number of rebels who were willing to work under the table (and take the risk of being written up) for the chance to make the high wages that we paid.

We sold a remarkable amount of art at the auction, and by the end of the sale, I was ready for a long break after juggling the quadruple duties of running paintings to the auction block, reorganizing the golden-painted easels, alerting Alex of bidders, and then recording the bid numbers and bid amounts on our auction sheet.

At the close of the auction, Alex pointed to me and said, "Please see *him* for your free prints." I grabbed the stack of prints off a back table. A stampede of passengers rushed toward me. I felt like a cruise-ship ice cream machine on the first day of a cruise. Before I had time to turn around and leap over the cruise ship rails, I was surrounded by a sea of hands grabbing prints from the stack.

I tried to summon the voice that I used to control crowds during the passenger emergency drills. "Folks, please, single file line."

But it was no use. The passengers started shouting. "I want the print of the house in the garden!" And then others, "I want the ship on the coast of Santorini!" A brawl nearly erupted when an English woman with a silk scarf around her neck was nearly knocked over by an older Indian man who wanted to get his hands on a colorful print of a cruise ship surrounded by idyllic Greek isles.

"Please stand back!" I said.

Passengers shouted as they tried to fight their way to the front of the crowd. I was pushed against the wall by the feeding frenzy of the art-loving school of passenger fish. Prints flew from the stack, passengers grabbed three and four at a time.

I tried to get them to form into a line again, but no one listened. Half of them didn't understand English. I looked past the crowd. Alex laughed. I set the stack of prints on a table, walked away, and watched the feeding frenzy from a distance. Then, faster than a crew member can say, "Yes, I'd like another chicken knuckle, please," the prints were gone. There was nothing left behind but the ripped paper bags that had once held the dollar-store quality artwork. Little white tickets for free prints lay scattered across the lounge floor.

A few passengers complained, saying they didn't get their free prints. They were headed straight for the purser's office in protest. I tried to subdue them, but there is no tranquilizer powerful enough to pacify an unsatisfied cruise ship passenger, unless you have a few extra bottles of Duck Nipple on hand, which we unfortunately did not.

I don't know how much those prints were worth, but to me they looked about as worthless as putting a digital scale at the end of the gangplank on disembarkation day. Cruise director to passengers: *Hey! Anybody want to see how much weight they gained during their fourteen-day cruise along the coast of Italy and France!*

I was ready to ride those donkeys of Santorini that Gertie

had talked so much about. I was ready to ride them right off that ship and gallop straight off into the dusty, Greek sunset, holding a bottle of Santorini wine in one hand, and a fat, juicy gyro in the other. *Hee-haw! Hee-haw! See you later, you scallywag suckers!*

Lucky for me, Gertie approved of this plan. She had even written it down in her little pink notebook of travel fun. Donkey town, here we come. *Hee-haw! Hee-haw!*

CHAPTER TWENTY-ONE

The Penguin And His Cappuccino At Sea

After the auction, I went back to our crew cabin and woke Gertie up. She had fallen asleep clutching her little pink notebook while watching reruns of *The Love Boat* on the crew channel. "I still only made it through half an episode," she said.

She rubbed her eyes and ran her fingers through her tangled hair. "I want a coffee," she said.

I dressed down, from my all-black sea monkey suit to tan slacks and a yellow polo. She dressed up, from bird's-nest hair and frumpy sweatpants to perfectly-curled brown locks and a snow-white dress with a pattern of tiny blue shrimp boats and pinkish-gray whales swimming in a sea of aquamarine waves and love-red hearts.

I looked at the whales on her dress, and they raised a very serious question. *Why do people always draw whales the way they do?* You know, with the big bulbous heads and the skinny tails that fan on the end. There's not a single whale on this planet that looks like that.

We walked up to a coffee shop on the promenade, Gertie walking in front in her white dress. I ordered a couple of mochas, each with an extra shot of espresso.

As we waited for our coffees, an Italian officer walked up to the counter beside us. He was the kind of Italian man that women dream about meeting when they leave their husbands after reading *Eat, Pray, Love*. Mysterious and dark cappuccino–

colored eyes, a mouth that tastes like cappuccinos when he kisses women with his full Italian lips, the scent of cappuccinos swirling around his cappuccino-colored hair.

He ordered a cappuccino.

So, this Italian cruise ship officer walked into the coffee bar and said, "I'd-ah like-ah cappuccino please-ah." He turned to Gertie and made the same face that he made every time his mama prepared a big bowl of spaghetti and meatballs for him back home in his house in the Tuscan hills. Then he saw me standing beside her and asked, "How-ah is-ah your contract-ah going-ah?"

I started coughing, and so Gertie answered for us, "Not so good, actually."

He grabbed his cappuccino and took a sip. "Why-ah are things going so bad-ah? We are sailing in Italy and France and Greece? What-ah could be better than sailing in-ah Italy?"

I completely agreed with him. No one truly understands and fully appreciates the arrogance often associated with Italians until they spend the proper amount of time in Italy and realize that the place and culture is actually much more beautiful than most places in the world and that perhaps Italian arrogance is actually just well-placed confidence.

Gertie explained the situation with our cabin, the smoke, and our manager. By the end of her story, the Italian officer was leaning in toward her. "This is-ah not-ah right-ah. I hate-ah the way-ah this is happening on-ah this ship-ah. I-ah want to help-ah you-ah."

Oh, this was a more wonderful sight than the fertile slopes of Banana Mountain. The best thing a crew member can have on a cruise ship is a friend who is an Italian officer. Well, other than a world-class maritime lawyer and a life raft, of course.

He led us both to a small table next to a wall of floor-to-ceiling windows, where we could see the sun just starting to dip behind the taller Greek isles that were gliding past, causing the sunlight to pulse through the ship's windows as we passed each island, like Morse code sent from God as the sun fell behind the islands and then slipped out into the open again.

The Italian officer laid out his plan. "We-ah have a monitoring device-ah. It will measure the smoke-ah in the room-ah. The next time you smell this smoke-ah, I will come by and get a reading from your vent-ah."

"You would do that? For us?" Gertie said.

"Yes-ah, of course-ah. You are crew members. I am a crew member-ah. We are all in the same boat-ah. We are all breathing the same air-ah. It is my responsibility to make this right-ah if I can-ah. I will do whatever I can-ah. Believe me. You are not the first crew members to complain to me about-ah this problem-ah. It is unacceptable, the way-ah crew members are living on this ship-ah."

I thought it was a rather good idea. Once we got a clear reading from our vent, then perhaps they would be forced to move us into a new cabin, and maybe we could make some actual positive change for the other crew members aboard the *MS Barnacle*.

"I will do everything that I can-ah. Unfortunately there is nothing I can do-ah about your manager-ah. You are on your own-ah with that one-ah."

Gertie and I couldn't thank him enough. Maybe he had just pulled us from the grip of whatever Kraken was living in our toilet drain.

The Italian officer waddled away like a penguin, with his three yellow-stripes shining in the sun, the smell of Drakkar Noir, cappuccinos, and olive-oil-based hair products swirling around him as he went.

CHAPTER TWENTY-TWO

Just Put de Lime In de Coconut

On the morning that we sailed into Santorini, Gertie told me to go see the shipboard doctor.

But crew members would rather jump overboard during a winter cruise through Alaska's Inside Passage than go see a ship doctor. Why? Because crew members don't like being treated as if they're third-class passengers, even if they are.

Ship Doctor: Oh, you have Ebola, huh?

Crew Member: I think so, sir. I believe that I'm dying.

Ship Doctor (dancing): Well, you put de lime in de coconut, and den you mix it all up. Put de lime in de coconut, and then you call me in de mor-or-or-or-nin. Come on! Dance with me!

Crew members also don't want to be put in quarantine, which is about as much fun as being locked in a crew cabin with no portholes, way down below the waterline, and being fed trays of Jell-O and saltine crackers through a slot in the door for five or ten days straight.

Wait. That's actually what quarantine is for crew members. So you can understand why I wanted to go see the doctor about as badly as a cruise ship passenger wants to see the ghost of the Unsinkable Molly Brown aboard their ship telling them to hurry up and don their lifejackets. I had donkeys to ride, wine to drink, and fresh vegetables to eat. I didn't want to be put in quarantine.

Gertie seemed to be recovering a bit, but the night before,

Alex had told me to leave the gallery because I was coughing too much. Alex had actually looked sincerely concerned, and Alex sometimes seemed to have about as much empathy for people as a shark circling a life raft.

So after a small naval battle ensued between Gertie and me, I finally hoisted the white flag of surrender and walked down the I-95 to the shipboard infirmary. One of the nurses on duty rolled her eyes as I walked through the crew entrance to the sickbay. She reached for another bottle of cough syrup, but I stuck out my hand and, through a series of deep coughs, managed to get out the words, "I need to see the doctor. No more cough syrup."

The nurse shook her head as she took my personal information and then pointed to the medical center waiting room. I was able to read an entire issue of *Porthole Cruise Magazine* before they called my name and led me into a small examining room.

Now, before we go any further, I would like to say that I have the utmost respect for doctors and the medical community, on land and on ships. While the shipboard nurses and doctors do have a tendency to treat crew with a bit of dismissiveness, not all the doctors and nurses that I have encountered while working aboard cruise ships have provided inadequate treatment or mistreated crew members in any way. In fact, I have received some rather stellar—and free, mind you—medical treatment from the cruise ship infirmary in the past, and some of my shipmates have too. I understand that cruise ship doctors are overworked. They're like lifeboats on the *Titanic*: there aren't enough of them for everyone on the ship, and when disaster strikes, everybody wants a free ride.

I sat down on the edge of the bed as a ship-nurse walked into the room. He left the door open behind him, and through the doorway, I could see an elderly man, a passenger, getting his blood pressure checked, a light-blue band wrapped around his arm.

"What seems to be the problem?" the nurse said, and then he sat in a swivel chair in front of me.

I explained my symptoms and added that I didn't want any more cough syrup. I told him that I thought my symptoms could have been the result of the cabin that Gertie and I were living in, and I let him know that Gertie was dealing with the same problems, too.

And then I added, truthfully, "And I'm concerned that this could be coronavirus. I'd like you to run some tests. Just to be safe."

The nurse looked at me as if I had just flushed his favorite stethoscope down a ship's toilet. *Whooosh.* He stood up, closed the door, and then turned to me. "Don't *ever* say that in front of passengers. Why would you say that?"

I was rather surprised. "I think it could be coronavirus. This ship just came from Dubai. We are sailing in Italy and France, where the virus—"

"How could you just say that in front of passengers?" The nurse seemed more focused on preventing any potential panic on the ship than in treating a crew member. "Why would you think this is coronavirus? That's *impossible,*" he said.

"Impossible? We're on a cruise ship. Viruses spread on these ships all the time."

I told him that I wanted to be tested.

"You won't be tested," the nurse said. "We received

direct orders from the head office not to test anyone for the virus."

I wondered why the head doctor of the cruise ship company would refuse to test anyone for a virus that was rapidly spreading through the countries that the ship was sailing to. Why would the nurse get so upset with me simply because I had mentioned the name of the virus in front of a passenger? The doctor had chosen to leave the door open. I was meeting with the doctor to tell him what I thought may be wrong with me. Why wouldn't they want to test crew members? Was the ship company attempting to mitigate liability in the event that a passenger or crew member died aboard their vessel as a result of the virus?

And what about the crew member that Bartek had told me about, the one that had died after getting sick and leaving the ship? Was he ever tested for the virus? Was the cruise ship company more concerned about protecting their busy, high-profit Mediterranean cruising season than protecting the lives of their passengers and crew? Was it possible that the cruise ship company would send out a memo to all of the doctors and nurses in the fleet, directing them to avoid testing anyone for the virus, just to remove themselves from any blame and potential lawsuit that could have arisen out of a positive result? Were they just trying to prevent panic? Were they willing to put the lives of their crew and passengers at risk just to avoid a reduction in cruise sales?

I didn't have the answers to any of those questions. Yet I did know, thanks to the honesty of the Lorax, the HR director, that this cruise ship company was willing to make choices that would put their profits ahead of the health of their crew and even ahead of their passengers.

Was this the kind of company that I wanted to work for? Were these the kinds of people that I wanted to generate profits for? Are these the kinds of companies that passengers want to entrust their lives with?

What side of the cosmic force had I found myself fighting for? Was I sailing on a ship with the patriots, the good guys? Or was I swimming in a sea of profit-hungry sharks and blood-sucking sea monsters? I know it's not always black and white, but I wondered if I had unknowingly grabbed the hand of the dark side and walked up the gangway of the death star.

I asked him again to test me for the virus.

"It's *impossible* for this virus to spread on this ship. We are *not* going to test you." The nurse pointed toward the door, and I walked out of the room.

The elderly passenger sitting behind the blood-pressure machine looked at me. He had probably heard our conversation through the thin walls, and he asked me with a very calm, very British accent, "Is everything all right? Should we be worried about anything?"

I looked at him. I didn't know what to say. I walked out of the sickbay and went back to our cabin.

When I walked in the door, the anchor chain was clanking as it was deployed. We had reached the coast of Santorini, where we could take a tender boat to the coast. Gertie and I packed two backpacks with a few bottles of water and some cash and then jogged down the I-95 toward the gangway. We needed sunlight and fresh air again. As we passed a crew hallway, I caught a glimpse of Svetlana Sosexyhotkova. She had her arms wrapped around the neck of her soap opera friend. *Where the hell was Squid?* But we didn't have time to stop. We had a pair of donkeys to catch.

CHAPTER TWENTY-THREE

The Donkey Days of Santorini

We finally found our big, orange Greek sun, and it was much hotter than we could have ever imagined. Gertie had talked about riding the Santorini donkeys for so long, and now we were finally there. It was one of the few self-fulfilling prophecies that we had realized during our time aboard the *MS Barnacle,* even though we had believed that our ship life was going to be so much better, even though we had tried to have things turn out so differently. I felt as if we were struggling against a deep ocean current that wanted to take us somewhere other than where we wanted to sail.

We took the tender boat across the emerald water of the Aegean Sea and drifted toward the steep rocky cliffs of the volcanic island. Gertie looked up at the chalk-white and sea-blue Greek village sitting atop the Santorini slopes.

We jumped off the tender and jogged up to the base of the steep, rocky hillside. I knew very little about Santorini, and I was surprised to find a long line of passengers weaving around in front of the shops that lined the coast. "Are they all waiting for donkeys?" I asked.

"No," Gertie said, looking up above us. "They're waiting for the tram."

I looked a few feet up the hillside where people were climbing inside a tramcar. The tram would safely and comfortably deliver cartloads of smiling passengers to a large white-and-blue marble building sitting atop the volcanic-mountain slope.

"They're air-conditioned, too," Gertie added.

"And you want to take the donkeys?" I asked.

"Of course I do. Let's have an adventure," she said, and I honestly wanted to have an adventure too.

"Where's the line for the donkeys?" I asked.

She pointed to a small opening between two stucco buildings, where an archway led to a dusty, narrow alleyway. Hanging on a large, rusty nail was a small wooden sign that looked as if it had been hand-painted by a donkey: *DONKEY RIDES. FIVE DOLLARS.*

Gertie grabbed me by the shirt sleeve, dragged me into the alleyway, and led us up a spiral of sandy marble steps to the top, where we found a man sitting at the edge of a donkey pen. A hand-rolled cigarette dangled from his bottom lip. He had the tanned skin of a shipwreck survivor who had been living on a secluded island for the past fifteen years without shade.

"Are you the donkey keeper?" Gertie asked. I didn't know what to call them, either.

The man looked up and mumbled something that I didn't understand one bit. "Five dollars," he said.

He put out his hand, leathery and calloused, his fingertips brown with tobacco stains. Gertie passed him a ten-dollar bill, taking us one step closer to donkey dreamland. The Santorini man, master of donkey-ville, began singing what sounded like an old traditional Greek tune, something I imagined that ancient Greek mariners may have sung as they sailed across the rolling Aegean Sea aboard their curved-hulled, multi-sail Minoan ships.

He led us through a herd of donkeys, slapping their

backsides as he walked by so that the stubborn beasts would move out of our way. He glanced back at us and smiled, and then he began to sing louder:

The maiden, oh, the maiden oh.
The sailor loves the maiden, oh!
So early in the morning,
The sailor loves the maiden, oh!
A maid that is young,
A maid that is fair,
A maid that is kind and pleasant, oh,
So early in the morning,
The sailor loves the maiden, oh!

Puffs of cigarette smoke drifted back toward us as we fought our way through the donkey herd. *HEE-HAW! HEE-HAW!* I lost sight of our fearless donkey general. The thick herd of mangy gray-and-brown-haired animals blocked our view. Eventually we emerged from the mess of pack animals and saw the Santorini man holding the reins of a donkey so fair, so perfect, that I thought I was walking into some sort of Santorini dream.

I had never known a donkey to be beautiful, but oh so beautiful, this donkey was. It had a bristled-hair coat of pure white fur. It stood tall and proud among the other lesser donkeys, as if it knew that it was an exceptionally special beast, a mare among the common burros, the Kim Kardashian of asses. It stuck its mouth of massive-teeth and its snout of moist-nostrils high toward the great, big, blue Mediterranean sky—an act of donkey snootiness, to be sure. It was a strong donkey indeed, its sinewy muscles rippling across its legs, all the way to its muscular donkey hind quarters.

Lying across its back, atop a vibrant-color-striped blanket with intricate tassels woven on the ends of its fringe, was a masterfully carved leather saddle with a repeating pattern of Aegean-style waves, so stunning that it was fit for a Santorini queen. A golden bell hung around its muscular neck.

"Woooooow," I said, my mouth dropping open.

The donkey man of Santorini bowed to us and put out his right hand, smiling at Gertie. "For you, my dear. A maid that is so fair."

Gertie had fallen under the spell of the gorgeous donkey and was already ambling toward the animal as if she were sleepwalking. The man helped her onto the saddle and gently pulled the donkey a few feet up the hill. Then he slapped the donkey on its backside, and the donkey went charging up the hill, Gertie bouncing and smiling and laughing as she went.

Gertie giggled and chortled as she sat atop her white-furred donkey, the two trotting together up the steep cobblestone path that zigged and zagged all the way to the top of the mountain. Her yellow sundress blew in the light Aegean breeze, tufts of white donkey hair swirling behind her as she went. Gertie and her donkey: a princess and her marvelous mule, each as beautiful and stubborn as the other.

Then the great donkey whisperer of Santorini turned to me. "For you, my young American man." He stepped out of the way and gestured to the donkey that had been hidden behind him. The donkey's head was hanging low to the ground, just like a crew member after a long contract of eating nothing but chicken knuckles and rice in the crew mess. The animal was thin and shriveled, looking as though it had contracted some serious donkey disease. Large patches were missing from its matted, prickly-looking hair. Swirling around the pathetic mule was a large flock of Greek flies, like vultures circling an animal they knew would drop dead any minute now.

There was no special saddle—just a mess of leather, like the rest of the hee-hawing hill climbers. No beautiful blanket. No golden bell.

"Come on," I said. "Put me on a different donkey."

The donkey whisperer laughed. "Your donkey. Your donkey," he said pointing.

Then he waved me forward and nearly threw me on top. I grabbed the reins. The donkey looked back at me and hee-hawed in a sickly, pathetic voice, the *hee-haw* containing as much enthusiasm as a group of passengers at the end of a 42-day cruise when their cruise director asks them to "come on, people, make some noise," for the millionth time.

I heard the donkey whisperer slap the mule on the rear, and with all the speed that Stanley Lord and the *SS Californian* used in aiding the sinking *Titanic,* the donkey went slowly wobbling up the hillside. The donkey's breathing became disturbingly heavy, and after a few steps, the donkey clumsily stumbled to the right before slowly staggering onward up the cobblestone path.

I looked up, and I could see Gertie's head sticking out above the low-built retaining wall that zigzagged up the hillside. She was smiling and laughing as her donkey stallion barreled up the mountain with ease.

My donkey stumbled to the right again, nearly scraping my leg against the jagged, dusty rocks on the mountainside. The donkey stopped and looked back at me with a dejected look, as if to say, *Hey, why are you still on my back, you knucklehead?*

My donkey took a few clunky steps, stumbled to the left, and then staggered to the right. His head suddenly went limp, and then the donkey leaned hard to the right like a ship listing in stormy seas.

My donkey was dying. I was sure of it. The donkey disease that had been ravaging his internal donkey organs had finally spread too far. He let out another agonizingly slow and raspy *Heeeeeeeee-Haaaaaaaaawwww*. I felt the muscles in his back twitch and then go limp. I caressed his neck, gently stroking his mangy fur. But what does one say to comfort a dying donkey in his final dusty moments?

"That'll do, donkey. That'll do," I said. It was all I could come up with.

Suddenly, I heard Gertie screaming, "Whoa, donkey! Whoa!"

She was coming straight toward me, coming back down the hill in the wrong direction. She looked terrified. She was leading an entire herd of donkeys that were carrying cruise ship passengers back down the hill. Gertie was bouncing and clutching the horn of the saddle as her beautiful snow-white donkey bolted down the hill back toward the donkey whisperer's donkey pen.

"My donkey. It's confused!" she said as she zoomed past, her donkey trotting faster than any donkey I had ever seen. It was the burro Seabiscuit of Santorini. She turned around to yell toward me as she disappeared down the trail. "A group of donkeys ran by! My donkey turned around! Help!"

And then they were gone, her and her donkey and the whole herd behind her, leaving nothing but a cloud of dust and donkey hair behind them.

"Come on, old sport," I whispered in the stinky ear of my dying donkey pal. "Can you make it up the hill one last time? I paid five dollars for you."

My donkey farted and then stumbled hard to the left, its hooves tripping over each other. I nearly lost my balance but managed to pull myself back toward the neck of the scrawny animal before I nearly went tumbling to the ground. The donkey stumbled hard to the right. He tried to take one more step but just staggered forward then came to a stop. His head sank down again.

There was a rumbling from behind me. I turned around to see Gertie atop her white majestic donkey, engulfed in a cloud of Santorini dust, another herd of donkeys behind her. They were charging toward me, like a cavalry of war mules. Gertie came galloping toward me aboard her war horse. I stood there, frozen atop my dying donkey.

Gertie was screaming. Half of her looked absolutely terrified, the other half looked like she was having the time of her life.

I slapped my donkey on the rear. "Come on! Hah! Hah, you mule! They're going to kill us! They're going to run us over!" My donkey stumbled toward the wall again, pressing my leg up against the sharp rocks. I let out a little yelp and then covered my head to protect myself from the fall that was sure to come next.

I heard the sound of stampeding donkey hooves all around me, and the sound of a hundred hee-haws as they kicked up a mound of dust. I could feel the hard-hitting hinds of donkey flesh as the herd scurried past me and my wobbly donkey friend.

After the dust settled, I opened my eyes. My donkey

sluggishly moved its neck around to look back at me. His donkey lips hung loosely around his massive donkey teeth, as if they were dangling in a depressed frown. The donkey's eyelids drooped low so that the entire top half of his brown donkey eyes, as big as chocolate-covered donut holes, were concealed beneath his lazy lids. His head fell down and hung so low that his flappy lips touched the dusty trail.

"Okay," I said. "You win. I'll walk the rest of the way." I lifted one leg over the poor donkey's back and jumped down to the ground.

The donkey suddenly lifted his head, his eyes as wide and awake as a Columbian mule that lives off a diet of espresso beans and coca leaves. The beast let out an energetic *"Hee-haw!"* and then turned around and galloped down the path, back toward the donkey whisperer's pen. As he ran away, the donkey turned around and looked at me, a big, toothy donkey grin beaming in the Santorini sun.

HEE-HAW. HEE-HAW! He seemed to laugh as he ran away. I had been duped, I thought—no, it was worse. I had been donkey duped.

I started my long, hard climb up the steep hill in the heat of the big, blazing, Greek sun. I reached the top about an hour later and found Gertie sitting in the shade of an olive tree, smiling and sipping on a cold glass of water.

"What took you so long?" she asked.

I had run out of water a half hour ago. I had been duped by a stupid donkey. The dust of the hillside was caked on my arms. It had mixed with my sweat and turned into a special form of Greek cement that, when wet, was as thick as tzatziki sauce and, once dried, was as hard and heavy as marble. "I'll tell you later. Let's find some vegetables. I want fresh fish and fresh fruit and olives and vegetables and Santorini wine."

Gertie perked up. "Yes. Wine. Mmmmm. Let's."

We found a small café on the edge of the hill that overlooked the sparkling Aegean Sea. We ordered mounds of food and two bottles of wine.

By afternoon, we were blissfully whistling in the Santorini sun, but no matter how much wine I drank, I couldn't forget the sight of that donkey running down that dusty, steep path, looking back at me and laughing the whole way with his big, floppy, donkey tongue hanging out the side of his wide-grinning, donkey mouth. Of all the donkey pens, in all the Greek Isles, in all the world, I just had to walk into his. *Dear Santorini Donkey, you still haunt my dreams.*

After our donkey adventure, Gertie decided to scratch everything from her schedule in her little pink notebook. We spent the rest of our afternoon feasting on fresh food, sitting in the sunlight, breathing the fresh sea air, and drinking the local wine.

It was the best plan that Gertie had ever made.

As the day was coming to an end, Gertie looked out over the sea. Our cruise ship was anchored off the coast like an unwelcomed foreign battleship—something we could never quite escape, no matter how far we traveled up the hill.

"It wasn't what I expected it to be," she said.

"No, but it's okay. We'll have other adventures. Maybe other ships, too."

"I can't believe it ended up like this. You know," she said and looked down.

I took a sip of the Santorini wine, the sharp flavor of the local grapes swirling with a slate and mineral touch.

Gertie looked up. "I've never been this unhappy in all my

life. It's this ship. We should be happy."

I nodded and agreed. We talked about how we didn't want to trade our health for money. We didn't have to be there. We had a choice, and we both felt it was foolish to throw our health away. It's all we really had. At the time, neither of us really cared that much about money, anyway? There would always be ways to make money, but we knew we couldn't always buy our health back. We couldn't always make more life, or more time.

"We can still travel," she said.

"Of course, just maybe not as crew members," I said. We knew this wouldn't be our last time on a cruise ship. We decided in our next life, our land life, we'd come back as passengers one day.

"Yeah, as passengers," she said then nodded. She looked past me as if she were suddenly lost in a daydream.

I thought back to my very first day aboard my very first cruise ship. I had promised myself I wouldn't let myself get dark. I promised I would know when it was time to move on from ship life. I wanted to keep that promise. I was grateful for everything ship life had taught me and how much it had helped me grow. It felt as though now was probably the right time to sound the alarm, abandon ship, and find the nearest lifeboat before the sea swallowed us whole. And being happy wasn't the most important factor in our decision. Staying healthy was much more important to me, and this ship was an unhealthy place to live.

I looked down at my watch. "Oh, wow. Doesn't the last ferry leave in twenty minutes?"

Gertie looked down, too. "Yes! Let's go!"

We ran down the hill, laughing and smiling and yelling

as we went. I felt free as I ran, free as the Santorini sun—that big orange, Greek sun. I wasn't just running down that hill. Gertie wasn't just racing down that mountainside. We were running home. We felt as if we were running down the gangway, running to the pier, running toward freedom, anywhere that was far away from that ship.

We caught the last ferry, and it felt as if that tender really was our last chance to get back home—at least, it felt that way to me, and I was happy to start sailing. I was ready to catch that strong sea current, to capture those winds that were guiding us off the *MS Barnacle,* off the ship of darkness. I was ready to catch that sea breeze that was blowing us back home.

CHAPTER TWENTY-FOUR

The Sinking Ship And The Silver Lining

We were standing on the I-95 as the ship pulled into the Port of *Bar-the-lona.* I had told Alex I was signing off as soon as we sailed back to Spain. There were a few friends to say good-bye to, but Alex didn't show up. I wasn't surprised. He was done with us now. He got what he wanted, and now he was on to the next person he could exploit for money and work.

Before we left, we wrote Ronald a note and left him a nice tip. Gertie had to go back to the crew cabin one more time. She still had a few loose ends to take care of. I heard the thrusters ignite. The ship shook and rumbled, and then the cruise liner finally knocked against the edge of the concrete pier. I listened as the ropes were thrown down to the dock. The engines were shut off, and the ship finally went quiet.

It was early in the morning, and as the Indian security guard opened the large gangway door, a beam of sunlight splashed into the *MS Barnacle.* The morning mist rolled onto the ship, smelling sweet in the way that only land can smell after you have been at sea for a long time. It smelled like grass and flowers and dirt and steel and wood. It smelled like life, and I wanted nothing more than to jump right in and grab back hold of it. I wanted to kiss the dirt. Yeah, I wanted to run across all the beautiful land that stretched out before us.

I heard two voices behind me, and I turned around to see Svetlana Sosexyhotkova and Squid. They were hugging and kissing.

Svetlana's eyes were welled up with tears. She held his hand and kissed it, as if she never wanted to let it go. "I'll miss you so much," she said.

Squid and I had become good friends toward the end of our contract. He even said that he was planning a trip across America, and that he wanted to come and see me when he did. I never expected to see him again, but I told him that he should keep in touch. I never could bring myself to tell him about what I had seen with Svetlana. I think he knew anyway, so I felt it really didn't matter.

I watched as the Indian security guard rolled out the gangway, then he walked over and handed me a sign-off packet that contained my passport, the plane tickets I had bought, and other shipboard documents that I would need on the trip back home.

I could hear Svetlana sniffling. "If it's meant to be, then it will work out. If we really *want* things to work out, then they *will*. I love you."

Squid let go of her hand.

I walked down the gangway of the *MS Barnacle* for the last time, and once on the pier, we had to wait for a crew bus to transport us to the airport a few miles away, one last hurry-up-and-wait from the cruise company. Squid lingered for a while at the dark threshold of the ship's gangplank, and then he waved and disappeared back into the shadows of the ship of darkness.

Svetlana wiped the tears from her eyes, took a deep breath of fresh air, and then smiled. She reached into her pocket, pulled out a pack of cigarettes, popped one in her mouth and lit it up. "That ship," she said. "What junk. What bullshit. *Bred sivoy kobyly*." Her Russian accent was sharp and biting. She parted her lips just a bit, letting a thick stream of smoke snake out from her mouth. She smiled at me, flashing her dimples. Then she stared forward, squinting, her face hardening, her fists clenched. "Worst ship I have ever been on."

"Yeah, it's dark," I said.

She took another drag on her cigarette. "I so happy to leave. I ask for transfer since I walk on board."

"You going to miss Squid?"

She shrugged. "Meh. He's just boy."

"Looked like you two were pretty close back there at the gangway."

She rolled her eyes. "Ship romance. You know how it is. I can't wait to leave ship. I so happy. That was ship love. It mean nothing." She made a waving motion with her hand. "Just like that and, *poof*, done. Then new ship. New ship life. New love. You know how it is." She winked at me and smiled as she blew out a stream of smoke.

Yeah, I knew how it was. All too well.

"This is dark ship," Svetlana said. "It like a sinking ship."

I nodded. "Yeah, it's like a sinking ship." I knew that sometimes we all find ourselves sailing in rough seas, battling through heavy storms that beat against our hulls and rip at our sails, and sometimes it does seem as if our ship is about to sink.

But there's a silver lining here too, I thought. The great thing about a sinking ship is that right before the ship goes down, all the rats jump overboard.

Sometimes we're able to salvage our ship. Sometimes we can patch the holes in the hull and we can activate the bilge pump and get all the water out of the cabin. Sometimes we can save ourselves from sinking, and then the next day, we wake up to calm seas and the bright light of the sun shining on our sails, and we find ourselves on a new ship, a ship without all of those filthy rats on board.

Maybe it's through that process that we learn how to identify the scavenging, parasitic stowaways aboard our boats. Maybe that's the way that we learn who's on board to help us navigate *all* the way through the storm, and also identify all the rats that have climbed aboard our ship just for the *cheese* down in the storage room, down there in the slop chest. Sometimes it's good to be on a sinking ship. We learn whom to trust. We see who people, and companies, really are, deep down beneath the surface. Perhaps we must dive down and see the deepest fathoms for ourselves, or we'll never know and truly believe just how much beauty or darkness there really is beneath the surface of the sea.

CHAPTER TWENTY-FIVE

Message In A Bottle

We never did find out exactly why we had become so sick on the *MS Barnacle,* but we did slowly recover after sleeping for nearly five days straight, taking long walks in the sunshine in leafy parks, and eating mountains of fresh fruits and vegetables.

Many months later, I was walking down a long wooden pier that reached out into the Atlantic Ocean from the coast of Myrtle Beach, South Carolina. Squid had come for a visit, to start his travels across America, to visit with shipmates that were now scattered across the country. He had left the *MS Barnacle* before his contract was over too, not long after I had walked down its gangway. A winter had passed, and now the spring was fighting to reemerge on the Carolina coast. It was one of those southern nights where the fog rolled ashore, sailing off the ocean in one giant wave of swirling mist, the humid air as thick and sweet as honey. The spring-blossom scent of honeysuckle, jasmine, and rose spun from the shore out into the salty ocean breeze.

Squid and I walked to the end of the pier where we could see the cold, choppy waves of the ocean fading into fog. The dim lights on the pier pilings illuminated a fuzzy halo of foggy mist. As we held onto the wooden rail of the pier, looking out toward the dark ocean with the wind blowing in to shore, it was easy to feel as if I were standing on the bow of the cruise ship once again. In the dark tide that stretched out before us, I could almost hear the sound of the waves slapping against the hull, and hear the creaking and stressing of the ship's walls as we swayed through the surging sea, and the deep, thundering sound of the ship's horn blowing through the abyss of the gray haze.

Squid was looking out toward the ocean, his pale skin clammy and cold, holding his arms crossed, the wind rippling the dark blue windbreaker flapping at his sides.

"I wonder," I said, "if it would have turned out better if we would have stayed on board. If we would have just stuck it out on that ship."

Squid was a fellow cruise ship crew member, so he understood me in a way that no one else really could. He understood the complex emotions and experiences that ship life presented to any person who really had their eyes open, who at some point found a way to pull off the ship goggles and see ship life a bit more clearly.

"You know, I loved ship life," Squid said. "But now I realize that falling in love with ship life is like falling in love with the worst type of person, the kind of person that doesn't have the capacity to love you back."

I laughed, and then I thought about how I loved so many aspects of ship life, and how wonderful ship life could be, if only the cruise ship companies would care about the well-being of their crew as much as their profits.

I looked out over the waves. The ocean looked so dark. I thought about how interesting it is that the ocean is always changing colors. Almost every day it's a different shade.

I turned to Squid. "Do you think the cruise lines are exploiting their crew?"

I heard a clinking sound behind me, the sound of metal

tapping against metal. I turned around to see a security guard walking up the pier, his flashlight beaming through the fog. He walked to the end of the dock and shined his light into the mist that swirled above the southern ocean.

I looked at the security guard and pointed south down the sandy coast of Myrtle Beach. A string of lights reached out over the ocean in the distance. "What's down that way?" I asked. "We haven't walked down there yet."

The guard kept his flashlight shining into the churning fog. "Just more piers. They're all the same," he said then turned around and walked off. The set of keys hanging on his belt clinked softly as he went.

I thought about how when it came to cruise-ship piers, that wasn't true at all. Each pier is completely different. Crew members never know what kind of ship is going to be roped up to that pier until they climb aboard and get beneath the waterline, get past the beautiful exterior and really explore deep beneath the surface. After the *MS Barnacle,* I believe that it's not the ship that is dark—it's the character of the people and the character of the company that are on board your ship. Are they honest? Do they care about your well-being? Are they true men and women? Are they rats? What's in their hearts? What's in their minds?

I turned to Squid, "While we were out at sea, we talked a lot about staying positive, about how your perception creates your reality. What do you think about that now? Looking back?"

Squid laughed and then looked down into the water below, waves slapping against the pilings. "I think the darkness on the ship was real, no matter how you wanted to perceive it, no matter what kind of reality we tried to create in our minds. I think of people in countries right before war arrives. There is a reality in those countries at that time, an objective truth, and a lot of people don't want to see it. They don't want to believe it. Maybe there are people who believe that if they just stay positive, that everything will be okay. However, some people get the heck out of those countries. They have their eyes open, and they take action. They realize that there *is* evil in the world, and that it's not something you can always just think away with a self-fulfilling prophecy or a wish upon a star. But here's the thing." Squid looked over the ocean. "Once you find yourself in that war, perhaps then you need to hold on to the positive. Maybe then you need to find the beauty in everything you can and hold on tight to your hopes and dreams of something better. I think that when you're in circumstances that you can't change, you have to look for the positive, but if you can change your reality, then you need to make the *decisions* that you need to make in order to improve your circumstances. You need to take the *actions* you must take in order to make your life and the lives of those around you better."

I thought about how it was like a ship in a storm. There's a huge wave coming, and the captain needs to use all of his knowledge, every bit of his skill, to get over that wave. He has to believe that he can do it. He has to believe that God can help him. He has to be positive and fight through the storm, but no amount of wishful thinking is going to change the fact that there's a huge wave coming that could split the ship in half.

I thought about how there was something positive about sailing on board that ship of darkness, after all. It's good to know that the darkness is real. Maybe we all sometimes have ships of darkness in our lives at some point. Maybe it's unhealthy relationships, or abusive people, neglectful people, or destructive addictions. It's good to know that the darkness is real, and that it's not something that can just be thought away. It's not something that we can just drink away with endless rum and Tings and giant glasses of wine and vodka cranberries in the crew bar. I learned that I needed to confront the darkness. I needed to battle the sea monster in whatever form it may take. I needed to sail out into the stormy sea and shine a big, yellow light in its eyes from the deck of the ship and defeat that black seadog.

I thought about how sometimes we can't just stuff our problems away, like a message in a bottle, and throw it out to sea, because the ocean currents have a mysterious way of always making sure those bottles wash right back up on shore.

The truth would always rise to the surface of the sea, no matter how far down below the waterline they tried to hide it.

And perhaps these ocean tides are always there to remind us, to give us an eternal hope, that whatever is pulled away from us will always come back to us again; that whenever our life falls apart, no matter how badly, it will always come back together, given time, if we simply allow the mysterious ebbing-and-flowing forces of the universe to guide us and to guide our ships upon the sea.

I nodded. "You're right, Squid."

I closed my eyes and thought about the *MS Barnacle*. In the end, I thought it was a seaworthy ship, worthy to be an artificial reef. The *MS Barnacle* was more fit for the onboard garbage incinerator than any ship I had ever met. I imagined the ship sailing away, and then I opened my eyes, and I never thought about that ship of darkness, that SOD, the *MS Barnacle*, ever again. I never thought about her again.

And then Squid asked, "Do you think that was your *last* contract?"

"Hey, never say never, right?" And as bad as the ship of darkness was, I knew we couldn't let the past define our future. We couldn't let the ports that our ship had anchored at define the harbors that our ship would sail toward. We had to keep sailing forward.

A few months later, after the winter had iced-over our tree branches again, and the snows had blown all across the Carolina Blue Ridge Mountains outside our window, I heard the sweet song of the sea siren once more. As I sat writing at my desk, I looked out as a blustery, cold wind blew fragile brown leaves down our icy, black road. I let the song gently drift into my seadog soul. It was a song of waves and ships and sun and sea, a song of palm trees swaying in the breeze on the edge of sandy Caribbean beaches.

I looked out across the dark, gray mountains. This was no place for a couple of pirates. We belonged in a land where summer never ends, where the ship sets sail and points its bow toward beautiful island harbors, where the mountains are never cold and are often made from bananas, where tropical shirts and margaritas are always in style.

I heard the phone; it was ringing. I heard the siren; she was singing. I heard the sweet ship, and she was calling me back home. It was a call back to the deep blue. It was the call back to the sea.

But then, for the first time in my ship life, I finally listened to that little voice in my head that loudly yelled, *"Don't do it! Don't go!"*, and I hung up the phone immediately.

AFTERWORD

I still miss ship life, even many years later. Well, I still miss the good parts. I don't miss the dinners of chicken knuckles and noodle cups, but I do miss the free food when it was edible. I don't miss Rice Mountain, but I'll never forget Banana Mountain. I don't miss the poor air quality in my crew cabin and the unhappy managers, but I miss the fresh sea air when we stood out on the open decks and all the friendships that I'd make on the ships. I especially miss that feeling of family while out at sea, especially when I worked with a cast of dancers and musicians. But most of all, I miss the travel, the adventure, and sailing through the sea; all the sights, sounds, and just that feeling of the ship crashing through the waves.

If you've never been on a cruise, I whole-heartedly encourage you to go and take one. It's really one of the best vacations you can ever take, and they're not as expensive as you may think they would be. And if you're thinking about going and working on a cruise ship, I encourage you to do that as well. My advice though: Don't let ship life get you down. Surround yourself with good people of good character and focus on making friends, working hard, and having fun. Don't let your ship life days pass you by without doing everything you can do to enjoy them. I guess that might be good advice for land life too. We all know life is short, but perhaps it's worth saying that most crew member's ship life is much shorter. My ship life went by faster than a passenger can say, "I'm eating whatever I want on my cruise. Cruise calories don't count."

And if you're on a cruise ship right now, make sure and tip those crew members well. They work harder than you might think, and on some ships they don't have it so good.

I hope you found this book entertaining and fun to read. I hope it brightened your life just a little and maybe put some wind back in your sails. This book was definitely a labor of love, and one that I hope captures what it's really like to work aboard cruise ships. And I hope this book can play some part in bringing positive change to the lives of cruise ship crew members. There's really no reason, with all the money that cruise companies make, that crew members should be living the way they do on some ships. I hope this book will bring some of these issues to light, make some positive change in cruise liner land, and make ship life better for the hundreds of thousands of cruise ship crew members sailing out at sea right now. If you're reading this and you have the ability to make some positive change for crew members, I encourage you to do that. Maybe if we all pull together as a team, as a real crew, we can make ship life much better for crew members all around the world.

In closing, I'd like to say thank you for reading my book. I really appreciate it.

And now I'm going to take a nice, long cruise…this time as a passenger, thank God.

*******~~~~~~~*******

The following is an excerpt from:

ON THE APPALACHIAN TRAIL

A nonfiction book about a hiking on the Appalachian Trail by Joshua Kinser

Now available at Amazon.com as an eBook and in print

1

A FLUFFY BALL OF TROUBLE

Our Appalachian Trail adventure started in a most unlikely way. Mowgli came from Georgie, and because of this I should have known that Mowgli was going to be highly intelligent and just a bit mischievous. Georgie was a cool Jersey kid who lived in the Florida neighborhood where I grew up. He was astoundingly intelligent, could master any magic trick, win any gambling game, and turn absolutely anything he could find with combustible properties into remarkable explosions, which made him the absolute best friend a teenage boy could ever have.

And I will forever be indebted to him, because Georgie brought me Mowgli. Now, I very much want to start this story somewhere out on the Appalachian Trail, on a foggy stretch of dirt path that's meandering past a rocky outcropping that has a view like a Kinkade painting, but for you to really understand this story, you have to understand Mowgli, fleas and all. And to understand Mowgli, we have to start at the beginning.

One afternoon, Georgie walked into my yard. In his hands, he held a little fluffy ball of trouble. Mowgli was definitely the cutest thing you ever saw, but he had a certain mangy quality that helped you visually identify him as one of the bad kids in the neighborhood. There were little tufts of hair missing here and there, and he had this naughty twinkle in his eye that seemed to say:

Dear Humans,

I have a sordid past that involves destroying entire couches. I refuse to eat dry dog food, and I only accept canned food with real vegetables or table scraps, but if you take me home I will be your best friend forever.

Sincerely,
Mowgli

His was a young puppy, small and cute, with large black paws, dark brown eyes the size of chocolate-covered donut holes, and long droopy ears that hung down past his neck. There is a scale of cuteness in this world, and Mowgli shared the most positive side of the spectrum along with wobbling baby pigs with tiny snouts the size of peas, fuzzy newborn bear cubs, and Cameron Diaz.

"I found him outside my house the other day," Georgie said. "He's been hanging around, and I thought maybe you'd want him since you're about to go hiking on the Appalachian Trail."

I couldn't think of a better companion than Mowgli (other than Heidi Klum) that I would rather have bouncing alongside me on the trail. *What dog wouldn't want to be explore the American wilderness?* I thought. *Everybody needs a sidekick. Mowgli will be perfect.*

"So, what do you think?" Georgie asked. "He's pretty well behaved. Seems smart. He'd make a great dog."

Mowgli was a German Shepherd and black Lab mix, which turned out to be an exceptional pairing. He had the high-intelligence and the eagerness to be trained that you find in

German Sheperds, and the gentle personality, desire for affection, and the love of water that is often associated with black labs.

I looked down at Mowgli, He looked up at me and then stretched out his floppy paws and yawned wide, making his tongue curl backwards.

"Absolutely," I said. I took him from Georgie and held him in my arms.

"You're a sweet dog," I said.

Mowgli bit my finger.

Our Appalachian Trail adventure had officially begun.

Also By Joshua Kinser:

Cruise Ports Caribbean, published by Lonely Planet (Nonfiction, travel guide)

On the Appalachian Trail (Nonfiction, memoir)

Art Heist on the High Seas (Fiction, novel)

Eat Bark Fetch (Fiction, novel)

Extraterrestrials on the Appalachian Trail (Fiction, short novel)

Hiking South Carolina: A Guide to the State's Greatest Hikes, published by Falcon Guides (Nonfiction, travel guide)

Five Star Trails: Raleigh and Durham, published by Menasha Ridge Press (Nonfiction, travel guide)

Five Star Trails: Charlotte, published by Menasha Ridge Press (Nonfiction, travel guide)

Florida Gulf Coast, published by Hachette Book Group (Nonfiction, travel guide)

The Florida Keys, published by Hachette Book Group (Nonfiction, travel guide)

Tampa and St. Petersburg, published by Hachette Book Group (Nonfiction, travel guide)

For an updated list of Joshua's books, visit his Amazon.com author page.

About the Author

Joshua Kinser writes about cruise ships, travel, and music. He is the author of more than ten books, including a travel guide to Caribbean Cruise Ports published by Lonely Planet, and several other travel guides to Florida and the Southeast US published by Hachette Book Group, Falcon Guides, and Wilderness Press. You can contact him at joshuakinser@gmail.com.

If you've enjoyed this book, please go to Amazon and write a review. This helps writers tremendously.

If you're interested in receiving a **FREE** eBook of one of the books below, just copy the link to your review of this book on Amazon and email it to me at Joshuakinser@gmail.com, and let me know which one of the following eBooks you would like to receive:

On the Appalachian Trail (Nonfiction, memoir)

Art Heist on the High Seas (Fiction, novel)

Extraterrestrials on the Appalachian Trail (Fiction, short novel)

Eat Bark Fetch (Fiction, novel)

27332757R00317

Printed in Great Britain
by Amazon